Peter van der Linden's Guide to Linux®

Peter van der Linden's Guide to Linux®

Peter van der Linden

PRENTICE
HALL
PTR

Prentice Hall Professional Technical Reference

Upper Saddle River, NJ • Boston • Indianapolis • San Francisco
New York • Toronto • Montreal • London • Munich • Paris • Madrid
Capetown • Sydney • Tokyo • Singapore • Mexico City

The publisher offers excellent discounts on this book when ordered in quantity for bulk purchases or special sales, which may include electronic versions and/or custom covers and content particular to your business, training goals, marketing focus, and branding interests. For more information, please contact:

U.S. Corporate and Government Sales
(800) 382-3419
corpsales@pearsontechgroup.com

For sales outside the U.S., please contact:

International Sales
international@pearsoned.com

Visit us on the Web: www.phptr.com

Library of Congress Cataloging-in-Publication Data

van der Linden, Peter.
      Peter van der Linden's guide to Linux / Peter van der Linden.
          p. cm.
      Includes index.
      ISBN 0-13-187284-2 (pbk. : alk. paper)
    1. Linux. 2. Operating systems (Computers) I. Title.
      QA76.76.O63V35815 2005
      005.4'3—dc22

                               2005015342

ISBN 0-13-187284-2
Text printed in the United States on recycled paper at Courier in Stoughton, Massachusetts.
First printing, August 2005

*This book is dedicated to
Josh van der Linden, who helped me learn
to read and, more importantly, helped me
learn to love reading.*

Quick Contents

Complete Contents

Preface

Maybe you're thinking back to the last time you tried something new, and got less-than-happy results.

Maybe you've been burned by technology before, like Sony's hated and costly MiniDisc format, Dell's troubled Movie Studio Plus bundle from 2002, or the original Pentium from Intel with the faulty multiplier.

Whether your concerns arise from past experience, or from fear of an unknown future, it's a reasonable question: Am I going to be OK with Linux?

This has three components:

- Will Linux **run** on my PC without problems?
- Can I **learn to use** Linux easily?
- Will Linux **install** on my PC without problems?

Running Linux Linux works with IBM PC-compatible computers, and on a great many more computer architectures too. Linux is a mainstream technology in the business world, and that's a place that quickly drops things that aren't cost effective. As long as you have a PC that runs at 800 MHz or more, with at least 256 MB memory, you're good to go.

Learning Linux So how easy is it to learn Linux? That depends partly on you. How much interest do you have in learning a new skill? How much time can you put into it? Since you're reading this book, the answers must at least be "some" and "a bit." I don't want to trivialize the effort to master a new operating system, but it's really not that big a deal. The Linux installed base overtook the Macintosh installed base in 2004, and a large number of people taught themselves to be Mac-savvy.

All current windowing systems—all window-based GUIs—do pretty much the same things in the same ways. If you can find the main navigation button in Linux (bottom left of the window, same as in Windows, labeled **Launch**), you can find all the applications. If you can find the applications, you can learn by doing.

With the help of this book, the Linux customer support forums, and online documentation, you don't need to worry about getting stuck. You can learn Linux at your own pace and with a safety net.

Installing Linux "Ah!" I hear you ask, "What about installing Linux?" Here, I have to acknowledge, lies an area that can cause frustration. The issue is that a few peripherals on your PC may be supported only under Windows. You might find that your modem or wifi card works on Windows and not on Linux. I'll get into the remedies for this situation in due course, but prepare yourself now for the possibility.

The easiest way to make all Linux installation issues disappear entirely is to acquire Linux the same way you acquired Windows—preinstalled on a PC by the vendor. A number of mainstream vendors will sell you a Linux PC, including Walmart, CompUSA, Staples, and MicrotelPC. Whether you buy a preinstalled Linux system, or re-use an existing PC, installation is a manageable problem, with the answers in this text.

The answer to the question Here's the bottom line. I know a lot of people who have successfully learned Linux. I don't know anyone who has tried to learn Linux and failed.

Yes, you are going to be OK with Linux too.

Acknowledgments

My profound thanks go to Bob Lynch, Chris Costello, and Bill Camarda, who read the manuscript, provided encouragement, and suggested numerous improvements.

I appreciate technical help from Terry Carroll, Robert C. Cumbow, Frank Florianz, Elizabeth Garner, Phil Gustafson, Atsushi Onoe, Brian Scearce, JoAnne Schmitz, Kevin Switzer, Szakacsits Szabolcs, K.J.Titcomb, and Paul Tomblin.

I'm very grateful to the software engineering and marketing staff at Linspire who put up with eight months of grilling from me, so that you could have the most complete information. In particular, Kendall Dawson read the entire manuscript in one sitting, and even handed over the keys so I could race the CEO's Segway scooter around the Linspire offices late one night.

Thanks to Clifford Beshers, Georgi Damyonov, David Fox, Duane Maxwell, Sean Meiners, Will Von Reis, Adam Wang, and all the talented, hard-working software developers at Linspire. I'm grateful to Vice President of Marketing Kevin La Rue and Vice President of Development Randy Linnell who "made things happen" for me.

I would also like to mention the Linspire fans around the world who make the Linspire forums such a practical, friendly source of help for new users. The forums are at https://linspire.com/forums. Among the many unsung heroes and heroines of the Linspire forums are:

- Bro.Tiag (Samuel J. Getty)
- CaptainTux (Patrick L. Green)
- CloudyWizzard (Patrick Kox)
- Daniel-Ec (Daniel Illingworth, in Guayaquil, Ecuador)
- ~deadcats (Ken Miller)
- DebLynne (Debbie Sanford)
- dre@dangerousron.com (Ron Meinsler)
- Exigentsky (Alex Radu)
- frank754 (Frank Florianz, http://viewoftheblue.com)

- Mr.Gigabytes (Josh Tordsen)
- Hawkeye52 (Larry L. Davis)
- hqlinux (Harvey Quackenbush)
- jcd@umd.edu (Sean D. McNamara)
- JLT (J.L. Townsend)
- mats (Mats Ekblom)
- medico_2001 (Dr. Chris J. Ramaglia)
- nokernel (Daniel Paquet)
- richard.a@internode.on.net (Richard Ashton)
- seeker 5528 (Don Mills)
- SmileyDon (Himself)
- Tekmate (John Pisini)
- The Kraut (Dave Groenig)
- Willem (Willem Fortuin)
- Zoic (Kevin Switzer, http://pcaid.ca)

I'm fortunate to work with skilled publishing professionals Greg Doench and Solveig Haugland.

About the Author

Peter van der Linden has worked in the computer industry since before there were PCs. He holds an M.S. in computer science from Yale, and has programmed computers in England, Germany, and on both coasts of the United States. For the last twenty years he has worked in Silicon Valley, for Sun Microsystems, Apple Computers, a storage start-up, and everything in between.

Peter wrote the best-selling *Expert C Programming* (Prentice Hall, 1994), and *The HandBook of Practical Jokes* (NAL-Penguin, 1991). His *Just Java* was twice nominated for Java Book of the Year. Peter teaches, writes, and consults on Linux and software generally. He gets a real kick out of figuring out how things work, and explaining them more clearly than anyone else.

Hello Linux

Why Linux Now?

When do we reach the point that enough is enough?

How do we conclude that a once-trusted tool is no longer up to the job?

For my uncle Josh that moment came last spring, when he called me for help with his Microsoft Windows PC. Here's a picture of uncle Josh. That's not his Rolls-Royce, but he's trying to kid me that it is. I'm onto him, though. One of his pleasures in life is surfing the Internet and emailing entertaining photos to family members.

For several years, Windows was adequate for Josh. But lately, his system ran slower than it used to. He could see the modem "in use" light flickering when he wasn't doing anything. Josh noticed that his virus protection software had somehow been disabled. Was someone interfering with his computer from across the Internet? When Josh discovered his password had been changed from under him, he called me for help.

Does any of this story sound familiar? With Linux, these Windows woes disappear completely.

Windows Woes

Here are a few of the Windows woes I think are the most important to understand.

Windows Security Problems

Microsoft's Windows products have always been deficient in security. Before the Internet was widely used, Microsoft's default policy of "no security" was convenient for home PC users. If you never went online, your data remained safe and private because your PC was locked up in your home.

Today, when you surf the Internet, you connect your computer to a gigantic global network of other computers. When you can see web sites, other people on the network can see the presence of your computer. Some of these people have malicious and even criminal intentions. They prey on the unprotected and the unknowledgeable. It's no longer enough to physically lock up your PC in your house. You also need to secure your Windows PC from electronic access over the network. As Josh found out, Microsoft's default "no security" just isn't good enough any more.

From the start, Windows has been far more vulnerable to computer viruses than other operating systems. As network use surged in the mid 1990s, crackers adapted Windows viruses to spread over the net. Some viruses really sink their teeth into your Windows system—the best way to get rid of a virus may be to reinstall everything from a backup. You might have big problems if you don't take regular backups of your data. Microsoft installs backup software with XP Pro but omits it from XP Home Edition, the market that needs it most. *Making Backups* on page 484 explains in detail how to back up a Windows or Linux PC.

Jargon update: viruses and worms

Originally, the definition of a computer virus was a program that copies itself into other program files. When an infected program ran, the virus also ran. Those copies would copy themselves, and so the virus spread to many files. The virus tried to get into lots of programs, so that eventually it would be in a file that was moved to another system and the virus would spread there too.

That "copying" definition is no longer relevant today. The Internet makes it trivial for viruses to move to new hosts automatically. They don't need to copy them-selves to many different files. Viruses spread to a new host (such as your PC) by sending email there, or requesting a service, or accessing a network drive on your PC that has been shared to the world.

Viruses that move to new hosts without human help are called worms. Since all current viruses spread automatically, the two terms virus and worm are synonymous these days. Using the net, viruses can spread very rapidly. They can attack millions of PCs in hours.

 At work, you probably have fewer problems with Windows viruses. At work, there should be computer staff paid to look for and block viruses, to keep up-to-date with security software patches, to notice and solve problems before they get out of hand, and to make backup copies of vital data. Few users want to spend time and money taking the same precautions at home. Nor should we have to— other operating systems don't have these problems.

A Typical Windows Virus

Whether you are at work or at home, virus writers are very skilled at exploiting defects in Microsoft software. Their goal is to take control of your PC and use it for sending spam or attacking web sites that don't pay protection. Here's an email I got recently:

From: support@symantec.com

Subject: Re: Virus Sample

Date: July 22, 2004 6:44:34 AM PDT

To: pvdl@afu.com

The sample file you sent contains a new virus version of mydoom.j.

Please clean your system with the attached signature.

Sincerly,

Robert Ferrew

1 Attachment, 29.1 KB, datafiles.zip

That looks pretty straightforward. Helpful, even. Except... I had not sent any "sample file" to Symantec. So it's unlikely that this email really came from them. Let's find out what the email really is, and who it's from.

Most mail readers have a way to show you the entire raw message, so you can see all the lines at the top known as the email headers. For example, in Outlook 2000, right-click on a message without opening it and choose **Options** > **Full Headers**.

Each email header line starts with a word-and-a-colon (like "From:"), then some text that describes the message or helps route the email to its destination. This header line was part of the email:

Received: from unknown (HELO afu.com) ([66.240.65.194])

The "Received:" header line shows the address of the computer that sent me this Windows virus. It came from address 66.240.65.194. This is an IP (Internet protocol) address—a unique identifier that is convenient for computers, less so for people.

An IP address is like a phone number for a computer: anyone can use it to reach whoever has that number. An IP address looks like four groups of numbers separated by periods.

Here's an example of an IP address:

66.240.65.194

Every one of the millions of computers connected to the Internet is given its own IP address. I'll look at IP addresses more in Chapter 2, "Running the Linux Live CD," on page 25.

Any header lines and text in an email can be forged, with one exception. The IP address of the computer that handed the email to your mail server cannot be forged. It must provide its IP address truthfully, otherwise your mail server cannot talk to it to accept the email. So the mail came from IP address 66.240.65.194, although not from Symantec because that is not one of their IP addresses.

Using the web site www.samspade.org, anyone can translate an IP address into the organization that owns it. The email really came from Orlando, Florida-based ISP FDN Communications. One of their customers has this virus. It probably found my email address in his online address book or a spammer's list and sent the virus to me. A question for another day is: "Why isn't that ISP filtering mail to prevent transmission of known viruses?"

Safely reviewing the attachment on my Linux system, I unzipped it to find it contained a single binary file with the strange name "details.txt   .pif". The spaces in the middle of the file name are trying to hide the true file extension of .pif from you. A PIF (Program Information File) tells Windows how to run a DOS application and in this case also contained the DOS program.

Searching Google for the text in the email "new virus version of mydoom.j." brought up several links suggesting this was the Netsky-P virus. With that knowledge, the real Symantec site had enough additional information to definitively confirm the virus identity as Netsky-P.

Because of bugs in Microsoft's Internet Explorer, the Netsky-P virus described previously will silently install itself on unpatched Windows systems. The user doesn't have to click on the attachment, merely preview the email in Outlook, and the virus gets installed on his/her computer. Read that again, if you can believe it: *buggy Microsoft code allows the virus to install itself!* This is by no means unique or even rare. You can learn more about this Windows bug by searching for article Q290108 at http://support.microsoft.com. So even when you run virus-checking software and avoid clicking on attachments, your Windows PC can still get plenty of viruses without you realizing it.

I'm not suggesting you bother with this kind of analysis yourself; I'm just pointing out how vulnerable Windows is. Virus-checking software is reactive: it can only shut the stable door after the horse has bolted. New viruses have to attack large numbers of victims before they come to the attention of security companies, and it takes further time to analyze the virus and issue software updates.

Windows Viruses "Arms Race"

Whether everyone realizes it yet or not, viruses and other malware are out of control in the Windows world. *Information Week* (June 3, 2004) reported that the number of new viruses released on the Internet in the previous month rose to a two-and-a-half-year high.

According to a study completed back in 2001 for the UK Ministry of Defence by Dr Nic Peeling and Dr Julian Satchell: "There are about 60,000 viruses known for Windows, 40 or so for the Macintosh, about 5 for commercial Unix versions, and perhaps 40 for Linux. Most of the Windows viruses are not important, but many hundreds have caused widespread damage. Two or three of the Macintosh viruses were widespread enough to be of importance. None of the Unix or Linux viruses became widespread."

We have gradually arrived at a point where the viruses have the upper hand over Windows. In June 2004 the U.S. Government's Computer Emergency Response Team (a government computer security clearing house) had to advise users to stop using Microsoft's Internet Explorer. See Appendix A for more information on this and Windows viruses in general.

Didn't XP's Service Pack 2 Solve the Windows Security Problems?

If only! The first new flaws in the SP2 patches were discovered within days of its August 2004 release. Chuck Adams, Chief Security Officer of NetSolve in Austin, Texas, declared "SP2 is certainly a step in the right direction. However, in practice, SP2 oversimplifies security management tasks and will likely cause significant disruptions to normal operating processes due to poor user choices". PC specialists Assetmetrix surveyed 136,000 PCs in 250 North American corporations, eight months after SP2's release. They found that less than 25% of Windows XP PCs also had SP2 installed.

Victor Wheatman, managing VP of the Gartner Group, was blunter in his comments on Microsoft's perpetually lagging work to repair its software flaws, "We've been in the biggest beta test there is, for years. We call it Windows."

Worse, Microsoft has a misguided new policy: they won't let you install service packs unless you can convince them that you have a licensed copy of Windows. It appears the revenue stream is more important to Microsoft than reducing cyber attacks caused through its own defective products.

This is an arms race between virus writers and security companies. Windows users are in the middle of the battle zone, and the security companies can never pull ahead. They can't guarantee a fix until a virus has established a presence. And virus writers are incredibly creative and ingenious: they examine new security patches and use them as blueprints to create attacks on unpatched systems.

Other Windows Problems

This isn't a book on security, and if you stick with Windows you'll need to guard against plenty more security problems: spyware, cross-site scripting, poison cookies, phishing, web bug GIFs, script kiddies, popup ads, cyber-stalking, and so on. You can find a checklist of procedures for cleaning up Windows malware at http://securitytango.com. You can find a longer explanation of home PC security issues in the excellent book, *Computer Security*, by Thomas Greene, published by Apress 2004, ISBN 1-59059-316-2.

Windows PCs compromised within minutes

In late 2004, a security research group connected numerous PCs to the Internet in eight different countries to study attacks on them. The findings present a stark factual contrast.

Unpatched Windows PCs are often compromised within minutes of connecting to the net, though their owners might not realize it. The average unpatched Linux system goes for months on the Internet without being hacked.

A second research group confirmed the average survival time of several versions of Windows was now down to just four minutes before the PC was located and taken over by automated cracking software! On the other hand, the report brought the welcome news that default installations of Linux are becoming harder to penetrate due to improvements such as enabling fewer network services. You can read the details at http://project.honeynet.org/papers.

Microsoft explains its poor showing by claiming that Windows presents a more popular hacking target than Linux. It sure does! And that suggests what you can do about it, too: take the Windows bullseye target off your back.

New Windows exploits come out every week, and patches are slow to arrive. Firewall software combined with antivirus software and regular patching of your Windows system is something, but it's far from enough. Windows viruses can no longer be avoided by not clicking on mail attachments. It's no wonder that Uncle Josh lost control of his PC.

Windows viruses are no longer about mindless youthful vandalism. They are now about professional criminals making money through spam, through identity theft, and through extortion. Windows viruses will be an ever-increasing problem in the years ahead.

Why Linux Is More Secure

Linux has several big security advantages over Windows:

Linux is less complex than Microsoft's "kudzu vine" architecture of intertwined products. Linux's window system and applications are simpler to work on; they have not been intermingled with the operating system.

Outlook uses Internet Explorer libraries to display email. But Microsoft artificially transplanted the Internet Explorer application into the operating system in a legal ploy to try to beat the rap in its monopoly abuse trial. The ploy was unsuccessful, but Explorer remains stuck as part of the Windows operating system. Explorer today still has inappropriate access to administrator privileges instead of only user privileges.

Linux doesn't rely on "security through obscurity". The Linux source code is published; open to scrutiny and improvement by all. When theoretical security flaws are uncovered, they are often patched within hours.

Linux doesn't have Outlook, Internet Explorer, and IIS, three of the buggiest, least-secure applications in use today. A network break-in at a credit card processor led to a surge in fraudulent transactions in 2005. More than 40 million Visa, Mastercard, and American Express accounts were potentially compromised. The card-processing company uses the Windows 2005 operating system and MIcrosoft IIS Server 5.0.

Linux, like MacOS, is just a far less popular target. When you have a choice, why ride on the bus that everybody pelts with garbage?

Improved PC security isn't the only reason to move to Linux. But it's a compelling one, and it's the one that motivated me to write this book. I didn't like finding out how Josh had been taken advantage of. *Advantages and Disadvantages of Linux* outlines pluses and minuses of moving to Linux.

Advantages and Disadvantages of Linux

You might already use Linux more than you realize. Two thirds of corporate web servers are already running Linux because it is faster, cheaper, and more reliable than Microsoft alternatives. This is from the MIT Technology Review Sept 2004, http://www.technologyreview.com/articles/04/09/roush0904.asp.

Every time you place a bid on eBay, you are using servers at eBay that run Linux. Whenever you do a Google search, you are tapping into Google's network of thousands of Linux servers to find your information. When you buy a book or consumer product at Amazon, your transaction is completed on processors running Linux. Linux is fully established in the commercial world of data processing and is quickly gaining ground among consumers.

IBM, the largest computer company in the world, is a huge supporter of Linux, and has tasked its internal IT organization to upgrade from Windows to a Linux-based desktop by the end of 2005. The government of Brazil plans to move all federal and state organizations to open source software. The city of Munich, Germany, is switching all its 14,000 desktops to Linux. If non-technical council workers can switch to Linux, you can too.

There are tradeoffs to everything in life. You'll be in the best position to judge what Linux holds for you if you understand the benefits, the drawbacks, and the things that stay the same when you switch.

Things That Are About the Same in Linux and Windows

This section covers things that are about the same in Windows and Linux. Switching one way or the other won't give you a relative advantage.

Ease of Installation

Linux installation used to be something best done with the help of an expert. That's improved remarkably in recent years.

Linux installation is now simpler and faster than the equivalent Windows installation. (Some experienced users actually compete to see who can do the fastest Linux installation; the current record is 4 minutes 15 seconds.) But most people only do a handful of installs, so a better installer doesn't count as a big advantage for Linux.

You don't have to register Linux with anyone, or activate it, or buy an additional copy for every PC you own. You can start running Linux with zero installation effort by booting from CD and ignoring the hard disk. A Linux CD that does this is called a live CD, which makes trying Linux very easy. There is a live CD included with this book.

You don't even need to install Linux. You can buy a PC with Linux preinstalled from Fry's, Walmart, and many other vendors. See *Linux with Zero Effort: Buying Linux Preinstalled* on page 440.

Operating System Stability

Microsoft has pretty much caught up to Linux levels of stability with XP. Microsoft's "blue screen of death" is a thing of the past. Apart from Windows security problems, Microsoft no longer lags behind in operating system quality.

What You Gain by Switching to Linux

Here is what you can expect to gain by switching to Linux:

Security

I've already discussed Windows viruses at length. Linux systems are completely immune to Windows viruses and there are essentially no Linux-specific viruses on the loose.

Privacy

Linux applications don't "phone home" the way so many Windows applications do. By default, details on every video or audio file you play with Windows Media Viewer are sent to a server at Microsoft.

No Digital Restrictions

The next release of Windows, code-named Longhorn, has controversial restrictions on digital media. Microsoft spins its next-generation secure computing base (NGSCB, previously known as "Palladium") architecture as one that protects you from viruses.

Its actual purpose is to control access to digital music and films, preventing you from playing them on your other PCs. NGSCB will also hinder file sharing with non-Windows systems. Linux does not impose restrictions on its users.

Cost Savings

Windows XP Professional Edition costs $299 and it can be installed on only one computer. The home edition of XP costs $199, again for one PC. The price of Microsoft Office 2003 Professional edition is $499. Antivirus software costs around $50. These are retail costs, but even at discounted manufacturer rates Windows is typically the single most expensive part of a new PC.

You can legally download many versions of Linux for free from the web. You can legally download a Microsoft Office-compatible suite called OpenOffice.org for free. OpenOffice.org runs on Linux, Windows, and the Apple Mac. The Dutch town of Harlem was faced with licensing costs of $670,000 to move its two thousand council employees to the current version of Microsoft Office. The city chose instead to adopt OpenOffice.org and completed the migration spending just $67,000 on training.

Microsoft pays for a lot of skewed studies to "prove" that Linux somehow costs more to administer than Windows. They do this by ignoring the costs of Windows security issues, overstating retraining effort, and selectively manipulating other expenses. Don't be fooled: almost every PC user will reduce their software costs by switching to Linux. Amazon.com revealed in an SEC financial filing (so this was not marketing hot air) that it saved $17 million, or about 25% of its computing budget, by switching to Linux.

Expect to spend a little time to learn some minor GUI differences, and a little effort to unlock your data from Windows. Expect to spend a lot less money than you have in the past on Microsoft applications.

Freedom

Linux has developed as a collaborative venture of software professionals. The source code of Linux is freely available to anyone. Students can read it to see how it works. Universities can teach it. Computer companies can freely adapt Linux for new hardware projects. Any programmer can improve something he or she doesn't like by writing some better code. None of this is true for Windows.

The freedom that Linux brings has created a dynamic and active community of Linux supporters. Like fans everywhere, these people are keen to make new converts, so they go out of their way to help Linux beginners.

Knowledge

Linux is on the verge of crossing over from hobbyist to mainstream use. It's similar to the situation in the early days of cars. There were a lot of enthusiasts for whom learning was an interest and a goal in itself. Nothing in Linux has to be hidden or proprietary.

If you want to, you can use Linux to explore how computers and networks work. If you don't want to, you can use Linux as a reliable black box. I say put the fun back into the fundamentals and use Linux to learn more about your PC.

Linux Runs on Everything

Linux runs on far more types of computer than Windows does. Linux is available for products made by Intel, AMD, Via, Sun, SGI, Apple, Hitachi, Motorola, and many more. Linux operates large supercomputer clusters with hundreds of processors. It runs on Personal Digital Assistants and cell phones that fit in your pocket. A few years ago, IBM built a wristwatch that ran Linux as a demonstration project. (Sadly, they never made it into a product, so you can't buy one.)

People who bought 64-bit (very large memory) Intel or AMD processors were promised a corresponding version of Windows for 2003. Microsoft eventually rolled out a 64-bit version of Windows Server two years late in mid 2005. Linux has shipped a 64-bit version since the day the chips became available.

Professionals who learn Linux are adding a broad and important skill to their repertoire.

What You Give Up by Switching to Linux

Here is the downside—some things that you might give up by switching to Linux:

Wide Selection of Commercial Software

Unquestionably, Windows has a wider range of application software than any other platform. But how many different word-processing packages do you need?

If you are looking for the latest game software, Linux is the sixth platform it will be ported to (after PlayStation 2, GameCube, Xbox, Windows, and the Mac), so Linux is not a good match for your needs.

How to get around this – The core applications you need for day-to-day work are available for free on Linux. They are often included with the Linux distribution, so you don't need to install them separately. Popular Linux software includes the OpenOffice.org office suite, the Firefox browser, Gimp photo editor, and Thunderbird email application. These applications are similar in use and appearance to the Windows-only equivalents; your skills are readily transferable.

If you have a specialized application that is only available for Windows, you can set up a dual boot system, which can boot up in either Windows or Linux. That lets you fall back to Windows when you need to run the stranded application.

Alternatively, several products emulate the Windows environment on Linux. Evaluate whether the Win4Lin, VMWare Workstation, Codeweavers or WINE emulation software can run your Windows software under Linux. However, using commercial emulation software changes the cost of Linux and is a short-term workaround rather than a long-term solution.

Windows Hardware Support

All computer peripherals (printers, scanners, disk, keyboard, monitor, etc.) need a piece of software called a *device driver* to control their operation and manage the flow of data between the peripheral and the computer.

Each peripheral needs its own specific driver (a video card driver won't do anything for your Ethernet card). Each operating system has its own conventions for device drivers to follow. So, just like most other software, a video card driver written for Windows won't work on Linux.

Some device manufacturers do not yet see the commercial justification for producing a Linux version of the driver for their device, and they do not want to publish the details of their device that would enable others to write the driver.

If there is no device driver software for Linux, you will not be able to use that peripheral on a system running Linux, though it will work perfectly when you run Windows (with the necessary Windows device driver) on the same PC.

The kinds of hardware most afflicted by not having Linux drivers are input/output devices that are new to the market (less than six months old), exotic (some graphics cards), or where the manufacturer refuses to release the hardware information needed for the Linux community to write a driver (some wifi cards, and essentially every cheap modem).

How to get around this – If a device manufacturer makes available the specifications of its device (and many do), the Linux community will quickly create the necessary device driver, and the problem is solved. If the device details are kept secret, all you can do is write to the CEO of the company explaining that you would like to buy their products, but cannot as they do not work with Linux. Ask them to provide Linux drivers or share product specifications with the Linux community.

By the way, the CEO of notorious Linux laggard Texas Instruments is Tom Engibous, at P.O. Box 660199, Dallas, TX 75266-0199.

I'll show you how to find out exactly what devices you have on your system, and how to do a web search to identify Linux drivers for all of them. If there is no driver, that device will not work under Linux, and you might want to consider buying a cheap replacement that does have a Linux driver. I'll take a look at this in detail in Appendix B.

Comfort in Numbers

There are major advantages to Windows having the largest installed base. New hardware and software products appear first (sometimes solely) for Windows. Books, training courses and support are readily available for Windows.

How to get around this – Use the resources of the Internet to seek out Linux-capable alternatives. Linux has far more online documentation and support than Windows does. If you want more detailed, task-oriented documentation that typical computer users look for, books like this fill the need.

You might be surprised at how quickly Linux is moving into volume platform status. In 2004 Linux crossed over to gain a larger market share than MacOS, and its market share has only increased since then. A lot of people anticipate a "tipping point" after which Linux will be supported as a mainstream choice by all vendors.

Investment in Learning

Plan to spend a little time learning to use a new window system and new applications. Most Linux applications are similar to their Windows counterparts, and can be picked up quickly. All GUIs (the window interface) do essentially the same things, and you can retrain your fingers within a day or two.

This book will steer you through the rocky patches. It's good to develop new skills, particularly in blooming areas of technology.

The bottom line is to be aware of the advantages and disadvantages. If your WinModem hardware doesn't work under Linux, you'll be prepared and know what to do. When your network is a "notwork", this book walks you through the steps to resolve it. When you have a technical question, you'll know which newsgroups or forums to go to for an answer.

Linux Background

For all its power and market share today, the Linux operating system came from a humble beginning. It started as a student project, when Linus Torvalds (a computer science student at the University of Helsinki in Finland) wanted to get programming experience with a new chip from Intel. To speed things along and make comparisons easier, Linus chose to make his system software project compatible with the well-established and proven Unix operating system. Hence the name: Linux is "Linus' version of Unix".

Linus Torvalds, originator of Linux

Linux is pronounced "Lee-nucks" (not "Lie-nucks" or "Lih-nucks"). You can hear a recording of Linus himself clarifying this in English and Swedish at the web site http://www.kernel.org/pub/linux/kernel/SillySounds.

It takes many person years of effort to implement an operating system. Linus was helped by standing on the shoulders of giants.

A much earlier project was already underway, led by Richard Stallman of MIT. He, too, planned an operating system, and had cloned the compilers and user-level utilities of Unix, making the source code freely available to all. Stallman (officially a genius, as a recipient of a MacArthur Foundation genius grant) named his project "GNU" for "Gnu's Not Unix".

Linus used the GNU compiler and utilities, which allowed him to focus on the operating system kernel (the core, privileged part of the operating system). Like Stallman, Linus also published his work openly and invited others to join in the effort. Linus even chose to share his work under the GNU Public License that Stallman had created.

From these roots, GNU/Linux has steadily grown in stature to the point where it is now backed by all major computer companies, with just one exception. Microsoft correctly sees Linux as a threat to its long-standing monopoly and conducts a well-funded, relentless, and basically dishonest PR campaign against Linux. However, Microsoft is on the losing side of history and will eventually be forced to reach an accommodation with Linux, probably by creating its own Linux-based product or applications.

Linux development is carried out cooperatively but independently by a broad-based collection of companies, volunteers, professionals, and graduate students. When anyone makes a change to their copy of Linux the change can be submitted to a small number of "gatekeeper" programmers who decide if it is good enough to bring into the core Linux source code. The Linux source code is open to all to download and view. It is kept at http://www.kernel.org.

GNU/Linux Distributions

Today the Linux kernel of the operating system and the GNU tools and commands are combined with applications, utilities, installation scripts, and other software (like the Apache web server) to provide a complete product. The complete bundle is called a "Distribution", usually abbreviated to a "distro".

The GNU-contributed parts of a distro are usually the biggest single component of a distro, sometimes about ten times as much code as the Linux kernel's four million lines of code. To get proper credit, the GNU folks ask that the system as a whole be referred to as "GNU/Linux"—a reasonable request that is not always honored.

GNU software, plus a Linux kernel, plus installation utilities and other software, make up a complete GNU/Linux distro.

Anyone can create a distro and offer it from a web site. My friend "Dangerous" Ron put one together, reflecting his interests by leaving out applications he'll never use. He put it on his web site www.dangerousron.com so others can make use of it.

There are about ten significant distros, each of which is the starting point for dozens of specialized sub-distributions. Web site www.distrowatch.com keeps a list of all distros and their key attributes. It's worth a visit when you want to learn more about other distros.

A distro may be assembled by a commercial company such as Red Hat Inc., Sun Microsystems, or Novell, and offered for sale. Or it may be a volunteer effort, such as Slackware Linux, which can be downloaded for free. Each user picks the price point and level of support he is most comfortable with. Some of the more significant distros are shown in Table 1-1.

Table 1-1   Some popular Linux distros

Distro	Created	Remarks
Slackware	1992	Oldest and most complete distro. Slackware is intended for knowledgeable users who don't mind editing configuration files.
Debian	1993	Noncommercial and free. Debian favors stability over cutting-edge code.
Red Hat Enterprise	1994	Commercial distro intended for corporate customers, very widely used for servers. Red Hat offers paid user support.
SuSE	1994	Developed by a German company, and very popular in Europe. SuSE bundles a huge amount of software with the distro. Bought by Novell in 2003.
Mandriva (formerly Mandrake)	1998	Originally based on Red Hat Linux, a French company evolved this into an independent distro. Mandriva has a number of tools to simplify system administration.

Table 1-1   Some popular Linux distros (Continued)

Distro	Created	Remarks
Linspire	2001	Based on Debian Linux, and specialized for desktop use with a simple robust installation process. This distro is pre-installed on some Linux systems sold by WalMart.
Fedora	2003	Cost-free distro; a spin-off from Red Hat Linux, focused on desktop users.
Knoppix	2002	Another Debian-based distro that popularized the use of live (bootable) CDs.

While the different distros provide choice and competition, they have two drawbacks:

- **Software might not be binary compatible between distros** – Changes in library versions and packaging might require you to recompile a program if you want to move it to another distro. That might be quick and easy, or you might run into problems, but it's an extra step. It means that you can't always take a program from a PC running one distro and "just run it" on a PC that uses a different distro.

- **Linux is fragmented into dialects** – You cannot rely on each distro having exactly the same commands and utilities as all the others. There are competing GUI window managers and administrative tools. The installation utilities are different. Moving from one distro to another may require a modest amount of re-learning on your part. It's about the same amount of effort as learning a new release of Windows.

There is a Linux initiative called the Linux Standard Base or LSB, which has set standards for important aspects of Linux. LSB has set a goal of complete application portability between distros. Unfortunately LSB members were over-partial to Red Hat Linux in the formative stages, and the emerging standard favors Red Hat even where other distros have better technology (e.g. in software installation scripts).

While I'm not dismissing the drawbacks of distro incompatibility, they tend to be an occasional nuisance rather than a fatal flaw. Most people and organizations pick one distro and stick with it.

The Linspire Distro

In this text, the Linspire distro of Linux is used. However, apart from the Linspire-specific tools (like Click-N-Run), pretty much all of this book applies to any Linux distro.

Why I Chose Linspire

In choosing a distro, I wanted one that was aimed solely at desktop users, so out went Red Hat, Mandrake, and Novell's SuSE. The distro had to be suitable for home as well as office desktop use, and play essentially all the media content (music, DVDs, etc.) that Windows does. Out went Sun's Java Desktop system.

Many excellent distros focus exclusively on the desktop user: Lycoris, Knoppix, Mepis, Xandros, among others. The chosen distro had to be up-to-date with the current revision of the Linux kernel (out went Lycoris), and the KDE window library (out went Xandros). The "up-to-date" criteria is not overwhelming; these releases all leapfrog each other over the course of several months.

Much more important is that the organization behind the distro should offer professional customer support, not just customer forums (out go Fedora and Knoppix). The distro should be based on Debian Linux, because Debian is arguably the best overall distro and certainly one of the most established. Debian emphasizes the best of the open source culture and mature software discipline. Debian uses the very best packaging technology available for any operating system, supporting online distribution of applications and software updates.

Several distros are still in the running at this point, all of them very good, but the Linspire distro stands head and shoulders above the others. They have licensed the players needed to play more file types than any other distro. Linspire is a commercial sub-distribution of Debian Linux. It doesn't rely on hobby or volunteer effort; the Linspire company has over 100 employees dedicated to the company mission. And Linspire's mission is simple: *to provide the world's easiest-to-use Linux desktop*.

Linspire and the Linux Community

Linspire works hard to welcome Windows users to the Linux experience. For example, just as in Windows, CDs are represented by a desktop icon that you can double-click to show the CD contents. In some other distros, users need to run a command to make the CD files accessible.

Some hard-bitten Linux old-timers disparage changes that make Linux easier for non-technical people (as with any club, there are a few elitists). A few even resent the commercial nature of Linspire, building on GNU-licensed software acquired for free. The source code for the Linux part of the Linspire distro can be downloaded for free, as the GNU license requires. But a big part of the value of Linspire is in its online software installer, known as "Click -N-Run", which is proprietary and not available for free download. Customers have to pay to get a complete copy of Linspire. As a business, Linspire follows ordinary business conventions and charges for products so it can stay in business and fulfill its mission of providing the world's easiest-to-use Linux desktop.

The majority of Linux supporters realize that Linspire represents the best shot at bringing Linux to mainstream users. That in turn will go a long way to restoring competition to the computer industry.

Linspire organizes an annual Linux conference concentrating on Linux desktops, and partners with numerous hardware vendors to provide systems with Linspire preinstalled. Linspire is the Linux leader in pre-installed PCs. That's an important enabler for mainstream use.

Linspire, the company, is a model citizen in the Linux world. Linspire funded several key Linux projects, such as the Reiser 4 filesystem debugging and the Nvu web editor. The company made important improvements to the Mozilla browser. Linspire created and gave to the community the Lphoto and Lmusic open source applications. Linspire really does a great job of investing back in the Linux community in a way that some other bigger and richer companies conspicuously have not.

Additional Linspire Advantages

Linspire supports more media file types than any other distro, right out of the box. If you browse a web page with Flash content, it plays perfectly. Linspire supports all the non-encrypted Windows Media Audio formats and is the only distro that has licensed all the source code from Microsoft to achieve this.

Two major distros, Fedora and SuSE, ship without the ability to play MP3s files due to license concerns about the patents that encumber them. Linspire takes the approach of paying for necessary licenses, just the way Apple does where necessary.

The Linspire customer forums are unquestionably the best and most active Linux forums that you'll find anywhere on the web. Those forums are a terrific source of support and encouragement for new users. The president and the CEO of Linspire post to the forums regularly. You certainly don't see that with other distros. The forums are reached from the support tab on www.linspire.com, and I'll describe them in more detail later.

Linspire provides "one-click installation" of Linux applications, downloaded and installed automatically from a Linspire server. Microsoft have promised this kind of feature for the release after XP; Linspire Linux has it working for users today with Click-N-Run.

Linspire Linux tries to avoid unnecessary differences from Microsoft Windows, so you should find Linspire quite familiar. All these factors together make Linspire the best distro for Windows users who want to try Linux.

The Significance of Open Source Software

I've mentioned a couple of times that Linux is an "open source" product. That means Linux software is developed according to the "scientific cooperation" mode, not the "trade secret" model. Scientific researchers achieve status by sharing their results with the world. The more peer-reviewed publications one has, the more status one has. Other researchers read the papers and can use the work as the starting point for their own efforts. The scientific model of open cooperation has worked for more than three hundred years, and is a major factor in Linux's success.

Openness Versus Restrictions

The openness and sharing of Linux source code contrasts with traditional proprietary software products that are kept secret or restricted with patents. When a vendor does that, nobody else can (potentially) profit from his work, but neither can anyone benefit from improvements made by others. In other words, there is less overall software development and competition in the closed source model.

Linux is part of a strong popular movement in the computer world to follow the open scientific model, rather than the closed proprietary model, for some software. A number of great things flow from open source products: lower costs because of more sharing, better security because of inspection by many independent eyes, technology available to more people more quickly because it is not tied to any one vendor, and better compatibility with other products because the implementation can be seen and adjusted by software professionals.

The GNU General Public License

The openness of Linux is assured by the terms of the license that accompanies it. Linux is licensed under the GNU General Public License or GPL. The GPL is a thoughtful license developed under the leadership of Richard Stallman. It requires that when a GPL-licensed program is distributed, it must be accompanied by the source code. When you take a GPL-licensed program, add more features, and distribute it, you must place your additions under the GPL and provide the source code for your changes, too.

This ensures that all the source code remains available for each GPL-licensed program. If you do not want to distribute the source code for your changes to a GPL-licensed program then you have two options: one, don't distribute the changed program at all (you may use it solely in-house), or, two, do not use a GPL-licensed program as the starting point for your software changes. The GPL basically says that if you distribute a GPL-licensed program, you have to pass on the same rights and responsibilities that you got with it.

You may charge a fee for making a copy (such as a CD) and for offering warranty protection (such as software support). You can't make any other charges for GPL-licensed software. After all, it came to you for free, even if you later added a lot of code to it. It's only fair that others benefit from your code just the way you benefited from the original program.

Some Linux distros (like Red Hat) are commercial and charge for a copy of the CD and for support. They have to supply a free copy of their Linux source code changes to anyone though. Other Linux distros (like Debian) are developed, assembled, and released by committed volunteers, completely for free.

Of course, any distributor can bundle additional software that's not part of the GNU utilities or the Linux kernel, and ship those under whatever license they like. But no one can convert GPL-licensed software into proprietary software, no matter how much they add to it.

People sometimes talk about "free software" in the context of open source software. It doesn't mean "no monetary charge". Free software means the liberty to run the program, the liberty for people to study it, to modify it, to improve it, and to redistribute it.

What Next for Uncle Josh

You're probably expecting me to say that I solved Uncle Josh's Windows-related problems by switching him to Linux and sending him the manuscript of this book.

Well, I didn't. For one thing, I hadn't written it yet. For another, Josh is in his eighties. If his computer fails in some way in future, he wants to talk to one help line that will solve all hardware and software issues. We're prepared to pay for that level of support. *PC Magazine* runs an annual survey of customer support. Apple always places at or near the very top.

The point is that Linux, like Windows, isn't right for every user on every occasion. You've got to review needs, priorities, budget, and readiness to learn something new.

Josh's needs were best met with an Apple Macintosh system. For many other mainstream users, Linux is the right answer. Linux lets you re-use your existing PC hardware and fall back into Windows just by rebooting. If you wish, you can pace yourself and learn Linux in a series of sessions, a couple of hours at a time.

Apple MacOS and Linux computers are both reliable, well-designed systems with innovative features that are usually copied into Windows eventually. Both Apple and Linux systems are immune to Windows viruses and have far fewer security issues of their own.

What Next for You

People who want world-class hardware, software, and support from one vendor, who expect everything to work perfectly right out of the box, and who don't mind paying a modest premium for these qualities, usually get an Apple.

For people eager to get rid of Windows' security problems, ready to learn something new, and happy to save a bundle, there's Linux. Read on for the inside information.

Running the Linux Live CD

Getting Started

You'll start using Linux in this chapter. Some Linux books try to take readers through a full installation onto your hard disk at this point. But successful installation can require an understanding of low-level details, like disk partitioning. These details are usually hidden from most Windows users. There's enough new stuff coming at you right now, without getting into the intricacies of installation.

You'll do something faster and simpler in this chapter—boot Linux from the live CD that accompanies this book. That gets Linux running on your PC, without installing anything.

Note – If you have a PC with Linspire preinstalled, you don't need to use the live CD. Go right on to Chapter 3, "The KDE Desktop," on page 43.

The easiest way to get Linux running

I want to mention, especially if you've heard stories about the difficulty of getting Linux running in the first place, that there is a foolproof, easy way to get Linux with no effort at all.

Just buy a Linux computer. Fry's, a large United States electronics retailer, in June 2004 was selling a PC with 128 MB memory, a 40 GB hard disk, a CD drive, and a modem, all with Linspire preinstalled. The price was $149—less than the retail cost of Windows by itself. Web sites that sell PCs with Linux preinstalled include Walmart.com, sub300.com, microcenter.com, koobox.com, gigabytescs.com, *and* vtlinux.com. *HP in Europe sells PCs with Linux preinstalled. In the United States, you currently have to go through HP's Factory Express web site to configure a PC purchase with Linux (no big deal, but everyone wishes they'd move it into the mainstream — "$100 off any PC that we preinstall with Linux instead of Windows" and they'd fly off the shelves.*

Here's what you'll encounter next in the book. Chapter 3, "The KDE Desktop," on page 43, is about using the Linux GUI. Chapter 4, "Onto the Net," on page 93 explains how to get a network connection.

Chapter 12, "Installation and Boot," on page 439 deals with installing Linux to your hard disk. You can easily skip ahead to Chapter 12 at any time as you progress through the book.

The rest of the book is a series of tutorials on the applications you will use. Those chapters are quite self-contained, so you can read them in any order. Several appendices containing reference material that you can dip into as the need arises.

System Requirements for Running the Live CD

This chapter has two goals:

- To let you boot up Linux using the "zero installation" live CD that comes with the book.

  First you'll learn a few prerequisites for the live CD. Next comes an explanation of how the live CD works, and its limitations. It's likely that the live CD will boot just fine, in which case you can skim through the description of support alternatives, and move right on to Chapter 3, "The KDE Desktop," on page 43.

- To inform you of all the Linux support alternatives that are available.

  These include web searches, the Linspire online forums, Usenet Linux newsgroups, and paid professional consulting.

The rest of the chapter contains troubleshooting help, in the event that the live CD did not boot for you, or did boot but came up with something missing, e.g. no working audio. Several common issues are described, along with their resolution.

Some Hardware Requirements

Modern Linux will run with acceptable performance on just about any PC bought new since the year 2000, when 600MHz Pentium 3's came on the market. That was the year that all PCs got the ability to boot from CD. The "boot from CD" ability is a requirement for installing XP and a requirement for running from a Linux live CD, too. If your PC is not able to boot from CD (because it is too old, or you don't have a CD drive) then it is not the right PC on which to learn Linux. When "CD drive" is mentioned in this chapter, it includes DVD drives.

The more memory you have the better, with 128 MB as the barest minimum. Thankfully, memory is cheap and keeps getting cheaper. It was about $60 for 1 GByte of the cheapest PC2700 DIMM memory in Spring 2005.

You can read your PC's CPU speed and memory on Windows 2000/XP by choosing **Start > My Computer > View System Information > General**. That brings up the System Properties panel showing CPU speed and memory in its lower right corner as in Figure 2-1.

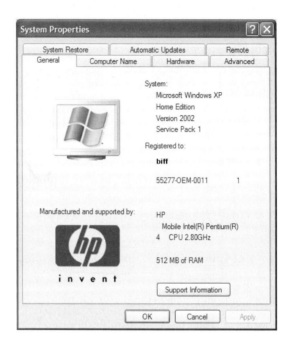

Figure 2-1   Windows' System Properties window, General tab, reveals CPU speed and memory

Confirm your PC's speed and memory now. If it's less than 600 MHz/128 MB, you can carry on but you will have a suboptimal and slow Linux experience. It won't work at all with too little memory.

Linspire Hardware "Must Nots"

As well as the hardware requirements of CPU speed, memory size and CD drive, there are some hardware "must nots". Please review the list and confirm that your PC is not configured with any of them. If it is configured with any of these, you will need to remove them to use the Linspire live CD. If you're not sure whether you have any of these or not, you probably don't. They are all extra cost options that won't be on a system by default.

Linspire is a desktop distro, and there are a number of server configurations that it does not support. These are:

- Linspire 5.0 does not support SCSI or fibre channel disk.

- Linspire 5.0 does not support RAID hardware.

- Linspire 5.0 does not support multiprocessor systems. A multiprocessor-capable Linspire kernel is available separately from Linspire's web site.

- Linspire 5.0 does not support overclocking (game players artificially speeding up the CPU by installing a faster clock chip).

How a Live CD Works

A CD with a bootable operating system on it is called a *live CD*. The live CD makes it very quick and very easy to start using Linux. No disk installation is necessary. You will put the CD in the drive, then reboot the system.

What Happens When You Run the Live CD

When the PC boots up, instead of loading the Windows software from your hard disk, it will load the Linux software from the CD. (You might need to adjust your BIOS settings to ensure that the PC looks at the CD when booting. I'll get to that shortly.) Voila! Your PC is now running Linux with zero installation effort.

When running from a live CD, if you save a file, it is saved to main memory, not disk. The contents of main memory are discarded when you later power down the PC, losing any work that you "saved". If you set a bookmark in the browser while running from the live CD, the details are kept only as long as your system stays powered on. A live CD is convenient for exploring Linux, less so for doing work that you want to save.

A Windows live CD from Kootwijkerbroek

Talented software engineer Bart Lagerweij from Kootwijkerbroek has created a live CD that boots into Windows XP.

Bart's web site is at http://www.nu2.nu/pebuilder. *You can download some of Bart's software and instructions there. The instructions tell you how to make a (perfectly legal) backup copy of certain files from your Windows XP CD, and where to put the files from Bart on the same CD. By an amazing happy chance, the resulting backup CD also works as a live CD for booting*

Windows. This can be very useful for inspecting, comparing, and repairing a Windows disk installation after a virus infection.

Are you wondering where Kootwijkerbroek is? It's in the Netherlands, just a Gouda cheese ball's roll away from Walwijk where Uncle Josh was born and raised. Everything in the universe really is connected if you look closely enough.

Limitations of Running Linux from a Live CD

Until you install Linux onto your hard disk, you'll need to re-enter configuration data about your network and your account each time you boot up from the live Linux CD. It is possible to set things up so that your files are saved to disk, but the whole point of a live CD is to avoid system administration. Don't forget—as soon as you feel confident in using Linux, you can follow the instructions in Chapter 12, "Installation and Boot," on page 439 to permanently install Linux to your disk.

There are a couple other limitations when running from a live CD.

- The Linux live CD needs to stay in the CD drive until you are ready to power off, so that CD drive isn't available for you to use for something else.

- CD and DVD drives are about four or five times slower than hard disk drives. Running Linux from a CD drive will thus be slower than running Linux from a hard disk installation. It won't be four to five times slower, but it will be noticeably slower. It might take five minutes to boot up instead of 90 seconds.

The key is to be aware of these constraints and set expectations appropriately. The live CD will be slower than running from a hard disk installation, you can't save work over a reboot, and it consumes a CD drive.

Advantages of Running Linux from a Live CD

Offsetting the limitations, Linux on a live CD has some really compelling advantages.

- You can use Linux from a live CD to do real tasks, like sending email and using the office applications. You can gradually get comfortable with Linux.

- You can learn at your own pace and with the safety net of knowing that you haven't made any changes that might affect your Windows installation.

Just pop in the live CD and learn some Linux for a while. When you're finished, reboot, remove the CD, and drop effortlessly back to Windows.

Booting and Running Linspire from the Live CD

Finally, the step everyone is ready for. Get the live CD that is bundled with this book, and follow these steps:

1 Make sure that you are running under Windows.

2 Put the Linux CD in the CD drive.

3 Restart your computer by clicking on the **Start** button and choosing **Turn Off Computer** > **Restart**.

4 If everything goes according to plan, the screen will go dark, then your PC will start to boot up. The screen will display a choice asking if you want to boot from the live CD or something else.

Use the cursor keys to highlight the **Live CD** choice and press the **Enter** key. The screen will display a progress bar for a couple of minutes as it boots up.

5 The screen will go dark for a minute, then you will see the Welcome to Linspire display shown in Figure 2-2. The icons on the screen indicate different activities in starting the desktop environment. The icons are highlighted one after the other in sequence to indicate the progress.

Figure 2-2   Welcome to Linspire

6 When this sequence completes, it will show the desktop seen in Figure 2-3.

Then the Linspire click-through user license will be displayed (Figure 12-13 on page 473). Accept the license by clicking **I Agree**, then **Next**.

7   The next four windows (Sound Volume, Date/Time Timezone, Advanced Settings, and Linspire Extras CD) are the same configuration windows that you'll also get after doing an actual installation to hard disk. When you run the live CD, just keep clicking **Next** to dismiss these windows without setting anything. If you want to know more about the settings, they are illustrated in Figure 12-14 on page 474 through Figure 12-18 on page 477.

8   At last, you'll reach the main desktop window.

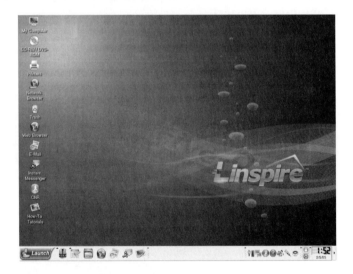

Figure 2-3   The Linspire desktop

Congratulations! This is the Linspire Linux main window. You have successfully launched the Linspire distro of Linux.

9   If you do not see the window shown in Figure 2-3, there is a problem to troubleshoot. *Getting Help* describes the tools for troubleshooting.

Even when the Desktop window comes up perfectly, I suggest you briefly review the *Getting Help* section. These techniques will get you moving again should you hit a problem in any of other chapters, too. The section also suggests some avenues for learning more about Linux.

Getting Help

I'll start with the most common problems with booting from a live CD.

- *PC Didn't Boot Linux*
- *Linspire-Specific Help*
- *Solving Other Problems*
- *BIOS and Device Driver Troubleshooting*

PC Didn't Boot Linux

Use the following sections to pin down the problem if your computer didn't boot the live CD.

Problem 1: The Screen Goes Dark Before Displaying a Progress Bar and the PC Hangs

This is sometimes caused by too little video memory, particularly on laptop systems. Some PCs have a BIOS setting allowing you to increase the amount of memory allocated to graphics. The factory setting might be as low as 1 or 2 MB.

Appendix B, "Making Your Hardware Obey You—BIOS and Device Drivers," on page 507, explains how to make BIOS adjustments. If you're having problems with the screen staying dark early in the boot process, look for this BIOS setting and increase it to 8 MB.

Problem 2: PC Gets Stuck in Boot Loader

One possible failure happens when you try to boot from the live CD. A few seconds after putting the CD in the drive, you'll see a message reading

grub>

This is the command line prompt of the GRUB boot loader. The boot loader is responsible for loading the operating system into memory and transferring control to it. If the GRUB boot loader cannot find the operating system, it doesn't know what to do, so it stops and asks you with the prompt.

Using an external CD drive (for instance, a drive connected to your PC by USB or FireWire, not fitted inside your computer's case) can cause this problem. Some PCs have a BIOS that is not capable of reading storage media connected via USB or FireWire. The operating system proper must be running in order to access these devices. A Windows installation from external CD on such a PC hits the same issue. There are other causes for this problem, too, so you might see it even when booting from an internal CD drive. The workaround is given in hint 378 at the Linspire Hints forum https://forum.linspire.com/forum/postlist.php?Cat=&Board=Hints. It involves making a disk partition, copying the CD contents to it, then using that instead of the CD.

Problem 3: PC Hangs

Another possible failure mode is for your PC to freeze, either with a blank screen, or in one of the Lindows windows, or to not successfully display the Linux main window within five minutes.

If this happens, turn your PC completely off (pull the power cord or battery out). Then wait thirty seconds, restore power and start again at the beginning of *Booting and Running Linspire from the Live CD* on page 31.

You can usually find out where it's getting stuck by pressing the ESCAPE key at the point where booting starts. (It's OK to tap it two or three times to be sure you get it at the right moment.) That will show hundreds of lines of log messages as booting proceeds. When your system freezes, the last three or four lines shown indicate what it's trying to do when things go wrong. Using those messages as search terms, you can search the Linspire forums for more detailed information.

Problem 4: PC Still Boots into Windows

By far the most likely failure you will see is that your system simply boots up into Windows, ignoring the Linux CD. This is also the easiest failure to fix.

This problem usually means that your PC is not configured to boot from CD. Most PCs ship with the BIOS configured to try to boot from floppy disk, CD-ROM, then hard disk, in that order. The PC boots from the first device that has an operating system stored on it. You can change this order in the BIOS setup utility. Since you boot from hard disk 99.9% of the time, booting will be slightly faster if you make the disk the first or only device the BIOS looks at. And that of course will cause the "boot from Linux CD" not to work.

Appendix B explains in full how to change the order in which devices are looked at, so you can move the CD drive to the top of the list.

Linspire-Specific Help

For issues with Linspire, including live CD issues, the first port of call should be the Linspire community forums. Make sure you can clearly describe what you were trying to do, what you're seeing, and how that differed from what you expected to see. There's a huge context that you take for granted about your own PC, and people trying to help don't have that information.

Linspire really does a great job of nurturing its user community. Because the help is web-based, you'll need to be up and running on the network before you can tap into this help. If the problem is that you can't connect to the network, then you'll need to go down to the library or to a friend's house and use their computer.

When you visit the Linspire support URL http://support.linspire.com, you'll see a web page like that shown in Figure 2-4. The critical pieces here are the column headings and the search function (both circled in Figure 2-4). These are the support resources on the Linspire site:

- Search and FAQs

- Forums

- Tutorials

- My Support

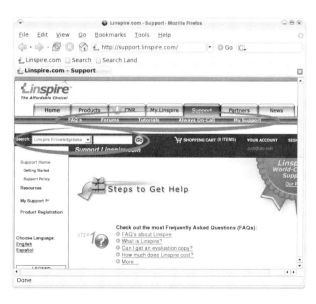

Figure 2-4   Linspire support web resources

Note – The web pages for Linspire were accurate at the time of writing, but of course web pages change quickly and might not look the same when you visit the site. If so, look around for the main menus, use the search field, and you should be able to find the resources I recommend.

The support resources appear in this order because this is the sequence you should follow when you have a problem. You should try to eliminate simple problems first before calling on the help of others.

Linspire plans to introduce pay-per-incident support at some point. They currently have it as an unimplemented place holder on the web site ("Always On-Call"). That will be a positive development for everyone.

linspire.com web site—Keeping busy

Linspire's web site is somewhat overwhelming at first, and uncomfortably Byzantine to navigate. The search engine is spectacularly poor.

Linspire should take the Apple.com web site as their model. When Linspire improves the web site, the screenshots presented here will be outdated, but the approaches described will still be relevant. The design is too busy, but the content is good.

Search and FAQs

This part of the support system is shown in the lower of the two circles in Figure 2-4.

The drop-down list lets you select several alternative places to search. The Knowledgebase is the most useful choice, but it's quicker to *explore* than to *search*. If you search, use plus signs for multiple terms, such as +term1 +term2. Don't leave a space between the plus and the search term!

Note the Date Range on searches defaults to Newer Than One Week. Most of the useful material is far older, so change it to the past year. Results older than 2005 probably aren't useful because they apply to obsolete versions of Linspire.

The best way to access the Linspire knowledge base is to enter a search term that won't be found, like *Lord Lucan* or *Jimmy Hoffa*. That will catapult you to a window with a big button marked **Explore**. Click it, and you'll go to a window listing the topics in the knowledge base (see Figure 2-5).

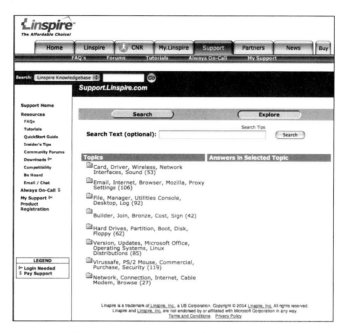

Figure 2-5   Exploring topics in the Linspire Knowledgebase

Now you can see all the topics in the knowledge base. Click on the one of interest.

- The column headed **Resources** (on the left in Figure 2-5) mostly consists of duplicate links to things you can reach in other ways.

- **FAQs** leads to a couple of pages of mixed technical and non-technical Frequently Asked Questions. It's not clear why these aren't simply merged into the knowledge base.

- **Tutorials** is a link to the same Flash tutorial that starts automatically after a new installation. It is well worth reviewing these tutorials once to get the big picture.

- **QuickStart Guide** dumps you into an immediate 30 MB PDF file download. I hope you've got broadband. The Guide is the kind of "Read This First" that you get with a new computer, describing how to plug it in, connect to the net, and run a few applications.

- **Insider's Tips** and **Community Forums** – Sends you to the Linspire user forums, which are described in *Support Forums*.

Support Forums

Linspire hosts a large interactive forum in the form of a web-based bulletin board where Linspire users can post and respond to messages, using their browser. The forum is a significant and very helpful undertaking. As you use Linspire, you should make time to visit the forum, and get a feel for the kind of postings there.

You can reach the forum by the links described previously or by browsing the web site http://linspire.com/forums.

Figure 2-6 shows how the forums will appear in your browser. Click on any of the links in the left column to be taken to a page of threads on that topic.

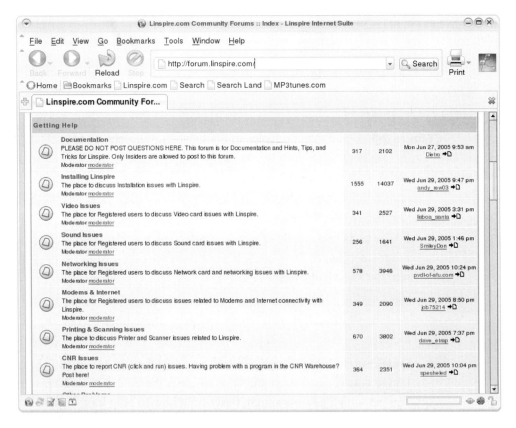

Figure 2-6   Linspire Forums main page

The Linspire community forum is the collective term for a couple of dozen individual forums each devoted to a specific topic. The forums most likely to be of immediate use to you are these ones, all under the heading Getting Help.

- **Documentation** – The accumulated wisdom from knowledgeable users. For example, I contributed hint number 368 on backing up files to USB flash memory.

- **General Discussion** – Discussion of Linspire products, and it includes many technical questions and answers.

- **Installing Linspire** – For people who have got stuck on some installation or boot problem.

- **Video Issues** – Issues relating to monitors, screen resolution, and graphics cards.

- **Sound Issues** – Audio problems and questions.

- **Networking Issues** – Questions on topics like how to use Samba, how to configure a network adapter, and why doesn't wireless work.

- **Modems and Internet** – Dial-up problems.

- **Other Problems** – Anything not covered by the other items, such as USB or scanner problems.

Register to Post in the Forums

Anyone can read the forums, so it's easy to search for an answer before posting a question. To post a question, you need to register by clicking on the link to join the forums. You supply an email address and some other information. You need to be a CNR customer to post questions or answers in some of the forums. It's not immediately obvious how you log in from your browser to be able to post. You do it through the Support tab.

Through careful nurturing, Linspire has created a positive atmosphere in these forums. New users pose questions, and more experienced users reply to them. Over time, new users gain more experience, and start answering questions themselves.

Some very skilled people are in these forums, who want to see Linux succeed, and who give freely of their time and expertise to help that happen. Some of those people are listed in the acknowledgments section of this book.

You might also find a few people with more enthusiasm than knowledge, so apply a little common sense, just like you do for everything else you read or hear.

In all question-and-answer forums, like the Linspire community, or Usenet newsgroups, or the http://www.linuxquestions.org site, the way you ask a question

makes a huge difference to the quality of answer you get. Open source supporter
Eric Raymond penned some advice on the subject at http://catb.org/~esr/faqs/
smart-questions.html. While not excusing the huge side-helping of attitude that
many Usenet posters have, the key points are:

- Make a serious effort to find the answer on your own first, with a web search,
  FAQs, etc.

- Remember you're asking busy people for free advice, so don't act like it's an
  entitlement.

- Give enough relevant detail on the problem so that helpers can envision what
  you are seeing.

- Try to give back, by helping others in turn.

Don't overlook the Linspire Wiki (cooperative writing venture) at the web site
http://www.linspireguide.com. Started in late 2004 by Linspire enthusiast Mats
Ekblom, the Linspire Wiki has quickly attracted many volunteers and grown to be
a substantial resource. Click the **Index** link on the home page to get an idea of
what's in the Wiki.

When all else fails, you have the opportunity to call on Linspire support. This is
found by clicking on the **My Support** sub-tab. This will take you to a page where
registered Linspire customers can create incident reports, or pose a question by
email (with a 3–5 day turnaround).

You might also find the Linspire Consultants Program helpful. The web page at
http://linspire.com/insiders lists hundreds of independent Linspire consultants
around the world. These people offer services for hire, and can often solve thorny
technical issues that are difficult to resolve oneself. If you have a broadband
connection, they can use desktop sharing to solve the problem remotely. In many
cases using a consultant is the fastest and most effective way to get results.

Most Linspire consultants belong to the Insiders Program. By paying a one-time
admission fee, Linspire users can join an elite circle enjoying the benefits of
additional communication between themselves and Linspire. Insiders get early
access to test releases of forthcoming products, and several forums are exclusively
for insiders. You can sign up for insider membership; just go to the web site at
http://www.linspire.com/insiders.

Solving Other Problems

If you encounter a problem not described here, or if you've tried the approaches described previously without solving the problem, you can look other places for help.

Use the Linux Documentation Project at http://www.tldp.org. The LDP is a loosely knit team of volunteers who provide documentation for many aspects of Linux. They produce guides, how-tos, manuals, and FAQs. In Unix generally, the pages of manuals are universally referred to as man pages. There is a man page for each command, each type of file, each programming interface and so on.

The LDP archives are translated into several languages, and are searchable. The most effective way to use the archive seems to be to find the right guide for that topic, and read it in depth. There isn't any feature for posting questions and getting them answered.

Search the Linux newsgroup archives using Google. One of the earliest applications on the Internet was a large electronic bulletin board for exchanging information and ideas. This is called Usenet and the individual forums are known as newsgroups. Usenet has dropped in use a little as people turn to simpler and more easily accessible web sites. It still has a large group of core users. Anyone can post questions on Usenet (you can do it from your browser at Google), and anyone can answer them.

To search the Usenet archive, go to http://groups.google.com. Click on the link on the top right labeled Advanced Groups Search. That brings up a web form, shown in Figure 2-7 on page 42, where you specify three things:

- All of the words to search for.

- The newsgroup to search in. Specify comp.os.linux.*

- The date range to search in. Linux improves so quickly, it is not worth searching more than two or three years in the past.

Usenet can be a bit of a kid's playground full of anonymous posters with no adult supervision. It's like a game where a lot of players cheat. Expect the good, the bad, and the ugly, and learn how to tell them apart. You have to ask questions in a respectful way, to encourage knowledgeable volunteers to give you helpful answers rather than merely make fun of you.

Figure 2-7   Using Google to searching Usenet for Linux information

These suggestions of where to find more help apply to all Linux questions, not just installation problems. You can find out how to register at Google and post questions to Usenet by reading http://groups.google.com/googlegroups/help.html.

BIOS and Device Driver Troubleshooting

It's extremely unlikely you'll still be having problems with the CD. If you are and you would like to pursue troubleshooting, see Appendix B, "Making Your Hardware Obey You—BIOS and Device Drivers," on page 507.

The KDE Desktop

Getting Started

There are several alternatives for a desktop GUI environment in Linux. This chapter will introduce you to the most popular: the KDE desktop environment. As you'll shortly see, it's not that different from what you're using now. And that's true whatever you're using now.

Different Operating Systems, Similar GUIs

Take a look at these examples from some popular operating systems. Figure 3-1 is Windows-95, around a decade ago. Figure 3-2 is Windows XP, today. (The windows have been configured with a neutral background, so you can see the windows and icons more clearly.)

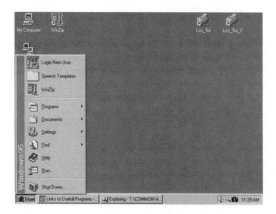

Figure 3-1   Windows 95 GUI, from ten years ago

There's not a lot of difference between Windows-then and Windows-ten-years-on. Buttons now have round corners and menu entries are rearranged, but all important elements are the same.

Files, folders, and applications are still represented by icons. You run applications by clicking on the Start button and descending through menus. There's a graphical file manager program that lets you explore your directories. You can drag popular files or folders to your desktop. The desktop holds files or links to them for quick access.

Figure 3-2   Windows XP today, showing the Firefox browser

Figure 3-3 is the MacOS X desktop. It is very similar in use to the Windows GUI.

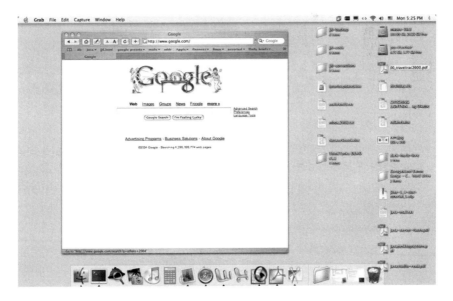

Figure 3-3   MacOS X window system, showing the Safari browser

GUIs Are Mature Technology

One recent idea in GUIs comes from Sun Microsystems. Sun has previewed its Java-based Looking Glass project, which makes windows into three-dimensional objects (more like a box of paper than a sheet of paper). Figure 3-4 shows a Linux desktop running Looking Glass.

Figure 3-4   Sun's innovative Looking Glass GUI on Linux

In Looking Glass, a user can spin a window around and type notes on the back of it! Sun is developing Looking Glass as an open source project, and plans to release it on both Linux and its own Unix-based operating system Solaris, probably in 2006.

Microsoft's biggest GUI innovation so far is the "Clear Desktop" button—a tiny refinement. Overall, very little serious GUI innovation has ever occurred on Windows or on Linux. That's not what they're for. They are both followers, primarily of Apple. It takes a while for Apple's inventions to be copied by others, so the lack of innovation in Windows and Linux GUIs means they are still quite similar to each other.

At the user level, just about every GUI has:

- A desktop display that represents the content of some specific folder with icons for applications, folders, and files.

  Clicking on an application icon runs that program. Clicking on a file or folder icon runs a program that lets you view the file or folder content. KDE has exactly the same concept, and its icons are quickly recognizable too. There are only so many ways to represent the concept "trash can" in a thumbnail-sized picture.

- A Start button in the lower-left corner of the screen that provides a menu containing icons representing programs. You progress through more menus to start a program. (OK, the Mac does this a little differently—all the programs are in one folder, and you get to it using the file explorer known as Finder.)

- A panel or task bar, by default at the bottom of the screen. The panel shows a small icon for each running program. This panel often displays other status items like date/time, and may have icons that are shortcuts to frequently used programs.

- A new window on the screen to contain each application you start. The window has menu items specific to that program; frequently the first menu item lets you select input and output files.

- Three small icons at the top right of each window. From left to right, these will iconify the window, toggle the window between supersize/normal, and close the application and window. The icons are the same bar, square, and X, that Windows uses.

The point is that, although there is some innovation taking place in the GUI world, window systems are fundamentally a mature technology. That really works in your favor as you learn KDE.

GUIs all do essentially the same things. Once you've seen how to configure the Linux desktop the way you want it, it's just a matter of finding your way around menus and retraining your fingers.

Introduction to the KDE Desktop

Figure 3-5 shows the KDE desktop. The name K Desktop Environment, or KDE, was chosen to distinguish the software from CDE, Unix's Common Desktop Environment. When the project started in 1996, the K briefly stood for Kool (as in *CDE is common but KDE is kool*). Now the K doesn't stand for anything. It has resulted in a large number of KDE utilities being named with an initial letter K, like Kmail, Kformula, KOffice, and so on.

There are several desktop environments for Linux. Another popular one is called Gnome—the GNU Network Object Model Environment. Among the twenty most popular distros, the majority prefer KDE to Gnome. Applications are generally compiled for one desktop environment, but they will run under any desktop environment as long as you have the right libraries installed.

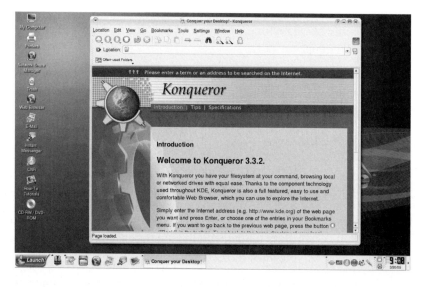

Figure 3-5   Linux's K Desktop Environment, showing a file manager window

KDE is more established than Gnome, and a little more Windows-like. Linspire and KDE are described in this book; I don't cover Gnome, but it's good to know that choices exist. Each distro decides for itself which desktop environment to include, and some distros include several.

Linspire version 5.0 uses KDE version 3.3.2. You can see the version number by choosing **Help** > **About** in many KDE applications, including the Control Center. (I'll get to that shortly; the Control Center is a configuration program like the Control Panel in Windows.)

KDE is completely open source software

KDE uses the Qt GUI toolkit (library), which used to incur license fees under some circumstances. That was a big sticking point for some users, and led to the launch of the Gnome project. Starting with Qt version 2.2 in September 2000, the Qt toolkit was released under the Limited GNU Public License. KDE is now completely free and open source software.

You can find the source code for KDE at the ftp site ftp://ftp.kde.org *or one of its mirror sites. You might not care about access to the source code, but it's an enabler for those who do care and can produce beautiful additions. Those updates and new versions benefit you directly and cost you nothing. Open source software is about professional cooperation, not the extraction of super-profits at the expense of customers.*

Figure 3-6 shows the **Start** button (Windows) and the **Launch** button (Linux).

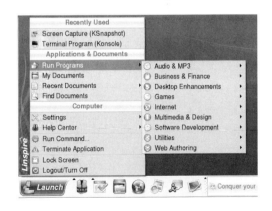

Windows   Linux

Figure 3-6   How to select and start an application, in Windows and Linux

KDE is noticeably better organized than Windows here. By default, Windows displays all the installed applications when you click the **All Programs** button. There might be one hundred of them, laid out in a long list from the top to bottom of the screen, in panels from left to right. I truncated the Windows display at the top and on the right to make this illustration fit on the page.

KDE has a more consistent menu under the **Start** or **Launch** button. KDE organizes programs into related groups, such as Business and Finance, which contains an application such as the office suite and a calculator. As in Windows, the black triangle at the end of a menu always means that selecting that item will expand to a lower level menu. So it's always safe to select it, as you will be seeing more choices rather than committing to an action.

The Windows icons for a trash can, spreadsheet program, folder, and picture file are shown in Figure 3-7. Figure 3-8 shows the KDE icons corresponding to the same concepts of trash can folder, application, folder, and picture file.

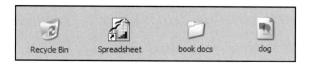

Figure 3-7   Some representative Windows XP icons

Figure 3-8   Corresponding KDE icons

Notice that the image file on Linux displays a thumbnail of the image. Windows will do this too, if in Windows Explorer you choose **View** > **Thumbnails**. There's a setting to increase the size of icons if you find these too small.

You will find that the concepts in KDE (and in Gnome, and in MacOS X) map quite closely to the concepts in the Windows GUI. Learning KDE is very quick for most Windows users. Just tour the desktop, try the pointing/clicking described here, and refer back to sections in this chapter as needed.

KDE notices which applications you are running when you log out, and starts them again when you log back in. If you log out with the browser window open, it will start the browser when you log in again.

The KDE Panel

Figure 3-9 shows the names given to pieces of the desktop in KDE. The main part of the desktop is just an expanse of screen where you can store icons representing files and folders that you'd like to keep handy. The more interesting part of the desktop is the bar along the bottom of the screen, known as the KDE Panel or Kicker.

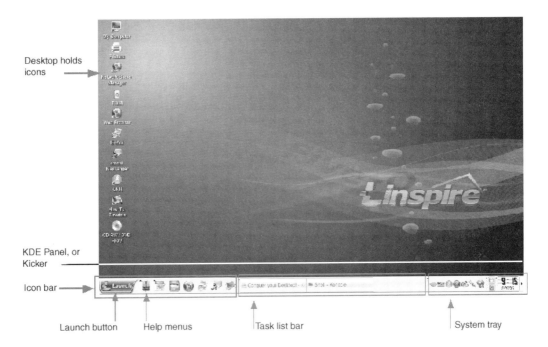

Figure 3-9   The entire bottom row of the desktop is the KDE Panel, or Kicker

The bottom row of the desktop, known as the KDE panel or Kicker has three distinct pieces: the icon bar, the task list bar, and the system tray. These three pieces do pretty much the same job as their counterparts that occupy the same places on the Windows desktop.

The icon bar has as its leftmost icon the KDE button or Launch button. The Launch button works just like the Start button in Windows. It brings up a cascading menu of programs you can run. The button is labeled **Launch** in the Linspire distro; most other distros label it with the letter **K** for KDE.

Next to the Launch button is a button that looks like a life-vest. Clicking on this brings up some help menus. Click once (only once) on an icon in the icon bar to start the application. Double-click on an icon on the desktop to start the application. You can correct the inconsistency by clicking **Launch** > **Settings** > **Control Center** > **Peripherals** > **Mouse**.

The rest of the icon bar is mostly shortcuts to programs you use often. From left to right, after the help menu life-vest (refer to Figure 3-10) come:

Figure 3-10   The icon bar is the leftmost part of the Kicker

- Lassist, a menu containing an address book, and calender applications.

- A blue file cabinet drawer, representing the Konqueror file manager and web browser.

- A globe for the Linspire Internet Suite browser (it's Mozilla with some neat additional features).

- The Mozilla email application, unfortunately with an icon showing a letter e confusingly close to Microsoft's Internet Explorer logo.

- The orange striding man/blue speech bubble instant messenger client.

- The "clear all windows from desktop/restore all windows" button.

Let your mouse linger over each icon to bring up a tooltip about each program.

The task bar contains a button for each GUI application you are running. Each task bar button provides a fast way to manipulate windows that may be buried under other windows. Try it now. Start the file manager application by clicking the file manager (file cabinet icon) in the icon bar.

A single left-click will bring up a new copy of the file manager and put a button representing it on the task list bar. When you click on an application's button in the task list bar, it opens the window for that application at the front of the desktop, on top of any other windows you have open. See Figure 3-11.

Figure 3-11   The task bar has a button for each running GUI application

Clicking on the button again will hide that window, by iconifying it. (The application window disappears from the screen, but the application keeps running; clicking the button in the task bar will restore the window to the front of the desktop.)

The system tray shown in Figure 3-12 is as quirky in KDE as it is in Windows.

Figure 3-12   The system tray gives you an icon to access demon programs

The original intention, with both Windows and KDE, was that the system tray would contain a few icons for demon applications (applications that run in the background with no user interface). When the user left-clicks on an icon in the tray, an application window appears that allows more user input. In practice, as on Windows, some applications seem to dump their icons willy nilly into the system tray just because they can. Most of the items in the system tray can safely be ignored, but here are some of the ones you might use.

* Linspire KDE puts a *green running man Click-N-Run icon* in the tray. Click-N-Run is the jewel in the crown of Linspire—it provides one-click installation of new applications from across the Internet. You'll learn about Click-N-Run in depth in *Introducing Linspire's Click-N-Run* on page 203.

* A notebook PC will show *battery status icon* in the system tray.

* There's a *red 0/1 button* to do a fast logout and an orange padlock to lock the screen. Together, these are called the lock/logout applet.

* The last icon is a *date/clock*. Left-click on it to bring up a calendar of this month. Right-click on the clock to bring up a menu that lets you adjust the clock appearance.

* The small *right-pointing arrowhead* at the far right edge of the system tray will remove the KDE panel from the desktop when you click it. It leaves just a similar left pointing arrowhead in its place. When you click that, the Kicker slides back into place. This is for people who just have to have that extra 5% of screen real estate and don't mind a few extra clicks to get it. Try removing and restoring the Kicker now.

How Your Folders Are Organized in KDE

When the Linspire team customized KDE for its distro, it called one of the predefined folders in each user's home folder My Computer. Windows has something similar that shows up in Windows Explorer. On Windows XP, My Computer is a panel that displays shortcuts to the home directories of all users, and has icons for various useful programs like the control panel, system information, and the install/remove utility. It also shows all the drives attached to a system.

In Linspire's version of KDE, My Computer is a folder, not a panel, and it does not have any links that start applications. It does show all the drives attached to a system. Linspire's My Computer folder also contains shortcuts pointing to half-a-dozen adjacent folders, indicated in Figure 3-13. I find these links confusing because of the name duplications, but it seems to be OK in practice.

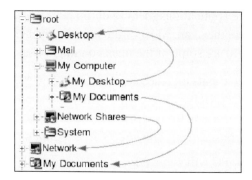

Figure 3-13   Your My Computer folder, which points to some of your other folders

The KDE file manager starts up in My Computer directory by default. The My Computer folder also appears on the desktop as an icon. Double-click to open it in the file manager.

Just as on Windows, pathnames can have spaces in them. The GUI tools understand this, but if you need to type a pathname containing spaces in a command window, either put the whole pathname in double quotes, or use a backslash to escape the space as in these two example pathnames:

```
"/root/My Documents/My Photos"
/root/My\ Documents/My\ Photos
```

When you escape a space the backslash tells the command line to treat the space as part of the string, rather than using it to end the string. It's named after the escape key on very old telex terminals that, when pressed, changed the meaning of the character that followed. Modern keyboards still have an escape key, but it is no longer used in this way.

File and folder terminology

File: A collection of bytes that belong together and form an application, a picture, a document, or some other kind of data. One definition of an operating system says that it is a program that maintains a file system and shares hardware resources on a computer.

Folder: This is a synonym for a directory. It is a special kind of file that contains a number of other files, just like a drawer in an office file cabinet can hold several paper files. Folders can be nested in other folders arbitrarily deep. We organize our files by putting related files in the same folder, and choosing meaningful file and folder names.

Link: This is effectively a synonym for a Windows shortcut. When you click on the icon representing a link, you get the same result as if you had clicked on the file or folder that is linked to.

Pathname: This is the series of folders that ultimately lead to a specific file on your system. The last component in a pathname is a file name if you are referring to a file. All the other components are folder names. Forward slashes / are used to separate the components in a Linux pathname.

Root directory: This is the topmost directory in the filesystem, referred to as / and pronounced root or slash. The term root is used in the sense of "most fundamental."

The Linux root directory corresponds to Windows C:\ but Linux doesn't use drive letters. Every file on every drive in Linux is reached through a pathname that starts at /. If Windows has a D: drive CD, the Linux equivalent is /mnt/cdrom0.

Home directory: Every user has a single top-level folder that contains all his or her other files and folders. This folder is called the user's home directory.

All the user home directories are put in a directory called /home. Each user's home directory is the same as their user name. So user peter has the directory /home/peter. User wendy has the home directory /home/wendy.

Root user: As well as a file called root, every Unix system has a user called root. This is the system administrator account, and it has permission to do anything.

The root user has his home directory at /root *pronounced* "slash-root". *Don't get confused over the three different things called root: the superuser, the* / *directory, and root's home directory* /root. *The context is always enough to tell these apart.*

The tilde sign ~ *is an abbreviation for your own home directory. You can refer to someone else's home directory by appending their username onto the tilde. Wendy's home directory is in* ~wendy. *So* ~root *is another way to refer to folder* /root.

Using the Konqueror File Manager

Linspire uses a popular application called Konqueror as the graphical file manager/browser. Used this way, Konqueror is roughly the equivalent of Windows Explorer, but Konqueror also has the capabilities of a web browser.

You can use Konqueror to move, copy and delete files. Later, you'll see how you can also do this with the command line, which is far faster and not the scary tool that some people have been led to fear. As a reminder, Figure 3-14 shows Windows Explorer.

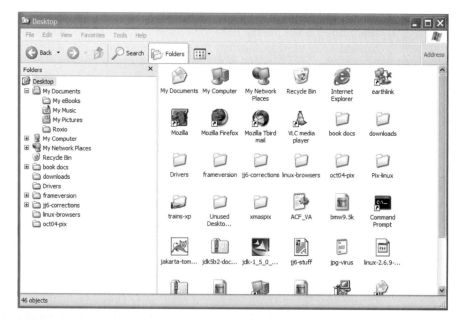

Figure 3-14   Windows Explorer shows folders and files

It has a left and right panel. The left panel list all the folders in the Desktop folder, plus a couple of others you might want to visit like My Computer and My Network Places. You can highlight any of these folders and/or expand the tree. The right panel shows all the files in the highlighted folder in the left panel.

Note – Here's a Windows tip. It's hard to pick out Windows Explorer from the menus on the Start button, as the entries are not in any useful order. Instead of playing "Hunt the program" in Windows XP, you can right-click on **Start** and select **Explore**.

Starting the Konqueror File Manager

Start the Konqueror file manager by clicking the **file cabinet icon** on the icon bar, shown in Figure 3-15. That opens Konqueror in a folder called My Computer

Figure 3-15   Konqueror main window

You can also start Konqueror by clicking the **Launch** button, then **My Documents**. That puts Konqueror in the My Documents folder, not My Computer.

Konqueror Basics Quick Reference

Although the program has some powerful features, the Konqueror basics are straightforward:

- You type pathnames and URLs in the Location field to see that directory or web page displayed.

- You can use the **Settings** menu to determine how much "icon junk" appears at the top of the Konqueror window.

- You can use the **Window** menu to determine how to "slice and dice" (split) the main window.

- You drag files and folders between windows to move them, or to the trash icon on the desktop to delete them.

- You can create new folders and rename them by right-clicking.

- You can rename files and folders by right-clicking, then choosing **Rename**, or by highlighting the name and pressing F2.

Like KDE itself, Konqueror is almost infinitely customizable. The **Settings** > **Toolbars** menu item (along the top of the Konqueror window) displays some of the choices you can make. You can show or not show: Toolbar, an extra toolbar (allowing easy splitting of the Konqueror window), Location Bar, and a bookmark. Figure 3-16 shows these features.

Make sure you have selected Main Toolbar, Extra Toolbar, and Location Toolbar, and that you can see them as in Figure 3-16. You can actually grab these toolbars by the dimpled bar at their left end, and drag them to new positions in or around Konqueror.

You can hide the menu bar, but then you lose the ability to select anything off a menu. Bring back a hidden menu bar by clicking in the Konqueror window to give it the focus, then hold down the control key and type m. This two-key combination is usually written as Ctrl-m.

The Konqueror Window menu allows still further customization: you can split the Konqueror window into two. This is useful for moving files from one folder to another.

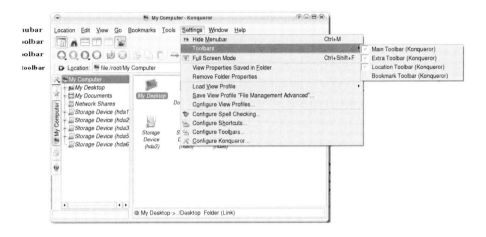

Figure 3-16   Toolbar names in Konqueror

Viewing More Information in Konqueror

Let's customize the Konqueror display a little more. Click the first icon on the left in the extra toolbar. This toggles on/off the Navigation panel (the Navigation panel is a table of shortcuts to folders that you don't need often).

Your display will now look similar to Figure 3-17 (perhaps with a different assortment of files).

Figure 3-17   Konqueror displays the folder /root/Desktop

Next, look at the main toolbar of Konqueror. See Figure 3-15 on page 57 for a refresher on which bar that is. Pause the mouse over each icon in turn on the main toolbar. A tooltip will pop up describing what the icon does.

The two icons at the far right end of the main toolbar change the view you get in the main window. If you let the mouse linger on either of these icons, they actually turn into a drop-down list of choices. If you look closely, you can see a black triangle under each icon—a subtle clue that the icon expands into a list.

You stay in the same folder, but depending on your icon choice, the files, folders, and links are shown as icons, as text, with additional information, and so on.

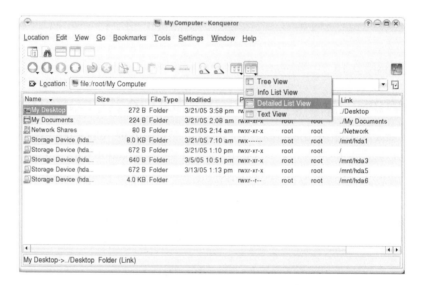

Figure 3-18   Konqueror displays a Detailed List View

I favor the rightmost icon's **Detailed List View**, shown in Figure 3-18. This is the view that tells you the most information about the folder contents. You can sort the view into order by clicking on the heading on any of the columns, Name, Size, File Type etc. You should look at all the view choices, and use whichever you like best.

Toolbar icons are intended to provide a shortcut to commands present on the menu. If you choose **View** > **View Mode**, you'll find all six views that the toolbar icons offer. You can change the width of the columns of information in a view by dragging left or right the bar that separates two column headings.

To see more of the display, drag the window wider by putting the cursor exactly on any corner of the window. When the cursor is in the right position, the cursor will change from a single-headed arrow to a double-headed arrow and you can click and drag. You can resize any window this way, not just Konqueror.

Moving Konqueror to Display a Different Folder

Just as in Windows, the desktop that you see as the main window of your GUI represents an actual folder on your system. On Windows, for user peter, that folder is C:\Documents and Settings\peter\Desktop.

Similarly, in KDE, most of the objects that are visible on the screen desktop are actual files, folders, and links in the folder called ~/Desktop. If you move a file out of that folder, it will disappear from the GUI desktop.

Both Windows and KDE fool you a bit by displaying some additional things on the GUI desktop that are not files within your Desktop directory. They do this because they think it will be helpful to you. The Network Share Manager icon is one of these things. So don't expect a perfect correspondence between what the desktop shows and what Konqueror shows in the ~/Desktop folder.

The Desktop folder is the GUI desktop and that's that!

It would be cool if you could select the folder that is displayed as the GUI desktop, and maybe change it on the fly, instead of being tied to the specific folder called ~/Desktop. But this would probably generate way too many calls to support lines asking "Hey, where did my files go?"

You're stuck with this one folder that's magnified to be the screen backdrop, and it's not even the home directory. If you want to look at directories other than the desktop, you have to use Konqueror, or some other file manager.

You can move display a different directory in a few different ways.

1   On the Konqueror menu bar, choose **Location** > **Open Location** and a dialog box will appear.

2   Type the pathname for the new folder in the dialog box. As you type, Konqueror will display a drop-down list of paths that match what you are typing. You can select from this list at any time (see Figure 3-18).

3   Click **OK**. Konqueror will now switch to display the chosen folder.

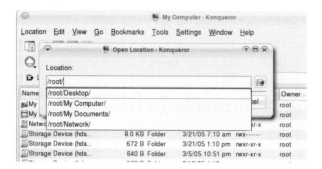

Figure 3-19   Moving Konqueror to a new location

4   In the Konqueror location bar (see Figure 3-19), overtype the text field, so it reads file:*path-to-new-folder*, e.g. file:/root/My Documents/My Photos. You can clear this Location field by clicking the white "X" on black arrow (again, see Figure 3-19) which is the leftmost icon in the toolbar. Again, Konqueror will show a list of possible path completions that you might select.

5   You can double-click on any folder that is visible in the main Konqueror window, to enter that folder.

6   In the Konqueror main toolbar, the first four icons take Konqueror to a different directory. You can see these icons in Figure 3-16. From left to right, they take you:

◆   Up to the parent directory

◆   Back to the directory you were previously in

◆   Forward to directory you were in before you pressed the back arrow

◆   Home to your home directory or URL

Konqueror, web browsing, and you

You might wonder about the meaning of the file: *prefix that Konqueror sticks on the beginning of pathnames in the Location field. It might remind you of the* http: *that gets stuck on the front of web addresses.*

In a fine example of the "creeping feature creature", Konqueror functions as a web browser, as well as a file explorer. The file: *prefix is the protocol that tells Konqueror how to deal with the string that follows.*

If Konqueror sees file:, *it will treat the string as a pathname in your filesystem (if there is no protocol present, it will default to this case). If Konqueror sees* http:, *it will treat the string as a URL. You can thus type a URL, such as*

http://yahoo.com, *in the Location field. As long as you have a network connection, Konqueror will display that web page.*

There are other protocols, too. The protocol google: *followed by some strings will do a search at Google, and return the results in the body of the Konqueror window. Figure 3-20 shows an example of this. The protocol* man: *followed by the name of a command displays the reference manual page for that command.*

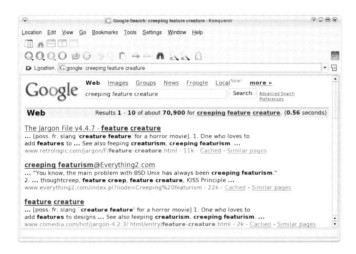

Figure 3-20   Konqueror: dessert topping, floor wax, and browser

When Konqueror displays a web page, the + and - magnifying glass icons will increase and reduce the font size, respectively. The binoculars icon lets you search for words in the web page.

Unifying the views of local and remote file access is a creative idea, and a great research project, but not mainstream yet. My advice is use Konqueror for file exploring, Firefox for browsing, and Thunderbird for email.

Splitting the Konqueror Window

You can move a file or a folder using a very handy feature of Konqueror known as the split screen view. On the Konqueror menu bar, choose **Window > Split View Top/Bottom** as shown in Figure 3-21. The top/bottom split has already been done in Figure 3-21. There's also a Split View Left/Right. Either choice divides the Konqueror display in half, and thus lets you show the contents of two different folders.

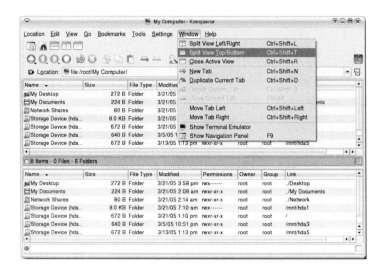

Figure 3-21   Splitting the Konqueror window

The extra toolbar also contains two icons that do the two view splits. There's also an icon to close a view. Move the mouse along the extra toolbar, pausing on icons to see the tooltip that pops up to identify the icons.

If the two views are too small for you, you might like to choose **Settings > Full Screen Mode** to maximize the Konqueror window. You lose the menu bar when you go into full screen mode, but you can revert to a smaller window by clicking the rightmost icon on the toolbar (a downward pointing red arrow). You might have noticed that the toolbar contents change according to the Konqueror view. This is called a context or context-sensitive GUI control described in the GUI terminology sidebar.

You can click and drag the dimpled bar between the two panels to change how much space each panel has. When you have split a view, notice that each panel has a radio button in its lower left corner. One of the radio buttons is filled in with a green color. That indicates that this panel is active, meaning that any changes you make to the location will be shown in this panel. The other panel won't change until you click on its radio button to make it the active panel.

Although several applications can run simultaneously, only one window at a time has the focus. The window with the focus will get any input typed on the keyboard. This window is also called the active window.

GUI terminology

A context menu or context-sensitive menu is a menu that pops up when you right-click on something. The list of items that the menu offers depends on what you right-clicked on.

If you right-click on a file icon on the desktop, your options are Open, Cut, Copy, Rename, Move to Trash, etc. If you right-click on the system tray, your options are Add, Remove, Size, Configure Panel, etc. The menu is sensitive to the context in which it appears. Other GUI controls can be context sensitive too, not just menus.

Moving and Copying Files

Once you have split the Konqueror window, you can copy or move files and folders just by dragging them between the windows. Use the Location field to make one of the windows show the source folder, and the other to show the destination folder. Drag the file or folder from source window to destination window.

To keep things sane, I like to set the view panels so that the source folder is always the upper panel, and the destination folder is always the lower panel. That way, I'm always dragging from the upper panel and dropping onto the lower panel.

As an example, let's move one of the sample photo files that accompany Linspire to your desktop. Follow these steps:

1   Split the Konqueror view, top and bottom, as in *Splitting the Konqueror Window* on page 63.

2   Change the location of the top view to be file:/root/My Documents/My Photos.

3   Change the location of the bottom view to be file:/root/Desktop.

4   Click and drag the file LphotoExample5.jpg from the top view, and drop it on the bottom view.

When you drop the file or folder into the destination window, Konqueror will pop up a small window asking if you want to move the object, copy it, or create a link to it, as illustrated in Figure 3-22. Make your choice by highlighting one of the choices, and Konqueror will do that action. Move is appropriate here.

You can equally well move and copy by starting a second copy of Konqueror, and dragging a file between the two instances. Many people prefer the split window approach because it avoids window proliferation, keeping your screen tidy.

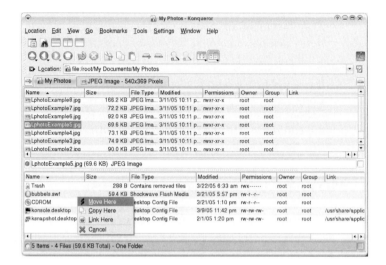

Figure 3-22   Using drag-and-drop to display the context menu with the options Copy, Move, and Link

You can view the photo file you just moved in a couple of ways:

- Double-click on the **file name**. It will open in that **View** tab. (Click on **Back** in the main toolbar to go back to the folder when you are finished looking at the picture.)

- Right-click on the **file name** and select **Open in New Window** from the context menu that pops up.

- To do simple image editing, right-click on the **file name** and select **Open With > KolourPaint**. KolourPaint is a basic image editor that supports image rotation, contrast/brightness changes, and cropping.

Deleting Files and Folders

You delete a file that is visible on the desktop or in the Konqueror file manager, the same way: highlight the file (or folder) with the left mouse button and press the **Delete** key on the keyboard. The first time you do this, you'll get a message asking you to confirm the deletion. Check the box in that message dialog to avoid future requests for delete confirmation.

It's safe to do unconfirmed deletes, because the files are not actually deleted. As with all modern consumer-oriented operating systems, files deleted using the GUI are just moved to a special Trash folder on the Desktop. You can open that folder by double-clicking on the trash icon. You undelete files by dragging them from the trash window back onto the desktop or into a Konqueror view.

You should empty the trash periodically to free up the disk space used by the files in the trash can. Right-clicking on the trash icon, or the open trash folder, brings up a menu with an **Empty Trash Bin** item. Another way to delete something is to drag its icon to the trash icon. You can do practically everything in KDE several different ways.

Creating Files and Folders

You'll usually create files using your applications. The spreadsheet program will create a spreadsheet file and so on. You might want to create additional directories to organize your files. You can do this either on the Desktop or on a Konqueror window. Right-click in either place, and select **Create New** to bring up a list of choices shown in Figure 3-23.

Figure 3-23   Right-click on the desktop or in a Konqueror window to create a new file or folder

Accessing Your Windows Files from Linux

When you run from the live CD, you can see and retrieve all your Windows data files. You might also be able to access these files after you install Linux, depending on the choices you make during installation.

When Linspire boots up, it will mount all the filesystems that it finds on your disks. A few pages earlier, I mentioned that Linux doesn't use drive letters. Instead of separate C:\ and D:\ drives, Linux will use /somepath/somename and /somepath/someotherdisk. Mounting a filesystem means attaching that filesystem to somewhere in the root filesystem.

In Konqueror, click on the home icon, or type file:/root/My Computer in the location. If there is a windows partition on a disk, it will typically appear with the name Storage Device (hda1).

Figure 3-24 (back) shows the view for hda1, the first partition on the first hard disk, which is a Windows partition in this case. If you have a second disk, it will be called hdb, and its partitions will be hdb1, hdb2, hdb3, and so on. The front Konqueror view in Figure 3-24 shows how you can navigate down to the files on the Windows desktop for user peter.

Figure 3-24   A Windows partition might show up as /mnt/hda1

You will typically find most of your Windows data on the Windows desktop, or under the folder /mnt/hda1/Documents and Settings/peter/My Documents. That's the good news.

The bad news is that you might not be able to write to these Windows folders using Linux. The older FAT filesystem (used in Windows 9x) is writeable, but the standard Windows XP NTFS filesystem presents problems. How can you tell which filesystem your Windows installation uses? Just try to create a file or folder there. If Konqueror gives you an error dialog box, you're using NTFS.

Microsoft keeps secret the details of its NTFS file system to hinder Linux people working for greater interoperability. Everything has to be laboriously reverse-engineered. The U.S. Department of Justice made a serious mistake in not requiring Microsoft to publish interoperability specifications for more interfaces as part of the legal settlement of Microsoft's monopoly abuses.

Nor will you be able to directly execute any Windows programs on Linux. Windows applications use operating system libraries that are only available on Windows. Chapter 1 mentions a couple of workarounds to this using the emulation software alternatives.

But all is not lost. You can copy your word-processing and spreadsheet files from Windows into your Linux home directory. From there, you can run the OpenOffice.org suite and update them. OpenOffice.org (described in *OpenOffice.org* on page 248) is an open-source Microsoft Office-compatible application, with millions of users. OpenOffice.org is preinstalled on your Linspire system, ready for use.

After you have finished updating your files, you can write them onto a CD, from where they can later be copied back into the Windows folders. Or just email a file to yourself, and read it when you are running Windows.

Basic Copy and Paste

You can copy text from one place, and paste it into another the same way you do in Windows. Click and drag to highlight the text, then press **Control-c** to copy. Click at the place you want to insert the copied text, and press **Control-v**.

You can also highlight the text, then right-click and select **Copy** or **Paste** from the context menu.

Accessing All the Strings You've Copied

Sometimes it's convenient to have access to all the strings you copied, not just the most recent one. Second, there's an unrelated bug in early versions of Linspire 5 that loses the copy contents when the application they were copied from ends. There's a way to address both of these issues: the Klipper clipboard tool.

Klipper is a small utility that you can add next to the system tray and that maintains a list of copied text. You can then paste any of the text that is on Klipper's list. It's easy to add Klipper or any of a half dozen other applets to the system tray. Right-click on a blank area in the system tray and from the menu that appears (see Figure 3-25), choose **Add** > **Applet** > **Klipper**.

Figure 3-25 shows the menu that appears when you click the Klipper icon (on the left of the system tray). The fours strings listed at the top of that menu (an example of copied text, etc.) have been saved by Klipper. Select any of them by highlighting it in the list. Your next paste will paste that string.

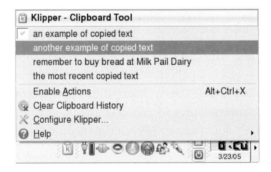

Figure 3-25   Choosing a string on the Klipper clipboard

Of mice and men

KDE works with the three-button mice common in Unix, so some documentation talks about the middle button. They don't mean the scroll wheel. You can simulate clicks from the phantom middle button on two button mice by clicking left and right mouse buttons together.

You can highlight text, then use the middle mouse button at the place where you want to paste it. Text copied this way is not saved by Klipper.

Advanced KDE Techniques

You can safely skip the rest of this chapter on a first reading. You can return if you want to see some advanced techniques for customizing the look of the desktop and making more use of its limited space.

Using KDE Settings and Themes

I mentioned previously that Linspire has customized their distro so the launcher button is labeled **Launch** instead of the letter K used in most other KDE-using distros. KDE is almost infinitely configurable, both by the distro, and by you the end user.

Configuring the Kicker

You can reconfigure the Kicker to run along any edge of the screen, not just the bottom. Right-click on the **Launch** button and choose **Panel Menu** > **Configure Panel** to change anything about the Kicker.

Brightening the Background

When you first start Linspire, it has a dark and busy background image. You can take a few steps immediately to brighten that picture.

1 You can press the **Windows button** on your keyboard (the button with a picture of four wavy squares) as a shortcut for bringing up the **Launch** menu, just as in Windows.

Or just click on **Launch** and choose **Settings** > **Control Center** as in Figure 3-26.

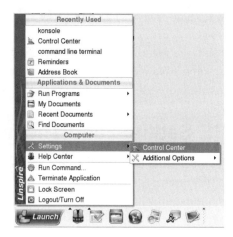

Figure 3-26   Launching the Control Center

2   That brings up the KDE Control Center. Like the Windows control panel, this provides one-stop shopping for many system and GUI configuration choices.

Right now, let's concentrate on the desktop appearance, so click on **Look & Feel**, circled in Figure 3-27. You can investigate the many other choices when you get around to it.

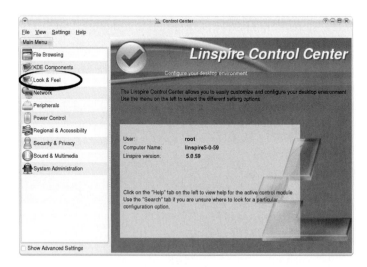

Figure 3-27   Choosing to adjust KDE appearance

3   This sequence brings up the control panel for Look & Feel. Click a couple of icons on the left side of this panel. Each new choice on the left will display further configuration choices in the right panel.

Figure 3-28   The Look & Feel panel after clicking on the Background icon

4   Figure 3-28 shows the circled icons to click. When you click on each of these icons in turn, the configuration is shown in the list under the name of that icon. Note that you will have to scroll down to reach the Window Decoration icon on the Look & Feel panel.

5   In the Look & Feel panel, click **Background**. This allows you to set the picture or pattern on your desktop. I normally use a picture of a landscape or an interesting vehicle as the backdrop. That's the Picture selection.

You can have the backdrop change every few minutes, cycling through a number of pictures. The **Slide show** selection gives you that and takes you to a panel where you can select the picture folder and how long to display each.

6   For this example, set the desktop to a bland color. Click on **No picture**, then click on the rectangle under the words **Single Color** to bring up a Select Color control panel shown in Figure 3-29.

Click anywhere on the color spectrum picture to select that color. I suggest a nice, restful, light grey. Click **OK**.

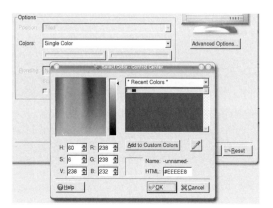

Figure 3-29   The Select Color window showing the Desktop background

7   The icons on the desktop are labeled in a white-colored font by default. This can be hard to read with a light background. Click on **Advanced Options** to bring up the **Advanced Background Settings** panel.

8   The **Text Color** option is circled in Figure 3-30. Click on the **color box** and a Select Color control panel will appear, allowing you to select another color that's different from the background.

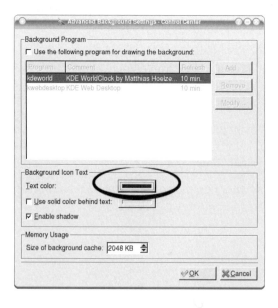

Figure 3-30   The Advanced Background Settings window for icon text

Using the Animated Desktop Background

It's worth taking a quick look at the Background Program checkbox. If you select that and highlight the line starting kdeworld, you get an animated picture of the world as your Desktop background. Part of the picture is highlighted to show the part of the globe that is in daylight. As the earth rotates, the section that is highlighted moves to match the area now in daylight. In Figure 3-31, the left edge of the light region is the dawn of a new day. It's midday in Australia, and dusk the previous night has just fallen on the west coast of the United States.

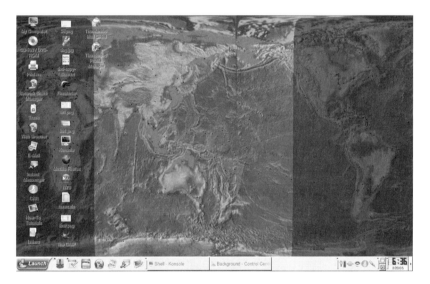

Figure 3-31   Is it day or night outside your windowless office?

If you can't see outside when you sit at your PC, this is a great way to tell whether it's night or day.

Choosing a Screen Saver

No one really needs a screen saver these days. Screen savers originated with an older generation of cathode ray tubes used in monitors. These kind of CRTs could be damaged by displaying the same pattern on the same part of the screen for an extended period. The phosphor coating would fatigue, permanently imprinting the pattern on the screen. It was very common to see a ghostly login prompt burned into the center of the monitor.

The current generation of CRTs is much more resistant to burn-in. All you have to really worry about is LCDs. On some LCD screens, a pixel is on when it's dark. So any screen saver that uses a black screen may actually be driving the LCD screen at full power.

Regardless of need, people have gotten used to screen savers, and Linux has some of the best available.

1   Click on **Launch > Settings > Control Center > Look & Feel > Screen Saver** as shown in Figure 3-28. That brings up the screen saver panel shown in Figure 3-32.

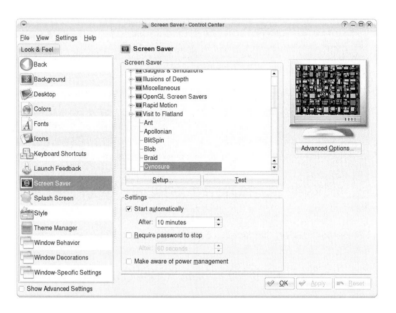

Figure 3-32   Setting the screen saver

2   Expand the tree of choices in the **Screen Saver** option. Highlight a choice in that box and click **Test** to see what it looks like.

3   Click the mouse to end the test. Not every screen saver works with every graphics card.

4   Many screen savers can be configured with the number of whim-whams, colors, speed, direction, and so on. Highlight a particular screen saver, then click the **Setup** button to go to its configuration screen.

5   Click **OK** to select a screen saver and dismiss the panel, or **Apply** to keep the panel open.

You might find that a notebook computer is given a VESA graphics device driver by default. This is done to help hibernation work. The VESA interface can be used to drive virtually any graphics adapter, but it doesn't use any fancy features that the adapter has. Some of the screen savers won't work with a VESA driver.

You can check which graphics driver you are using and what the alternatives are by clicking **Launch** > **Settings** > **Control Center** > **Peripherals** > **Display**. There is a drop-down list labeled Video Driver on that screen. If **vesa** is selected, you might get a crisper, faster display (albeit one that won't work with hibernation) by choosing one of the other alternatives.

Adding a Program to the Launch Menu

Other KDE customizations can change the underlying functionality. You ca add different shortcuts to the icon bar, add different programs to the launch menus, and put different objects in the system tray. You're most likely to want to add an application to a menu under the Launch button, so that's what I'll present here.

Just to give you the confidence that it really is easy to add new items to KDE menus, try one now. You'll add a menu item to open a console terminal window.

1   Right-click on **Launch** and select **Menu Editor** to open the KDE Menu Editor window shown in Figure 3-33.

Figure 3-33   KDE Menu Editor window

2   Click on the + **sign** to expand the **Run Programs** tree in the panel. These lines represent entries on the **Launch** button menu and expandable parts of the tree represent submenus.

3   Make sure that the **Run Programs** line in the tree is highlighted, as shown in Figure 3-33.

4   Choose **File** > **New Item** as shown in Figure 3-34.

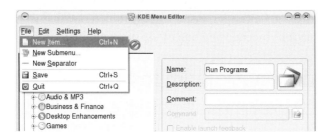

Figure 3-34   Adding a new item

5   The dialog box shown in Figure 3-35 will appear. Type the name that you want to see in the menu, in this case console terminal.

Figure 3-35   New Item window

6   Click **OK**. The dialog box will disappear.

7   On the KDE Menu Editor panel shown in Figure 3-36, in the **Command** field, type the command that will start the application. In this case, type konsole. (Here, you type *konsole*; in the New Item window, you typed *console terminal*. It's a confusing but correct difference between the command and the application.)

You can also drag the menu entry that you just added in the tree to a new place in the tree.

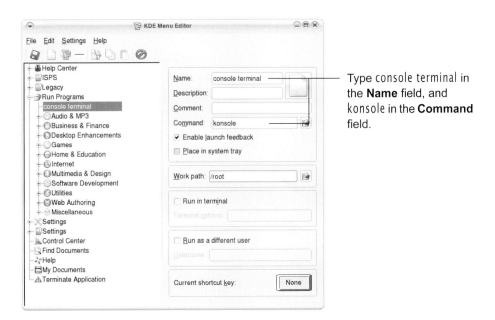

Figure 3-36   Providing information about the program the menu should start

8   Fill in the field labeled **Work path** with the path to the folder that you want the application to use as its current working directory. Use /root if you're not sure.

9   Select **Run in terminal** if you want a menu entry for a command line command, rather than a GUI application. Otherwise leave it blank, as here.

10 Choose **File > Save**, then **File > Quit**.

11 If you now click **Launch > Run Programs** as shown in Figure 3-37, you will see the new entry console terminal. (In a previous step, it was dragged to be the last entry on the menu, just to show it can be done.) Selecting console terminal will start the Konsole application.

Run through these steps now, and the command line program will appear on your screen. The konsole program is the Linux equivalent of a DOS shell, but the Linux shell is quite a bit more capable than MS-DOS; there is a tutorial on commands in Appendix D, "Commands for the Command Line," on page 531.

If you want to reconfigure the system tray or icon bar, see KDE documentation at http://www.kde.org/documentation/userguide/desktop-components.html.

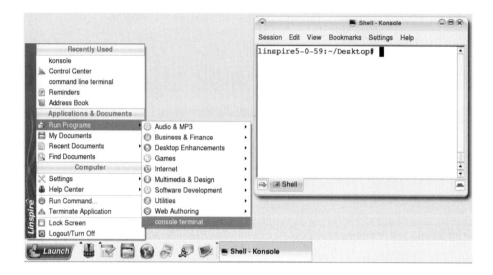

Figure 3-37   Selecting the new menu entry will start the command line console

KDE Often Has Several Ways to Do Something

There are usually several ways to do something in KDE.

- An alternative way to bring up a command line window is to use Konqueror File Manager, and choose **Tools** > **Open Terminal**. A console window will come up with its working directory set to wherever the Location field is pointing.

- A shortcut for this is to click on the **File Manager** window to make it the current window (where all input goes), then press F4. The menu items all list their shortcuts to help you learn them as you use the system. Unfortunately, some shortcuts change from release to release.

- Or click **Launch** > **Run Command** and type konsole in the text field.

Using Prepackaged Themes

I showed you how to use the Control Center to set individual look-and-feel characteristics of KDE. It turns out that KDE (and many window systems) have a way to group together many configuration choices and set them all at one go. Such a collection of settings is called a theme.

You install, change, and remove your themes. In the **Control Panel**, double-click
Look & Feel, then select **Theme Manager**. Figure 3-38 shows an example
theme. This is the Berlin Südstern theme, named after the Südstern station on
U-Bahn line 7, Berlin, Germany, where many of the pictures were taken.

Berlin Südstern has the same abandoned, edgy feel evoked by some Berlin-based
movies from the Iron Curtain days, like *Wir Kinder vom Bahnhof Zoo* or *Der
Himmel über Berlin*. The artist who created this KDE theme, Barbara Kaemper,
explained that the project was a spinoff of a photo calendar she created in 2003
with many pictures from stations on line 7. She wanted to reflect the atmosphere
of the U-Bahn (subway) in the KDE theme.

Figure 3-38   Berlin Südstern station theme

A desktop theme can be created in a couple of hours and perfected over months.
Barbara is not a programmer and taught herself how to do this by reading the KDE
documentation. You take a set of photos for the background, adapt the color
settings, and select a window decoration and an icon set. If you want to be
complete, you can create your own icons, application splash screens, and sounds,
too, though that's a lot more work.

Themes are volunteer-written, and they don't necessarily uninstall cleanly. To
reassure yourself on this point, you might want to first try a theme when you're
booted under the live CD. If it doesn't uninstall properly, you know you'll have to
change everything back by hand or reinstall the OS to get rid of the theme (if you
later install it to disk).

You can find many other KDE themes by searching the web and also checking the theme section at http://www.freshmeat.net and at http://www.kde-look.org.

Making Better Use of Screen Real Estate

The screen size (industry insiders refer to it as real estate) is one of the key limitations of your computer. As long as you have enough room on your desk, when it comes to displays, bigger is better. But not everyone can afford the $3000 plus purchase price of a really good, really big flat panel display.

That's where the desktop environment comes in. The desktop environment should provide features to help you organize your files and make the most of limited screen real estate. One choice that affects desktop real estate is whether to put an icon in the Kicker's icon bar or make it accessible from the Launch menu, or just make it a desktop icon. You can put a file in any of these places and get quick access to it. You've got more room on the desktop, but the desktop is often obscured by other windows. The icon bar is always visible but quickly fills up your precious screen real estate. The Launch button menus don't take up any space until you use them but they need a few clicks to reach them.

The KDE features that help you get more out of screen real estate are these:

- Desktop access button
- Windows shades
- Virtual desktops

I'll talk about each of these in turn. They are simple to set up and a great boon to use, so follow through the instructions on your PC while reading these sections.

Desktop Access Button

This button is at the screen and pencil icon at the right end of the icon bar (see Figure 3-39). Clicking it clears the entire desktop in one go. All the windows on the desktop are closed into icons on the task list bar, from where you can reopen them individually as needed with a single click on each.

Figure 3-39   The Desktop Access button at the far right of the icon bar

Windows XP also has this feature. You've got to reach for an unused portion of the XP task bar, right-click and choose **Show the Desktop**.

Window Shades

Everyone is familiar with the three small icons at the top of a window to iconify, maximize/restore, and close the window. Some KDE applications also put a help icon next to these three, denoted by a question mark. Window shades allow an additional choice for window size, between *iconified* and *open on screen*.

Figure 3-40 shows a shaded Konqueror window—just the title bar is visible. For comparison, an open on-screen Konqueror window appears below it. A shaded window springs open when you roll the mouse into the title bar. It's more accurate to think of roller blind than window shade but you get the idea.

You might keep your email window shaded like this. It's clearly visible on the desktop and ready to spring open when needed, but it hardly takes up any room.

Sharing a Window

To shade a window, right-click on the window's button in the task bar and choose **Shade** as shown in Figure 3-40. The body of the window disappears, leaving just the title bar on the screen.

Restoring a Shaded Window

Restore a shaded window by again right-clicking on the window's button in the task list bar to get a context menu, then click **Shade** again. The window will reappear at normal size.

I find shaded windows too fussy to control, and I don't use them. There are also several other keystrokes that operate them. But if you try them and like them, go ahead.

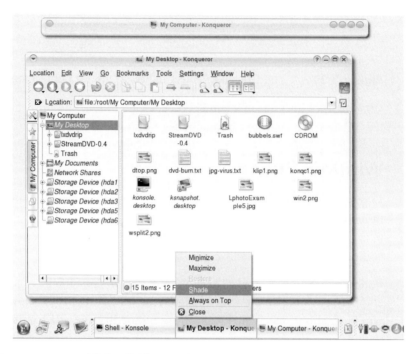

Figure 3-40   Right-clicking on the task list button for a window to shade it

Virtual Desktops

The last word in saving screen space must surely be the Pager. The Pager is another applet, like the Klipper. It supports several desktops, and lets you quickly switch any one of them onto the screen.

The idea is to organize yourself by opening different applications on each virtual desktop. You might decide to run email in desktop one, to have a game going in desktop two, and to run a browser in desktop three. You switch between virtual desktops by clicking on the Pager icon that you will add to the Kicker.

Turning on Virtual Desktops

Some distros come with virtual desktops already enabled, but the Linspire distro aims to keep things simple and avoid Kicker clutter. Here's how to turn on virtual desktops:

1   Start the pager applet by right-clicking on an empty space in the task bar or system tray. On the context menu that appears, choose **Add** > **Applet** > **Pager**.

That puts a Pager icon like the one shown in Figure 3-41 next to your task list bar. The Pager icon shows the number of virtual desktops you currently have. You start with just one virtual desktop, as shown here.

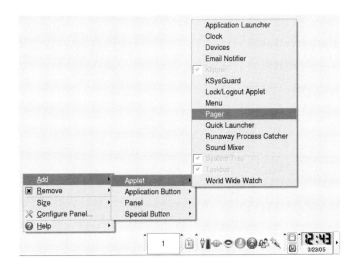

Figure 3-41   Starting the pager

2   Configure the number of virtual desktops you want.

Right-click on the Pager icon that you just created, and select **Configure Virtual Desktops**. That brings up a panel that allows you to set the number of virtual desktops. Four is a good number to begin with.

3   Click **OK** to dismiss the panel. The Pager icon in the Kicker panel will immediately change to show that you now have four desktops, shown circled in Figure 3-42. It gives them numbers, but you can also give them a more descriptive brief name.

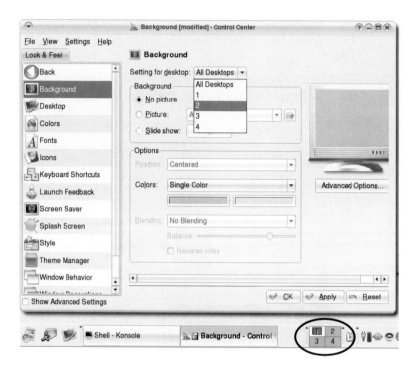

Figure 3-42   Clicking on a box in the Pager icon to switch to that virtual
desktop

Setting a Different Color Background for Each Desktop

I recommend that you set a different color background in each of your virtual
desktops to help distinguish them (they all start out the same).

1   Click **Launch** > **Settings** > **Control Center** > **Look & Feel** > **Background**
to bring up the Background setting panel.

2   There's a Setting for Desktop list at the top of this panel, as shown in
Figure 3-42. Go through all four numbers, set a different color, and click
Apply after each.

3   When you have set a different color background on all four, click **OK**.

Switching Among Desktops

Virtual desktops allow you to organize your work, and let you switch instantly to a new desktop by clicking the corresponding quadrant of the Pager icon. The Pager icon forms a pretty good *boss key*, allowing you to switch instantly from playing a game to something that looks more work-related when the boss springs into your office.

You can send any window to another desktop, or make a window sticky to appear in all desktops. Right-click on the window's task bar button, and you'll see both of these choices in the context menu.

The last point to make is that there are frequently several ways of arriving at a configuration screen or carrying out some menu action in KDE. There are command key combinations as shortcuts for lots of things. That's all part of the richness of the environment, and you don't have to learn more than one way to do something if you don't want to.

Linux and X Window

This section has a few under-the-hood implementation details for people who like to push their window system as far as it will go. GUI support on Linux and Unix is split into layers, just as it is under Windows, but the layers are quite different.

X is a protocol that sits in between the window manager layer and device drivers for devices that can draw. One big task X does is allowing the window system to run across a network. Compared with Windows, the Linux GUI implementation therefore has an extra library layer to provide network-independent windowing (read on for the details of what that means).

A second big design difference from Windows is that Linux GUI support runs as an ordinary user process, not a privileged kernel subsystem as in Windows. That means that the Linux GUI layers are simpler and can be changed independently to a certain extent. Linux GUI bugs don't subvert the kernel, the way they can in Windows.

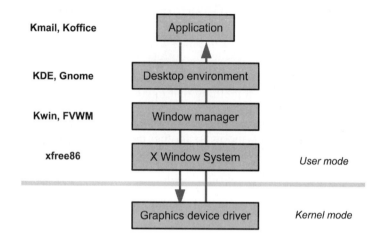

Figure 3-43   Linux's layered approach to supporting a GUI

Linux Layers

The layers in the Linux GUI implementation are shown in Figure 3-43. Applications run on top, and there are four main layers:

- The desktop environment is the top library level. It defines the look and feel of the icons, toolbars, and some other GUI elements. Several desktop libraries are available for Linux. KDE, Gnome, and XFCE are the three most popular Linux desktops, in that order.

- Underneath the desktop layer is the window manager. The window manager controls where application windows appear on the screen, and how they look (whether they have square or rounded corners, etc.). Kwin (previously called kwm) is the default window manager for KDE. Sawfish and Metacity are window managers often used with the Gnome desktop environment. Blackbox is a minimalist window manager that has fewer features but very snappy performance, and it is thus popular on low-powered hardware.

- The fundamental Linux GUI layer is known as the X Window System, commonly called X or X11. X is a protocol allowing the window manager layer to talk to devices that actually do rendering (drawing).

  X allows the Unix/Linux window system to run across a network, with a process running on one PC and its GUI appearing (by mutual agreement) on a completely different PC. The X Window System uses sockets to talk to rendering devices, and part of the identification of a socket is the IP address of the computer where it is located. The other end of the socket may be an X library on a remote host. Or it may be the graphics driver on the local host. The feature is known as network-independent windowing.

Two major libraries handle the X protocol: XFree86 and X.org. X.org is a fork from the XFree86 code, caused when XFree86 changed their licensing terms in 2004 to become incompatible with the GPL. Most of the developers disagreed with this philosophy, quit XFree86, and moved to X.org. The consensus is that X.org is the best and only way forward, and Linspire has switched to it already. You can tell if you are running X.org or XFree86 by looking for the X configuration file. If you have the file named /etc/X11/xorg.conf, you are running X.org. You are running XFree86 if you have the file /etc/X11/XF86Config-4. Only one of the two files will be on a system.

- The lowest Linux GUI layer is the graphics device driver. This part of the Linux GUI does much the same job as the Windows graphics device driver, though each operating system has its own unique driver framework.

Goals of X Window Architecture

Back in the mid 1980s when powerful Unix workstations set the standard for desktop computing, the X design was laid out at M.I.T. with two goals:

- Allow the window system to run across a network. The X Window System can display a window on any host on the Internet, not just on the host running the application.

- Provide a basic framework for a GUI library, but do not dictate anything about the way that application windows, icons, etc. should look on the screen. This was called *mechanism not policy*.

X Windows played to the core strength of Unix workstations: powerful, built-in networking. It seemed like a good idea at the time, but with the benefit of hind-sight, X Windows was a disastrous over-generalization that wasted a decade and a half of developer effort.

Both of its original goals were misconceived. Network-independent windowing meant that every program paid a performance penalty for a feature that was the rare case, not the common case of run-and-display on the same host.

Worse still, the "mechanism, not policy" approach led to proliferation of different GUI toolkits and incompatible code. X never had a good approach to printing exactly what was displayed on the screen. It ignored sound libraries, at a time when multimedia audio was becoming the most important trend on PCs.

When Apple switched to a Unix-based operating system, it rewrote the windowing support to get rid of the X Window System entirely. Nobody misses it. If you want network transparent windows on MacOS, you use the same approach that Windows does: install a product such as VNC or Citrix. (The X in MacOS X is the roman numeral for 10—a version number—nothing to do with X Window.)

X has now had sufficient effort applied, that it is "good enough". But everyone would have been better served if all that effort had gone into more productive ends. You probably won't need any direct interaction with X Windows or the window manager as you work with Linux, but you might see references to it occasionally in boot messages or as part of installation of other distros.

Troubleshooting X

X keeps a log of messages as you use it. Occasionally, you can find something in there that helps with troubleshooting. The file is ~/.xsession-errors.

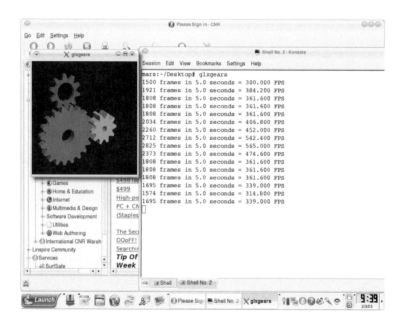

Figure 3-44   glxgears window

Your X Window stack should use the Direct Rendering Interface (DRI) to get 3D hardware acceleration. You can do a quick-and-dirty check on whether it does. Type glxgears in a command window. This will bring up a window with three spinning cogs (see Figure 3-44). Make sure no part of that window is obscured.

The command window where you started it will print out performance statistics every few seconds, showing the numbers of Frames Per Second (FPS) that it is drawing. If you're getting 10 or 20 FPS, you don't have hardware acceleration. A typical speed on a low-end graphics card is 2000 FPS. A high-end graphics card could double that. If hardware acceleration is not working, check the DRI Users Guide at http://www.xfree86.org/4.0/DRI.html.

Help Menus and More Information

Konqueror was designed to be easy to use. Of course, all programmers say that about all their programs, and ease of use means different things to different people. In the case of Konqueror, I think ease of use is a reasonable claim.

You have three great resources for learning more about KDE or Konqueror:

- The Help menu in Konqueror has a menu item called Browser Handbook that gives a good and easy-to-read tutorial on Konqueror's many features.

- The KDE home page is located at http://www.kde.org. The site has the most up-to-date information about KDE. They have a great user guide online at http://www.kde.org/documentation/userguide.

- As always, search Usenet for information on KDE features and problems. Whatever issue you hit, it's almost certain that someone else has encountered it before you, and posted on Usenet about it. There may even be a helpful answer for you. *Getting Help* on page 33 described how to use Google to search the Usenet archives. Check the newsgroup comp.windows.x.kde.

CHAPTER 4

Onto the Net

Getting Started

This chapter shows you how to connect to the Internet, which opens up a world of interesting possibilities like web browsing, online shopping, and email.

Bringing the Internet to Your Home

A 2004 survey reported about three-quarters of the adult population of the United States were online. Almost everyone uses one of two technologies to get an Internet connection into their home.

- **Broadband access** using phone or cable TV wiring. Broadband service is always on, and twenty to thirty times faster than dial-up. It uses your existing cable or phone line, but does not affect other family members who can also use the phone or cable TV at the same time.

  Broadband use is growing fast. The majority of online users in the USA now use broadband, and it's spreading at 47% year-on-year (estimate from Nielsen NetRatings, July 2004).

- **Dial-up access** to your Internet service provider (ISP). Dial-up service is sometimes called narrowband access to contrast it with the broadband alternative. When you go online, the modem on your computer places a regular phone call to your ISP. While you're online, no one else can use the phone (though the latest V.92 modem standard supports call waiting to put a modem on hold and take an incoming call).

  Dial-up access is the slowest kind of online service. At best, it can deliver a small text web page, or about one tenth of a typical image file, per second. Dial-up is cheap, about $10-$15 per month plus the cost of phone calls, but is rapidly heading for the scrap heap of technical obsolescence. The number of phone lines in the United States actually fell by 10% in the year to July 2004, as people dropped their second computer lines to switch to broadband. Many people also switched completely to cell phone service because of flexibility and cost.

The Future Is Fiber and Wireless

Other Internet connection methods are possible, none of which are yet widely used. The experimental "broadband over power lines" brings an Internet connection over the electricity utility line. The advantages of this are compelling: no home wiring changes needed; wherever you have power you have broadband. The power grid extends to more places than cable and phone service.

A few people, mostly in rural areas, have satellite access to the Internet using a dish receiver similar to dish TV.

The ISDN dial-up service went from being expensive and ahead of its time to expensive and behind the times, without ever really finding its time. ISDN always managed to be expensive, though.

Very high speed DSL (VDSL) is currently going through standardization and is offered by telcos in a small number of trial areas. Although only five times faster than standard broadband, VDSL may become more significant in future because it can support video-on-demand services. The phone companies really hope that video-on-demand will be the "killer app" for their VDSL service, although the service hasn't worked out that way for cable companies.

Why Don't We Have Super-Fast Fiber Networks to Our Homes?

Broadband connections have grown in popularity since the service became widely available. But surveys show that most people think broadband costs more than it should. They are right.

In the United States, phone and cable companies have a monopoly on the "last mile" segment of wiring from their central offices to each consumer's home. In Canada and many European countries, telephone poles are regarded as essential infrastructure, just like the power grid, city sewers, and roads. The phone company must share the right-of-way by renting access to competitors.

Outside the United States, competition means that many home consumers have access to optical fiber connections 100 times faster than broadband. Consumers in, for example, Sweden, Japan, and South Korea are well served with very fast fiber networks to the home at prices cheaper than broadband in the United States.

In the United States, the phone and cable companies keep pushing broadband instead of faster, better alternatives like fiber optic cable because broadband lets them re-use their existing network of (slow) copper cable. Competitors with much faster technology cannot get a foothold because the telcos won't share the existing infrastructure. So home users aren't offered the choice of super-fast fiber network service.

Some good may come out of this log-jam. We may get low-cost metro-wide wireless networks, like the pioneering ones in Philadelphia and Cork, Ireland. But the telcos are doing all they can to prevent competition. They are lobbying government to forbid cities from providing Internet access the way cities provide other infrastructure like libraries, sewers, roads, and schools. They won't provide you cheap broadband, and they won't let anyone else try. Phone companies are looking more and more like buggy whip manufacturers in the age of the automobile.

Networking Inside Your Home

Your incoming narrowband connection will be a phone line to a modem connected to your PC. The modem will either be a separate box or, more commonly, a card or chipset inside your PC. The modem converts between noises (noises can be sent by phone) and digital data (used inside a PC). A dial-up connection is far too slow to try to share among several computers.

A broadband connection to your home arrives at a cable or DSL modem. If you use DSL, you might see the names of the two different kinds, ADSL and SDSL, but the details of these are not important.

Broadband connections can usefully be shared among several nearby computers. If you have more than one PC at home, you can let them all have an Internet connection by setting up a local area network (LAN). Setting up a LAN used to be a task for gurus. Today, it's as simple as buying a $25 router, plugging your broadband modem into the router, and running an Ethernet cable from the router to each of your PCs.

Windows has a feature called Internet Connection Sharing that lets one PC share its network connection with one or two nearby computers. The computer with the Internet connection must have two Ethernet cards installed. Linux can be configured to do connection sharing like Windows, but in practice it's quicker and simpler (under both Windows and Linux) to use a router.

A router is the most common device for sharing a network connection among several computers. It's about the size and shape of a modem, but uses Ethernet cable not a phone line. The router takes the Ethernet connection from your ISP, and shares it across a number of your PCs. Other devices, like hubs and switches, can be used to share a network connection. A router is the one you want, because it has the right blend of features, performance, and cost for use with fewer than say six PCs.

A router is like a traffic cop that sends network traffic to its various destinations. Your router may connect to your other computers using Ethernet cable, or using a wireless signal. A lot of people like wireless connections at home because it is simple and very convenient to set up. You don't have to drill through walls or lift carpets to lay cable through the house.

A router also performs a valuable security function. It acts as a firewall to shield your computers from unsolicited network communications from the outside world. On the other hand, unsecured wireless networks can be accessed by other people near your home. I'll show you how to secure a wireless network a little later in the chapter.

In summary, three different kinds of Internet connection are in common use:

- Broadband using a hardwired cable
- Broadband using a wireless connection
- Dial-up phone service

These three kinds of connections to your home PC use different hardware, and you set them up in different ways in Linux.

What Are the Chances Networking Will "Just Work" on Linux?

To set your expectations correctly, some of these kinds of connection are more likely to "just work" than others. The phrase "just work" means *"after confirming that the cables are correct and the hardware operates OK, and after you enter the configuration data, you get a working network connection using Linux"*.

Roughly speaking, the probabilities are:

- Pretty much 100% that a wired Ethernet connection to Linux running on your PC will just work. That's great!

- Somewhat less than 100% that a wireless network adapter will just work under Linux. It's the old story about the availability of device drivers.

- Somewhat more than 0% that a dial-up modem will just work. But perhaps not a whole lot more than zero. All modems that contain true modem hardware will work fine. But the most common modems today are cheap and nasty Winmodems, which rely on Windows-only software to operate.

  In trying to shave a couple of dollars off the price, PC manufacturers have made the mistake of selling you modem hardware that requires Windows to operate. This is like Ford selling you a car without telling you it only works with Exxon gas.

Improving Your Chances of Successful Networking on Linux

If you are still using a dial-up network connection, this is a good time to think about upgrading to broadband. You'll have to do a bit of work to get most modems running under Linux. And when you do get it running, you've still only got inadequate modem performance.

If you currently use a wireless connection inside your home, I strongly recommend you revert to a wired Ethernet cable to get started with Linux networking. Temporarily run an Ethernet cable from your wireless base station (access point) to your PC. Ethernet cable costs 30 cents/foot on amazon.com, less if you buy it used, and is good for distances of up to 100 meters.

A wired network connection is virtually certain to work on Linux with almost no effort on your part. Later, after you have built up a level of comfort and familiarity with Linux, you can set up wireless networking. When you upgrade from a working wired connection, you will know that any problems relate solely to wireless and not to any other aspect of network configuration.

Whatever kind of network connection you want to use, use the following procedure to getting it working under Linux.

1 Boot in Windows, and confirm that your Windows network connection is working by browsing a web page.

2 Write down the details of your Windows network configuration (user name, phone number, etc.) so that they'll be ready to reenter in Linux. I'll tell you where to look in Windows to find these details.

3 Do not change anything. This is not the right time to add a new device, reconfigure your firewall, fit a new router, change passwords, or switch to a new ISP.

4 Boot up Linux and carry out the appropriate Linux configuration.

By rigorously following these steps, you can avoid trying to troubleshoot two unrelated problems at once. The rest of this chapter is divided into three sections:

- *Alternative 1: A Wired Ethernet Connection* on page 99

- *Alternative 2: A Wireless Ethernet Connection* on page 110

- *Alternative 3: A Dial-Up Network Connection* on page 127

If you have broadband, work through the section about wired connections first. When that's working, switch to wireless. If you're using narrowband, read the section about phone modem connections, and follow the steps there.

Alternative 1: A Wired Ethernet Connection

This section describes how to set up a wired Ethernet connection to your PC under Linux. It assumes that you have broadband service from your ISP, and that you already checked that the hardware works under Windows. Windows and Linux use the same network wiring and hardware, and it never hurts to check your configuration.

Here's the information in this section.

- *Find the Hardware*

- *Boot into Linux*

- *Set Up the Firewall*

- *Troubleshoot the Wired Connection*

Find the Hardware

The line bringing network service will run into a cable modem or DSL modem. A cable, known as cat-5 Ethernet cable, will run from the modem to the network adapter card on your PC.

An Ethernet cable looks a bit like a fat phone cable, but its RJ45 plug is too wide to fit into a phone socket. See Figure 4-1.

Ethernet cord ———————————   ——————— Phone cord

Figure 4-1   RJ45 Ethernet plug and RJ11 phone plug

Virtually all computers made in the last 10 years come with a network port as standard. If yours doesn't, install a network adapter card or use a different computer to work with Linux. If your broadband modem plugs into a USB port on your system, it probably won't have a Linux device driver and therefore probably won't work with Linux. Try it and if you don't get a connection, ask your ISP to exchange the modem for one that uses a standard Ethernet cable.

Make sure one end of the Ethernet cable is plugged into the broadband modem and that the other end is plugged into the network port on your computer. You might have a router in between the modem and the PC.

Make sure your broadband modem has power

I once wasted an embarrassing amount of time troubleshooting a network problem. Someone had dislodged the power supply from the broadband modem (it was you, Dale!). In a remarkably unhelpful design feature, the modem used the voltage on the Ethernet line to drive the status LEDs on the front. So the LEDs were on, even when the modem was not plugged into its power supply.

Because the LEDs were lit, I assumed the modem was powered up. In reality it did not have power, so nothing downstream worked. It was the ultimate "lights were on but nobody was home."

To troubleshoot a modem, boot your system into Windows and check that the network connection is active there. If Windows cannot get a network connection either, call your broadband service provider and get a support representative to walk you through the steps to connect on Windows.

When you power cycle your network to clear transient faults, restore power starting from the ISP end first: the cable modem, then your router, then your PC. Wait a minute or two on each device before starting the next one.

Boot into Linux

You can use the live CD, or if you feel confident, do the hard disk installation described in Chapter 12, "Installation and Boot," on page 439. When Linux is running, test your network connection by clicking Konqueror (the file cabinet icon in the KDE panel). When Konqueror starts, type google.com in the location field and press **Enter**.

In many cases your network connection will be fully working. The Google web page in Konqueror will come up and no network configuration is required. Set up the firewall described in *Set Up the Firewall*, then move right on to Chapter 5, "All About Email," on page 145.

If the web page doesn't appear, it means you don't have a working network connection. There is some help after the firewall section, in *Troubleshoot the Wired Connection* on page 102.

Set Up the Firewall

Part of the IP conventions that run the Internet give each computer 65,000 software ports that can communicate with other computers. Some of the worst Microsoft security failures have happened because Microsoft left unnecessary programs attached to one or more of these ports.

A firewall is a deliberate blocker that prevents other computers from connecting to any of your ports, except ones you specifically allow. Many firewalls can also be tuned to regulate outgoing connections or to only permit certain IP addresses to connect to you.

1   Linspire comes with a "broad brush" firewall utility that allows all, some, or
    no connections from other computers. To start the utility, click **Launch >
    Control Center > Network > Network Settings & Profiles.**

2   Click the **Firewall** tab in Figure 4-2.

3   The Firewall tab offers three different levels of firewall protection. Select the
    most restricted mode that still allows you to get your tasks done.

4   Click **OK**.

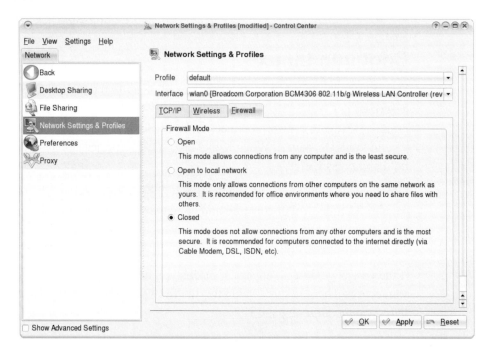

Figure 4-2   The firewall

It's so easy to update the firewall settings, you might wish to start with **Closed**
and only change it if you find yourself blocked from doing something.

Troubleshoot the Wired Connection

If the attempt to open location http://google.com does not bring up that web page,
then your network connection is not fully working yet. Here are the two likeliest
causes:

- Many DSL providers issue a username/password to their customers, and this has to be provided to the DSL modem. You can find out if this is the problem by following the steps in *Problem 1: Setting Up PPPoE*.

- Your ISP expects you to configure your PC manually with its IP address. This is called static IP address assignment. Follow the steps in *Problem 2: Setting Up Static IP Addressing for Broadband*.

Problem 1: Setting Up PPPoE

The issue here is that you might need Linux to specify to the broadband modem the username and password that your ISP uses to identify you. You will only see this issue when you are using broadband and not using a router (the router normally holds the sign-on details for you). It is straightforward to address, so if you are not using a router go ahead and try the remedy to see if it makes everything work.

Most users only type their ISP user ID and password combination once, and then the system remembers it. Because you use this name so rarely, it's likely that you do not have it on hand. If you don't have it, call your ISP support line and get them to tell you what your username and password are. The username will probably look like an email address, such as bobjohnson@earthlink.net.

1   In Linux, click **Launch** > **Settings** > **Control Center** > **Network** > **Network Settings & Profiles**. That brings up the configuration window shown in Figure 4-3, where you'll enter the ISP username and password.

2   In the **Configuration Mode** field, select **PPPoE** from the drop-down list (circled in Figure 4-3).

    The term PPPoE stands for Point-to-Point Protocol over Ethernet. It is a technique that many ISPs use to identify and authorize you for starting IP service.

3   You might find that the **Account Name** or **Password** fields shown in Figure 4-3 do not appear. If so, click and drag the Control Center window by one corner to make it bigger.

4   When the configuration screen shown in Figure 4-3 comes up, enter the user name in the **Account Name** field and the password in the **Password** field.

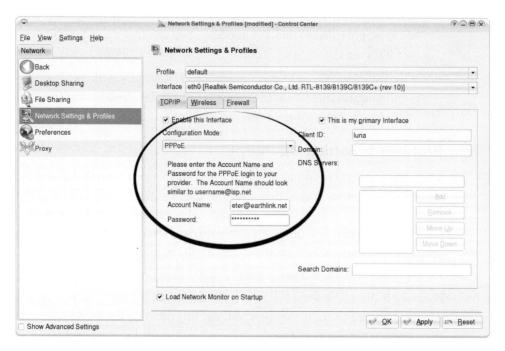

Figure 4-3   Entering your PPPoE user ID and password in the Network
Settings & Profiles window

5   Click **OK**. A confirmation dialog may come up, so click **OK** in that too.

There is no easy way to remove a name and password once you have entered
one in this screen. There should be a clear fields button, but there is not. If you
try entering PPPoE details, and then decide you don't want them, you might
have to reinstall to get rid of the details.

6   When your entries are saved (allow a few seconds for the settings to be saved
and the software restarted), repeat the connection test of opening a web page
in Konqueror.

If you can reach sites on the Internet, you now are finished with this chapter.

Problem 2: Setting Up Static IP Addressing for Broadband

Your PC needs to have an IP address to function on the Internet. Your PC can get
an IP address in two ways:

*   Manually configure your PC with a fixed IP address value (this is called static
    IP addressing).

- Or have your PC automatically request an IP address when your PC boots up (this is called DHCP). The IP address you get might be different each time you reboot, so this is not suitable for server systems. It's fine for desktop systems though.

Check DHCP Settings

Almost all consumer broadband providers use DHCP, but you can find out if yours doesn't by either calling their support line and asking, or by booting into Windows and looking at your settings there.

1   Boot up Windows. Switch to **Classic View** of the control panel if you aren't already using it. Click **My Computer** > **Control Panel** and double-click **Network Connections**. That brings up the Windows panel shown in Figure 4-4.

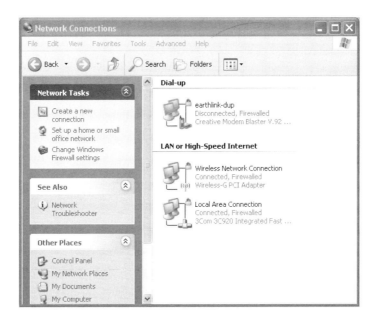

Figure 4-4   Microsoft Windows' Network Connections window

2   The Network Connections panel lists all the network interfaces that your PC has. The PC shown in Figure 4-4 has three network connections.

You want to get the details on the wired connection, which is the icon labeled **Local Area Connection**. Right-click on that icon and choose **Properties** from the menu that pops up. That will bring up the Local Area Connection Properties window shown in Figure 4-5.

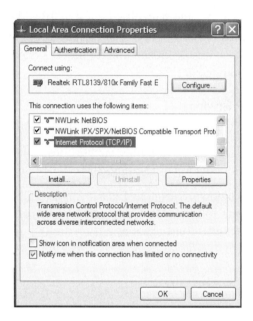

Figure 4-5   Windows' Local Area Connections Properties window, General tab

3   Scroll through the list and highlight **Internet Protocol (TCP/IP)**. Click the
     Properties button. That brings up the Internet Protocol (TCP/IP) Properties
     panel shown in Figure 4-6.

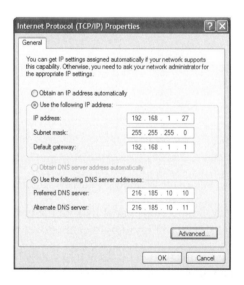

Figure 4-6   Windows' Internet Protocol (TCP/IP) Properties window, General
                    tab

4 Look at this panel closely to see if your PC is using static or dynamic IP addressing.

- ◆ If the choice **Use the Following IP Address** is selected, as in Figure 4-6, then you are using static IP addressing. Continue to *Copy Static IP Address Settings from Windows to Linux*.

- ◆ If the properties panel shows the choice **Obtain an IP address automatically**, then you are using DHCP, and you should not carry out the steps in *Copy Static IP Address Settings from Windows to Linux*. Go on to the advice for *Problem 3: Setting Up Your MAC Address* on page 108.

Copy Static IP Address Settings from Windows to Linux

Only proceed with this section if the window in Figure 4-6 shows that you are using static IP addressing.

1 Write down all the IP address values in that window (some values may be empty). Use Table 4-1 to record the values on your PC.

2 Now boot into Linux and manually copy these values into the appropriate network configuration screens.

Table 4-1   IP addresses and related values

Item	Information	Your value
Item 1	IP address:	
Item 2	Subnet mask:	Typically not used on a home network, but record it if set.
Item 3	Default gateway:	
Item 4a	Preferred DNS server:	
Item 4b	Alternate DNS server:	

3 In Linux, click **Launch > Settings > Control Center > Network > Network Settings & Profiles**. In the **Configuration Mode** drop-down list, select **Static**. Your display will look similar to Figure 4-7.

Figure 4-7   Setting static IP addresses in Linux

4   Enter in this window the IP addresses that you wrote down in a previous step.
Note that the fields in Linux are labeled with very similar, but not always
identical, names to the ones used in Windows.

5   Type the preferred DNS server in the **DNS Servers** field, then click **Add**.

6   Enter the alternate DNS server in the same **DNS Server** field, and click **Add**.

7   When you have completed this for all the values you collected in Table 4-1,
click **OK**, and click **OK** on any confirmation dialog.

When this completes (the setting needs a few seconds to take effect), repeat the
connection test of opening a web page in Konqueror. If you can reach sites on the
Internet, you now are finished with this chapter.

Problem 3: Setting Up Your MAC Address

There's one other possible problem. You won't see this issue if you followed the
advice to prove the hardware under Windows and keep the hardware unchanged
while switching to Linux. You'll only see this problem if you added a router at the
same time you moved to Linux.

Some Internet cable providers lock in the details of the computer that was first
connected to the cable system. They will then only allow future connections from
the same device. They do this to discourage you from using several PCs with your
broadband service. We all know how customer-friendly the cable companies are.

They use the MAC address to identify a computer, so to solve the problem, you need to assign your new router the same MAC address used by the PC you first connected to the broadband modem. (A MAC address is not related to the Apple Mac or Macintosh, though they have MAC addresses too.)

All modern routers have a menu entry during configuration that lets you set its MAC address. You can get the MAC address of the original PC by typing ifconfig in a Linux command line terminal and looking for the number in the MAC format that is shown in the following note.

What is a MAC address?

MAC is an abbreviation for Media Access Control—an uninformative name. The medium it accesses is Ethernet. A better, commonly used name for MAC address is Ethernet address.

An Ethernet or MAC address is a unique identifying number, with the general form of six pairs of hexadecimal digits separated by colons, like this:

`00:02:08:2D:CB:B0`

Such an address is burned into the ROM of every network device, card, adapter, and so on.

You might wonder why computers have both an IP address and this unrelated MAC address. IP addresses have a hierarchy (like the area code, then exchange, then line, of a phone number). A computer router thus knows which router to send a packet to, even when it cannot directly see the ultimate destination computer.

MAC addresses do not have this hierarchy, and they can't be used to route packets. MAC addresses are used at the local level to uniquely identify a box. Think of a MAC address as the social security number for a piece of hardware; you cannot mail an envelope to someone's social security number, but you can use it to identify them or tell them apart from other people. The technical way of saying all that is "IP addresses are routable, MAC addresses are not."

If you still don't have a working, wired network connection (and we're down to one in a thousand readers at this point), double check that you followed all the procedures here to the letter, check the book web site at http://afu.com/linux for any updates, then search the Linspire customer forums (described in Chapter 2, "Running the Linux Live CD," on page 25). Make sure you have a clear description of what you did, what you saw, and what failed.

Alternative 2: A Wireless Ethernet Connection

Wireless networks are a very popular modern choice because they cut down cable clutter, and let you move your PC around. You can use your laptop to do something creative while other family members watch TV. You'll take the cable coming out of the broadband modem and plug it into the wireless access point or base station.

The following information is covered in this wireless Ethernet connection section.

- *Know Your Wireless Options*
- *Know Your Wireless Basics*
- *Make Connecting as Easy as Possible: Turn Off Security*
- *Confirm That Linux Has a Device Driver for Your Network Adapter*
- *Set Wireless Security Options*
- *Troubleshoot the Wireless Network Adapter*
- *Alternative to a Wifi Adapter Card: Use an Ethernet Bridge*

Know Your Wireless Options

You have two basic options for going wireless—a wifi card or an Ethernet bridge. An Ethernet bridge is an alternative to using a wifi card at all. I'll give you the information about wireless cards first on the following pages. If you'd like to go with an Ethernet bridge or at least learn more about it, then see the end of this wireless section, *Alternative to a Wifi Adapter Card: Use an Ethernet Bridge* on page 126.

Know Your Wireless Basics

A wireless access point is a router that distributes its signal using radio waves instead of wires, indicated in Figure 4-8.

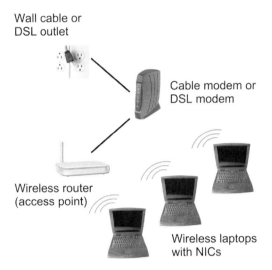

Wall cable or
DSL outlet

Cable modem or
DSL modem

Wireless router
(access point)

Wireless laptops
with NICs

Figure 4-8   A wireless network

More of the same: what the terms mean

The terms access point, base station, and wireless router all mean the same thing. The terms refer to the box that provides IP service over radio.

The terms radio, wireless, and wifi mean the same thing. Strictly, wifi is the radio technology for carrying an Ethernet signal, as opposed to Bluetooth or infrared technologies.

The terms network interface, network adapter, and network card mean the same thing. The terms refer to the circuits and chips in your PC receive the incoming messages from the network and send back your replies.

Wireless Standard

All modern wireless routers meet the 802.11 *wireless standard*. There are three variants of this standard, only two of which are compatible. Routers compatible with the 802.11g standard can also talk to devices that use the slower, older 802.11b standard. Most routers compatible with 802.11a can only talk to other 802.11a devices and this variant is rapidly dropping out of use.

Make sure the router and the wifi hardware you have on your computer meet the same 802.11 standard, whether that is the .a, .b, or .g variant. All .g routers are compatible with .b devices. A few routers are compatible with both .a and .g standards.

Mixing .b and .g devices—slow, slow quick, quick, slow

Wifi cards that implement the 11 Mbps 802.11b standard can be used with a router that uses the faster 802.11g 54 Mbps standard. There is a widespread belief that when you mix .b and .g devices on a network, everything runs at the slower .b speed. This belief is very common, and completely wrong.

It's based on an over-simplification. Two factors slow down wifi networks and neither relates to mixed devices. The first factor says that whatever the nominal communication rate of a device, it will be reduced when that will help maintain connectivity. When at the limits of wireless range or in the presence of interference, a .g device may run at a fraction of its maximum speed.

The second factor occurs when there is traffic waiting at the access point for more than one client. The clients will be served one after the other. That can lead to a fast device having to wait a long time while data is transferred to a slow device. Network throughput is reduced when slow devices are in contention for network bandwidth. But fast devices still communicate at their fastest practical speed once they get airtime. So don't worry about mixing .b and .g devices on the same network. Depending on traffic and network load, it may slow things down, but it doesn't make everything run at .b speed.

The current standard for wireless equipment is 802.11g, which is five times faster than the older 802.11b revision of the standard. The 802.11g standard is also known as 54g because its speed is 54 Megabits per second. That highlights how slow DSL/cable service is: you can send packets around your home fifty times faster than the phone or cable company can bring them to your door.

Two updates are available for the 802.11 standard: the 802.11i revision gives improved security, while the 802.11n revision is a speed improvement promising 100 Megabits per second. Preliminary versions of this are known as *Super G.*

Routers With Wireless and Wired Capabilities

Some routers have both wireless and wired capabilities. They can run a network that communicates with some PCs using Ethernet, and with other PCs using wireless. I run this kind of network at home using a Netgear model WGR614 v5 wireless router. The router cost me $45 in summer 2004. You just plug the Netgear router into your DSL line and talk to it using your browser and the URL given in the router manual. It self-configures with just a few mouse clicks.

Wireless Range

The radio waves spread out in all directions, and the signal has enough power to reach throughout most rooms of an average house. You need a wireless receiver attached to your computer to connect to the wireless network. The wireless receiver in your computer comes in many forms, but there is always some hardware to receive the wireless signal and convert it into the same kind of data carried on Ethernet cable. Microwave ovens and cell phones use the same radio frequency as wireless network equipment and may cause interference.

Wireless Hardware

The wireless card may be inside your computer, or it may be a removable PCMCIA card. PCMCIA cards usually cause a beep when you insert them into a Linux PC and often have two small lights that come on. These are indications that the kernel has found and loaded the device driver to operate the card.

Another alternative is an external wireless adapter that plugs into a USB port. Current Linux support for wireless USB adapters is preliminary and improving. Many USB wifi devices can be made to work by a very simple procedure that involves re-using a configuration file with the extension .inf included with their Windows driver. Search the Linspire forums for the term XYZZY to find the post I made describing this.

Make Connecting as Easy as Possible: Turn Off Security

The first step in configuring wireless access for any new computer is to turn off all security. After you have established a working connection, you should add back the wireless security mechanisms.

The settings on a wireless acccss point have to match the settings on all its clients. So you'll need to turn off security (described in the following steps) on the wireless router, on the Linux PC, and on all the other PCs that use this net.

Dig out the manual for your wireless access point (or download it from the manufacturer's web site). In most cases, resetting the wireless router back to the factory defaults will turn off security. Many routers have a pinhole in which you can poke an unfolded paperclip to make the device revert to factory default settings. You need to take these steps on the access point:

1   Give the wireless network a brief name like home or something similar. The
    manual probably refers to the name of a network as its SSID or ESSID; the
    designation is just arbitrary wireless LAN terminology.

2   Make it an open network, i.e., one that will accept unencrypted packets.

3   Turn off MAC address filtering. The MAC address gives every network
    device its unique identity. You can set up a router with a list of MAC
    addresses and tell it to talk to those devices only. Turn that off in the router
    and let the network accept connections from every device.

4   Turn off the WEP (Wired Equivalent Privacy) feature, or the WPA (Wi-Fi
    Protected Access) feature that newer wireless base stations use. Both features
    encrypt transmissions to discourage casual eavesdropping.

After you have configured the network access point for easy access, you need to
focus on the other end of the connection, on your PC. *Confirm That Linux Has a
Device Driver for Your Network Adapter* provides the information.

Confirm That Linux Has a Device Driver for Your Network Adapter

The wireless network hardware is easy to set up, but it can take a bit of effort to
find a wireless network card with a Linux device driver. Linspire has put in a lot
of effort to bundle the drivers for many of the newer 802.11g cards, as well as for
older 802.11b cards. But there is not 100% coverage. If you don't have a Linux
driver for your specific card, it won't work on Linux.

The easiest way to see if you have a working driver is to plug in your wifi adapter
and see if Linux detects it.

1   Make sure your wireless router is turned on and sending out a signal by
    booting into Windows and confirming you have wireless net access through
    the same adapter.

2   Boot up Linux. Click **Launch** > **Settings** > **Control Center** > **Network** >
    Network Settings & Profiles.

3   Look at the network adapters that the Linux kernel has detected. Click in the
    Interface list in Figure 4-9 to see all network interfaces the kernel has
    detected.

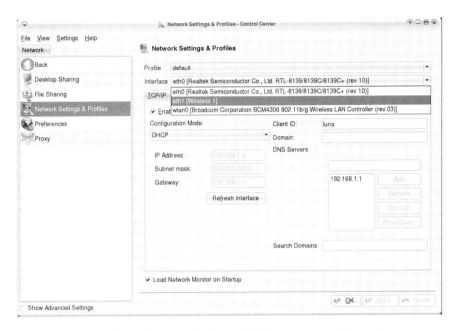

Figure 4-9   Choosing the wireless interface you want to configure

If a broadband network device appears here, the kernel has found a device driver for it. If a broadband network device does not appear here, the kernel has not found a device driver for it.

4   This computer has three network interfaces:

- ◆ eth0 (Ethernet zero), the hardwired Ethernet socket on this PC.

- ◆ eth1 (Ethernet one), a wireless PCMCIA card on this PC.

- ◆ wlan0 (wifi LAN zero), the integrated wireless chip on this laptop. More about this interface later.

These names are assigned arbitrarily by the kernel. Most computers will only have one or two network adapters, and eth0 is usually the hard-wired one. That means your remaining interface, if it shows up at all, is your wifi interface. Unlike Windows, Linux doesn't automatically classify the FireWire bus as a network adapter.

In the rare case that you have three or more network interfaces, match the chip description in the drop-down list against your hardware description, as obtained from Windows. See *Troubleshooting Balky Devices* on page 513. Or just remove one of the wifi cards and see which entry disappears from the list.

The good news is that when a wireless adapter shows up as one of the entries in the Interface list, it means that Linspire has a device driver for that adapter. So that's great! If your wireless adapter is plugged in, turned on, and still does not show up here, go to *Problem 1: Your Wifi Adapter Does Not Show Up in the Interfaces List* on page 120.

5   Make sure the **Configuration Mode** is set to DHCP. This is an abbreviation for Dynamic Host Configuration Protocol and means that the wireless base station will assign an IP address to your system. Wireless networks almost always use DHCP.

6   Now select the interface that you are going to configure from the Interface list in Figure 4-9.

7   In the demonstration of this step I configure the eth1 interface; you should select whatever entry in the list represents your wireless hardware.

8   Click **Enable this Interface** (obscured behind the drop-down list in Figure 4-9).

9   In the Network Settings & Profiles window in Figure 4-10, click on the **Wireless** tab. That switches the Control Center to a window where you can configure all aspects of this wireless interface, primarily the security features.

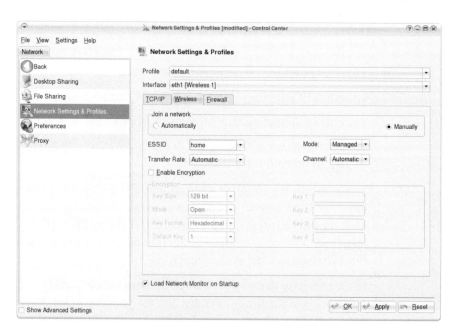

Figure 4-10   Network Settings & Profiles, Wireless tab

10 Since you temporarily turned all the security features off in the wireless access point, there is only one choice to make on this panel. Select one of the two alternatives for the **Join a network** setting.

♦ Select **Automatically**, which will make your system join the open network with the strongest signal. This is appropriate when you move your PC around several wireless hotspots (home, work, or coffee shop).

♦ Or select **Manually**, and fill in the **ESSID** field with the name of your network. This is the better choice if you are in a place where several wifi signals are received, or when you usually want to join a specific network.

11 Click **OK** to lock in your selection. It will take several seconds for the choices to take effect. You might be shown a confirmation dialog; if so, click **OK** there as well.

12 The last step is to test the wireless connection, by bringing up Konqueror and opening a URL. This should work correctly. If so, congratulations; you have successfully configured a Linux client onto a wireless network.

Complete *Set Wireless Security Options*, and you're done with your Internet setup.

Set Wireless Security Options

There is always a tradeoff between security and convenience. You need to decide for yourself what level of security is appropriate for your own environment.

When you use a wireless network, your network communications are broadcast by radio, and can be received by anyone in range. Some people actively drive around searching for wireless networks and use your bandwidth—an activity known as war-driving. That old saying comes to mind—*The devil finds work for idle bands—on open wifi networks without MAC filtering.*

After you have successfully set up a basic wireless network, you should turn on one or more security features. The wireless security features are:

• Wireless Protected Access (WPA) – An emerging standard that will appear as part of the 802.11i specification expected in 2005. It will appear in products from 2005 on. The Click-n-Run warehouse has add-on software for configuring WPA.

• Wired Equivalent Privacy (WEP) – An older and less-than-adequate attempt at security. You set up a secret key on your router and each client must provide the key in order to join the network. Packets are encoded using the key. The name is wildly optimistic, as it is a limited attempt at privacy, but not equivalent to that of a wired network. It can be circumvented by determined eavesdropping.

- Closed network – A wireless network may be closed or open. A closed network does not broadcast its SSID (network name). Therefore you need to know the name in order to join the network. It can be circumvented by determined eavesdropping.

- Restricted network – A wireless network may be restricted or open. A restricted network only accepts encrypted packets. Therefore you need to know the network key in order to join the network. It can be circumvented by determined eavesdropping.

- MAC address filtering – The access point maintains a list of MAC addresses of devices that are allowed to join the network. It can be circumvented by determined eavesdropping. The command iwconfig will give you the MAC addresses of your wireless interfaces.

- IP address filtering – IP addresses are allocated statically to each client, and the access point maintains a list of IP addresses that are allowed to join the network. This can be circumvented by determined eavesdropping.

All of these are breakable with enough effort. But you usually don't have to make your network impregnable, you just need to make it a little bit harder to break into than adjacent networks.

The Wireless tab of the Network Settings & Profiles panel is where you enter all the security settings of the network. But if security is truly a concern for you (you're a bank or a hospital or a teacher marking examinations, say), don't use wireless networking at all.

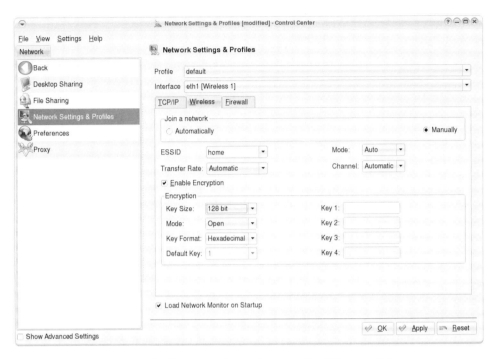

Figure 4-11   Setting security options on the Wireless tab

1 Since security choices are set on a per-network basis, select the **Manually** option for joining a network.

2 Fill in the **ESSID** field for the network to which these settings apply.

3 Click **Enable Encryption** and set the choices. Table 4-2 shows the descriptions of the encryption fields shown in Figure 4-11. Remember, your choices here have to match the settings in the wireless access point.

Table 4-2   Encryption fields and descriptions

Field	Description
Network Name (ESSID)	The ESSID (Extended Service Set IDentifier) is the name you give to the wireless network. Give it a simple name, like home.
Mode (mode field to the right of ESSID)	This field determines whether the adapter will act as a base station (master), an ordinary client, or a peer-to-peer station. Set it to **Managed** for an ordinary client.
Channel	Set it to **Automatic** and let the hardware take care of finding the channel.
Transfer Rate	Set it to **Automatic** and let the hardware take care of the speed.

Table 4-2   Encryption fields and descriptions (Continued)

Field	Description
Mode	Select **Open** (client can accept unencrypted packets) and **Restricted** (client only accepts encrypted packets).
Key Format	Select the key format you have used in setting the key in the wireless router. ASCII will look like Mary had a li. Hexadecimal will look like 4d61727920686164206120a206c69. You can get help generating and converting WEP keys at http://www.andrewscompanies.com/tools/wep.asp
Key 1	Enter the WEP key that you set in the wireless router. If you selected ASCII format, a 128-bit key will be 13 characters, like Mary had a li. A 128-bit hexadecimal key will look like 4d61727920686164206120a206c69. WEP keys are either 64 bits or 128 bits long. The encoding algorithm uses an initialization vector of 24 bits. You provide a WEP key that is actually 40 bits or 104 bits long. You enter 26 hexadecimal characters or 13 ASCII characters for a 128-bit key.

4   If wireless networking is now working for you, you're done. You can go on to Chapter 5, "All About Email," on page 145. Otherwise, additional sections in this chapter have some troubleshooting and resolution procedures.

Troubleshoot the Wireless Network Adapter

You can anticipate the problems covered in this section. Beyond that, there's no royal road to troubleshooting networking problems. You just have to methodically check and recheck every part of it.

These topics are covered in this troubleshooting section:

* *Problem 1: Your Wifi Adapter Does Not Show Up in the Interfaces List*
* *Problem 2: The Wifi Card Shows Up, But Won't Connect to the Internet*
* *Problem 3: Integrated Wifi Switch Problem*

Problem 1: Your Wifi Adapter Does Not Show Up in the Interfaces List

When your wifi hardware does not show up in the list of recognized interfaces (Figure 4-9 on page 115), it usually means the kernel couldn't find an appropriate device driver. You can :

* Get a device driver for your wireless adapter

- Get a different wireless adapter that you know works with Linux. You can find out which ones work with your distro by checking the distro's hardware compatibility list.

- Temporarily run Ethernet cable to this PC so you can continue your evaluation without getting sidetracked by wifi troubleshooting.

Finding Vendors of Wireless Adapters

Just five large vendors supply the majority of all wifi chipsets. The vendors and their product families are shown in Table 4-3.

Table 4-3   Wifi chip set vendors

Manufacturer	Product family	Linux friendliness
Ralink	RT2500	Very friendly
Intersil/Conexant	Prism	Very friendly
Intel	PRO/Wireless 2915 (Centrino)	Friendly
Atheros	AR5212	Somewhat friendly
Texas Instruments	ACX111	Very unhelpful

These five chip makers supply companies like Netgear, Linksys, Lucent, D-Link, and SMC, who package the basic wifi chip into a card or access point product. So when you look for a wifi driver, you're more interested in the underlying chip than in the make of card.

Unfortunately, it can be hard to identify the chip used in a product, as card vendors frequently change the chip without changing their product model numbers.

For example, some of D-Link's wifi G650 PC cards use a chip from Intersil's Prism family, some use a chip from Atheros' AR5212 family, and some use a chip from TI's AX100 family. But they all come in a box labeled G650. So even if you buy the same card that someone else has working under Linux, there's no guarantee you'll have the same success. You need to buy wifi adapters from a store that has a good return policy.

Intersil and Ralink released open source drivers for their respective chips. Intel sponsored the development of open source drivers for their wifi chips. Device drivers exist for Atheros because of open source volunteers like Atsushi Onoe,

Sam Leffler, and Greg Chesson; see Figure 4-12. Open source volunteer programmers from around the world get busy once (if) chip vendors release their product specifications.

Figure 4-12   Open source developers, like Tokyo-based Atsushi Onoe, create Linux wifi drivers

Some companies keep their product details secret, hoping to gain a competitive advantage. Linux users should write to those vendors and ask them to produce their own Linux drivers. In the meantime, avoid products based on chips from Linux-unfriendly vendors.

Getting a Device Driver for Your Wireless Adapter

When your wifi network adapter does not appear in the list of network interfaces shown in the Network Settings and Profile window in Figure 4-9, it usually means you don't have a device driver for it. You can try running the ndiswrapper utility using the Windows .inf file, described in the Linspire customer forum. (Search for the term XYZZY to find the post.) If that doesn't work, visit the web site at http://www.linuxant.com for a commercial version of the same software. Linuxant is a Canadian software company that sells device drivers for network adapters on Linux.

Linuxant sells a technically impressive library called DriverLoader. DriverLoader re-uses some driver configuration data from the Windows wireless device driver (an .inf file) to produce a driver that works under Linux.

Linuxant's DriverLoader works with almost all PCI and PCMCIA wifi cards, and many USB wireless adapters. Linuxant offers a 15-day trial period and the library costs about $20 if you do decide to buy it. The trial period lets you check without cost whether this solution will work for you.

You can also find a free, open source equivalent of Linuxant's DriverLoader at http://ndiswrapper.sourceforge.net/. That device driver is free, but it is only distributed as source code. That means that you have to compile it yourself to get it working, following the instructions included with the files.

Problem 2: The Wifi Card Shows Up, But Won't Connect to the Internet

So far I've talked about the GUI tools for configuring a PC to join a network. The GUI tools are based on underlying command line tools that have much finer granularity. You will find it helpful to use these commands directly when troubleshooting. They will help you localize a problem.

You can bring up a command window in which to type commands by clicking **Launch > Run**. Type xterm in the text field. Then you can enter commands.

You can get more detail about these or any commands by visiting the web site http://www.fifi.org/cgi-bin/man2html. Alternatively, search the web for manpage (it's Unix-speak for manual page) and the name of the command.

If you're really stuck, a good plan is to start running through the commands in Table 4-4, and see where things stop working. Appendix C shows sample correct output from each command. When you stop getting that, you've hit the problem area and thus know what to change.

Table 4-4   Command-line interface commands for troubleshooting networks

Command	Comments
ifconfig	This command is used to show and set the configuration of a network interface. When executed with no options, it displays details of all active interfaces, so this tells you if the driver can see the device or not. If a working device is plugged in and turned on and ifconfig cannot see it, the likeliest cause is that there is no device driver for it on your system.

This command will tell you your IP address, the name of the interface (it will be something like eth0, eth1, wlan0, etc.), and the MAC address for that interface. |

Table 4-4   Command-line interface commands for troubleshooting networks (Continued)

Command	Comments
dmesg –c	Prints out the buffer of system log messages and the -c option clears the buffer. Type the command once (ignore the output, this is just to clear the buffer) and plug in any hot-pluggable network hardware (Ethernet cable, removable wireless card, etc.). Type the command again. It will print all the logging messages associated with plugging in the hardware. This may point you in the direction of a problem.
iwconfig	Similar to ifconfig, but dedicated to wireless interfaces. It sets and displays the configuration details. Not all options are accepted by all wireless cards, but you can try. Read the man page for this. Example commands include:
	iwconfig eth1 essid home1
	to specify home1 as the name of the network that you want to join.
	iwconfig eth1 enc s:mypasswordis1
	will set the WEP key on the eth1 interface to mypasswordis1.
iwlist interface y	Specify interface, which is a network interface like eth0. This displays a chunk of information about that interface. The y part can be an access point or key, or other alternatives listed in the man page.
	An example of the command is
	iwlist eth1 key
	to display the encryption key in use for the eth1 network interface.
route	Prints the routing tables being used by the kernel. On a home network this will typically confirm that your system is successfully talking to the router.
dhclient	Requests an IP address (when using DHCP). Will tell you the IP address you have been given and the IP address of the device that gave it to you.
ifdown interface ifup interface	ifdown turns off the stated network interface. An example use is
	ifdown wlan0.
	The ifup command turns it on. Using both commands gives you new DHCP information including an IP address. This will tell you the IP address you have been given and also the IP address of the device that gave it to you.
ping –c 10 192.168.1.1	Sends a count of ten (-c 10) test packets to IP address 192.168.1.1. Use the IP address of your router to tell if you can send/receive packets on your network. The router IP address is shown by dhclient and is likely to be 192.168.1.1.
	Then ping IP address 216.239.39.99 (Google.com) to see if you can send/receive packets to an outside IP address.

Table 4-4   Command-line interface commands for troubleshooting networks (Continued)

Command	Comments
cat /etc/resolv.conf	Types the contents of file /etc/resolv.conf. This file contains the name of your DNS server. The DNS server (probably your router or a host at your ISP) lets you convert between domain names and IP addresses. If there is a sensible entry in this file, then the DNS service should be working properly for you.
ping -c 10 google.com	Confirms that DNS works for you. Pinging to a domain name rather than an IP address will work only if DNS is working.

Note – For sample output, see Appendix C on page 525.

Problem 3: Integrated Wifi Switch Problem

There is an issue with some laptop computers that have an on/off switch for integrated wifi networking. That switch controls the power to the radio side of the wifi device. As well as being a mechanical switch, on some notebooks, such as the Hewlett-Packard ZX Pavilion series, it is also a software switch. When you press it to enable wifi networking, it powers on the radio transmitter and also invokes a small program that kicks the transmitter into operation.

The problem is that a similar small program is required to make integrated wifi networking function under Linux. It is essentially a device driver for the switch, separate and unrelated to the device driver for the wifi chip.

You'll know if you have this problem because you will see your wireless interface show up in the network configuration panel, but nothing you do will make the interface communicate with the base station. Be sure to eliminate configuration errors before you decide you have this problem.

To make the integrated switch work properly, you need details from the PC vendor of what the switch is doing. Good luck getting that. The PC vendor has your money and no further interest in you.

Some people have uncovered the details for some notebooks and started a project to act as a clearing house for others. See http://rfswitch.sourceforge.net and click the link **Laptop support table**.

If you have the integrated wifi switch problem, you can solve it by buying new hardware. That's why two wireless interfaces are shown in Figure 4-9. In the case of my HP zx5070us, I bought a Lucent Orinoco Gold PCMCIA card, which works perfectly with Linux. It's wasteful to have to duplicate some circuitry that already works fine. It would be better if notebook vendors were more sensitive to the needs of Linux users.

Alternative to a Wifi Adapter Card: Use an Ethernet Bridge

A more flexible alternative to a wifi card is a hardware device called a *wireless-to-Ethernet bridge*. It consists of a free-standing wifi network device combined with an Ethernet interface. It receives the wireless signal from the router and sends the data out of a regular Ethernet cable that you plug into your PC. To your PC, it looks like an Ethernet cable running to the router, so little or no configuration is needed. To the router, it looks like just another wireless client.

The whole thing is built as a single unit, with a separate transformer power supply that plugs into a wall outlet. You plug one end of an RJ45 Ethernet cable into the standard Ethernet interface on the device, and the other end into whatever host you are trying to connect wirelessly. You do any necessary configuration of the bridge using a browser from any host on the network.

The wireless-to-Ethernet bridge frees you from any and all operating system dependencies. It is virtually guaranteed to work, as long as your standard wired Ethernet connection works. You do need a power cord to the bridge, so although it is wireless, it is not a totally untethered connection.

This approach is foolproof, easy, and instantly gives wireless access to any Ethernet-enabled device, such as a gaming console, printer, set-top box, point-of-sale terminal, desktop, or laptop computer. It is so much easier than all the other approaches that if you're willing to spend $50 to $90, you should try this first.

There are several different models of wireless-Ethernet bridge including the Zyxel Zyair B-400 and B-420, the Belkin F5D7330, and the Actiontec wireless-Ethernet adapter.

These units are currently a little pricey, but that will come down as the volume of sales rises. Don't overlook eBay. I bought a new Zyair B-400 unit for $25 on eBay so I could test it as part of writing this chapter.

Alternative 3: A Dial-Up Network Connection

The word *modem* in this section means a narrowband or analog modem which operates using a phone call to your ISP. We're not talking about a cable or DSL modem here. The modem converts incoming sounds into bytes of data, and outgoing bytes of data into sounds. The conversion is done by a technique called modulation, which has given its name to modems—they MOdulate and DEModulate. The modem might be implemented as a card that plugs into the bus inside your computer, or as a small box that plugs into a USB or serial port outside your computer.

The modem is connected to a standard phone line that runs to a phone jack in the wall. When you want to connect to the Internet, your computer makes a phone call to your Internet service provider (ISP). The ISP answers your phone call using a modem that has a wired connection to the Internet. The phone circuit connection between the two modems brings the Internet from the ISP onto your computer. Connections over a narrowband modem are very slow compared to other kinds of network connection. The peak speed that a modem can manage is about 5000 characters per second, and half that speed is more typical.

Here's the information in this section.

- *Evaluate Dial-Up Disadvantages*
- *Set Up the Modem*
- *Collect Dial-up ISP Data from Windows*
- *Set Up an Analog Modem Under Linux*
- *Configure the Modem*
- *Troubleshoot the Dial-Up Network Adapter*

Evaluate Dial-Up Disadvantages

If you have any choice in the matter, avoid modem service.

Slow Performance and Dim Future

Because of its low performance, modems are a dying technology. Modem service is being replaced around the world by broadband or better connections to homes.

Winmodem Woes

Worse than the slow speed, all modems in notebook PCs, and the majority of modems in other PCs, are now Winmodems. Winmodems are not true modems. True modems have hardware to do the conversion between sound and data. Winmodems are cheap and nasty partial modems, built down to a price. They use the minimum possible hardware and make up the difference with device driver software.

Because they lack a digital signal processing chip, Winmodems are a couple of dollars cheaper than a full modem. Instead of a chip, they do the signal processing in software, which takes resources away from your applications. Today's CPUs are mostly fast enough to cope with this additional work, whereas a few years ago they could not.

Winmodems are often created in batches of a few thousand, each batch needing a unique device driver. Then some cost reduction design change forces a change in the driver software. The manufacturers themselves come and go, and any documentation perishes with them. Getting a device like this working under Linux requires laborious reverse engineering. As a result, only a few of the higher volume Winmodems work under Linux. To change this situation, PC vendors will have to start demanding Linux drivers as well as Windows drivers. They won't do that until they hear from customers.

If you want to find out more about the type of modem in your PC, use some specialized Linux commands to extract various numbers from your hardware that you can later look up in a table. The details can be found at `http://start.at/modem`.

Set Up the Modem

Here are a few things to do before you get going.

Check Whether Your Modem Works with Linux

The quickest way to find out if your modem works under Linux is to configure it for your dial-up ISP and try it. If it doesn't work, there are a couple other approaches I'll describe later.

Add a Phone to a Modem Line

It's convenient to be able to add a phone to your modem line. The phone cable from the wall socket plugs into the RJ11 port, which is marked with the word line and/or a picture of a phone jack. A PC often has a second RJ11 connector, marked with the word phone or a picture of a phone handset, where you can plug in a phone. That gives you normal use of the line when it is not in use for Internet service.

If your PC doesn't have a second RJ11 socket, you can buy an ordinary 1-into-2 RJ11 adapter from any electronics hobby store for a couple of dollars. Plug the adapter into the RJ11 socket on the PC. Then plug the phone and modem lines into the two sockets in the adapter. That works equally well for using the phone while offline.

Collect Dial-up ISP Data from Windows

First, boot your PC into Windows, make sure your modem is connected to a phone line, and make sure that Windows can successfully dial out and make a usable network connection. Then collect the modem configuration information used by this successful Windows connection.

Collect Information

In this procedure, you'll collect all the information you need to make a dial-up connection and run TCP/IP networking over that phone call. Specifically, you want the following information:

- The phone number your PC should call to reach your ISP's modem bank.

- The account name and password that the ISP will use to identify you.

- How the ISP supplies an IP address to your PC. This will be either static allocation or dynamic allocation using the dynamic host configuration protocol.

- How the ISP tells you where to look up Internet addresses. This task is known as DNS resolution and again, you will either get a fixed IP address for this purpose, or you will get one dynamically when you need it.

Follow these steps to collect that information.

1   You can get the account name and phone number from the same panel in Windows. Switch to Classic View of the control panel if you aren't already using it. Click **My Computer** > **Control Panel**, and double-click **Network Connections**. That brings up the Windows panel shown in Figure 4-13.

Figure 4-13   Windows' Network Connections window

The Network Connections panel lists all the network interfaces that your PC has. The PC shown in Figure 4-13 has three network connections. The one under the heading **Dial-up** is the modem. The other two connections, under the headings **LAN** and **High-Speed Internet**, are the wireless and wired Ethernet connections on this PC.

2   Double-click the **icon for the modem connection** to display the window shown in Figure 4-14.

3   You can directly read the user name and phone number from this window. Here, they are peter@earthlink.net and 492-4002.

You cannot read the saved password; you have to remember that one. Remembering is difficult because the software can provide the password to the ISP automatically. You enter it once to set up the modem, and never type it again. You might have to call the ISP if you cannot recall it. They will authenticate you and give you a new password, which you can enter on this panel and write down for future use.

Figure 4-14   Window for a modem

4   Dismiss the panel by clicking **Cancel**.

5   Go back to the **modem icon** on Windows, Figure 4-4 on page 105. Right-click on the icon and choose **Properties**. The Properties window appears.

6   Click on the **Networking** tab to display a window like Figure 4-15.

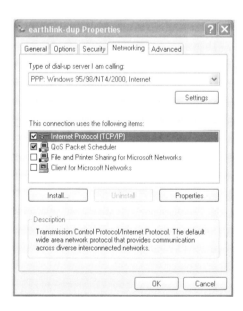

Figure 4-15   Windows Modem Properties window, Networking tab

7   At this point you might be wondering about the ease of use of GUIs compared with command line interfaces, but press on. Select **Internet Protocol (TCP/IP)** and click **Properties**. That (at last!) brings up Figure 4-16.

Figure 4-16   Windows TCP/IP Properties window, General tab

This is the panel that gives us two pieces of information: how your PC gets an IP address, and how your PC resolves domain names (like google.com) into IP addresses, like 216.239.37.99.

Note Windows' DHCP Setting

1   Look at Figure 4-16. You can see that the radio button labeled **Obtain an IP Address Automatically** is selected. This is the most common approach. It tells your PC to ask your ISP for an IP address, and accept the one it is given. The protocol by which this request is made is called Dynamic Host Configuration Protocol (DHCP). The name DHCP has come to be used for this choice, although the Windows description of it (**Obtain an IP Address Automatically**) is more easily understood.

2   The alternative, much less common choice, is the other radio button **Use the Following IP Address**. If the option **Use the Following IP Address** is filled in, make a note that your PC uses a static IP address and copy down the IP address.

Now go on to the second piece of information, the domain name server.

Note Windows' Domain Name Server Setting

Every computer connected to the Internet has an IP address. IP addresses are organized so that, given some IP address, routers know where to send information to reach it. But many computers also have a domain name, such as google.com. The automated service that translates between domain names and IP addresses is called the Domain Name Service (DNS) and it is essential to run the Internet. Your ISP will have one or more DNS servers running this service.

Your PC needs to know how to find your ISP's DNS server. As with IP address allocation, there are two possibilities.

The most convenient and most common choice is that your PC obtains the DNS server address automatically when it needs it. You almost certainly will find this choice (**Obtain DNS server address automatically**) selected on your PC. It means your PC will broadcast a request for the service, and listen to see who answers.

1   ISPs running very old software will require the other choice **Use the following DNS server addresses**, which is not selected in Figure 4-16.

2   If that choice is filled in, make a note that your PC uses a static DNS server IP address. Often there will be two server addresses, in case one is temporarily busy. Note the choice and copy down all the DNS server IP addresses.

3   In Table 4-5, record all configuration information you collect from Windows.

Table 4-5   Summary of the modem configuration information from Windows

Item 1	User name:
Item 2	Password:
Item 3	ISP phone number:
Item 4	Static or dynamic IP:
Item 4a (if static)	IP address:
Item 5	Static or dynamic DNS:
Item 5a (if static)	DNS IP addresses:

Set Up an Analog Modem Under Linux

By this point you've demonstrated that your phone connection worked under Windows, and you gathered the information needed to configure the modem for Linux. In this section you'll carry out that Linux configuration. Make sure your system is booted into Linux, then follow the steps in this section.

Get Documentation if You're Using AOL as Your ISP

If your ISP is AOL.com, then please refer to the instructions you get from clicking **Launch > Run Programs > Internet > Internet Connection Tools > Using AOL as Your ISP**. There are also entries for Earthlink and NetHere. If you want to use Linux, AOL is a suboptimal choice for your ISP. There are too many places where AOL assumes that you are using Windows.

Configure the Modem

Take the dial-up information you gathered from Windows, and enter it into several windows in the KPPP program. The windows are shown on the following pages. Table 4-6 is a summary of the windows and information to enter.

Table 4-6   Information to enter

Figure	Panel name	Data to enter
Figure 4-19	New Account, dial tab	Connection name, phone number
Figure 4-20	New Account, IP tab	Dynamic or static IP address
Figure 4-21	New Account, DNS tab	DNS configured automatically or manually
Figure 4-24	New Modem - KPPP	The type of modem you have, and where it is attached to your system (serial port, USB connection, etc.)
Figure 4-17	KPPP main panel	Dial-up login ID and password

Open the Internet Dial-up Tool Panel

1. Click **Launch > Run Programs > Internet > Internet Connection Tools > Internet Dial-Up Tool (KPPP)**.

2. This will bring up the window called KPPP as shown in Figure 4-17.

Figure 4-17   Launching the Internet dial-up tool, KPPP

Open the KPPP Configuration Window

The KPPP program for entering modem configuration data is almost as poorly designed as the Windows equivalent. As with Windows, you enter your set of dial-up data on several separate panes.

1   Click **Configure** on the KPPP window to bring up the KPPP Configuration window shown in Figure 4-18.

KPPP means KDE's Point-to-Point Protocol; KPPP is the program that maintains the connection in a dial-up session. The KPPP Configuration window has four tabs: Accounts, Modems, Graph, and Misc.

Figure 4-18   The KPPP Configuration window

2   You'll use the first two tabs. Make sure the window is showing the **Accounts** tab, then click **New**.

Enter Information in the New Account Window

The New button brings up a New Account window shown in Figure 4-19.

1 Enlarge the window to fully reveal all the tabs.

2 In the following steps you're going to enter the information you previously collected and laid out in Table 4-1 on page 107. Figure 4-19 shows the Dial tab of the Account window.

Click on the **Dial** tab. In the **Connection name** field, type the name you want to give this connection. Most people use the ISP name, such as earthlink.

Figure 4-19 New Account window, Dial tab

3 Click **Add**. This will bring up a text field. Enter the **dial-up phone number** that the modem should call.

4 In the Dial tab, leave the **Authentication** setting on PAP/CHAP. PAP/CHAP is the PPP Authentication Protocol and Challenge Handshake Authentication Protocol. CHAP is the protocol most commonly used with PPP to authenticate access. When you select PAP/CHAP, the modem dialer program can save the login and password that you will enter and use that on each connection.

If your modem starts to dial but refuses to authenticate you, use the Terminal-based setting instead. When you make a call, a window will be displayed with a login prompt, allowing you to see what is going on.

Enter Information in the Account, IP Tab

1 Click the IP tab on the Account window to display the window shown in Figure 4-20.

Figure 4-20 Edit Account window, IP tab

2 Select static or dynamic IP address allocation. Refer to *Note Windows' DHCP Setting* on page 132 if you need to refresh your memory on the details.

If your ISP requires static IP addresses, also enter the **IP address** you have been given.

You won't usually change anything in the Gateway tab. When you have several network connections active at one time, the Gateway tab allows you to specify which connection you want to use to send packets onto the network. Most users will only have one network connection active at a time.

Enter Information in the Account, DNS tab

1 Click the **DNS** tab of the Account window to display the window shown in Figure 4-21.

Figure 4-21   Edit Account window, DNS tab

2   Modern software uses automatic DNS configuration. But if your ISP still uses static DNS, take the details you wrote in Table 4-1 on page 107, item 5, and enter them here. Otherwise leave the **Configuration** set to Automatic.

3   Click **OK** to return to the KPPP Configuration window (Figure 4-18).

Select Your Modem

In the current version of Linspire Linux, KPPP may need to be told where to find the modem. It's perfectly possible in software to go and look in all the possible places that a modem might be, and ask each one (electronically), "is a modem connected here?" But this is not yet done. Instead you, the user, are expected to tell KPPP where to find the modem. If you don't know where it is, you have to resort to working through the list of possible places one by one.

The KPPP Configuration window has a tab labeled Modems; see Figure 4-22.

Figure 4-22   KPPP Configuration window, Modem tab

1   In the KPPP Configuration window, click on the **Modems** tab and then **New** to bring up the window shown in Figure 4-23. To change an existing configuration, (such as attempt-1 here) highlight it on the Modems tab and click **Edit**.

Figure 4-23   KPPP New Modem window, Device tab

2   In the **Modem name** field, provide any name you like, such as my-modem. This name is only used so you can later tell the modems apart when you have more than one on your PC (unlikely).

3   Click on the **Modem device** drop-down list, in Figure 4-24.

Figure 4-24   Edit Modem window, Device tab

The 20-some entries represent the possible pathnames identifying the modem.

* The first is /dev/modem, which represents an internal modem on the motherboard.

* The second entry is /dev/ttyS0, meaning a modem on the first serial port.

* The /dev/ttyI0 entry means a modem plugged into the first port on a RISCom serial port card.

* The /dev/usb/ttyACM0 entry means an ACM-type modem plugged into a USB port.

* The /dev/usb/ttyUSB0 entry means some other type of modem plugged into a USB port.

* The /dev/usb/tts0 entry means a serial port type of modem plugged into a USB port.

* The /dev/rfcomm0 entry means a Bluetooth modem.

* The /dev/ircomm0 entry means a modem communicating with your PC via infrared spectrum.

* The /dev/ttySL0 entry means a SmartLink-type Winmodem plugged into a serial port.

Select a modem device from the list. The first time through this step, select the first entry (/dev/modem). Keep reading, but you might have to come back to this step if you don't know what kind of modem you have and where it is connected. If this is the case, you'll have to methodically work your way down the list one entry at a time.

4   Click **OK** in this window.

5   Click **OK** in the KPPP Configuration window.

Add Your Account Details and Connect to Your ISP

At this point, you should be back at the KPPP window (shown in Figure 4-17 on page 135).

1   Now that you've set up some modem and account details, you will be able to enter the login ID and password that you harvested from Windows and recorded in Table 4-1. Make sure **Login ID** and **Password** are filled in on the KPPP screen.

2   Click **Connect** to place a call to your ISP.

  ◆   If the call goes through correctly, you're done.

  ◆   If you see an Error window, shown in Figure 4-25, click **OK** and repeat the steps you just went through, starting at *Select Your Modem* on page 138. This time select the next entry on the modem list shown in Figure 4-24.

Figure 4-25   Modem not found

If you have been through all the pathnames on the list, and every one of them gives you a screen like Figure 4-25, it probably means you have a Winmodem and should go to *Troubleshoot the Dial-Up Network Adapter* on page 143.

Connect Using the Modem

You've set everything up, so it's time to use it.

Connect Using Dial-Up

Use the KPPP program to place a dial-up call.

1   If you have just completed all the configuration in the previous section, the KPPP program will still be in the window, as in Figure 4-17 on page 135.

If it is not in the window, click on **Launch > Run Programs > Internet > Internet Connection Tools > Internet Dial-Up Tool (KPPP)**.

For greater convenience, you can click and drag the **KPPP entry** (or any entry) from the Launch menus to create a shortcut on the desktop. Drag it from the menu and drop it on the desktop.

2   A context menu will appear, asking if you want to move it, copy it, or link to it on the desktop. Usually **link here** is the right answer. You can then click the **KPPP icon** on the desktop to start the application.

3   When the KPPP window appears, the Connect button will be enabled because the modem configuration is complete. Click the **Connect** button to start a dial-up attempt.

End the Dial-up Session

You need to explicitly end a dial-up connection when you are finished. When you make a successful connection, KDE puts an icon representing the connection into your task list.

1   End the call by clicking that **connection icon** to bring up the window in Figure 4-26.

Figure 4-26   Keeping track of a dial-up connection

2   Click the **Disconnect** button to end the call and make your phone line available for other use.

Troubleshoot the Dial-Up Network Adapter

After you have double- and triple-checked that everything is connected and configured correctly, you have only two more things to try. You can try these in either order, but they cost about the same. Either get new software, or get new hardware.

Get New Modem Hardware

The approach here is to buy one of the external modems that are known to work. That means an external modem that is not labeled as a soft modem, and that connects via the serial port not via USB. A soft modem is another term for a Winmodem, and it is driven by Windows software.

The first choice is the $15 SmartLink modem from www.archtek.com. SmartLink is a manufacturer that supports Linux wholeheartedly. SmartLink's engineers work directly with the Linspire team to keep their modems compatible. There are two models. The V92 one is more modern. This is an internal modem, so you can only use it on a desktop, not a laptop. You need an empty PCI slot and the confidence to open up your PC case and plug a PCI card into it. Or visit your local Linux Users Group and ask for help.

A new external modem costs from $30 to $50. You can find used ones on eBay for half that. Dial-up Internet service is a dying technology so modems will get cheaper and cheaper in the years ahead as people dump the service.

If you buy a used modem make sure it comes with all the pieces you need: the modem itself, its power adapter, the cable that runs between the modem and your PC, a CD containing the Windows device driver (so you can check that it works on Windows), and a manual or guide. If the modem is not too old, you might be able to download the last two items from the modem manufacturer's web site.

Only buy a modem that works at the fastest speed: 56 Kbps. Anything slower is like waiting for paint to dry. A modem that meets the V92 standard is capable of working correctly with call-waiting phone service. If you have that service, you might want to get a V92 modem.

Many external modems that work through the serial port are compatible with Linux, so you need to confirm with the seller that this is a full hardware modem. If it's advertised as working with Apple PCs, it's a full hardware modem. Most internal modems and most USB modems are not compatible with Linux.

Another internal modem is the U.S. Robotics 56K model 3CP5610. A recommended external modem is the Modem Blaster V92 serial model DE5621 from Creative Labs www.creative.com. This modem plugs onto your PC's serial port, so it's trivial to install and get working.

Get New Modem Software

The same Linuxant company that sells a Linux device driver for some wireless cards also sells a driver for some analog modems. In particular, Linuxant offers a driver for Winmodems that use the Conexant chipset.

There is a way to find out exactly what chipset is used in your modem. It involves running a command to get a coded number, then running another command to get more details, and finally looking up the details on the web.

It's easier to download the trial driver from http://www.linuxant.com/drivers/. There is no guarantee that this driver will work, but the company offers a free trial. The trial version runs at 14Kbps maximum speed, which is fast enough for testing purposes. Linuxant also has some support for modems with USB connections.

If you run into problems with your modem, it is better to move on to a broadband connection than to invest much in trying to work around it. That's the final word on modems. You're now ready for Chapter 5, "All About Email."

All About Email

Getting Started

At this point you've completed all the steps to connect your PC to the Internet. This chapter covers Linux support for the two most-used network applications: email and web browsing.

I'll start with email, because an important player (Google) started providing free web-based email service in 2004. Before web-based email, email required a certain amount of configuration on your PC. You had to select an email client program, and tell it what protocol your mail server used.

Web-based email changed all that. For millions of people, email has became a service accessed through a browser, provided in exchange for looking at a few adverts. Web-based email takes no configuration to set up on your PC. You simply register a user name and password with one of the providers like yahoo.com, or google.com, and they handle all the mail server aspects. This works because all the communication between the mail server and your PC is handled by the browser, and the browser already knows how to talk to servers.

Better still, you can access your mail from anywhere and anything that can run a browser. That's not just a networked PC—it includes most PDAs, cell phones, and other mobile devices such as the Blackberry email organizer.

Use web-based email if it suits you. If it doesn't, set up regular mail by following the process described in *Using a Standalone Mail Program* on page 148.

Using Web-Based Mail

For several years, Yahoo, Hotmail, and others have offered good free email services. They have some virus and spam filtering capabilities. They provide limited free capacity for storing your mail, and will gladly sell you additional space. The main drawbacks are the low limits on free email storage, time wasted waiting for excessive advertising images to load, and the horrible clunkiness of a browser as an interactive user interface.

Then in spring 2004, the Google search engine people launched a free email service they call Gmail. The Google Gmail service has all the qualities that made the Google search engine the best in the world.

It avoids distracting images that take too long to load. You still run it from a browser, but the Gmail interface is simple and uncluttered. See Figure 5-1.

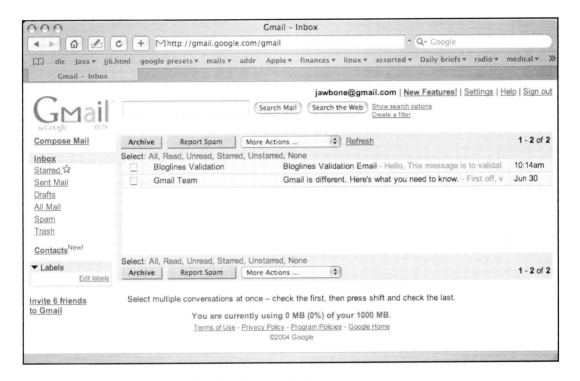

Figure 5-1   The Gmail user interface

All Gmail users get 1 Gigabyte of free email storage. This is a thousand times more space than other free email services, and for most people is several year's worth of email. In spring 2005, Yahoo was obliged to match this amount of storage for its own free mail service.

As you would expect, Gmail provides excellent tools for saving and searching old email. Gmail automatically filters out viruses and spam, and you can customize the basic settings. It is all paid for by unobtrusive advertising. Gmail scripts automatically process your email, and display ads whose keywords match topics in the email. If you get email from a friend talking about a ski trip, it will be accompanied by ads for ski rentals, and ski vacations.

Some people find this creepy. Others dislike the privacy implications of allowing one of the world's biggest advertising agencies (Google) to read their email. These people will want to avoid using Gmail.

Apart from privacy, there are a couple of other reasons why you might not want to move to Gmail. For example, you might not want to change your email address. Other people prefer to take responsibility themselves for storing and archiving their own data. Still other people prefer to use secure encrypted email.

For people who don't have these objections, and who want simple, capacious, spam-filtered, free email service with excellent sorting and searching, Google's Gmail is the clear answer. You can sign up at http://gmail.google.com.

Using a Standalone Mail Program

The alternative to web-based email is a standalone mail program called an email client or mail client that runs on your PC. Mail client software can be obscure to set up because you need to understand low-level implementation details.

Users are sometimes confronted with mysterious things called SMTP, IMAP, and POP. They are asked to provide information about the port number for servers. This section explains what it all those terms mean. Once you know that, configuring email is a snap.

Understanding SMTP, POP, and IMAP

Have you noticed that so many things in computing are a protocol, like Transmission Control Protocol (TCP), Internet Protocol (IP), or Dynamic Host Configuration Protocol (DHCP)? In the diplomatic world, a protocol is an agreed method of doing something, like a new ambassador presenting his credentials to the host government when newly posted overseas. Diplomats follow protocols so everyone knows what to expect and what to do.

Protocols have exactly the same role in computing. A protocol spells out the set of sentences that two different processes can communicate to each other, and says what a process is supposed to do when it gets a particular input. TCP describes in detail what a valid packet looks like, and what the various fields in the packet header mean.

SMTP, POP, and IMAP are three more protocols, all relating to email. The names can be confusing because they relate to what the computer does, not what the user does. It will help you set up your email client if you understand what SMTP, POP, and IMAP are.

By the way, even exposing these names to users breaks one of the top five rules of Human Usability: *never let the implementation leak through into the interface.* That's a lost cause in computing.

SMTP—Simple Mail Transfer Protocol

Simple Mail Transfer Protocol is a very old and basic protocol that defines how one mail server talks to another, to pass along files (email messages). SMTP is the protocol for the commands that one mail server will send to a second, in order to write files on the second server.

At first, SMTP was the only protocol for moving email messages. To get your email in those days, you either had to run an SMTP mail server on your own workstation, or you had to log into the mail server system. That wasn't very convenient or secure.

SMTP is still used today to transfer email messages between mail servers. However, SMTP is no longer used by individuals to get their mail. Two other protocols, POP and the more modern IMAP, are used by individuals to pull their email down from a remote mail server on demand. So a mail server runs at least two processes:

* SMTP to collect email from, and deliver email to, other mail servers. Outgoing SMTP and incoming SMTP might be run as two separate services, and might even be on separate computers.

* Either POP or IMAP to deliver email to the email clients (ordinary users).

In the technical literature, programs that implement SMTP are called MTAs (Mail Transfer Agents), and email clients are called MUAs (Mail User Agents). Users know them as mail servers and mail applications, respectively.

POP—Post Office Protocol

Consider how a post office box works for your paper mail. People send you letters and packages through the mail. These are held at the post office in a locked drawer (the actual P.O. box) to which you have access. From time to time, you call in at the post office, pick up all your mail, and take it home with you.

The Post Office Protocol for email works in exactly the same way. POP defines how email client programs (in contrast to mail server programs) check in with a mail server, and let users download their mail onto their own PC, PDA, or cellphone.

Because your email is downloaded to your PC, you can look at your old email even when you're not connected to the mail server. The protocol went through several revisions, and is currently at version 3, so it is called POP3. Figure 5-2 shows how POP lets you pick up your email.

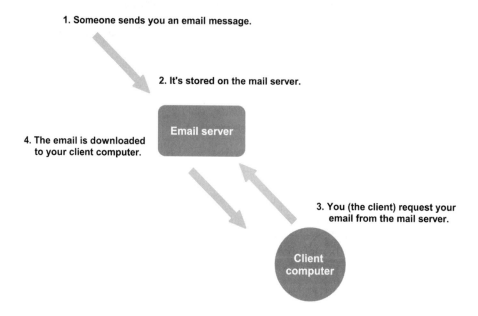

1. Someone sends you an email message.

2. It's stored on the mail server.

Email server

4. The email is downloaded to your client computer.

3. You (the client) request your email from the mail server.

Client computer

Figure 5-2   POP—How new email gets downloaded to the PC you read it on

The POP3 scheme had the virtue of simplicity, but it left all your mail isolated on the PC where you originally read it. If you wanted to read mail from a different PC, you could get new mail, but none of your old email could be seen. That had all been delivered to your original PC, and remained there. That was fine when most people only used one PC, but in a world where people use PCs at home, work, school, on the train, in airports, cafes, and public libraries, something better was needed.

The IMAP Giveth, and the SMTP Taketh Away

The computer industry soon came up with the obvious solution: keep all the email on the server, and just send a copy of any message (old or new) that you want to read, to whatever PC you are using at the time. Using the Internet, your messages can be accessed from any PC with this protocol. Hence the approach got the name Internet Message Access Protocol (IMAP).

IMAP is an extension to POP that allows mail folders on the server to be accessed and changed as though they were stored on the PC you are using. IMAP brings you your mail from your server and also supports attaching binary files, such as word-processing documents or image files, to messages. IMAP is a better, more flexible approach than POP3. Almost everyone who hasn't switched to browser-based email, now uses an IMAP mail-server. IMAP gives you everything POP3 gives, and more. Figure 5-3 is a diagram of IMAP.

With an IMAP-based email system, you can get your email from...

The PC in your office

The cell phone in your pocket

Your inbox on the mail server

Your Linux system at home or work

The Macintosh in your office or lab

Figure 5-3   IMAP—The inbox stays on the server and can be read from anywhere

The IMAP specification is in its fourth revision, so some people call it IMAP4. One quirk is that both IMAP and POP are only used to download mail from your mail server. Any outgoing mail that you send is uploaded to the mail server using SMTP.

This leads to a surprising asymmetry: it's easy to receive mail, as that is based on POP or IMAP. These protocols don't care what ISP you are using to reach the mailbox, as long as you supply the right user ID and password. But sending mail is based on SMTP and (to cut down on unauthorized use by spammers) the ISP server is always configured so it will only accept email from an account that it recognizes as a customer. SMTP servers that are misconfigured so they are visible outside their own network are known as *open mail relays*. The point here is that you'll check different settings depending on whether sending email, or receiving it, is broken. If you can't receive email, it's a POP or IMAP issue. If you can receive but not send, it's an SMTP issue.

Mail Server Port Number

An additional variable is the port that your mail server uses to talk to mail clients. A port number is like a telephone extension. Remote computers make requests for service to an IP address and a port number. If the server is running a program that listens for requests on that specific port, it will reply according to the protocol. Both ends of the connection have to agree in advance on the port and protocol to use.

Firewalls are there to shut ports

One key function of a firewall is to shut off ports so that your PC doesn't respond to unsolicited outside requests for services it does not actually intend to run. There's usually a way to specify the ports and services that you want to shut down. You can't do a blanket shut down of every port, because you wouldn't be able to get email (port 110 or 143), use your browser (port 80), or keep your computer clock synchronized (port 13).

For years, Microsoft shipped Windows with a dozen or more ports open and running completely unnecessary services. These frequently led to the penetration of PCs. It wasn't until Service Pack 2 for XP that users finally got a minimal firewall as part of Windows.

Another function of a good firewall is to scan outgoing network traffic, to flag anything that you didn't initiate.

Your email client thus has to know both the mail server host name, and the port number on that host that the mail server is using. It would be quite feasible to make applications, including email applications, self-configuring. Have them broadcast requests for service and lock on to whichever neighbor answers. This has been done for very low-level configuration of IP address and DNS server (it's the dynamic host configuration protocol of Chapter 4, "Onto the Net.") It isn't generally done for any application programs that use the network.

Retrieving Your Current Email Configuration

This section covers the steps to get the configuration data you need to set up your email client program. The basic approach is to start your current email program on Windows, visit the series of screens that allow you to edit the configuration data, and collect the settings that are shown in Table 5-1. Then boot into Linux and enter those same settings in whichever Linux email application you select.

As an example, you'll extract the data from Microsoft's Outlook program, but the principle is the same for all email programs. Find the screens that let you change the configuration data, and write down the values you find as shown in Table 5-1. Usually these screens are two levels deep starting at Edit or Tools. As always, an alternative way to collect the data is to call your ISP support line.

Table 5-1   The email configuration data you will collect

Item	Configuration data	Typical value	Your value
Item 1	Does your mail server currently talk to you using IMAP or using POP3 service?	IMAP	
Item 2	Your email address	peter@earthlink.net	
Item 2a	Your user ID (usually the first part of the email address)	peter	
Item 3	Your email password	Water-Melon23+>%	
Item 4	POP or IMAP server name for incoming mail	mail.earthlink.net	
Item 5	Port on incoming mail server	Default is 110 for POP3, 143 for IMAP.	
Item 6	SMTP server name for outgoing mail	smtp.earthlink.net	
Item 7	Port on outgoing SMTP mail server	Default is port 25. Port 5190 is sometimes used.	

The order in which these items appear will vary with different mail programs. Some of the items might have a slightly different name. **User ID** might appear as **User name**. **Mail server** might appear as **SMTP server**. As an anti-spam or load-balancing measure, some ISPs use two different mail servers for incoming and outgoing email. Other ISPs use one SMTP mail server for messages in both directions.

Capture the configuration data listed in Table 5-1. Not all mail servers use all these items, so Table 5-1 might have some blank entries after you have finished.

There won't generally be any other settings that matter, but if you see other settings, make a note of them (perhaps by printing out a screen shot). Then you will have the details handy as you set up your new mail program.

1 Running under Windows, start your email program. Outlook is the example here, but the process of collecting the data applies to any email client.

2 In Microsoft Outlook, choose **Tools** > **Accounts** as shown in Figure 5-4.

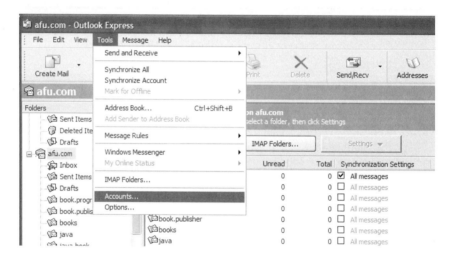

Figure 5-4   Opening Outlook's Internet Accounts window

3 The Internet Accounts window in Figure 5-5 will appear.Click the **Properties** button to open the Properties window.

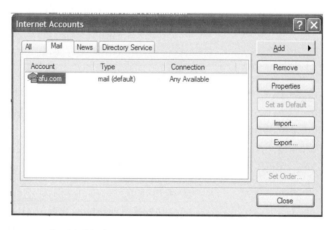

Figure 5-5   Outlook's Internet Accounts window

4   In the Properties window the information you need is spread out across several tabs. Figure 5-6 shows the three tabs where you will collect information.

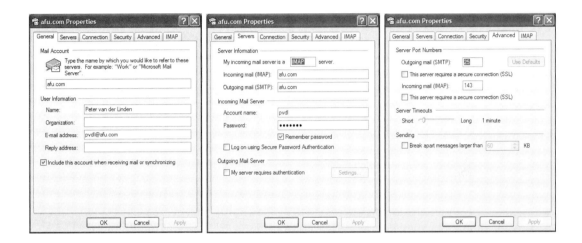

Figure 5-6   Outlook's Properties window—General, Server, and Advanced tabs

5   Copy your configuration information into Table 5-1 as follows:

- **General** tab – Item 2 (email address)

- **Servers** tab – Item 1 (IMAP or POP), item 4 (incoming server), item 6 (outgoing server) item 2a (user ID), and item 3 (password)

- **Advanced** tab – Items 5 and 7 (port numbers)

That completes the hardest part. In *Setting Up Mozilla Email*, you will reboot under Linux, and put the collected information into the mail program.

Setting Up Mozilla Email

The default email client in Linspire is Mozilla. This section reviews how to configure Mozilla with the mail information that you just collected.

- *History of Mozilla: The Mosaic Killer*
- *Setting Up Mozilla*

History of Mozilla: The Mosaic Killer

Mozilla has an interesting family tree. Mozilla was the code name used inside Netscape for their Navigator web browser. They likened it to the Godzilla monster and wanted Navigator/Mozilla to be the Mosaic Killer.

Mosaic was a competing web browser from 1994. Mosaic spun off from the University of Illinois into a company called Spyglass. Microsoft had no browser at that time, and bought Spyglass to form the basis of Internet Explorer. The guys who sold the Spyglass/Mozilla code to Microsoft asked for a per-copy royalty that was a percentage of Microsoft's browser retail price. They imagined they'd all get rich. Microsoft agreed to pay a percentage royalty, in return for a smaller lump sum payment to Spyglass.

Microsoft was secretly delighted to agree to a royalty based on the retail price. They knew they planned to bundle the browser for free to destroy Netscape, so a retail price percentage royalty would be worth...precisely nothing.

Businesses cannot assume good faith when they negotiate with Microsoft, and it all ended in tears for the Mosaic guys. They did not pass Go. They did not collect $200. Spyglass brought a lawsuit that Microsoft eventually settled to avoid further embarrassment during their monopoly abuse trial. To this day, Explorer's About window says *Based on NCSA Mosaic. NCSA Mosaic™ was developed at the National Center for Supercomputing Applications at the University of Illinois at Urbana-Champaign.*

By 1998 the Netscape company had been crushed by Microsoft's anti-competitive monopoly tactics (paying ISPs not to use Navigator, bundling Explorer with the operating system, deliberate incompatibilities, and so on). In a last-ditch attempt to gain public mind share, Netscape made Navigator an open source product.

Alas, the years of frantic development on Internet time left Navigator with a chaotic and crumbling source base. You couldn't even build the product from the sources that Netscape released. The source release was a spectacular flop, but it pointed the way forward. It taught everyone that open source wasn't a magic ingredient, but had to be applied to a product that was accessible with real value.

Netscape soon became a division of AOL, and to everyone's surprise eventually managed the necessary total rewrite of Navigator. It was launched in June 2002 under the name Mozilla, and became a reference implementation for many web standards. But the browser wars were long over, and about a year later AOL closed the browser division. Netscape was only ever a bargaining chip for AOL against Microsoft.

Some former Netscape/Mozilla staff set up the Mozilla Foundation to keep the software alive. The Mozilla Foundation is going from strength to strength today, under the leadership of Mitch Baker.

All the action now is in splitting Mozilla into a suite of smaller applications that share technology, such as the Gecko HTML display software. Although there is still a Mozilla all-in-one browser/news reader/mail client, it's not getting any further development. The future is with two other Mozilla-based products: the Firefox browser and the Thunderbird email client.

Setting Up Mozilla

1   Start the mail program by clicking the **email icon** in the KDE panel, circled in Figure 5-7.

Figure 5-7   Email icon in the KDE icon panel

2   That launches the Mozilla mail client window shown in Figure 5-8. The first time you do this, you will be offered a **New Account Setup** wizard.

3   You can cancel out of the wizard if you wish to poke around email before setting up an account. You can bring the wizard back by choosing **Edit > Mail & Newsgroups Account Settings > Add Account**. Those steps will bring up the same wizard shown in Figure 5-8.

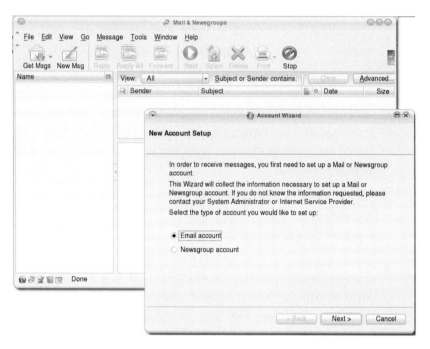

Figure 5-8   Mozilla mail client main window

4 Proceed from tab to tab through the wizard, entering all the mail details you collected in Table 5-1 on page 153. The final wizard screen is a summary of everything, shown in Figure 5-9.

Figure 5-9   Mozilla mail wizard summary window

Note that there is an **Enable Spam Filter** choice. You've got nothing to lose by accepting that. It's easy to turn off, if you later find you don't like it.

5 When satisfied with the information, click **Finish**.

6 The wizard goes away, its job complete, and the mail client presents a Password Required dialog shown in Figure 5-10.

Figure 5-10   Mail Server Password Required window

7 Type your mail password in the **Enter your password for home mail** field. Since I'm the only person that uses my PC, I typically like the convenience of having Password Manager remember my passwords. Click **OK**.

8 There's a deficiency in Mozilla you might have noticed at this point: the wizard doesn't provide any way for you to enter port numbers if your mail server uses non-default ports. Should you need to, you can specify non-standard port numbers after you have completed the wizard.

In Mozilla Mail, choose **Edit > Mail & Newsgroups Account Settings**. Click on **Outgoing Server (SMTP)**. That changes the right part of the window to let you specify the SMTP port, if it is something other than the standard port 25. Figure 5-11 shows the Port field where you enter the number.

9 Click the **Server Settings** line at the top left of the Account settings window. That lets you specify the IMAP or POP3 port.

10 Click **OK** when you have changed the settings. This completes your email set up. Send yourself an email of congratulation.

If you still can't send email, take this tip: it seems to be more reliable to delete the faulty email account and re-enter the details from the start, rather than try to modify the settings.

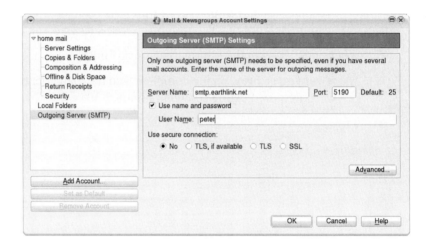

Figure 5-11   Account Settings window, Outgoing Server (SMTP) Settings

Using spell check and more

*Mozilla (and its replacement, Thunderbird) is a powerful email client, with many more features than the basic send/receive. One great feature is spell checking for mail. When you click the **New Msg** button to bring up a Compose email window, you might notice that it has an **Options** menu item.*

*One of the choices on the Options menu is Check Spelling. The item will be grayed out until you have typed some text in the body of the email. Then you can either choose **Options** > **Check Spelling**, or hold the Control (Ctrl) key down and type the letter k. That's a shortcut to bring up the email spell checker.*

You can learn more about the spell checker and Mozilla's other features at http://www.mozilla.org/docs/end-user. *The site has a lot of links to various guidebooks.*

There is also a really comprehensive Mozilla help site put together by Mozilla supporter Gunnar Jurdzik. Gunnar's help site at http://mozilla.gunnars.net *is so good that the* mozilla.org *web site has a pointer to it!*

You can find the full Thunderbird documentation at this site:

http://www.mozilla.org/support/thunderbird.

Using Other Email Clients

The Linspire distro uses Mozilla as the default email client, but there are lots of alternatives. Some of the fun of Linux lies in sampling the alternatives and choosing the exact blend of applications that you like best. Since most applications are free, you don't have to spend a fortune trying alternatives.

Available Linux Email Clients

Table 5-2 on page 162 shows some of the free Linux email clients. I use the Mozilla derivative Thunderbird for email. I like the fast and lean philosophy that the Mozilla developers now favor. I like it so much that when I have to use Windows, I use Thunderbird there too. Here's some good news: Thunderbird is set up by a wizard that is pretty much identical to Mozilla Mail's wizard! You can download and install Thunderbird from Linspire's Click N' Run warehouse, which is described in Chapter 7. So now you know how to try Thunderbird, too. (Start the Thunderbird wizard by choosing **Tool** > **Account Settings** > **Add Account**.)

People who are used to Microsoft Outlook should try Ximian Evolution. Evolution has similar features to Outlook, including support for email, calendar management, contact lists, and to-do lists.

You can obtain all of the software in Table 5-2 from Linspire's one-touch Click-N-Run process. That downloads and installs the software with the single click of a mouse. If you want a more up-to-date version than the one in the Click-N-Run warehouse, download the software from the web site shown in Table 5-2, and install it manually.

Table 5-2 is a list of selected programs; many others are available on Linux.

Table 5-2   Alternative email clients you might enjoy trying

Email	Client	Home web site
Ximian Evolution	Ximian is owned and run by the Novell Corporation. The Evolution mailer integrates mail, calendar, and address book features. It will be readily familiar to Outlook users.	http://www.novell.com/linux/ximian.html
Sylpheed	A lightweight email client, similar to Outlook Express (but without the virus propagation and infection features).	http://sylpheed.good-day.net
Thunderbird	A lightweight email client derived from the excellent Mozilla browser, but higher performance because it does not have any browsing capability.	http://www.mozilla.org/products/thunderbird/
Kmail	A full-featured email client specialized for the KDE desktop. It is part of an integrated suite of personal information management (so it may be overkill if all you want to do is read mail).	http://kmail.kde.org
Opera	A very good browser with a built-in email client combined with a news reader, mailing list organizer, and RSS newsfeed reader. Opera is so good and so popular that Microsoft changed one of its web sites specifically to make it give bad results to Opera users!	http://www.opera.com/products/desktop/m2

Transferring Data from Windows Email Clients

Many email programs store an address book containing email details for the people with whom you want to exchange email. You can use a couple of techniques to import a Windows address book into your Linux email application.

While you are still running under Windows, decide what Linux email client you will use. If you don't want to install anything or you're just feeling lazy, use Mozilla (which has been rebadged as Linspire Internet Suite). Mozilla is a combined browser and email application pre-installed as part of Linspire. If you want an email client with a more modern design and better performance, use the Thunderbird email program, which is a descendant of Mozilla.

Exporting Data from the Windows Email Client

You can get your Windows email client to disgorge your address book into one of three standard file formats so that you can import it directly from Mozilla or Thunderbird. The three formats that Mozilla understands are:

- A tab-delimited file, with the file extension .tab or .txt

- A file of comma-separated values, with the file extension of .csv

- A file of data exported from LDAP (a directory of key/value pairs popular on Windows), with the file extension of .ldif or .ldi. It's unlikely you will use LDAP on a home PC.

Use your current Windows email program to export the address book in one of these formats. The export function is typically under the File or Tools menu. After creating the file under Windows, write it to a diskette or CD so you can make it available to Linux. Or email it to yourself.

Importing Email Data into a Linux Email Program

Here are some approaches for importing email data.

Importing into Mozilla

Boot up in Linux, start the Mozilla email program, then use the wizard available by choosing **Tools** > **Import** to bring the data into Mozilla.

A Trick to Import Everything into Mozilla

There is another technique for importing data into Mozilla. It's a little bit of a trick, so while it might seem to work OK, it could stop working at any time.

1   If you are going to use Mozilla on Linux, then first install the Windows version of Mozilla on Windows.

2   When you do this, the Windows version of Mozilla looks to see if you are using Outlook, and automatically offers to import all your settings. Accept the offer. If Mozilla doesn't make this offer, in Mozilla choose **Tools** > **Import**, then select **Mail and Outlook** to get the data into the Windows version of Mozilla.

3   Once all the data is in the Windows version of Mozilla, find the folder where Mozilla keeps this data, and copy it to the corresponding place used by the Linux version of Mozilla.

This works because Mozilla stores the data in the same format for different operating systems, but it is not guaranteed for the future.

On Windows, look for a folder called **Mozilla**. The Mozilla data you want is in a folder underneath there. On my Windows PC the full pathname is

c:\Documents and Settings*user*\Application Data\Mozilla\Profiles\Default*XXX*.slt

where user is the username you chose in Windows, and *XXX* is a random name chosen by Mozilla. (On my Windows system it is qa49fz4k.slt.)

4 Save the contents of that *XXX*.slt Windows folder to a floppy disk or CD, then boot up Linux. Now copy those files into the corresponding Mozilla folder on Linux. All settings for the Mozilla suite (Linspire Internet suite) are kept in a folder underneath your home directory with the pathname

~/.mozilla/default/*YYY*.slt

on Linux.

5 The path to this folder has changed a little with recent releases, so you might need to explore a little to pin down its location. Again, *YYY* is a random name chosen by Mozilla (on my Linux system it is hieypity.slt) The .mozilla folder name starts with a dot (**.**) so it will be hidden by default. Check the **Show hidden files** option under **View** option in File Manager to see it.

If you are running as root, the full pathname is /root/.mozilla/default/*YYY*.slt. If you are running as an ordinary user, the full pathname is /home/*username*/.mozilla/default/*YYY*.slt. Quit out of all copies of Mozilla, browser, email, etc.

Use File Manager to copy the Windows version of the *XXX*.slt folder to the Linux version of the *YYY*.slt folder. When prompted, select **Overwrite All Files**.

Because Mozilla is an all-in-one suite, this will replicate all the settings of the browser, email, bookmarks, and so on, from Windows over to Linux.

Importing to Thunderbird

If you are using the Thunderbird email client, the folder to look for is called Thunderbird on Windows, and .thunderbird on Linux. Copy all files and folders to the following:

c:\Documents and Settings*user*\Application Data\Thunderbird\Profiles\default.hhq

Put them into the Linux folder called ~/.mozilla-thunderbird/rqkbtbi2.default/ where the rqkbtbi2 may be some other random collection of letters and numbers on your system. The pathname has changed in recent releases, so look around nearby folders to find the one with the right name form.

Junk Mail Control

Whatever email client you use, you'll probably want to configure some protection against the unsolicited commercial email known as spam.

Mozilla has two different mechanisms for filtering email:

- A simple approach that gradually improves, based on your feedback about which messages are or are not junk. This approach to weeding out junk mail uses an algorithm called a Bayesian Filter. See *Simple Spam Control Setup* on page 166.

- A sophisticated set of rules that you specify in detail. These rules can filter any kind of email, not just junk mail. You might use them to move all email from family members into a special folder. See *Sophisticated Email Filtering* on page 167.

Who put the "Bayes" in Bayesian filtering?

Bayesian spam filters are named after Thomas Bayes, an English clergyman from the 1700s who studied probability theory. His most famous formulation is known as Bayes' Theorem. It calculates the probability of something, based on the occurrence of related events.

Today, the term Bayesian means applying the laws of probability to any statement, not just those involving numbers and events. A Bayesian spam filter is one that classifies a message on the basis of how much it has in common with known spam, and thus how likely it is to be spam itself. For some reason, probably the unfamiliar name, "Bayesian spam filters" have become the fad of the moment. Everyone's falling over themselves to proclaim their filter is more Bayesian than the next guy's.

Bayesian filters are good, but not that good. It's far better to filter spam out at the mail server, rather than download it to the mail client, scan it, and discard it there. By definition, all good ISPs offer the option for spam filtering on the server. If you haven't heard about this, ask your ISP.

*Bayesian filters work on probabilities, rather than iron-clad rules. That
means that a Bayesian filter might be wrong occasionally, but it will adapt to
the kind of spam you receive and become more accurate over time.*

Simple Spam Control Setup

Mozilla mail automatically flags incoming mail that it thinks is spam. It displays a
little pink trash can icon on the summary line of the email, next to the date. An
example is shown in Figure 5-12 with the first two messages marked as spam.
This is indicated by a tiny spam icon on the summary lines (inside the oval ring).

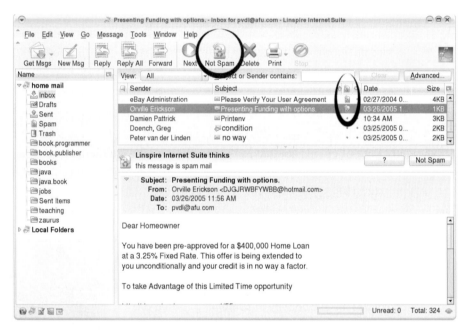

Figure 5-12   Use the Spam icon to toggle the spam status

Training the Filter

You train the filter by marking messages as spam or not spam. **Highlight a
message** in the summary window, then click the **Spam/Not Spam** icon (circled,
Figure 5-12) to toggle the message's spam state.

As you classify mail as spam and not spam, the filter records the characteristics of
each—the length, words used, origin, and so on. Each new classification tells the
filter more about what spam looks like to you. Eventually it gets pretty good at
detecting spam for itself.

Turning on Automatic Spam Filtering

Once Mozilla mail is correctly identifying spam, turn on automatic spam filtering.

Figure 5-13   Accessing spam control from Mozilla email's Tools menu

Do this by choosing **Tools** > **Spam Mail Controls** > **Enable spam mail controls**. All the settings on the Spam Mail Controls window (Figure 5-13) are safe defaults, but review them to make sure you are happy with all of them.

Reviewing the Results of the Spam Controls

After you turn on spam mail controls, you must periodically review the spam folder, and correct any non-spam that has been sent there by the filter. Correct misclassified mail by right-clicking on the summary line for that email, then choosing **Mark** > **As Not Spam** and drag it back to your inbox folder. If you don't do this, real email will occasionally be misclassified as spam. You will lose more and more of it if you allow the filter to learn to recognize good mail as spam.

Sophisticated Email Filtering

As well as plucking the spam, you can do additional automatic filtering on your mail inbox, in advance of reading the email. For example, you can automatically place incoming email from certain addresses into specific mail folders. This is a tool for people who get a lot of email, and who want some help from their mailer in organizing it.

Exclude Real Correspondents from Filtering

To minimize the chances of the filter learning the wrong thing, you can stop it looking at mail from regular correspondents. You can, if you wish, exclude senders who are in your email address book from spam checking. It's assumed that you want to hear from them if you put them in your address book.

You can put someone in your address book by displaying an email from them, and right-clicking on the name or address to the right of **From** (in the preview window that shows the body of the email). That brings up a menu whose first entry is **Add to Address Book.**

Other Filtering

Choose **Tools** > **Message Filters** to create new filters. A filter can look for particular words in particular fields (such as "tax preparation" in the subject line) and move it to a folder, or take other actions.

Many people use message filters to pre-sort their email, so that email from various senders is directed into certain folders automatically. For example, I am on a couple of astronomy mail lists. I use a message filter to divert all email from those lists into a single astronomy mail folder. That prevents me being interrupted by hobby-related email. When I want to read it later, it's all in one handy folder.

Spam is out of control

Whatever approach you use to try to reduce spam, there is no foolproof automated answer. I want to be able to get email from colleagues, classmates, and former students who have never emailed me before. That means that some Viagra salesmen, fake Rolex peddlers and Nigerian 419 scammers will always get through, too.

Perhaps you haven't yet heard of the Nigerian 419 scam? It starts with plausible email from someone claiming to have a large amount of valuables just out of reach, and offering you a share if you help him retrieve it. It's a standard confidence trick, run by email.

The only money that really changes hands is from you to the scammer for advances, license fees, bribes, taxes, etc. The Nigerian 419 scam (named after the section of the Nigerian legal code that prohibits it) is said to be the fifth largest export earner of that country. Amazingly, the Nigerian 419 scam finds enough gullible marks that the scammers pull in millions of dollars each year.

Although there's no permanent technical solution to spam, law enforcement occasionally takes a spammer off the net. Jeremy Jaynes of Raleigh, North Carolina, made history in October 2004 when he was sentenced to nine years in prison in the first felony spam case. Jaynes was one of the top ten most prolific email spammers on the Internet, responsible for wasting vast amounts of other people's time, money, and bandwidth. Jaynes made millions of dollars from his spam. He was found guilty and sent to prison for sending unsolicited junk mail and forging IP addresses to hide his tracks. Most of us would like to see a few more go down, including some of the 419ers.

Conclusion

That completes this chapter on email. Chapter 11, "Keeping Your Data Private," describes how you can use encryption to make your data files and email messages more difficult for eavesdroppers to read. That chapter also shows in detail how to compile and install new application programs. So much Linux software is supplied in source form, it is useful to know how to process it to create an executable binary. So even if you don't want to use encryption, you might want to skim Chapter 11 and come back to it later.

The lore of Linux—Trademarks for pleasure and profit

From its earliest days, the philosophy of Linux (and founder Linus Torvalds) was one of cooperation, learning, and sharing. The software was freely given away, and programmers could join in and help develop it, sharpening their own skills, learning from and teaching others. Linus Torvalds started the project in 1991, and within a couple of years it was clear that the system had great potential.

The Linux potential was clear even to people who were outside the open source community and did not share its lofty goals. In August 1994, one of these people, a Boston lawyer named William R. Della Croce Jr., decided to register "Linux" as a software trademark that belonged to him.

U.S. trademark law is definitive on one point: the right to exclusive use of a commercial identifier depends on the identifier not being similar to pre-existing brand names in the same field. You have to be the first one to use that name in that field. In addition, state and federal laws forbid the use of any trade name that is likely to cause confusion or to deceive. Of all people, a lawyer will understand these requirements.

Unfortunately for Della Croce, there were many examples of the commercial use of the name Linux prior his bright idea of trademarking a name in prior use by someone else. To avoid wasting everyone's time, the U.S. Patent and Trademark Office insists that people conduct a search to make sure they don't conflict with an existing name, before registering a trademark. However, the Patent Office doesn't do a thorough search of its own, and perhaps foolishly, relies on the honesty of applicants.

Della Croce was granted the trademark to the name Linux on September 5, 1995. The first time anyone noticed was in 1996, when IDG Books did a trademark search on the title for their latest book, Linux Secrets. *Finding that it was registered, they printed a cover footnote saying Linux is a registered trademark of William R. Della Croce, Jr. That confused readers of* Linux Journal, *commercially published since March 1994. When Linux Journal contacted Della Croce, he told them that Linux was owned by him, and they'd be hearing from his attorney.*

But wait, it gets even better! In 1996 Della Croce sent letters to the top Linux distributors, claiming to own the Linux trademark and demanding 10% of their turnover in royalties. The distributors quickly joined together, and appealed to the Trademark Office against the original trademark assignment. Della Croce was on quicksand here. If the trademark was judged to be falsely obtained, its use to demand money (royalties) under false pretenses was mail fraud—punishable by up to five years in prison. Della Croce dragged it out for a year, but in August 1997 he got off scot-free by assigning the trademark to Linus. The distributors actually reimbursed him his trademark filing fees.

A small non-profit organization, the Linux Mark Institute, was immediately set up to administer the Linux trademark on behalf of Linus Torvalds. They have their hands full busting greedy, dishonest opportunists around the world, and have fought successful trademark lawcases in five other countries so far. But to this day, LINUX® remains a registered trademark of Linus Torvald.

Web Tools

Getting Started

This chapter introduces you to two Linux applications that you'll use with the web. The idea is to let you know these applications exist, to tell you what they can do, and to show you the basics of using them.

The first application is the Firefox browser, which is enormously popular and gaining widespread use on Windows as a safe replacement for Internet Explorer. If you're not already using Firefox, you might want to switch to it on both Linux and Windows. In mid-2004 the U.S. Government's Computer Emergency Response Team advised users to stop running Internet Explorer because of its security flaws.

The second application is Linspire's Nvu program, which helps you create your own web pages.

Firefox Browser

Linspire 5 comes with the Linspire Internet Suite bundle of tools. This bundle includes the Mozilla open source browser. It's a fine tool, but the Mozilla people are now all working on Mozilla's next generation browser, Firefox. The Firefox browser is available for Linux, the Mac, and Windows. Firefox is where the action is now. The www.w3schools.com web site ranked Firefox with a 20% browser market share in early 2005. That's probably representative of their customers rather than the overall Internet, but it's a clear indication of how things are changing.

Linspire Internet Suite and Hot Words

The Mozilla-based Linspire Internet Suite has a new feature called Hot Words. Hot Words lets you do a Google search on text from a web page you are browsing, without taking all the steps of opening a new tab, going to Google, and pasting the search term.

With Hot Words, select the search term in the page where you're reading it, then right-click and choose **Search Web**. (You can also select the Lookup dictionary.com entry to get the dictionary definition of the word.) Hot Words will automatically open a new browser tab with the results of the search.

There is also a spelling checker in the Linspire Mozilla email client and in web forms. It follows along as you type and suggests corrections for words it does not recognize. The spell checker does not work with Firefox yet, nor with the Thunderbird email client. It starts automatically, and you can click the Spell button on the email toolbar to see a list of suggested replacements for misspelled words.

It's great to have a browser with integrated spelling checks and web searching. But I still prefer the leaner, faster feel of Firefox over its ancestor Mozilla. Firefox will get these features soon. Spell checking is available now as a browser extension, described in Spelling Check on page 195.

Downloading Firefox

Firefox is based on the Mozilla browser, simplified and improved. It has tabbed browsing for faster, easier web page displays. I recommend you use the Firefox browser instead of the older Mozilla suite that is bundled with Linspire. Firefox is in CNR (the Click-N-Run warehouse), and you can also download it from the web at http://www.mozilla.org/products/firefox.

Firefox is shown in Figure 6-1.

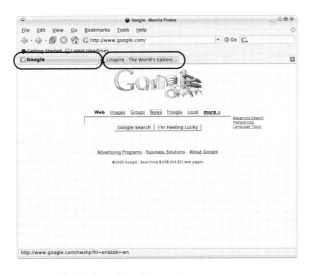

Figure 6-1   Firefox's tabbed browsing

Getting to Know Firefox

The areas highlighted in Figure 6-1 show tabbed browsing, which might be new to you if you've mostly used Internet Explorer. The main window of Firefox displays a single web page, but you can easily switch to another web page by clicking one of the tabs.

The browser does not have to open and fill a complete new window (which is slow). It only has to bring the new tab to the front (which is very fast). If you want to browse half a dozen web sites at once, your screen stays manageable without windows open everywhere.

In Figure 6-1, two web pages have been opened. You create a new empty tab by right-clicking on the bar in which the tabs appear (or on a tab itself). That brings up the context menu shown in Figure 6-2.

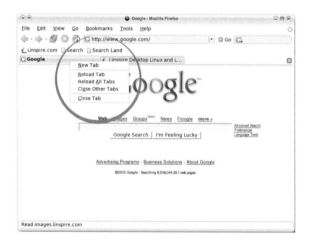

Figure 6-2   The tab control menu

- You can create a new tab by choosing the **New tab** menu item. You can close the tab you are on or all the other tabs.

- You switch to a new tab by clicking on it. The active tab is the one with the lighter colored tab label. In Figure 6-1, the tab labeled **Google** is the active tab (the tab shows as much of the web page title as will fit). The URL text field displays the URL for the active tab.

- You can right-click on a link in a web page and select the displayed option for opening it in a new tab. You get the same effect by holding down the control key on the keyboard and clicking on the link in a web page. This is particularly useful, as it allows you to continue browsing on the original web page while the new one loads in a new tab. The new tab gives an indication of when the page has finished loading.

Associating Applications with File Types

It's one thing to install Firefox (or any application). It's quite another to make Firefox the default application used whenever the system needs to handle an HTML file. This section explains how to make a permanent association between a file type, and the application that you want to handle it.

Making Firefox the Default Browser

1   You use a panel in the control center to make file/application associations. Reach it by clicking **Launch** > **Control Center** > **File Browsing** > **File Associations**.

2   That brings up the window shown in Figure 6-3.

Figure 6-3   Using the Control Center to associate applications and files

3   Type **html** in the **Find filename pattern** field. A tree-list of known file types is the second column. Out of all the categories of file types in that second

column, you'd guess correctly that HTML files are probably under Text. So click on **Text** to expand the tree.

4   Now find **html** in the expanded list, and click on it. That sets the file type you're dealing with.

5   It causes a third column to appear, (shown in Figure 6-3 with the two tabs General and Embedding). This third column gives the list of applications that the system knows about that can handle HTML files. (You can add another application by clicking the **Add** button.)

Instead, click on **Mozilla Firefox**, and click the **Move Up** button repeatedly, until Firefox is at the top of the Application Preference Order list.

6   Click the **OK** button to lock in the change.

Associating Any File Type with an Application

You can make this kind of association for any file type that is listed in the Known Types, to state your preferred program for handling it. For example, you could associate K3b with the .iso file type. Clicking on the icon for an ISO file would then launch the K3b application to burn an ISO CD as described in Chapter 9, "Filesystems and Optical Storage (CDs and DVDs)."

Fill in **iso** in the **Find filename pattern** field, and when that brings up the application entry in **Known Types**, click to expand it. My system shows a type x-iso. When highlighted, the description confirms it is an ISO9660 image file. You can then set K3b or another application to deal with it automatically by clicking the **Add** button of Application Preference Order. In case you're wondering, there's an industry-wide standard for these file types; anyone can change or add handy new ones that aren't in the standard, and the convention is to stick "x-" on the beginning to signify that.

Making That Application Preference Stick

Reports indicate that sometimes this procedure is not enough to make your chosen application be used for this file type.

1   If you see that problem, then call up the File Associations panel again.

2   Click **Launch** > **Run Programs** > **Utilities** > **Screen Capture** to save a picture showing the existing settings. If you want to switch back, you'll have all the old details shown in that screen dump.

3   Remove all other applications except your selection from the Application Preference Order list. Click **OK**.

If you still can't associate Firefox with html, type these in a command tool.

```
mv /usr/bin/mozilla /usr/bin/mozilla.old
ln -s /usr/bin/mozilla-firefox /usr/bin/mozilla
```

The first command moves the Mozilla program to one side. The second command puts a link from the place where Mozilla was, so that it now invokes the Firefox binary. Admittedly a fierce and ugly kludge, but it will force the system to do what you tell it if you run up against this bug.

Making Email Open Links with Firefox

Once you're using Firefox, you'll probably want your Thunderbird email application to use Firefox to open any links in email messages. The configuration file that controls this is /usr/lib/mozilla-thunderbird/defaults/pref/all.js and the root user can open it with any text editor. To open one text editor, just choose **Launch > Run Programs > Software Development > Advanced Text Editor (Kate)**. You'll see two lines in the file like this:

```
// pref("network.protocol-handler.app.http","mozilla-firefox");
// pref("network.protocol-handler.app.https","mozilla-firefox");
```

Remove just the two slashes at the start of each line (the slashes make the lines into comments). Save the file, and restart Thunderbird. It will now use Firefox to open links in email messages.

Changing Font Size

You can enlarge or reduce the typeface used in Firefox using the following approaches.

- Control with "+" key increases the font size – Pressing the control key and the "-" key will make the typeface smaller. I like this approach because it works the same way under Windows and Linux.

- Control and mouse scroll wheel – Scrolling the wheel toward you while holding down the Control key increases the font size for a zoom-in effect. Control-scrolling away from you reduces the font size. You have very fine control over the end result, and get there quickly using this method.

- Firefox's color preferences window – Choose **Edit** > **Preferences** > **Fonts and Colors**; the resulting window lets you set the font minimum size. This sets the minimum type size permanently, while the other two approaches only affect the browser window you are in.

Configuring Firefox with Browser Extensions

The Firefox browser is probably the most customizable browser on the web. To see one aspect of this, type about:config in the URL field. Firefox will display scores of its configurable settings.

When you install it, Firefox is basic, fast, and simple. Hundreds of little programs known as browser extensions are freely available; they add some new feature or appearance to Firefox. It's your choice whether to add them or not. Some people prefer an uncluttered look. Others want to keep track of the latest information from the web. Everyone gets what they like best.

Some of the best Firefox extensions have been collected and put on the web site https://addons.update.mozilla.org/extensions.

Here are a couple of useful extensions; you can find more on your own.

The "ForecastFox" Weather Icons

I live in Silicon Valley, California. They say there are just two seasons here: green and brown. For eight months of the year, the daily weather forecast is always the same: mild and overcast early, with temperatures reaching into the 90's by noon as the cloud cover burns off, sunny for the rest of the day with light winds from the west. I don't know how the weather clowns on TV here justify their salary. But if you live in a place where the weather does vary, take a look at the ForecastFox extension.

You can reach ForecastFox by searching at the Mozilla extensions site mentioned previously. When you install this extension, it will display the weather forecast for the next few days as little icons in your browser. See Figure 6-4 for an example.

Silicon Valley was in the green (rainy) season when I took this screendump, and the icons are saying today will be sunny, and the next two days rainy.

I briefly mention Mozilla browser extensions in Chapter 11, "Keeping Your Data Private," and explain they are blissfully simple to install: you just browse the link to an .xpi file and it installs automagically.

Figure 6-4   The local weather forecast in your browser

1   Once you arrive at the ForecastFox web page, you'll see a button on the page marked **Install Now**. Click it to start the process, and you'll get a dialog box like that shown in Figure 6-5.

Figure 6-5   Software Installation window

Heed that warning when you see it on other sites. It's probably safe to install extensions that are from the same web site as the browser itself. But you need to really think about whether you trust a web site before allowing it to install something on your computer, and the default response should be cancel. One of the problems with Internet Explorer is that you can't rely on it to warn you of outside attempts to install software on your PC. When Microsoft smuggled the Explorer application into the kernel, they also opened a door to all kinds of self-installing horrorware.

2   When you click **Install**, you'll get the dialog box shown in Figure 6-6. You use this to customize what kind of weather forecast is shown, what area the forecast is for, and so on.

Figure 6-6   Customizing ForecastFox

3   Click the button marked **Find Code**. That lets you type in the name of your town (or airport). It fills in the corresponding weather code representing that area. All the information for ForecastFox comes from the www.weather.com site, and it's possible that they will block it eventually rather than supply free weather forecasts without the chance to beam ads at you.

4   The other tabs in Figure 6-6 allow you to set the kind of weather data you want to appear, and where on the browser page you want it to appear. Just experiment to get the effect you want. As you might guess, this configuration window will reappear when you right-click on one of the weather icons and select **Options**.

5   Finally, completely exit the Firefox application, and restart it to see your weather forecast. Just don't bother with it in California from March to November.

Dictionary Search

This extension lets you look up the definition of any words you find in web pages. It provides the same service as Linspire's Hot Words, but for Firefox.

1   From the Mozilla extensions site, look for the DictionarySearch extension, and install it by clicking as explained previously. Remember to exit and restart Firefox.

2   Now when you see a term you want explained, highlight it and right-click, then select **Dictionary Search**, as shown in Figure 6-7.

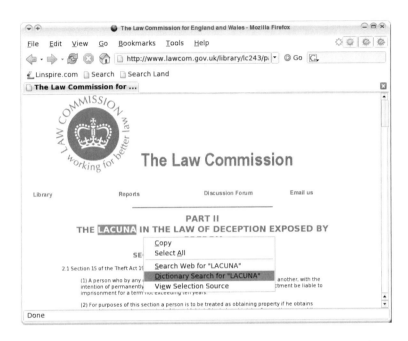

Figure 6-7   Choosing to do a dictionary search

3   In the example you're doing a dictionary search for the word lacuna. Selecting the Dictionary Search menu item opens a new tab with the results of the search, shown in Figure 6-8.

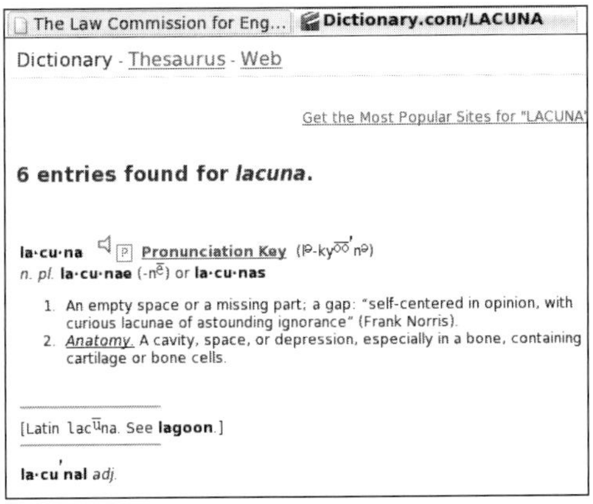

Figure 6-8   The word search results

4   From this you can see that a lacuna is a medical or legal term for an empty space, a missing part, or a gap. You can get roughly the same service by typing define:lacuna in the search web text field at Google.

BugMeNot—Site Registration

How do you feel about sites that require free registration before they'll let you look at their web pages? It's very common on news sites—the more they know about their reader demographics, the more they can charge advertisers.

Many people find it a burden to provide a page of personal information, in order to read a few paragraphs of news story. Some people get creative and register fictitious details (you'd be amazed how many 94-year old millionaire Peruvian goat herders read the New York Times).

Figure 6-9 shows what happens when you try to access a story on the New York Times web site; it challenges you for registration details.

Figure 6-9   Site with registration required

Now there's an alternative in the form of a Firefox extension called BugMeNot. You can find BugMeNot at http://extensions.roachfiend.com/index.php#bugmenot. This site maintains a database of existing registrations. When you install the extension, and you are confronted with a free registration required page, use BugMeNot to automatically get the name/password of a pre-registered account filled out.

Try it! Install the BugMeNot extension, restart Firefox and visit any page that requires free registration. Quite properly, BugMeNot doesn't work for paid registration sites. Right-click on the user name field. You'll see a pop up menu similar to that shown in Figure 6-10.

Figure 6-10   Choosing BugMeNot to get a name and password

Select BugMeNot from the menu, and a user ID/password combination will be filled in automatically, allowing access without an additional registration. If the site has already revoked that user ID/password (to cut down on readership among wealthy Peruvian goatherders), then right-click in the field again to obtain another name/password pair, as shown in Figure 6-11.

Figure 6-11   BugMeNot fills in the name and password

Some people feel that providing genuine registration data is a fair price to pay to view other people's web sites. Others believe in discouraging data fishing expeditions by web site operators, and maintain that they should not have to provide any personal data to view content that is laden with ads. Personally, I think it's all gone downhill since cable TV started showing ads. Every web site already has a traffic log showing volume and geographic location of readers, and many surfers think that should be enough.

Smarter web sites are already making data capture less of an imposition by providing a small, optional form at the top of the desired web page asking for age, gender and zip code. I don't expect BugMeNot to keep working indefinitely (registration-required sites hate it), but whatever your views on registration data, BugMeNot is a clever Firefox extension and more fun than a big barrel of really fun things.

Spoofing the User Agent String

An extension for Firefox changes the user agent to an arbitrary string. The user agent is a string that your browser sends to server sites, identifying itself and the system it's running on. A typical user agent string is Mozilla/4.0 (compatible; MSIE 5.5; Windows NT 5.0) which comes from Internet Explorer 5.5 running on Windows 2000.

The Microsoft browser still identifies itself as Mozilla from the days when Microsoft bought it from the Spyglass company. Some misguided web sites use the agent string to identify the browser you are using and will disable access if it's a browser they haven't tested with. Spoofing the user agent string allows you to access the site anyway.

Visit http://extensionroom.mozdev.org/more-info/useragentswitcher to get the extension that allows you to let your browser identify itself to servers as anything you like. Internet Explorer-specific code such as ActiveX won't run, not that you should have that enabled in Explorer, but you'll be able to do more than if you can't see the site at all.

Removing an Extension

In Firefox, choose **Tools > Extensions** to display the extensions that you have installed. Click on one extension to highlight it, then click **Uninstall** to remove it.

Reviewing Firefox Settings

Firefox has an excellent mechanism for reviewing and changing custom settings. Type about:config in the URL bar, and press **Return**. You'll see a window like the one in Figure 6-12.

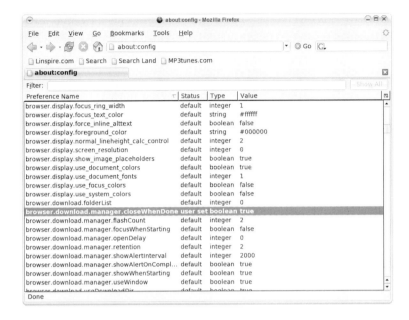

Figure 6-12   Firefox configuration

The browser displays a list of dozens and dozens of Firefox settings. To change one, right-click on one and select **New**. Then select **String**, **Integer**, or **Boolean** according to what kind of field it is.

A web search will reveal what a setting does, if it is not obvious from the name. Figure 6-12 shows that I have changed the default setting that leaves the download manager window open after a file download completes. That window will now close on completion. After changing a setting, save it and put it into effect by completely exiting the Firefox program and restarting it.

Nvu Web Page Editor

Nvu is an editor that lets you create web pages without having to know HTML. It's like the old Netscape Composer, or Macromedia's Dreamweaver or Microsoft's FrontPage tool. Nvu is best for relatively simple web pages, and can't do some of the slick stuff that Dreamweaver can do. Nvu only deals with HTML and CSS files, and not other kinds of web content such as .php files.

OpenOffice.org also has an HTML editor, but Nvu is generally simpler to use.

To open Nvu, click **Launch** > **Programs** > **Web Authoring**. Figure 6-13 shows how Nvu looks when you start it, and also indicates the names of various controls.

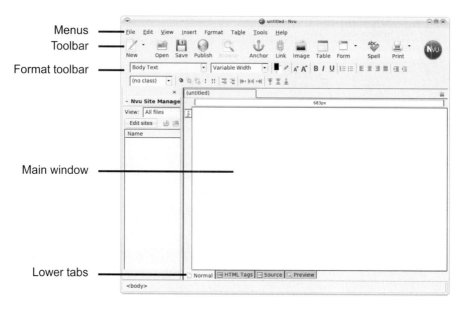

Figure 6-13   Names of the Nvu GUI components

After you have finished creating or editing a web page, Nvu can automatically upload it to your web site.

Who do you thank for Nvu?

The lead developer on the Nvu project is Daniel Glazman, who was the chief architect on Netscape Composer. Nvu started from the Composer code base. It's an open source project that will eventually be merged back into the main Mozilla code base.

The Linspire organization is backing Nvu financially, and with server space and technical expertise. Because of this backing it is very likely that Nvu will become the premier web authoring system for Linux. The Nvu site is http:// www.nvu.com. *They also have a forum where you can pose questions and talk to other Nvu users at* http://forum.nvudev.org.

Nvu is a WYSIWYG editor, meaning you don't have to know much about HTML tags. You just type what you want into the Nvu window, then format the layout and text using the **Format** menu. The HTML tags that control page formatting will be generated automatically. When you are satisfied, click the **Publish** button to put the page on your web site.

Create a Web Page

Figure 6-14 shows a finished web page I created in Nvu to showcase Gray's Beach on Cape Cod, Massachusetts. You can look at this finished web page at http://afu.com/beach/swim.html.

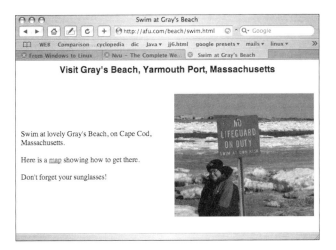

Figure 6-14   The finished web page created by Nvu

Walk through all the steps to create this web page.

1 Create a new page by clicking on the **New** button at the left of the toolbar (the toolbar is the strip of icon buttons near the top of any GUI).

You can work on an existing page by choosing **File** > **Open File**. You can even use an existing web page (such as http://afu.com/beach/swim.html) as your starting point by choosing **File** > **Open web location**.

2 Type the text for the heading of the web page Visit Gray's Beach, Yarmouth Port, Massachusetts in the main window of Nvu.

3 Highlight the line you just typed, so you can select a format. In the drop-down list on the top left side of the Nvu window, select **Heading 3**.

4 Choose **Format** > **Align** > **Center**. Both choices are shown in Figure 6-15

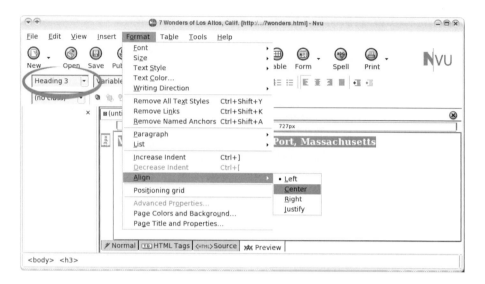

Figure 6-15 Formatting a line of text as a heading

5 Put a table on the web page. The table will have one row and two columns. Each entry in the body of the table is called a cell. You can put anything you like into a cell: a link, some text, a picture, or any combination of these. Put the words in the left cell, and the picture in the right cell. It's common to use a table to space and separate elements on a web page.

Click the **Table** button on the toolbar to bring up the Insert Table window seen in Figure 6-16.

6 Roll your mouse over the table grid to highlight cells starting from the top left. When you have highlighted the exact number of rows and columns you want, click the mouse and click **OK**.

Alternatively, you can click the **Precisely** tab, and set rows and columns by typing numbers. Your action fills in the blank frame of the two-cell table in the main window.

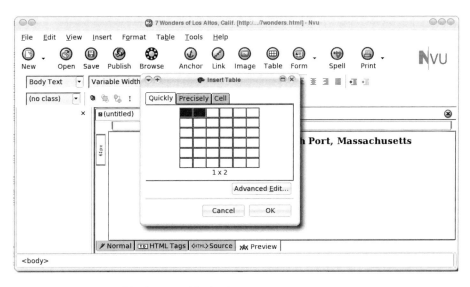

Figure 6-16   Placing a table in the web page

7 Click on the right cell in the table; this becomes the place where things are entered. Click the icon marked **Image** in the toolbar to bring up Figure 6-17.

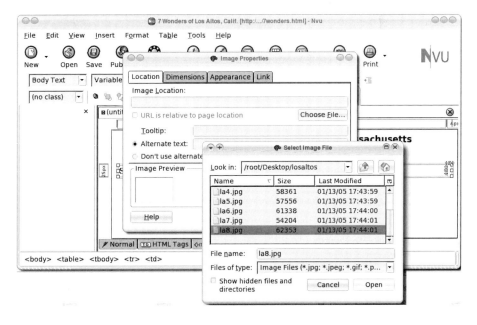

Figure 6-17   Adding the Image file

8   Click the **Choose File** button on the Image Properties window to open the Select Image File window also shown in Figure 6-17. This allows you to browse for the image file that you want to go on the web page. Select an image file in GIF, JPEG or PNG format, since these are displayable by most browsers.

9   After selecting the image file, click the **Open** button.

10   Click in the left cell of the table and in the space that appears, type a few words describing the image, as shown in Figure 6-18. This is for people who are using text-only browsers that can't display pictures. This should be an optional field, but you currently have to enter something.

Figure 6-18   Adding the text to the table cell

11   You're ready to add a link to a web page that displays a map of access to Gray's Beach.

The easiest way to find street maps for U.S. addresses is to type the address into the Google search field of your browser. Google will offer links to maps as the very first choice of search results. Street maps for Great Britain and many other countries are at the excellent web site http://www.multimap.com.

In this example, I happen to already know the address of Grays Beach; the address is 499 Center Street, Yarmouth Port, MA. When I type in that address, I get the map shown in Figure 6-19.

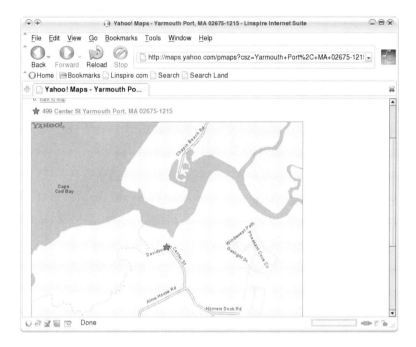

Figure 6-19   Finding the URL for the map to the beach

You don't need the map itself, though; you need the link to it. To get the URL, place your cursor in the URL field of the browser displaying the map. Highlight the entire URL, right-click, and select **Copy**.

12 Now create a link from your web page to the map web page. Click the **Link** icon on the Nvu toolbar to bring up the Link Properties window shown in Figure 6-20.

13 Paste the link from the previous step into the field labeled **Link Location**. You can right-click at the point where you want to paste the text, and select **Paste**.

14 Enter the text to display for the link in the textfield labeled **Link Text**. Something like Map of Grays Beach is sufficient. Then click **OK**.

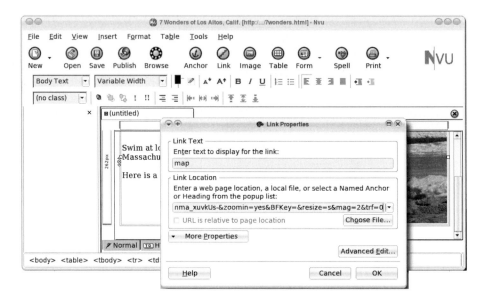

Figure 6-20   Clicking the **Link** button to add the link

15 That table would look better without a visible border. You can edit a table after creating it; click on the edge of the table, then choose **Table** > **Table Properties**. That brings up the tabbed window shown in Figure 6-21.

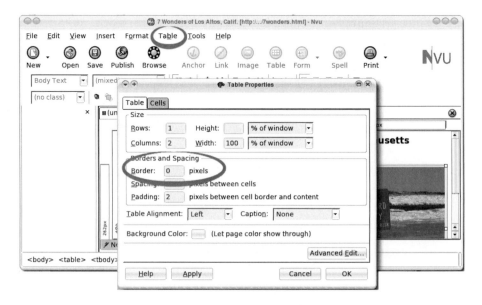

Figure 6-21   Removing the table's visible border

16 One tab lets you edit table properties, the other tab lets you edit an individual cell (highlight it before bringing up the window). Make sure the **Table** tab is selected. Set the **border** to zero pixels, and click **OK** to exit.

17 Now review the web page, and if satisfied, save it to disk. Click the toolbar icon **Save** shown in Figure 6-22 to bring up a Save Page As dialog.

18 Select a folder and file name, and click **Save** in the dialog to put the file on your local disk.

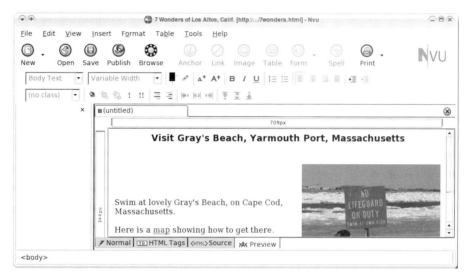

Figure 6-22   Reviewing the finished page in the Preview window

Let's mention the function of the lower tabs (refer back to Figure 6-13). These four tabs display four different views of the web page you are constructing. You can edit the web page in any of these views (you've been using the Preview view so far). These are the differences:

- Normal – This is how you will see the web page in a browser, but with tables outlined in red, to make it easier to see where they are, and to select them. Spelling mistakes are underlined in red (I'll tell you how to turn that feature on in just a minute).

- HTML Tags – This has the features of the Normal window, and also displays a little icon next to every HTML tag (the tag itself is not displayed). This makes it easy to edit any tag, including ones that otherwise require precise clicking, such as a table versus a cell within a table.

Click on any of the tag icons to bring up the appropriate window for editing that tag. This is a clever and powerful editing feature.

◆   HTML Source – This view allows you to see (and edit) the HTML tags that control how a page is displayed in a browser. Tags aren't that hard to decipher. They are enclosed in a pair of angled brackets so a browser can easily tell them apart from regular text.

◆   Preview – This is how you will see the web page in a browser.

19 The last step is to upload your web page (HTML file and images) to your web site. Click the **Publish** button in the toolbar. It brings up the Publish Page window shown in Figure 6-23.

Figure 6-23   Providing access details for your web site

20 The first time you publish, you will have to fill in all the details of where your web site is, and the account name/password that you use to access it. This information is entered on the Settings tab.

21 Then click on the **Publish** tab shown in Figure 6-24. Fill out the details, saying whether the images need to be uploaded too (unless they are already on your web site, respond Yes).

22 Click the **Publish** button, and the window will be replaced by one showing progress bars for each file being uploaded.

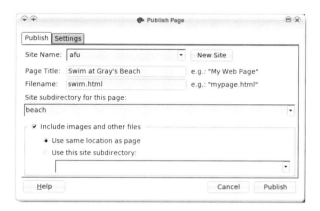

Figure 6-24   Uploading the files to your web site

Nvu is a wonderful program: it has a good combination of features, and is easy to use. By paying for its development, and keeping the program open source and available for all distros, Linspire is showing its commitment to Linux and its willingness to invest back in the open source community.

Additional Nvu Tips

Here are a few additional tips for using Nvu.

Settings Are Reset

If you install a newer version of Nvu, all your existing publish settings are wiped out. It's either a bug or a very unhelpful design feature, depending on who you talk to. If you plan to install a later version of Nvu, you might want to bring up the publish window first, and write down the settings (or just take a screen snapshot, using the Screen Capture utility).

Spelling Check

Choose **Tools** > **Preferences** > **Advanced**. Click on the option labeled **Underline misspelled words** shown in Figure 6-25.

Figure 6-25   Turning on spell checking

In passing, let's elaborate on the words in the **Special Characters** drop-down list: *Output the following characters as entities: All characters having an entity equivalence in the HTML 4 specification*. It looks like some kind of scare-the-newbie joke. It actually means use the symbolic name, not the numeric code, for a special character (like a trademark symbol).

If you select that choice, Nvu will put ™ in the HTML instead of ™ to represent the trademark symbol ™. The numeric form of characters was part of HTML 2, but the named form was introduced with HTML 4. This feature lets you be friendly to older browsers, that's all.

I asked Daniel Glazman (Nvu chief developer) about the wording. He gave me a candid reply, "Peter, the answer is easy: I am just a geek, and geeks rarely find the best or simplest wording in user interfaces. ;-)" This suggests a great way for non-programmers to contribute to open source software: review the user interface and suggest constructive improvements; write better documentation; participate in testing early releases.

Program Errors Are Logged

Nvu is still under development. The version that I used while writing this chapter was version 0.70, and later versions will be available by the time you read this.

It's possible that you will find a bug in Nvu—something that doesn't work properly. You can get more information about what Nvu is doing by bringing up the console. Choose **Tools** > **Web Development** > **Javascript Console** to bring up the window shown in Figure 6-26. Repeat the action that caused the bug, and see if it generates a message in the console.

Figure 6-26   Looking at errors

If a message does appear in the console, you can provide more information when you post an enquiry/bug rcport in the Nvu user forum at http://forum.nvudev.org. As ever, the better the information you provide, the more likely you are to get a useful answer.

Correcting Web Pages Produced by Microsoft Tools

Microsoft has many different tools that produce HTML. Unfortunately they often output incorrect and unportable HTML. Sometimes Microsoft's own browser cannot read Microsoft-generated HTML, and Microsoft deliberately writes HTML that is incompatible with browsers from other organizations.

Research scientist John Walker got fed up with this situation, and he wrote a software utility to, as he put it, "Remove the moronic parts of Microsoft's HTML output." If you have some HTML files that were originally produced by Microsoft tools, you might be able to bring them back to standard portable form by using John's program at http://www.fourmilab.ch/webtools/demoroniser.

Advanced Users Only

Advanced users might like to note that Nvu supports the following features, not described here.

- Nvu can call W3C's HTML validator to check that the web page under construction is portable and correct. Choose **Tools** > **Validate HTML** to run the validator.

- Nvu has a CSS editor. Cascading Style Sheets (CSS) are a way of customizing HTML tags in a document. Choose **Tools** > **CSS Editor** to start the editor.

- Nvu can edit several documents at once using a tabbed window. This is the function of the option labeled **Upper tabs** in Figure 6-13.

- Nvu supports the creation and editing of web forms. Web forms provide a simple GUI for collecting information from the browser user. Nvu will only help you create the form, not do any of the server-side wiring needed to make it run.

Legends of Linux—The name game

The Linspire distro jettisoned its former name of Lindows in exchange for a $20 million payment from Microsoft. Some of the other Linux distros have names with amusing or surprising origins, too. Here's a selection for your entertainment.

Slackware is the oldest distro still in existence. Founded by Patrick Volkerding in 1993, Slackware is a no-frills distro that emphasizes installing and working without a GUI. For this reason, running Slackware as your main desktop is considered a mark of studliness among many in the Linux world. These days, Patrick tells questioners that all the good names were already taken then changes the subject. But actually, Slackware was named after 1980s counter-culture icon J.R. "Bob" Dobbs of the Church of the Sub-Genius. For a while Dobbs' pipe-smoking paternal face could be found in the most unexpected of places, and would-be revolutionaries bought into his message of "Slack". Today, we'd call it "tilt". Since the Great Big Tech Bust of 2000, www.subgenius.com is just another web site hawking (as they put it) doo-hickeys and geegaws. But the concept lives on in Slackware.

Gentoo *Although Slackware has the reputation, Gentoo is the distro that real studly nerds run. Most users install Gentoo by compiling it from scratch, resulting in the highest possible performance by matching the hardware they have. But where does the name come from? It's from Pygoscelis papua, commonly known as the Gentoo penguin. Gentoo was a penguin species long before it was a Linux distro. Gentoos are the only breed of penguin with a white stripe on the top of the head and an orange beak. They are also the fastest underwater swimming penguins and can reach 36 kph. And speed is the reason the name was appropriated for a distro.*

Debian *is the distro on which Linspire and many other sub-distros are based. Debian adheres very strictly to the philosophy of open source software, and will not ship any code that is not openly licensed. Another key tenet of the Debian distro is stability. The project is organized and run to favor stable code over the latest new developments or early release dates. The Debian project was started in 1993 by Ian Murdock while he was still a student at Purdue University. He combined the first names of himself and his girlfriend (now wife) Debra to coin the project name Debian. Debian is very highly regarded in the Linux community, and has over one thousand programmers volunteering their labor to work on different aspects of the project.*

Red Hat *While still an undergraduate, Marc Ewing, the eventual founder of Red Hat Linux, was given his grandfather's Cornell lacrosse team cap. The Cornell lacrosse cap featured dazzling red and white stripes. In spite of its striking appearance, Marc managed to lose the historic cap and searched for it with increasing desperation. The manual for the original Red Hat Linux beta contained an appeal for readers to return Marc's red hat if found. By rights, this distro should be called Red and White Striped Cap Linux.*

SUSE *Originally a spin-off from Slackware founded by some programmers in Germany, SUSE acquired the same name as their software company, S.u.S.e. That was an abbreviation for Software-und System-Entwicklung (Software and system development). Later the distro was rebranded as "SUSE" which was deemed not to be an acronym for anything. In 2004, the Novell company bought SUSE and has focused it on corporate computing.*

Adding Software

Getting Started

This chapter looks at some of the ways that software is packaged for Linux, and the tools that you use to download and install it. Unlike the Windows world, most Linux software uses a more efficient distribution mechanism than CDs—the Internet itself.

Mostly you download the Linux software you need, free of charge, from a number of trusted web sites. Sometimes only the source code is available, so you have to compile the software. When the majority of Linux users were enthusiasts and computer industry professionals, it was reasonable for users to build the software they wanted to use.

Now that Linux is gaining market share among home users, it is no longer so reasonable. Let's review the ways you can obtain new applications on your computer. Only one involves compiling.

- Linspire's Click-N-Run installer. I'll demonstrate using it to install the GIMP, a popular image editor.

- Debian Linux's Advanced Package Tools. I'll demonstrate using it to install bzflag, a popular game.

- Many popular Linux programs, including the distros themselves, are available on CD. Anyone can order an OpenOffice.org CD on Amazon or eBay, or from the www.openoffice.org site. Macromedia Director and Quark Express are available for Linux on Amazon. Many books include CDs for Linux or Linux applications.

- Downloading source code from the web, and compiling it. I'll demonstrate using this approach with gpg, a popular encryption program, in Chapter 11, "Keeping Your Data Private," on page 395.

These approaches to software installation are listed in increasing order of the effort involved. You should generally start looking for software from the top of the list and work your way down.

Introducing Linspire's Click-N-Run

The Linspire distro solves the problems of software installation with a program called Click-N-Run. It runs using a server at the Linspire web site. Click-N-Run, usually abbreviated as CNR, provides access to a library of applications that have been built and tested on Linspire. Linspire customers can download and install any of these applications with only one mouse click. Click-N-Run is a unique innovation from Linspire that is now being more widely copied. Microsoft plans support for over-the-Internet software distribution, starting with the "Longhorn" release that replaces XP. The Mandrake distro has the Mandrake Club, where membership buys you forum access and one click RPM installs.

CNR is far superior to the installation wizards used on Windows. With CNR, you go to one web site to find your applications. You click one button, and the application is installed automatically. There is no configuration, no CD to lose, no software registration, and no rebooting needed. CNR is a paid subscription service that includes access to updates of Linspire OS without further charge.

Figure 7-1 shows the CNR icon that appears on your desktop. Double-click the **CNR icon** to start the CNR application.

CNR

Figure 7-1   Click-N-Run icon

You can better appreciate the advantages of CNR if you look at the steps needed to install an application from source code. Say I want an image-editing program for Linux. I know from reading Linux magazines and the Linspire Forums that Linux has the GNU Image Manipulation Program, invariably called the GIMP. The GIMP is a free-of-cost, open source program roughly equivalent to Adobe Photoshop. Photoshop has a few more features, costs $649, and doesn't yet run on Linux.

Installing Applications from Source Takes Effort

The hands-down easiest way to get the GIMP on your Linspire PC is to install it using Click-N-Run. Other Linux distros don't have CNR, and the easiest way to install it is to download it as a package. However, not all applications have been organized as packages. Some are only available as source code.

If the GIMP application were only available as source code, I would have to go through all these steps to install it on my system.

1   Do a web search for download sites for the GIMP.

2   Go to the GIMP download page at http://www.gimp.org/unix. Note that the GIMP people do not include a tested executable with the bundle they put together. If you want to be sure of what you're getting, you have to build it yourself from source code.

3   Go to the nearest mirror site and download the 18 MB file gimp-2.1.7.tar.gz and the file containing the checksum total. A .tar.gz file is essentially a zip file for Linux.

4   Run the md5sum utility on the downloaded tar.gz file, and check that it matches the figure given in the checksum file. This gives you confidence that the file was not corrupted during the download.

5   Repeat this process of download-tarfile and review-checksum for eight other libraries that the web page says are needed to build the GIMP. Unpack and install all the libraries.

6   Unpack the gimp tar file into a folder where you will build it.

7   Make sure you have the g++ compiler already installed via CNR. Run the configure script to configure the build scripts for this distro of linux. Then run the *make* command to build the application. Then run the *make install* command to put the binary, help files, etc., in the right folders on your system.

There's nothing in there that is particularly difficult. It's just time-consuming. One of the reasons that I have a computer is so it can do the grunt work, not me.

With CNR, Adding Software Is Easy

Now look at how you install the GIMP image editor on a Linspire system using Linspire's Click-N-Run.

Note – Some versions of Linspire come with the GIMP preinstalled, so if you CNR install it as well, you might see two menu entries for it. It's not a big deal; the application is only on the system in one place. Use the menu editor described in Chapter 3, "The KDE Desktop," to delete any menu entry you don't want.

Adding New Software

1 Bring up the CNR client program by clicking on the **CNR icon** in the system tray.

2 Sign in to CNR if you are not already signed in, using the Sign In button on the toolbar.

3 There is a search field at the top of the right-hand panel of CNR. Make sure the search field label is set to **CNR Warehouse** (in the drop-down list).

4 Type GIMP into the CNR search field (the field is not case sensitive) and click the **Go** button.

The CNR program will display the search with a page similar to Figure 7-2.

The search shows a list of ten or twenty GIMP-related programs in the CNR warehouse. The very first entry is the GIMP program itself. The other entries are various add-ons, utilities, and manuals for GIMP.

5 Click the **CNR** button that appears next to the left of the first search result. That starts the 3 MB GIMP download and install.

6 The CNR icon in the system tray shows animated arrows while the download is taking place, so you know when it has finished. The GIMP download will take a couple of minutes if you have broadband, and several hours if you have a dial-up connection.

Figure 7-2   Finding software in the Click-N-Run warehouse

That's all! The GIMP is now installed and ready for use. The GIMP program can be reached from the **Launch** button, as shown in Figure 7-3.

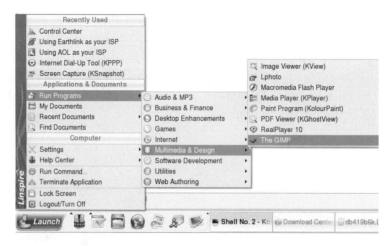

Figure 7-3   Starting the GIMP

Running the New Software

In spite of the name, Click-N-Run doesn't run the program (unless you configure CNR to do so). You start a newly installed program by clicking through the menus available from the **Launch** button, just as usual.

Adding an Icon for the New Software

You'll probably want CNR to add an icon to the desktop for downloads so that you can find them easily.

1 In the CNR application, at the right-hand end of the icon bar, click the **Configure CNR** icon to display the Configure CNR window.

2 Click on the **Status** icon in the left panel of the window. (This is misnamed; it should really be called something like "CNR preferences".) Select **Add an icon to the desktop**.

3 Click **OK**.

4 Then configure the desktop to show all icons, by clicking **Launch > Control Center > Look & Feel > Desktop > Behavior > General**. Make sure **Show icons on desktop** is selected, then click OK.

> If you don't get an icon for some CNR download, then it means the download isn't something that can be started by clicking. It may be a library, or an application run from a console.

After the CNR installation finishes, you can launch the GIMP program. Once the GIMP was running, I chose **File > Open** to bring in the JPG image shown in Figure 7-4.

This is a photo taken at the 2004 Charity Concours car exhibition at Stanford University, California. I used the GIMP features to label the picture with text at the top left, identifying the location and date. As Figure 7-4 shows, the GIMP tiles pretty much the whole screen with windows. Like Photoshop, it's a big program to get your arms around.

CNR is spectacular. Without CNR, it took more than an hour to get all the libraries right and to build the GIMP software. Using CNR, it took a couple of minutes to get to the point where I could run the application, and I didn't have to worry about dependencies on other libraries or packages. CNR supplied everything that was needed and put it in the right place on my system.

Figure 7-4   Editing an image file with the GIMP

More CNR Details

This section covers a few more useful features in CNR.

The Aisle and Info Buttons in CNR

You used the green running man button to download and install software located in CNR. You might have wondered about the other buttons.

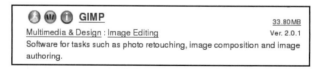

Figure 7-5   Other CNR buttons

You can see in Figure 7-5 two other buttons next to the green running man button.

- The orange button in the middle is the aisle button. The icon is intended to depict aisles (lanes in a supermarket).

  Aisles are effectively folders of CNR software that you can keep on the CNR server. You can share your aisles (your software picks) with other CNR users if you wish, and they can share theirs with you. Someone teaching a class might publish an aisle for all the students. I have a standard set of downloads that I want on all my Linux systems (the gcc compiler, the man pages, GIMP, Firefox and so on). I keep these in a personal aisle accessible through the URL http://www.linspire.com/aisles/pvdl.

  Feel free to CNR it, if you want to try the aisles feature. If you install the PvdL aisle, you'll have everything you need to build applications and device drivers. But it's 65 MB of goodness, so dial-up users be warned.

- There is also the blue *more information* button bearing the letter **i** next to the name of the software. Click this, and CNR will go to a web page that gives more information on that piece of software. It allows you to find out more about the software without installing it.

Later Updates

CNR keeps a record of software that you have CNR installed. If there is an update in the CNR warehouse, it will inform you by overlaying the running man in the CNR icon with a blue up arrow in your system tray. The up arrow suggests the topic of upgrades. This is shown as the fourth icon from the left in Figure 7-6.

Figure 7-6   CNR has updates for an installed application

When you click on the running man with blue up arrow icon, your CNR-installed software will automatically be updated.

The icons in the system tray shown in Figure 7-6 are (left to right): Ethernet connection, CNR download in progress, sound volume, and CNR updates ready.

Click and Download

The green running man icon is used for executable applications. A different icon, the green down arrow icon, is used for products that are not standalone executables. Examples are software such as libraries and files that support playable content.

You click the green down arrow icon to install the software on your computer. The slightly different icon gives you the hint that this is not an application, but an application helper.

Click-N-Run Extras

CNR Extras is a cache of applications, intended for users with dial-up connections. Twenty or so large, popular applications are preloaded either on a CD or on your system.

If you decide to CNR install one of these applications, you don't have to wait for all the necessary files to be retrieved through a slow modem. CNR only has to read the CD, then retrieve the latest updates to the application. The tradeoff for the faster install is that these applications may take up megabytes of storage on your disk, even if you don't use any of them.

You can get CNR Extras on your computer three ways:

- If you buy a PC preinstalled with Linspire, it may have CNR Extras preinstalled too.

- You can order a CD containing CNR Extras by going to the My Products section of http://my.linspire.com. You will need to pay the shipping costs.

- You can download a file that contains the CNR Extras application and software, again from the My Products section of http://my.linspire.com. You might do this at work or at the library where there is a fast connection, and transfer the .iso file to CD for use at home.

If CNR Extras is installed on your computer, the CNR download icon changes to a green letter E icon for extra applications. If you have a broadband network connection on your Linspire computer, you probably won't get CNR Extras.

Click and Buy

Products that display prices beneath them are available for Click-N-Buy. These are largely products from third-party vendors that Linspire makes available through the CNR warehouse. This is an exciting enabler for commercial software on Linux. If I write a valuable Linux application, I can negotiate with Linspire to sell it using their e-commerce site, instead of having to build my own. Costs are lower, and everyone benefits.

When you download a Click-N-Buy product, your credit card is charged for the purchase. An example Click-N-Buy product is the DVD player software. This includes licensed software to play commercial DVD movies. The DVD player is an alternative to VLC software freely available from http://www.videolan.org/vlc.

Figure 7-7 shows some Click-N-Buy software in the CNR warehouse.

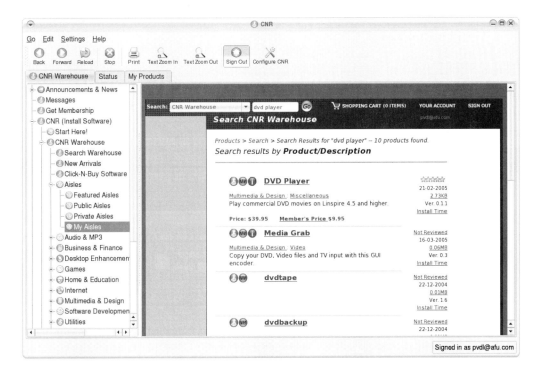

Figure 7-7   Click-N-Buy software

Note – You do not have to have a CNR (click-and-run) subscription to use the CNB (click-and-buy) service. Some products are available at lower prices to CNR subscribers. You do need to use a credit card.

Using whatever DVD player you choose—a warning

Software like VLC contravenes section 1201(a)(1) of the Digital Millennium Copyright Act. Incredible as it seems, the Motion Picture Association of America has succeeded in making it illegal to play a DVD that you own, using software that they don't approve of. They object to software that can play copy-protected DVDs, without a license from the DVD Copy Control Association.

The DMCA is a sad, bad law because it tilts the balance between consumers and copyright holders too heavily in favor of copyright holders. Most kinds of otherwise-legal uses of DVDs, such as playing them with your DVD player of choice, or making a personal backup copy, have effectively become illegal under the DMCA.

Many people think that the Digital Millennium Copyright Act will eventually be found unconstitutional, just as other bad laws have been over the years.

Uninstalling Click-N-Run Software

If you ever need to uninstall some software you installed with CNR, follow this process.

1   Start CNR, log in (if necessary), and select **My Products**.

2   Highlight any product that is listed as installed.

3   Right-click and choose **Uninstall**. That software will be removed from your system.

Click-N-Run: The Bottom Line

For me, the bottom line on CNR is paying a small monthly fee for convenience. Sure, I can download and build all my own programs. For that matter, I can write them from scratch if I want, but why spend my time on that when Linspire has done the work for me, and I can access it for pennies a day? The CNR warehouse has more than 2000 programs and libraries, which is plenty for most people. You can nominate Linux programs that should be added to the CNR warehouse by sending email to warehouseideas@linspireinc.com.

With CNR, software installation is even easier than on Windows. Just one click, and the software is installed. CNR contains libraries, application software, and a small number of OS updates.

CNR is the centerpiece of the Linspire ease-of-use experience. If you don't like it, or never install new applications, or believe that software should always be free of charge, you could be happy using a different distro such as Debian. But be ready to put in the time needed to make it work.

To subscribe to CNR service, go to http://www.linspire.com.

Linux Packages

If anything characterizes Linux, it is the state of continuous evolution and improvement. But it would be burdensome if you had to download and install an entire Linux distribution to get some new library or bug fix. To address this issue, most distros have been administratively split into small, independently updatable software chunks called packages.

A package might contain an application, a utility, a library, a set of desktop themes, or operating system components like a device driver or kernel patch, plus the scripts to install it. Packages contain all the files relating to a single piece of software (the application files, help files, configuration data, documentation and so on). Some packages are source packages, containing the source code that must be compiled before you can use it. Other packages are binary packages that have already been compiled. When you install a package, the contents are all moved into the correct folders.

Dependency Checking

Packages are so handy for system administrators that all modern operating systems use them in some form. To work properly, application software in one package often relies on library software in a different package. You might not have enough to run an application if you only install the application package itself, but not the supporting libraries.

Packaging bundles a few extra files in each package that describe the contents of the package: its name, what it does, the version number, what other packages it relies on, and so on. The Debian package manager, known as APT or the Advanced Packaging Tool, uses this extra data to understand the dependencies between packages.

When you use APT to install a package, it will automatically also install any prerequisite packages that you do not yet have. APT will remove any packages that conflict with your new package. (For example, older kernel patches that are rendered obsolete by a software update.) Before removing anything, APT will warn you and give you the chance to decline the change.

Avoiding DLL hell

Package dependency checking might not seem like a big deal. But Microsoft's failure to do it on Windows led to the problem known as "DLL hell". DLLs—dynamically linked libraries—are libraries that support applications. Sometimes the Microsoft programmers working on Word would change a system DLL to fix a bug or add a feature. They would ship the new DLL with Word, and Word would only work with that DLL in place.

Microsoft's DLL problem arose when the Excel team made their own adjustments to the same library, and shipped their own version of it, which did not have the changes needed by Word.

Whichever of the two products had been installed first on your computer would thus have its version of the DLL overwritten by the second one, so that application would fail at runtime. There's no error message or other indication of what's wrong, or which library caused the problem. The application just silently fails to start, or starts and fails in use. Help desks soon christened this problem DLL hell because it can take many unproductive hours to solve.

Package Manager Choices in Linux

The different distros use several different packaging systems. It's a bit like the metric system versus Imperial measurements. The same basic information is present in both systems, but it takes effort to convert between them, and you never use a mixture of systems on the same job.

An unfortunate mixture

Using a mixture of systems on the same job was the blunder that led to the loss of the $125 million Mars Orbiter in September 1999. The Lockheed Martin team provided thruster firing figures in foot-pounds of force per second. The NASA team calculated the orbiter's new position using those raw numbers as if they were metric grams of force per second. That meant that the craft was not where they thought it was. The Mars Orbiter dipped 15 miles too low in orbit, and became the "Mars Plummeter" as it was sucked down by Mars' gravity. "No one wants to do any finger pointing here," commented a NASA spokesman as he handed out copies of the official report blaming the flight operations team at Lockheed Martin.

Some of the leading Linux packaging tools are shown in Table 7-1. There are others, too. Although this may seem like a wasteful duplication of effort, competition improves the packaging products for everyone.

Table 7-1   Linux packaging tools

Distro	Tool	File	Comment
Debian	APT	.deb	The gold standard for software packaging. APT—the Advanced Packaging Tool—is built on top of Debian's earlier dpkg design. When you install a package using APT utilities, it does full cross checking to make sure all other required packages are present, fetching and installing them if necessary. APT also has excellent quality and package naming standards.
Red Hat	RPM	.rpm	RPM allows installation and removal of packages with a single command. It does not do the vital check for other packages that are required by the package you are installing. Red Hat bundles a tool called YUM that adds this missing feature. But some Red Hat users have standardized on a port of APT to Red Hat, so there are several alternatives here.
Mandrake	URPMI	.rpm	URPMI is built on top of RPM and adds package dependency checking.
SUSE	YAST	.rpm	YAST ("yet another set-up tool") is built on top of RPM, and adds some package dependency checking. YAST includes other features that enable it to be the main tool for installing SuSE Linux. But it sometimes has problems installing software that comes from a third party.
Slackware	TGZ	.tgz	This is one of the oldest Linux distros. TGZ is just compressed file archives, like zip files, with no attempt to identify other required software.

There is no easy compatibility between APT and RPM, although there are some prototype tools that may be able to convert a package in one format into a package in the other format. If you have a package with an .rpm file extension, it is in Red Hat Package manager format.

You might be able to install that on Linspire or any Debian distro by processing it with the software called Alien. Alien can be found in the CNR warehouse. The command is alien -i nameofpackage.rpm. But be careful—you have no dependency information, so you might have to add prerequisite packages by hand.

Standardizing Linux

An industry standard called the Linux Standard Base or LSB has standardized key aspects of the internal structure of variants of Linux. The goal is to enable applications compiled for any distro to install and run on any other distro. With different library versions, packaging conventions, and configuration file names, this goal is not met today.

Alas, the initial stages of LSB were too heavily weighted to Red Hat, which will hold back LSB's general acceptance as an industry-wide standard. As an example, the LSB standard specifies that software packages should be delivered in Red Hat's RPM format. That doesn't mean that Debian cannot use its superior .deb package format, only that it must also be able to install the less-useful .rpms as well (and using Alien is fine for this).

The LSB standard also specifies the content of key libraries, a number of commands and utilities, the layout of the file system, the order in which the system comes to life when the operating system starts, and so on. These are all good things to standardize. Linspire will inherit LSB standardization if and when Debian (the distro on which Linspire is based) does so.

Some top Linux vendors have come together in a group called the Linux Core Consortium to pool resources in implementing LSB. The Linux Core Consortium is made up of industry players like Novell (SUSE distribution), Red Hat, Hewlett-Packard, Sun Microsystems, and the Open Source Development Labs (a Linux clearing house where Linus Torvalds now works).

Using Debian's Advanced Packaging Tool

The Debian distro ships packages in file archives that have a file extension of .deb. There is a basic package handling utility called dpkg, which works directly with .deb files. If you know what .deb file you want and you download it, you can install it onto your system using dpkg.

The main APT utility that you might use is called apt-get. Like dpkg, it is a command line tool, but it is more sophisticated and does more than dpkg. Many apt-get commands are built on underlying dpkg features. Through its utility programs like apt-get and several others, APT provides an easy way to search for packages, download and install them, or remove them.

Be careful with apt-get

The Linspire CNR feature works like a GUI version of the text-oriented apt-get command. In fact CNR is built on top of apt-get, but it does not strive for compatibility with apt-get. As a result, using apt-get may overwrite a Lindows-specific package with a later Debian version that does not have the Linspire changes.

This could cause some Linspire-specific parts of your system, like CNR, to stop working. Whether this happens depends on what you install. There's no easy way to tell in advance—although you can look for the string CNR in the proposed to-be-replaced packages. If present, that's a big clue that installing a new version will blow away CNR.

You might not hit the problem if you only use apt-get to put standalone programs on your system. However, you're still at risk because a common underlying library might be replaced. If you prefer to avoid the risk, then either use apt-get exclusively, or use CNR exclusively.

Tell APT Where to Look for Packages

On Debian-based distros, the file /etc/apt/sources.list lists the sources (meaning *locations*, not source code) where packages can be downloaded. On Linspire, until you change it, the sources.list file looks similar to this:

```
# If you uncomment the lines below you can use apt-get to install packages
# from the Debian distribution.  However, PLEASE NOTE that you may pull in
# packages which are incompatible with the LindowsOS distribution, and will
# cause the CNR installer to stop working.
#deb ftp://ftp.us.debian.org/debian sarge main contrib non-free
#deb ftp://non-us.debian.org/debian-non-US sarge/non-US main contrib non-free
```

In the sources.list file, a # at the start of a line makes the line a comment, which is ignored when the file is processed. If you want to use apt-get, you must edit the file to uncomment the last two lines. Do this by removing the hash signs that are the first character on the last two lines. Do this by clicking **Launch > Run Programs > Software Development > Advanced Text Editor** to open a GUI editor.

As well as uncommenting those lines, you could also edit this file to tell it to look in other places, such as a CD you have, or other Debian package servers around the world. After changing sources.list, you must run the following command.

```
apt-get update
```

This tells APT about the new sources you specified. It will take a minute or two to run and produce a few lines of output. Run this once each time this file is changed to tell APT the new remote sites from where it can retrieve packages.

Listing Packages

About 9000 packages are available for the Debian distro (of which Linspire is a sub-distro). You can see a list of them at the following web site:

http://packages.debian.org/stable/allpackages.html

About 600–700 packages installed in the basic Linspire distro. That indicates the tremendous amount of additional software that's available, over and above what is pre-installed. You can list the packages on your Debian-based system by using the command:

dpkg -l

The -l option tells dpkg to list the installed packages. That produces 650 lines of output on my system, so you might want to redirect the output into a file, by adding the redirect-to-a-file operator > like this:

dpkg -l > my-list-of-pkgs.txt

That will put the output into a file called my-list-of-pkgs.txt in your current directory. You can now edit that file, email it somewhere, review it at leisure, drag it to the trash, or whatever.

For completeness I'll mention that if you have downloaded a package onto your PC, you install it from the command line tool by typing

dpkg -i *filename*.deb

where *filename*.deb is the name of the downloaded file. You'll shortly see a better way to install packages, without needing to download them in a separate step.

Searching for a Package

It's all very well to learn the names of packages that are already installed, but how do you find out the name of the package that contains some software you want? You need to know the name of a package to install it, but luckily it's easy to find out. You can visit any Debian web site or mirror that has all the packages, and search through the lists of packages using the web pages. One such web site is mentioned previously, http://packages.debian.org/stable/allpackages.html.

An alternative is to use one of the APT utilities to search for a certain string in a package name. Let's take as an example a Linux game. A quick web search told me that a very popular Linux game is bzflag. It's "gone platinum" with over one million downloads.

bzflag game

I'm not really a game player, but because bzflag is such a popular game I used it as the example here. bzflag stands for Battle Zone flag. You ride around in a tank and shoot at other tanks. It's a multi-player game running over the Internet: the tanks that you see on your screen are controlled by other players. If you object to first-person shooter games, use Tux Racer or Step Mania as the example instead.

bzflag has a home page at http://www.bzflag.org, *where you can download the source code, if you want to know how games like this are written (or if you want to write new code so you can cheat). The game has been written in a portable way, so it can be recompiled for many different platforms. The talented developers, led by Chris Schoeneman and Tim Riker, made bzflag available to all under a GNU license. As a result there is an active user community, with bulletin boards, bug reporting, interactive personal help, and much more.*

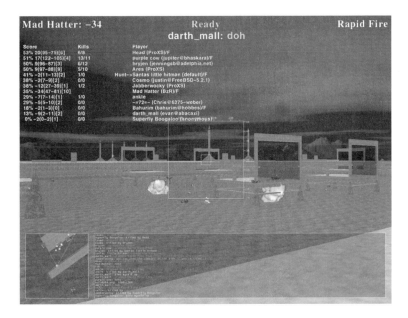

Figure 7-8   *bzflag illustration*

bzflag was inspired by Atari's Battlezone game from the early 1980s, but the graphics are much better today. The flags are tokens that you can pick up on the battlefield to give yourself extra powers, like high speed. Figure 7-8 shows a screen snapshot of bzflag.

The square at the bottom left is an aerial view of the battlefield that is referred to as "radar". The rectangle to the right of that is a log of who has run who off the road. There is also a chat feature, allowing you to taunt other players, form alliances, etc.

The APT utility that will search for packages is apt-cache. The command to search for all software with bzflag anywhere in the name or package description is as follows:

```
apt-cache  search  bzflag
```

If you try this command, you'll get output similar to the following.

```
bzflag - a 3D first person tank battle game
bzflag-server - bzfs - BZFlag game server and proxy
```

Bingo! You got it in one. Now you know the package name is just bzflag, so continue to installing.

Installing a Package with APT

The apt-get command lets you bring additional packages to your system and install them. To install the bzflag game on your computer, type apt-get install with the package name, like this:

```
apt-get  install  bzflag
```

If you try this command (don't worry, this particular package won't affect CNR), you will see output similar to the following:

```
Reading Package Lists... Done
Building Dependency Tree... Done
The following extra packages will be installed:
libadns1 libgcc1 libstdc++5
The following NEW packages will be installed:
bzflag libadns1
2 packages upgraded, 2 newly installed, 0 to remove and 439  not upgraded.
Need to get 3983kB of archives. After unpacking 5661kB will be used.
Do you want to continue? [Y/n]
```

After reviewing what will be installed, type **Y** if you want to proceed. Approximately 4 MB of files will be downloaded, so if you're doing this by phone plan on a minimum of fifteen minutes. (You can transfer about 5 KB per second on the fastest dial-up line, slightly more if the modem does compression).

APT will search its database for the most recent version of this package and get it from an archive site you specified in the sources.list file. APT will also check what other packages this software depends on, and it will install everything that is needed.

It prints out progress as it goes along, so you'll see some lines starting like this:

```
Do you want to continue? [Y/n] y
Get:1 ftp://ftp.us.debian.org sarge/main libgcc1 1:3.4.2-2 [78.5kB]
Get:2 ftp://ftp.us.debian.org sarge/main libstdc++5 1:3.3.4-13 [293kB]
Get:3 ftp://ftp.us.debian.org sarge/main libadns1 1.0-8.2 [51.3kB]
Get:4 ftp://ftp.us.debian.org sarge/main bzflag 1.10.6.20040516 [3561kB]
```

This is all done over regular Internet connections, so if you can't reach one of the sites (perhaps because it has hit its bandwidth limit), repeat the installation for that package later. If you get really stuck, remove the package as shown in *Removing a Package*, then try again.

Removing a Package

The apt-get command has a couple of options to let you completely remove a package.

Package Removal Command

You can remove bzflag by typing this:

```
apt-get --purge remove bzflag
```

The --purge option gets rid of every part of the installed package. If you wanted to keep the configuration files but get rid of everything else, perhaps because you want to install a newer version of the software but keep your old settings, you can omit the --purge flag.

When you install a package, APT first downloads the files to the folder /var/cache/apt/archives, and then does the installation. Over time that folder can end up with a lot of files and occupy a lot of disk space. APT provides tools for managing its local cache. If you use APT a lot, you might need to clean up that folder occasionally with the command

```
apt-get clean
```

The apt-get clean command removes everything (except lock files for downloads in progress) from /var/cache/apt/archives. After clearing out the cache, if you need to reinstall a package, APT will have to download the package and all dependencies again.

Where Did APT Put the App?

The bzflag installation could, but doesn't, add a menu item in KDE. So you have to find the folder that contains the program. You can use the find command to locate where any file is located on the system. Find the bzflag executable by typing:

```
find / -name bzflag -print
```

Alternatively, you can find a file by using the Konqueror File Manager GUI in Chapter 3. Choosing **Tools** > **Find File** brings up a window (see Figure 7-9) where you can enter a file name and a place to start looking. If the file could be anywhere on your system, start looking in /. Wildcards are acceptable in search strings if you only know (or guess) part of the file name.

You can use the **Contents** tab in Figure 7-9 to look for files that contain some string that you specify. The **Properties** tab in Figure 7-9 lets you look for files by size, ownership, or date ranges for when they were created or changed.

Either technique (command line find, or Konqueror) will tell you the executable is stored in /usr/games/bzflag. When you start bzflag, there are a couple of screens of easy one-time setup. The program will give you a list of game servers. For the best results, you want a server that has plenty of bandwidth, and whose domain name suggests it might be near you.

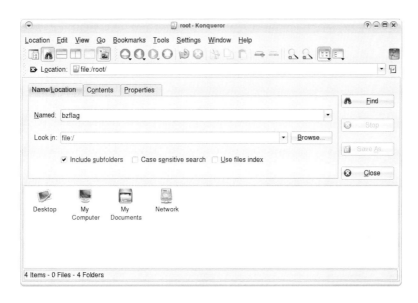

Figure 7-9   Choosing Tools > Find File to find a file you know the name of

Using Man Pages

There is a lengthy man page for the bzflag program, which you can see by typing man:bzflag into the location field of the File Manager. That tells File Manager that you want to look at the man page (Unix-speak for the manual pages) for the bzflag program. If you CNR install the manpage package, or the PvdL CNR aisle, you can also look at man pages with the command

man   bzflag

Every Linux command line command has man pages, and most of the administrative files. Man pages are (alas) not a good way to learn about new features of Linux; they are mostly intended as reminders to people who already know about the features. A good way to find out about Unix commands is to read Appendix D, "Commands for the Command Line," on page 531 of this book. Then review *Linux Desk Reference* (2nd edition) by Scott Hawkins, published by Prentice Hall PTR, ISBN 0130619892.

After running bzflag you might find a diagnostic message

Xlib: extension "XFree86-DRI" missing on display 0:0

You can ignore it, unless and until you get sucked into playing bzflag competitively. That message is X Windows' cute way of telling you that you'll get higher performance if you can find a driver that supports the Open GL commands for your graphics adapter.

The average amount of time that I drive the tank around before being crushed by another player is four to five seconds. See if you can beat this record. With practice and the right opponents, you might be able to self-destruct in three and a half or even three seconds.

Synaptic GUI Front End for Apt

If you like GUIs, you might want to try the Synaptic or kpackage GUI front ends to apt-get. You can download them through the Click-N-Run feature coming up shortly. Or you can use one of these two commands:

apt-get install synaptic or apt-get install kpackage

Synaptic is like the Windows Add/Remove Software control panel. Except it's easy to use, helpful, and works really well. After you use CNR to install Synaptic, type synaptic in a command terminal to bring up the GUI, shown in Figure 7-10.

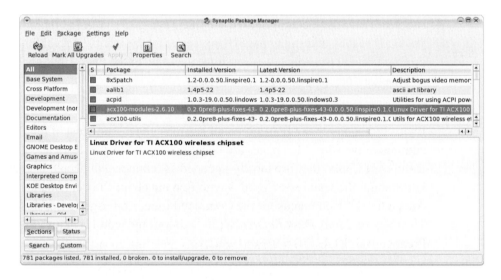

Figure 7-10   Synaptic, the GUI front end for apt

Practically everything in Synaptic is built on apt, so you do all the things you would do if you were using apt directly.

Synaptic doesn't carry out actions as soon as you specify them. Instead, it builds a list of things you want done and starts them when you click **Proceed** in the toolbar. This makes it easier to undo actions based on something you learn later.

You might not use Synaptic at all with Linspire because Click-N-Run offers the same functionality, plus a one-click install. Synaptic is an excellent tool for other Debian distros, however, and for inspecting packages on your Linspire system.

Note – Make sure that you never have more than one of apt-get, dpkg, CNR, or synaptic running simultaneously. Each of these wants to own the lock file /var/lib/dpkg/lock, and only one may have it at a time.

Adding a Menu Item for a New Application

Where appropriate, CNR will give you a menu item for the software you install. Other forms of installation might not update your GUI menus. It's inconvenient to have to remember the path to an application so you can start it from the command line. Here's how to add an application to the KDE menus you reach from **Launch**.

1   Right-click on the **Launch** button to bring up the small menu shown, and select the **Menu Editor** entry.

    You can right-click on any icon on the icon bar to adjust its menus, position on the bar, or size—not just the Launch button.

2   The KDE Menu Editor application appears as shown in Figure 7-11.

3   The left side of the KDE Menu Editor displays the same menu items that are reached by clicking the **Launch** button. Expand the display by clicking to get to the correct menu. Highlight the menu that will contain your new item. For this application it will be **Games**.

4   The previous version of KDE Menu Editor labeled the toolbar icons, but that feature has foolishly been dropped. Clearly, appearance of the toolbar icons is completely inadequate for determining what they do; they might as well be pictures of different puddings. To solve the "mystery of the icons," let the cursor linger on each toolbar icon until you discover which one is the **Add New Item** menu. It's the second icon from the left. Click **New Item**.

Figure 7-11   The KDE Menu Editor

5   A dialog box will appear; fill in the name to appear on the menu, bzflag, then click **OK**. The display will change to that shown in Figure 7-12.

Figure 7-12   Details of the menu item

The important fields are as follows

- Name – The brief name you want on the menu item, e.g., bzflag.

- Description – The text you type here also appears on the menu. If you type battle zone here, the full menu entry will be battle zone (bzflag).

- "Sheet of paper with folded corner" icon in the upper right corner of Figure 7-12 – This is the *select icon* icon. Click on it to select the icon you want for the application. It is a serious usability bug that the button's function is not labeled. You'll be able to walk through an example later.

- Comment – An optional comment about the application. This text may be used as a tool tip for the application.

- Command – The pathname of the executable program. You might also add any optional command line arguments to the program that you wish it to always start with (e.g., a particular file to work on).

- Work Path – If you want the application to use a particular working directory, such as ~/Desktop, enter the path here.

- Run in terminal – Some early text-based programs like the Pine mailer must run in an xterminal window. You would also use this if you wanted to create a menu item for a non-GUI command, such as ls. Select this option if necessary.

- Run as different user – Some applications need to run with particular privileges, often those of the root user. Stipulate that here. For security reasons, do not give an application root user privileges unnecessarily.

- Current shortcut key – Lets you define key combinations that will be a shortcut to the menu item.

6 When you click on the (unlabeled) **select icon** button, it summons the Select Icon window shown in Figure 7-13.

7 You can either select an icon from one of the many system icons shown, or you can choose **Other icons** > **Browse** to find a better icon. Many apps will have their own icon, such as the bzflag icon I found in the /usr/share/bzflag folder. Highlight the icon you want, then click **Open** to get back to the menu editor window.

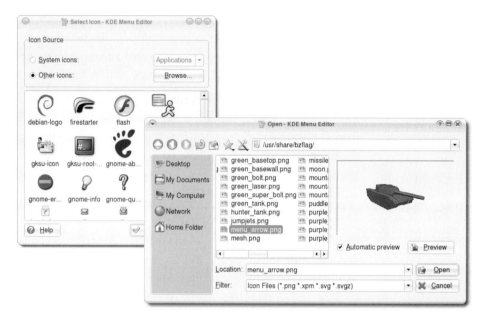

Figure 7-13   Selecting an icon

8   Click **File** > **Save**, then **File** > **Quit** to finish.

This technique of adding a menu item can be used for any application, of course, not just the bzflag example used here.

Note – This is also a very slick and quick way to create a clickable icon that runs a command or application. Follow the steps described previously to create a menu item for the program you want to run. Then drill down from the **Launch** button to the newly created item. Instead of clicking the item to start the program, click and drag the item off the menu, then drop it onto an empty area of the Desktop. A context menu will appear, offering the options Move, Copy, or Link. Select **Link**. Now when you click on that icon, the application on that menu entry will be run.

These are the three easy ways you can add software to Linspire:

*   Install from CD, if the vendor offers one

*   Linspire's Click-N-Run

*   Debian's apt-get

In general, you should always prefer CNR to apt-get because it is simpler and easier. But you've gotta love Synaptic. Check CNR first, before you install any software, to see if there is a version in the CNR warehouse.

You'll find both CNR and apt-get more convenient than the fourth alternative for installing Linux software: downloading the source code and compiling it. That's covered in *Compiling and Installing Software from Source Code*.

Compiling and Installing Software from Source Code

This section demonstrates how to compile and install software that comes to you in the form of source code; the example used is encryption software. Chapter 11, "Keeping Your Data Private," demonstrates how to use this encryption (coding and decoding) software on Linux. You encrypt a file or email to keep it private.

Source Code and Open Source

There is no connection between the "code" in "source code", and the code used to encrypt a file. (Well, except the trivial one that they are both hard to read.) Don't let the name throw you off. I'll start by reviewing what "source code" is, and why most Linux software is "open source".

Finished software products are made up of files of binary data. Low-level binary data is the easiest and fastest format for a computer to work with.

Source Code Basics

Source code consists of files of readable text which are easier for software engineers to work with. Source code is written in a programming language, such as C, C++, Java or Python. Most of the Linux kernel is written in C. Most of the Linux user-level applications are written in C, C++, Java, Python or other high-level programming languages.

Many Linux programs are distributed in source code form for two reasons.

- The Linux philosophy encourages sharing the source code.
- Linux runs on many different types of computer, not just the Intel x86 line. By distributing the source, the program can be compiled for whatever processor you want to run it on.

A program called a compiler translates source code to create a corresponding binary file. A library file is a piece of utility software that can be shared among several applications. Binary files and libraries are linked together to create a finished executable. Figure 7-14 illustrates the process of compiling and linking.

When you get a Linux program in source form, you need to compile and link it yourself. The commands to do this are generally provided in a file called a *makefile* for you. Make is a command line utility that follows the instructions in a makefile to create an executable. Instead of typing many individual compile and link commands with all their options, you can issue one or two simpler make commands. The make command will read the makefile in your current directory, and carry out the compiling, linking, and installing tasks listed there.

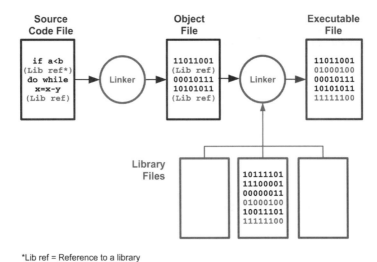

*Lib ref = Reference to a library

Figure 7-14   Compiling source code, linking object code

Why Does Open Source Matter?

One of the features that distinguishes Linux from many other operating systems is its open source nature. That means, along with the finished software product, the source code used to create it is readily available.

Why should users care about this? The majority of users don't need to care directly about source code. On the other hand, I usually keep a workshop manual for my car, even though I don't service it myself. I want to know how my car works, and I want the freedom to adjust it myself. The Linux source code provides the same freedom to software users.

Open source software is really just an expression of the scientific cooperation model, which has worked very well for three hundred years, adding greatly to the public well being. It doesn't preclude for-profit enterprises, and it doesn't force anyone else to adopt the model.

Closed Source Restricts Your Choices and Costs You More

Vehicle makers don't follow the philosophy of open source code. They jealously hoard the information and diagnostic codes needed to service modern cars. As cars acquire more and more computerized control systems, they become serviceable by fewer and fewer mechanics.

Vehicle systems like emission control, air conditioning, and door locks frequently involve computers, but the data that is vital for servicing is not released to the public. Third-party repair shops have to turn away the business, and owners are forced to use the monopoly of factory-authorized dealers.

The stakes are high: more than $200 billion is spent annually on car repairs and upgrades according to industry analysts. After the warranty period, about 80% of that business goes to independent mechanics. In 2004, the Motor Vehicle Owner's Right to Repair Act was introduced to require automakers to provide the data to anyone who needs it, but the bill has not yet passed into law. The requirement would apply to any make of car sold in the United States.

Although only a very small fraction of drivers will service their own cars, open access to the servicing information is an important issue for all drivers. It works exactly the same way with computer software.

Open Source Doesn't Mean Noncommercial

The philosophy of being open means that source code should be included with the program, or at least be readily available. Openness is separate and unrelated to whether the software is commercially distributed or not. As it happens, the majority of the major Linux distros are commercially distributed for profit, and they are all open source, too.

Open Source Means Experts Can Examine the Software

Open source code can be examined by experts outside the originating company so that they can find bugs and security holes. Linux has a far better record of generating and issuing security patches than any other operating system.

Microsoft periodically issues press releases purporting to show otherwise; they cherry-pick the numbers, and compare just the Windows kernel against the Linux kernel and all its applications. They engage in all kinds of deceptive flim-flam. Don't be fooled. Linux patches are sometimes issued within hours of an defect being found, before crackers have a chance to exploit it. Windows XP SP2 took 22 months to appear.

Open Source Is More Open to Users

Another aspect of having access to the source is the ability to search or grep through the source for error messages. Say you're trying to run a new program, and you get a mysterious error message Error 54. Not all users will have a passing familiarity with software, but if you do, you can look through the source code and see where that message is printed. You might be able to tell from the comments in the source code what the program is trying to do at that point. And that in turn may help you zero in on the general area of the problem: hardware, software library, permissions, etc.

Creating GIMPshop from open source

Graphic artist Scott Moschella loved the GIMP editor, but hated going back and forth between Photoshop at work, and the GIMP at home. Photoshop is not an open source application, so he couldn't do anything to improve that. But he could download the source of GIMP and reorganize its menus to match Photoshop much more closely.

And that's exactly what Scott did. He hacked GIMPshop into existence: the GIMP editing application but with all tools, options, windows, and menus updated to closely resemble Adobe Photoshop's menu structure and naming conventions. The goal is to make the Gimp accessible to the many Adobe Photoshop users out there. Figure 7-15 shows menus for rotating an image, with Photoshop.

Scott succeeded brilliantly, but the story doesn't end there. As a graphics guy, he naturally prefers a Mac to Windows. He created GIMPshop only for the Mac platform. But the Windows and Linux community of Photoshop users wanted this too. No problem—GIMPshop is open source! GIMPshop was recompiled for Linux by Anshuman Gholap and for Windows within hours of its release in March 2005. It's richly ironic to see Windows (Photoshop) users clamoring for a port of Linux (GIMP) software.

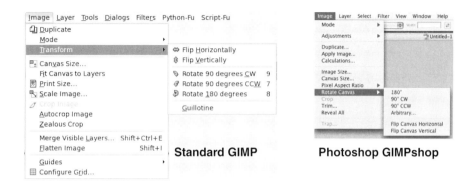

Figure 7-15   Standard GIMP and Photoshop GIMPshop

Building a program from source code is straightforward for those who have been shown the tricks. Shipping the source encourages professionals to improve the code and add useful features. If you don't like the way a feature works, ask someone to change it.

Although only a small fraction of Linux users will modify the source code, the principle of open access is important to everyone. One of the easiest ways to ensure that everyone has access to the source code is to make the source code (rather than the executable program) the piece that is distributed and downloaded.

To reduce the size of the download, often the executable program is not even included—Linux users are expected to build it themselves from the source code.

Downloading the Compiler Tools

To build an application from source code, you need a compiler and related software tools. The encryption application you'll use is written in the C programming language. Some Linux distros bundle the C compiler as part of the basic installation, but the Linspire distro does not. The first step is to download the C tools.

The C compiler tools are in a package called gcc. It originally stood for GNU C Compiler, but as support was extended to more and more languages, it was revised to mean GNU Compiler Collection. The gcc package has been refined over several years, and there are several different revision levels in existence. In preference to gcc, you should install g++, which contains everything in gcc plus support for C++ libraries. C++ is a development of C, extended to support object-oriented programming.

Note – You must install the same version of gcc or g++ used to compile your version of Linux. That ensures the applications you compile will be compatible with the libraries on your system.

Check the Version of Your Linux Kernel

Run this command to see what version of gcc was used to compile your kernel.

```
# cat /proc/version
Linux version 2.6.10 (root@khrystal) (gcc version 3.3.5 (Debian 1:3.3.5-3)) ...
```

You can see gcc version 3.3.5 was used to build (compile) this kernel. Your kernel may have been built with this, or gcc 3.2, or something else again. Download the gcc version that matches the command's output on your system.

The easiest way to download and install the compiler tools (and much other software) is to use the Click-N-Run process. You need to sign up for a Click-N-Run subscription to use the service. Alternatively, read *Alternative Ways to Get the gcc Compiler Tools*.

Alternative Ways to Get the gcc Compiler Tools

If you are not using the Linspire distro, or you do not want to pay for the CNR convenience of downloading working software, you can get the g++ compiler using apt-get as explained in *Using Debian's Advanced Packaging Tool* on page 216. First, do an apt-cache search on g++ to find the different versions that are available. You'll get pages of output, because almost every package mentions g++ somewhere. Cut it down to just the relevant ones by using the command

```
apt-cache search g++ | grep g++
```

The grep command filters out lines that do not contain the search string (here g++). Then use apt-get to install the right version on your system.

You can visit the gcc main web site at http://gcc.gnu.org. They offer much documentation and information about gcc and compiling on Linux. You can also download the compiler from there in source code form (only).

Think about that: you're downloading a compiler so that you can convert source code into finished applications. What tool will you use to turn the gcc compiler source code into a finished compiler application that you can run? A compiler is the one application that you absolutely need in ready-to-use form! Without a working compiler, the compiler source code is no use to you.

It's a chicken and egg problem, and the gcc folks seem to take a perverse pride in not providing binary downloads. They half-heartedly provide a few links to other sites and tell you to buy the CD if you want a binary (but not the latest binary).

The gcc folks don't make the binaries available primarily because they want to do compiler development, not compiler customer support. This is the downside of non-commercial software: if no one is paid to do it, there is no one to blame if it doesn't happen. The solution for Linux users is to get gcc from the web site of their distro and support that distro by buying its products.

Get g++ Using CNR

The easiest way to install the compiler tools on Linspire is to CNR install my aisle of software at http://www.linspire.com/aisles/pvdl. If you don't want to do that, because you want to install only g++, follow these steps.

1   Double-click the **CNR icon** on your desktop to bring up the main CNR window shown in Figure 7-16.

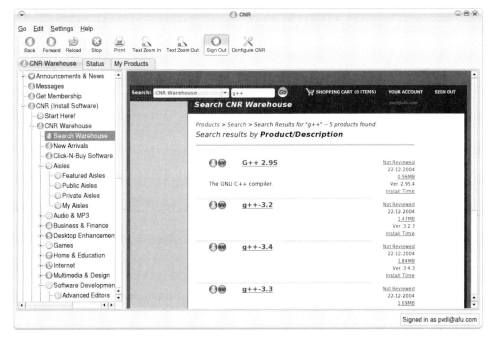

Figure 7-16   Get g++ through Click-N-Run

2 The left side of the CNR window has a tree component displaying the categories of software in the CNR warehouse. Click on the category **Search Warehouse**.

3 That brings up a text field; enter the search term g++ as shown in Figure 7-16.

4 Click **Go**.

5 Scroll through the search results in the right-hand panel to find the g++ version that matches the one used to build your compiler; in this case g++-3.3.

6 Click the **CNR icon** next to the version you want, to download and install the compiler tools on your PC. It will take a little while to download the megabytes of compiler software.

7 After the progress bar at the bottom right of the CNR window shows the download has completion, test that the compiler installed correctly.

Open a command line window. Click **Launch** > **Run Command** and type xterm. Type the command gcc -v. If the compiler is now installed, you will see a version message similar to the one shown in Figure 7-17.

Figure 7-17   A test-run of gcc in a command line window

That completes the installation of the compiler tools. This was a one-time set-up activity and does not need to be repeated for each application you build from source. You're now ready to download the application source code, then build it.

Building from Source: GNU Privacy Guard Application

Say you have some files that you wish to keep private; perhaps they contain your family tax records or medical information. The powerful Linux utility called gpg (meaning GNU Privacy Guard) can keep it private. It allows you to encrypt and decrypt files, and helps you generate the keys (passwords) needed to do so.

Gpg is an open source re-implementation of the PGP "Pretty Good Privacy" software, which has become a commercial product. Gpg provides military-grade encryption for your use at home.

The gpg utility is our example, but the steps apply to downloading and building most Linux application software that comes in source form.

Remember that Linspire provides the CNR warehouse, where you should check first for software you want. If you can download what you want from CNR, it saves you the trouble of building it yourself. Let's pretend that gpg is not in the CNR warehouse.

Basic Steps for Building Software

In most cases, source code comes with a script that builds it, known as a makefile. After you have installed the compiler and tools, most applications and drivers are built by following these command line steps:

1   Download the archive file containing the software. In many cases this will be .tgz file. That extension indicates that the file is a tar archive that has been compressed with gzip. When you have the file, check any MD5 or SHA1 checksum against the one on the download site, then unpack the file to a directory. See *Download gpg* on page 238.

2   Move to the directory with the source files and read the README file and any INSTALL file. You might need to adjust the subsequent steps according to the information you read. See *Move to the Directory with the Source Files* on page 241.

3   Create the makefile that matches your configuration (the compiler tools and libraries that are installed on your system). Typically you do this with a command like ./configure or make config. See *Create the Makefile* on page 241.

4   Build the application. Typically you will type the command make. See *Create the Makefile* on page 241.

5   Put everything in the right place. Type the command make install to move the newly created executable to the right folder. See *Put Everything in the Right Place* on page 242.

Download gpg

1   You will find the gpg program at http://www.gnupg.org. As you can see in Figure 7-18, the download page offers several versions of gpg. (You can bypass this work by searching for gnupg in Click-N-Run, but the point here is to demonstrate the process of building something from source code.)

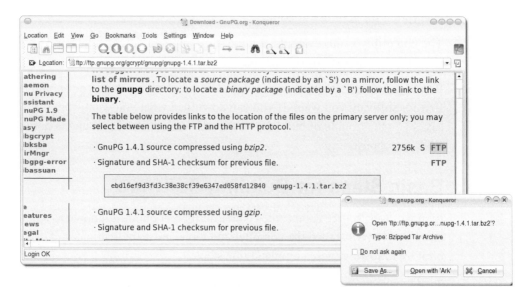

Figure 7-18   The download page at the http://www.gnupg.org site

2   You want to download the most recent release of the gnupg source code. When these screen snapshots were taken (March 2005) the most recent release was version 1.4.1. GNU offers you the download as either a .bz2 file or as a .gz file.

3   To spell their names in full, bzip2 and gzip are alternative algorithms for compressing a file. Bzip2 can compress some files smaller than gzip, but it takes longer to do the work. In this case, the bzip2 file is only three-quarters the size of the gzip version (2756 KB versus 3964 KB), so that's a better choice to download.

The file extension .tar.bz2 tells us the download is a tarball (tape archive file) that has then been compressed by bzip2.

4   Click on the bzip2 link labeled **FTP** to start the download going, and you will be offered the choice to save the download to a file or open it with the Ark archive extractor.

5   Save it to a file on your desktop, where you can easily find it, and not to some other directory like My Documents. You will see a download progress window, shown in Figure 7-19.

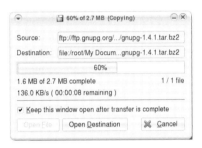

Figure 7-19   The download progress window for the gnupg gzip file

Check the Integrity of the Downloaded gpg File

1   After the file has finished downloading to your system, run the SHA1 checksum program, shown in Figure 7-20 and confirm the checksum matches the one shown on the web page (Figure 7-18). The command is as follows:

```
sha1sum gnupg-1.4.1.tar.bz2
```

For a file with an MD5 checksum, the command is md5sum filename.

2   If it does not match, you need to repeat the download until it does.

Figure 7-20   Confirming the SHA1 checksum

The Secure Hashing Algorithm #1 (SHA1) crunches all the bits in the file and comes up with a number that represents them. SHA1 is not so secure anymore. It was cryptographically broken in 2004, but it's still good enough for many low-security uses, like some checksums.

A change of even one bit in the file will produce a different checksum result. You compare the number calculated from the downloaded file on your system with the number calculated from the master copy on the web site. If they match, you very likely have a good copy of the download.

3   If they do not match, make sure you are comparing the right checksum for the file you downloaded. If they still differ, your download was not good and you should discard the file, and repeat the download with this site or another one until you get a matching checksum.

The checksum check is particularly important for encryption software. It guards against deliberate subversion, as well as ordinary transmission errors. If hackers managed to infiltrate some of their code into the GNU Privacy Guard software, they might be able to send themselves copies of your secret files because you encrypted them.

You might question why you should trust a checksum from the same web site where you're getting the file. You shouldn't. If one file has been illicitly changed, the other could have been too. But in general, you download the (large) software file from a mirror site, and get the (small) checksum from the main development site. The checksum is mostly to detect errors introduced by network transmission problems.

Unpack the Downloaded GNU Privacy Guard Program

1   If the file archiving tool, Ark, does not start automatically, click **Launch > Run Programs > Utilities > Archiving & Zip Tool (Ark)**.

2   In Ark, click **File > Open,** then click the name of the file you just downloaded. You will see a display like Figure 7-21.

3   Choose **Action > Extract** and provide the extract to pathname. Select **All Files** and extract them to /root/Desktop.

You now have all the files that make up the source code of gnupg in the folder /root/Desktop/gnupg-1.4.1 (or whatever pathname you used, and whatever later version number is available when you follow these steps).

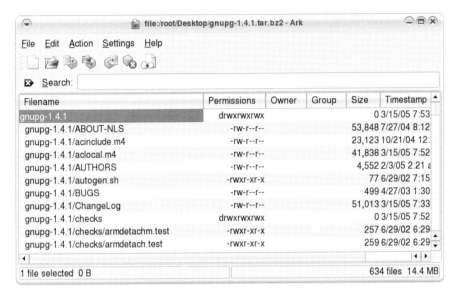

Figure 7-21   The ark utility for unpacking files

Move to the Directory with the Source Files

The following command puts you in the directory containing the source files.
Don't type the # sign, which represents the prompt.

```
# cd /root/Desktop/gnupg-1.4.1
```

List all the files in the directory with the command ls. Read any files with readme
or install in the name. These contain information about building and installing the
application. You can page through a file called readme.txt with this command:

```
# more readme.txt
```

Create the Makefile

Now run the script that examines your system to create various configuration files
used in building. Gpg runs on many different platforms, so the first job is to
collect information about the libraries and capabilities of this platform and create
a customized makefile that will build the application.

```
# ./configure
```

You'll see dozens of output lines, ending in a few lines like these:

```
config.status: creating po/POTFILES
config.status: creating po/Makefile
config.status: executing g10defs.h commands
g10defs.h created


        Configured for: GNU/Linux (i686-pc-linux-gnu)
#
```

Build the Application

In this step you'll type the command make. The make program will look for a configuration file called makefile that contains the individual commands needed to compile the source files and to link the binaries together creating the executable.

```
# make
```

You'll see hundreds of output lines, ending in a few lines like these:

```
make[2]: Leaving directory `/root/Desktop/gnupg-1.4.1/checks'
make[2]: Entering directory `/root/Desktop/gnupg-1.4.1'
make[2]: Nothing to be done for `all-am'.
make[2]: Leaving directory `/tmp/gnupg-1.4.1'
make[1]: Leaving directory `/tmp/gnupg-1.4.1'
#
```

Put Everything in the Right Place

The final step in creating the program is to install the binary and help files into the correct system folders. To install programs into the system directories (the usual place), you need to do the installation as the super-user. Again, you invoke the make program, with an argument of install, as shown.

```
# make install
```

You'll see a couple of hundred more output lines, ending in a few lines like these:

```
make[2]: Nothing to be done for `install-exec-am'.
make[2]: Nothing to be done for `install-data-am'.
make[2]: Leaving directory `/root/Desktop/gnupg-1.4.1'
make[1]: Leaving directory `/root/Desktop/gnupg-1.4.1'
#
```

That moves the gpg executable to the folder /usr/local/bin. The last step in installing is to invoke the program and make sure that it runs. Invoke programs by typing the pathname of the file that contains the executable. Just as on Windows, there is an operating system setting called path that contains a list of folders to search if someone just types the file name and not the whole pathname.

As long as your path variable contains /usr/local/bin (it does by default on Linspire), you can test-run gpg by typing the following command.

```
# gpg --help
```

You will see some help output lines, ending in a line like this:

```
    Please report bugs to <gnupg-bugs@gnu.org>.
#
```

If you see the message bash: gpg: command not found, it means that gpg is not in one of the standard folders that the system looks in when you type the name of a program you want to run. Appendix D, "Commands for the Command Line," on page 531 has more information on this. To fix it, when you are in the gpg directory, type this command:

```
cp g10/gpg /bin
```

That puts a copy of the gpg program in a standard place where the system will always find it.

Whenever you want to compile a program from source, read the README and/or INSTALL files in the top directory. They usually have vital information on how to compile the software. Most of the time you'll simply use these three commands one after the other:

```
./configure
make
make install
```

But occasionally something different is supported. Some programs let you add an option to ./configure . For instance, you'd use ./configure --prefix=/usr to install the program in the /usr/bin and /usr directory. The README or INSTALL file will explain this.

You've successfully downloaded, built and installed the gpg encryption software. You're good to go. In Chapter 11 you'll learn how to use the gpg program.

The lore of Linux—Tux the Penguin

This is Tux the Penguin. He's the official mascot of Linux created in 1996 by Texas A&M student Larry Ewing. Appropriately enough, Larry used the GIMP image editor to craft Tux.

The inspiration for Tux came from Linus Torvalds. Linus explained that he "just likes penguins" and that a lovable, cuddly penguin, gorged on herring would be a flexible and practical mascot. Linus added the enigmatic detail that while on vacation in Australia, he was nibbled on the finger by a Fairy penguin at Canberra Zoo.

Figure 7-22 Mistook his finger for a herring, and bit it

```
  ,-_|\
 /     \
 \_,-._*   <--- Canberra Zoo
     v
```

The Fairy penguin is the smallest and most vicious of all the carnivorous penguins. Linus said it was feeding time at the zoo, and his finger looked like a herring to the feathered predator. But, who knows, maybe the cranky little marine dweller thought Linux was, uh, giving him the finger.

Tux got his name from the resemblance between penguin plumage and a tuxedo jacket. Linux supporter James Hughes was quick to suggest that the name could also represent "Torvald's UniX".

In the spirit of open source software, Larry made Tux available to everyone, and he appears in many guises and forms throughout the world of Linux. Zach Greenberger of ThePaperShaper.com created the cut-and-fold Tux shown on the next pages. You can get the full color version from the site http://www.thepapershaper.com.

Assemble the head (tabs 1-13), bending the paper so the tabs line up with the corresponding tab-less region.

Glue all tabs in the number they are ordered. Some tabs may be glued at the same time.

Assemble the body (tabs 15-29), following the numbers.

Make sure your assembly leaves holes for the wings.

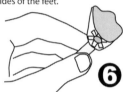

Asslembe the wings (tabs 30-35), following the numbered tabs.

Apply glue to the wings' joint tabs and squeeze them through the wing holes at the same time.

Flatten the joint tabs against the inside of the body to secure the wings.

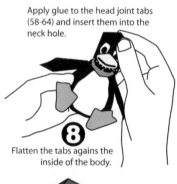

Build the legs by rolling them into cylinders and gluing their tab.

Insert the leg tabs (46-55) through the foot holes. Fold the tabs flat against the undersides of the feet.

Apply glue to the undersides of the feet and attach the foot bottoms.

Apply glue to the leg joint tabs (56 & 57) and insert them into the body's leg holes.

Flatten the tabs against the inside of the body, making sure the feet will point in a nice direction.

Apply glue to the head joint tabs (58-64) and insert them into the neck hole.

Flatten the tabs agains the inside of the body.

Seal up the body by gluing the remaining tabs (65-71).

A toothpick can be used to apply pressure to the last few tabs until the glue holds.

Keep your penguin out of direct sunlight as they're used to the cold Antarctic days.

CHAPTER 8

More Applications

Getting Started

This chapter introduces you to more Linux applications. The idea is to let you know these applications exist, to tell you what they can do, and to show you some of what they look like.

Most of these applications need a book of their own to be fully presented. Some of them *have* a book of their own. So admittedly, I'm skimming the surface by covering several in one chapter, but it's plenty to get started. Frankly, the effort involved in changing from a Windows application to the equivalent Linux application is about the same as the effort in moving from one release of a Windows application to the next; not really a big deal.

The first application is an entire suite: the OpenOffice.org package that replaces Microsoft Office. Next you'll learn about Instant Messaging and finish up with Linspire's Lphoto application and digital photography in general. Don't overlook Appendix D, "Commands for the Command Line," on page 531, which summarizes twenty frequently used Linux commands.

If you're wondering how to find other applications—an astronomy program, a bank account balancer, games, etc.—the answer is as near as your browser. Do a web search on likely key words plus "linux" and see what comes up. Check if any of the results are in the CNR warehouse. Double-check on the favorites by asking for recommendations in the Linspire discussion forums described at the end of *Support Forums* on page 38.

OpenOffice.org

Linspire bundles the OpenOffice.org suite of applications. The OpenOffice.org office productivity suite is comparable to, and compatible with, Microsoft's Office suite. You can open Microsoft Office-format documents using OpenOffice.org, and create Microsoft Office-format documents using OpenOffice.org, as well.

Versions of OpenOffice.org are available for Linux, the Apple Mac, Solaris, and Windows.

OpenOffice.org Applications

OpenOffice.org includes these capabilities:

- Word processor

- Spreadsheet

- Image editor (similar to CorelDraw or Visio)

- Slide show presenter (similar to PowerPoint)

- Mathematical equation layout package (specialized word processor)

- The ability to connect to and read from a variety of databases, including Access, Oracle, or plain old spreadsheets

These programs are found by clicking **Launch** > **Programs** > **Business and Finance** > **OpenOffice.org**.

Table 8-1 is a quick-reference guide to the main OpenOffice.org programs, Microsoft equivalents, and some of the file extensions they open. In general, OpenOffice.org will open just about anything Microsoft Office will open and more besides.

Note – In OpenOffice.org 2.0, the file extensions such as .sxc and .sxw will change to file extensions indicative of the new file format.

Table 8-1   OpenOffice.org-compatible applications and file formats

OpenOffice.org application	Microsoft equivalent	Selected OpenOffice.org-compatible file formats
Calc	Excel	.xls, .xlw, .sxc
Draw	CorelDraw or Visio	.jpg, .png, .gif, .bmp, .eps, .dxf (AutoCad interchange format)
Impress	PowerPoint	.ppt, .pps, .pot, .sxi
Writer	Word	.doc, .rtf, .sxw
Data source connections to databases	Connectivity to Access	.txt, .csv, .xls, .sxc, .mdb, and other databases

Windows doesn't come with a good lightweight image editor for JPG, GIF, and PNG files, but the Draw application is bundled with OpenOffice.org. People often use Word or PowerPoint for picture editing, and then they end up with an unportable Word or PowerPoint file, not an image file. OpenOffice.org Draw has about the same capabilities as Word for editing raster (bit image) file. But Draw will also let you save the results as a JPG or other portable format.

OpenOffice.org use—Case study

In 2003, the University of Detroit Jesuit High School and Academy decided to upgrade to OpenOffice.org instead of Microsoft Office 2000. Before taking this step, the IT director there conducted an extensive evaluation to determine if OpenOffice.org could meet the school requirements for quality and feature set.

Not only did OpenOffice.org meet the requirements, the school found that in some cases OpenOffice.org had better compatibility with older versions of Word than Word 2000 had! The school moved some older PCs to Linux immediately, at a saving of $100,000 in Microsoft licensing costs. Newer systems running XP were upgraded with the Windows version of OpenOffice.org, so the same application was available on both Linux and XP. The school provides a 45-minute orientation at the beginning of each school year for teachers and staff to show them where to find the most commonly used features. That's all it takes.

The highly successful experience with OpenOffice.org gave the school the confidence to try other Linux software, and they are now happily using Mozilla, GIMP, the Apache web server, and the Moodle course management software. They recommended OpenOffice.org to other schools, and many have repeated the successful experience, reaping substantial savings of their own.

OpenOffice.org Basics

You can see from Figure 8-1 that the OpenOffice.org word processor interface is very similar to Microsoft Word. Because the two interfaces are similar, most skills in one are easily transferable to the other. As with any word processor, you type the words, insert pictures or figures using the Insert menu, and format using the toolbar and menus.

The OpenOffice.org user interface has these general parts:

- Look on the first row of the toolbar area (the menu bar) for menus

- Look on the second row (the function bar) for icons that are short cuts to commonly used menu items, such as New, Save, Print.

- Look on the third row (the object bar) for text formatting controls.

- Look at the vertical column main toolbar at the left of the window for icons that apply to the kind of file you are working on (image, text, presentation, spreadsheet, etc.).

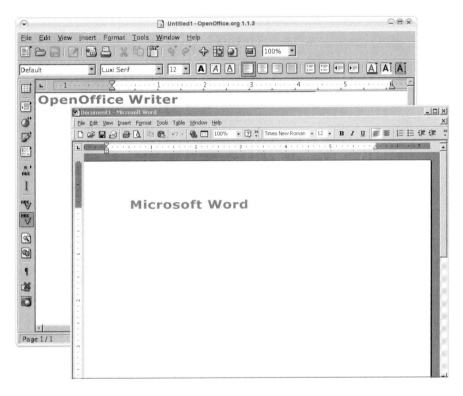

Figure 8-1   OpenOffice.org Writer word processing application (back) and Microsoft Word (front)

OpenOffice.org contains some really good online guides; choose **Help** > **Contents** or just press **F1**. The help files are available in several languages in the CNR warehouse. Search for the term openoffice.org-help.

OpenOffice.org doesn't have a personal information manager/email client, but Novell's Evolution serves that purpose. Evolution is available in the CNR warehouse. OpenOffice.org doesn't have the collaboration features of the kind seen in Microsoft Office, but OpenOffice.org is available on multiple operating systems, which is an important part of collaboration.

OpenOffice.org can create PDF files; Microsoft Office cannot do this. PDF files are used when you want to send high-quality documents to people, but not let them change the documents.

Each program in the OpenOffice.org suite has the same basic appearance, with the same customizable toolbar at the top of the GUI.

Figure 8-2 shows the OpenOffice.org spreadsheet, with Microsoft Excel overlaid on it for comparison. They are similar enough that most home users can immediately use OpenOffice.org. There may be some training needs for business users with particularly complex macros or formatting needs. If you are not familiar with any word-processing or spreadsheet applications, the web site http://www.openoffice.org/product has introductory information.

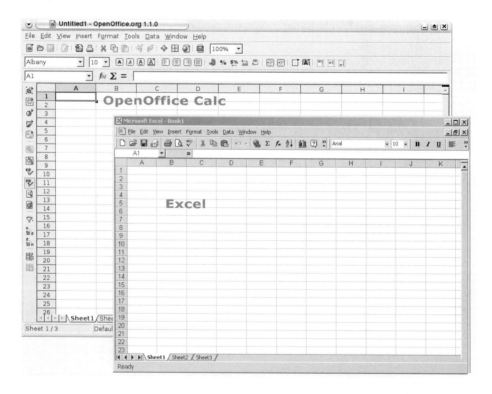

Figure 8-2   OpenOffice.org spreadsheet (back) and MS Excel (front)

Most of the buttons that are specific to a word processor or a spreadsheet are aligned in a column on the left edge of the main window known as the main toolbar. The toolbars at the top contains controls that are common to all the

OpenOffice.org programs. Separating out the specialized controls means that if you customize the toolbar along the top in one program, those toolbar choices carry through to the other programs in the suite. The other programs will still have their specialized buttons.

You can easily find out what a particular button does by letting your mouse linger on it. A tooltip will pop up, describing the icon and providing a name for which you can search in the help index.

Trying It Out: Curvy Text

The best way to learn OpenOffice.org is to start using it. I want to give just one tip here to demonstrate the feature equivalence between OpenOffice.org and Microsoft Office.

Many people like to print labels for their CDs and DVDs. Sometimes it's stylish to put the words in a curved arc, so they match the curve of the CD. You can do that in an obscure way in Word by using the word art toolbar to insert and then shape the text.

Here's how you get the same effect in OpenOffice.org.

1   In OpenOffice.org, create a new Draw document by choosing **File > New > Drawing**.

2   Click the **T icon** on the toolbar at the left edge of the window.

3   Click in the document and drag to draw a text box.

4   Type your label inside the text box, circled in Figure 8-3.

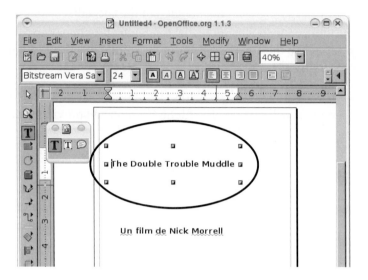

Figure 8-3   Typing your CD label in the text box (circled)

5   Optional: To change the appearance, select the text and select different fonts
and point sizes from the toolbar near the top of the window.

6   Choose **Format > Fontwork**; the Fontwork window in Figure 8-4 appears.

Figure 8-4   The Fontwork window

7   Make sure your text box is selected. (Click on the text box border, not on the
text inside.) Click on one of the eight arcs at the top of the Fontwork window.
The text will change to match that shape, as shown in Figure 8-5.

Figure 8-5   Bending text using a Fontwork arc

8   You can drag the text box by a corner to make the curve deeper or narrower.

You can download a free CD label template from http://www.worldlabel.com. You have to poke around their site, but it's there. Also keep in mind that, since OpenOffice.org opens Microsoft Office files, that you can open your existing Word, Powerpoint, and Excel templates in OpenOffice.org.

Saving Files in OpenOffice.org

All the OpenOffice.org applications store your documents in a zip-compressed XML file by default. The file format is an open industry standard, which means that no company can control it and use it as a proprietary lock-in the way Microsoft does with your Microsoft Office files.

Or perhaps you have had the experience of owning data files created by an old word processor, but you're no longer able to run the word processor to get at the data. If so, you will understand what a blessing it is that OpenOffice.org saves files in a text-based, industry-standard manner. You can decide instead to save your OpenOffice.org files in Microsoft Office format, if you are sharing documents with Windows users. OpenOffice.org files are typically roughly one tenth the size of MS files.

You can also use OpenOffice.org to open documents created in Microsoft Office. When you move a Microsoft Office document to OpenOffice.org, in some cases some advanced formatting may be lost. The situation improves with each new release of OpenOffice.org. It is unreasonable to demand more, because Microsoft purposely does not make its data formats public. Microsoft wants your data to be locked-in to their software. Sun has a white paper with more specific guidance at http://www.sun.com/software/whitepapers/staroffice/SO7Migration_wp.pdf.

Where OpenOffice.org Came From

OpenOffice.org is now a freely available open source program that many people are learning about for the first time. However, it's been around for years. Here's some background information and where you can learn more.

OpenOffice.org is Based on Sun's StarOffice

OpenOffice.org is based on the StarOffice suite of programs. StarOffice was developed in Germany by the StarDivision company, which was bought by Sun Microsystems in 1999. At the suggestion of StarDivision founder Marco Boerries, Sun donated all the StarOffice source code to the open source community and set up a web site at http://www.openoffice.org to act as a focal point for development and downloads.

Sun continues to develop and distribute a commercial version of StarOffice. StarOffice offers a few advantages over the open-source OpenOffice.org. It has more and better fonts, a well-stocked multimedia clip art gallery, the Adabas database program, and extensive platform testing and end-user support from Sun. Most home users will find that OpenOffice.org is enough for their needs.

Both StarOffice (in the Click-N-Buy warehouse) and OpenOffice.org (at www.openoffice.org) are under active development and share improvements with each other. OpenOffice.org 2 is in beta testing (May 2005) and is much faster than earlier versions. It also contains a lightweight database that works much like Microsoft Access.

Learning More About OpenOffice.org

The easiest way to learn OpenOffice.org is to fire up the application and start using it. Beyond that, I've already mentioned the extensive online help files. OpenOffice.org has a support forum at http://support.openoffice.org/index.html There is a documentation site at http://www.oooauthors.org/.

If you are not a technical person, but you want to give back something to the Open Source community, writing or improving documentation is a great way to help.

Many training and consulting businesses have sprung up to support OpenOffice.org and StarOffice; you can find them on the http://www.openoffice.org web site or by googling.

There are several OpenOffice.org/StarOffice books. I like the books by the author and instructor Solveig Haugland, including the *OpenOffice.Org Resource Kit*, a combined book and CD tutorial.

Where to Get OpenOffice.org

In addition to Click-N-Run and other approaches mentioned previously, you can get OpenOffice.org from the http://www.openoffice.org web site. Download it for free, or get an OpenOffice.org CD from one of the many vendors listed there.

Instant Messenger

Remember when you were a school kid, trying to pass notes back and forth in class without the teacher noticing? Remember how much fun it was? (For the kid, not the teacher.) That's exactly what instant messaging (IM) is like.

There are several different IM services with varying degrees of interoperability. By far the most popular IM service is AOL Instant Messenger (AIM), which is freely available to the 20+ million AOL users, and equally to non-AOL subscribers. The different IM operators support different services, and here are the kinds of things IM can do:

- Instant messages – Send text notes back and forth with a friend who is online.
- Chat – Create a private area where friends or coworkers can drop in, chat, and leave.
- Audio – Play audio files for others.
- Share files – Send pictures, programs, or other files directly to a friend.
- Voice over IP – Talk with a friend using the Internet instead of the phone network.
- Streaming data – Subscribe to near-real-time feeds of news or financial data.

Cell phones feature their own version of instant messaging called Short Message Service (SMS), allowing the display of a line of text from another phone, announced by a different ring tone. Most IM services, including AIM, can also accept IMs forwarded from your PC to your cell phone when you're away from your desk. It is an extra cost service for most cell phone plans.

There seems to be a generational thing going on with instant messaging. People who came online after the explosion of interest in IM in 1996 regularly use it. People who were online before IM broke out tend not to use it much. Because it is interactive, there is an immediacy to IM that is not present in email. (Some people say IM stands for Intrusive or Insistent Messaging).

IM started as a recreational tool to send fast brief notes, and that can be useful in a business environment too. IM can also be an intrusive time waster. Each of the three main IM services (AOL IM, Yahoo Messenger, and MSN Messenger) has its own topic-related chat rooms. All of these chat rooms are full of people you would definitely want younger family members to stay away from.

IM is not secure. Others can eavesdrop as the messages are passed on. The conversations can be recorded permanently at either end or anywhere along the way. The AOL IM terms of service grant AOL "The irrevocable, perpetual, worldwide right to reproduce, display, perform, distribute, adapt and promote (your words) in any medium." Keep that in mind, at least until you download the encryption plugin for IM from http://people.debian.org/~costela/debian.

A good Linux program for instant messaging is Gaim. The program described here is PhoneGaim, based on Gaim and with the additional ability to use voice communication over the Internet via VOIP. The phone features of PhoneGaim aren't described here; check back when this book goes to a second edition.

The developers of Gaim assert that the name doesn't stand for anything, isn't an acronym, has no meaning, etc. They have to say that to emphasize that the software does not have any affiliation with any trademarks (like AIM) owned by AOL. So wherever the name for this **G**tk-based **A**OL **I**nstant **M**essenger-compatible software came from, I'm sure it has nothing to do with **AOL**.

Get an IM Account

You need an account to use instant messaging. Since it has the widest user base, select AIM. You can get a free AIM account at http://linspire.com/getaimaccount as shown in Figure 8-6.

You provide a couple of pieces of information on a web form, including an email address where they will send a confirmation email. You click on a link in the email to activate your AIM account.

Select your own screen name. If someone else hasn't taken that one, you can have it. For some reason, probably because they can, people create whimsical names for their IM accounts. Just ask my brother Paul, AIM screenname the-real-vicar. Your screen name is used as your address by people who want to instant-message you. Once you have an AIM account you are free to IM and be IM'd by others.

Figure 8-6   Getting a free AIM account by filling in a web form

Set Up Your Instant Messenger Application

1 Start the Gaim instant messenger program by double-clicking on the orange man icon at right, or click **Launch** > **Programs** > **Internet** > **Instant Messenger**. That brings up Figure 8-7.

Figure 8-7   Login window

2 The first time you do this, click the **Accounts** button shown in Figure 8-7, which opens the window shown at the top of Figure 8-8.

Gaim is compatible with the IM services from these vendors: AOL IM, Yahoo, and MSN. Shamefully, AOL had a spate of introducing deliberate incompatibilities into Gaim to shut out competing IM services. They seem to have stopped trying that nonsense now.

3 Click the **Add** button in the Accounts window to open the Add Account window.

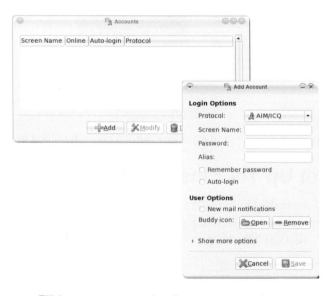

Figure 8-8   Fill in your account details to get started

4   Fill in the screen name and password that you chose, and select the **Remember password** and **Auto-Logon** choices. The password is stored in an unencrypted file on your computer, so don't use the same password that you use for anything else.

You can also fill out an alias or nickname, in case you chose your screen name unwisely.

5   Half the fun of IM is representing yourself in imaginative and dramatic ways, so you definitely want to select a **Buddy icon**.

This is a thumbnail picture, no more than 48 x 48 pixels, that represents you. It can be a GIF, animated GIF, JPG, or PNG file.

You can create your own icon using OpenOffice.org Draw or GIMP. Or you can find a suitable icon by doing an image search at Google for a term with which you self-identify, such as mechanic, love nut, zombie, or wood nymph. Select an image from the clip-art that's freely available for public re-use.

Save the file locally and scale it down to 48 x 48 pixels using your favorite image editor.

6   Give the pathname to the file by clicking on the **Open** button.

7   Click **Save** in the Add Account window. That will take you back to the Login window, shown in Figure 8-7, but with your account information filled in.

8   In the Login window, click the **Sign on** button and sign yourself in. The main window will now appear, the Buddy List window shown in Figure 8-9.

9   Choose **Buddies** > **Add Buddies** to add the IDs of everyone you want to chat with frequently.

Figure 8-9   Use the Buddy window to list people you want to instant message

10 That brings up a window (not shown) where you can add details of your buddy; the only essential detail is the screen name. It's useful to set the **Show Offline Buddies** option so that you can see the friends on your list, and be notified when they appear online.

Start Annoying Your Buddies with Chatter

All IM services allow you to create a list of people you talk to frequently. To demonstrate how to set up IM and engage in IM chatter, and because my brother theRealVicar was unavailable, I asked a friend to create an ID and join me online. He created the ID theBogusVicar and we engaged in conversation that you'll see in this procedure. My own ID here is just an email address, pvdl@mac.com.

Here's how to get started chatting.

1 Make sure you are logged in and that you've set up buddies as described previously and shown in Figure 8-9.

2 Select the person you want to chat with. A quick way to start communicating with someone is to click on their entry in the **Buddy List**, then click **IM** at the bottom of the Buddy List window, as shown in Figure 8-10. My friend theBogusVicar has decided he wants to talk to me, pvdl@mac.com.

Figure 8-10   Starting a conversation with a buddy (the*BogusVicar*'s view)

3   If your buddy is online, a window will appear (see Figure 8-11) in which you can type messages. Type in the lower text field. When you press Enter after each new line, your message will be sent and written into the upper text field, along with your buddy's subsequent replies. Each message line is prefixed by the screen name or alias of the person who sent it.

Here my friend the*BogusVicar* has messaged a loan request to me, pvdl@mac.com. Figure 8-11 shows the*BogusVicar* seeing his own words on his screen.

Figure 8-11   TheBogusVicar sees his message to pvdl@mac.com

4   Over on my PC, wherever it is on the Internet, if I am running a compatible chat program, I (pvdl@mac.com) will get a window announcing that the theBogusVicar wants to IM. I accepted the vicar's chat, saw his loan request, and messaged back my terms for the money.

5   The vicar receives the answer to his message. Figure 8-12 shows how this message appears in the vicar's IM client window.

Figure 8-12   TheBogusVicar gets back an IM reply from pvdl@mac.com

6   When the conversation has finished, choose **Conversation** > **Close** to end the conversation and close the window.

A good portion of the appeal of IM is messaging back and forth in clipped words and abbreviations that are not readily understandable to those not in the know. Tho, OMG, U cn overdo 1337-spk, IMHO. Thank heavens Microsoft is here to help parents get "clued-in" to the "hip" new slang their kids are using, with a primer at http://www.microsoft.com/athome/security/children/kidtalk.mspx.

There is a user manual for Gaim at http://www.alphamonkey.org/gdp/files/gaim-manual-1.0/gaim-manual-html-1.0/t1.html.

Instant Messaging and Phone Service

The Linspire IM client also has support for Internet phone service. When you start the program, it will pop up a window asking if you want a free SIPphone account. This account will allow you to make free calls to other SIPphone users and cheap calls to the regular telephone network. Click the **Ask me Later** button until you are ready to deal with this.

To eliminate the message permanently, replace the preinstalled AIM with the Instant Messenger from CNR. It is the same program without the SIPphone integration and nagging.

SIP is the Session Initiation Protocol that defines the back-and-forth of message exchange, just as HTTP defines the conversation between a browser and a web server, and IP defines how two Internet computers can send packets to each other. When SIP is used to send voice traffic, it is termed Voice Over IP (VOIP). Currently an area of emerging technology, VOIP has a real chance of making the entire telephone network obsolete over the next few years. At the very least it will force phone companies to charge flat monthly fees for most land line phone use, instead of metering per call. Cell phones as we know them today (2005) will probably disappear completely within a few years (so don't buy any expensive new ones). We'll still be able to make telephone calls on handheld devices, but the signal will travel over TCP/IP networks that handle data of any and every kind, not private single-purpose voice phone networks.

A SIPphone can be a real phone, modified to plug into your broadband connection, or it can be a program that runs on your PC and displays a picture of a phone. The sound subsystem on your PC has to work correctly if you intend to use the software simulation. You will also need a microphone for your PC. There is more information at the SIPphone site http://sipphone.com.

Lphoto and Digital Photography

As Linspire says, "Lphoto is the complete desktop Linux solution for digital photo management." Lphoto is an open source application created by Linspire, and given to the Linux open source community as a whole.

Start Lphoto by clicking **Launch** > **Programs** > **Multimedia and Design** > **Lphoto**. The first time you do this, a window similar to Figure 8-13 will appear. It's easy to import image files later, so click **Don't import anything right now**. Let's focus on getting comfortable with the interface first.

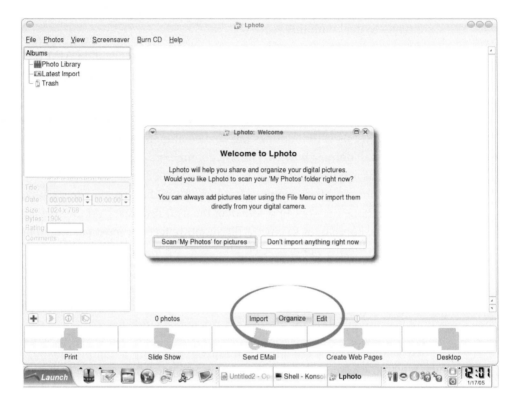

Figure 8-13 Lphoto main window

Just as Lsongs looks virtually identical to Apple's iTunes application, the Lphoto GUI is a near duplicate of Apple's iPhoto GUI. Apple's suite of iLife applications sets the standard for the entire computer industry, and in this case imitation is the sincerest form of flattery.

Take note of the three tabs circled in Figure 8-13. These three tabs control different views of the main window, and Import, Organize, and Edit correspond to the steps in processing a set of pictures.

Importing Your Pictures into Lphoto

Practically all digital cameras tell you to upload your pictures by connecting a cable between the camera and a USB port on your PC. Don't do it! A far better approach to uploading your pictures is to use a $10 USB card reader such as the one shown in Figure 8-14.

Figure 8-14   USB card reader for uploading your pictures

Connecting Your Storage Card to the Computer

Remove the storage card from your camera, plug it into the card reader, and plug the card reader into a USB port. There are three reasons to do it this way.

• The camera needs to be powered on if you upload direct from the camera. If the camera battery expires during an upload attempt, you will corrupt the card filesystem and risk losing the entire batch of pictures. If you plug the camera into a power source, you will partially charge the battery and reduce the number of lifetime charges it has left.

• Many cameras are not recognized by PCs or require special driver software. Essentially all card readers are recognized as USB mass storage devices.

• Card storage media are designed to be repeatedly plugged and unplugged. Be gentle with them anyway, and you won't run into problems.

Camera storage media

There are half a dozen formats for the storage media in digital cameras: Compact Flash I and II, Secure Digital card, Smart Media card, Multi Media card. Apart from proprietary memory sticks from Sony (too expensive), they are all broadly similar in price and performance. You don't know what type of storage media your next camera will use, so your best bet is to buy a multi-way card adapter that accepts many or all of these cards.

Whichever card you use, it will be formatted with Microsoft's FAT32 filesystem. In a short-sighted decision, over much better open source alternatives, FAT32 was universally adopted by the digital camera industry. When Microsoft noticed this, they leveled license fees of up to $250,000 from each camera maker, even though no Microsoft code was used. The basis for this demand was the five patents on trivial aspects of FAT32 (like the code to support long filenames) that Microsoft holds. The camera makers now pay a lot more attention to software patents and the possibilities of open source software than they did in the past.

Plug the card reader with card into a USB port, and wait a couple of seconds for the icon to appear on the desktop. Before you ever import your photos into any photo application, you should make a separate backup copy of them. This ensures that you never suffer from "data lock-in" where your documents are held by some application that you no longer wish to use. Write them off to CD or DVD periodically, so you can delete them if you need to free up some storage.

Archiving Photos Before Handing Them Over to an Application

Create an archive directory as follows:

1   Double-click on the desktop icon representing the card reader, and drill down through the directories to your image files.

2   Choose **Window** > **Split View Top/Bottom**.

3   Right-click in the empty window and choose **Create New** > **Folder**, giving it a name of Picture.archive.

4   Click that folder, and create a folder in it named for the current year and month, such as 2005-09. Each new month, as you save your pictures, you'll make a new folder for that month.

As you upload pictures throughout the year, copy them into folders by the date of the upload (you'll go nuts trying to put them in folders by the date the picture was taken).

5   Select all the pictures on the USB device.

6   Right-click on one of the pictures and select **Copy**.

7   Move the cursor over to the icon for the year/month folder in the other view window. Right-click on the folder and select **Paste**. For a large amount of data, a progress bar will appear. Wait until the copying is complete.

Now you have a separate copy of your unedited pictures. If you screw up your photo editing, you'll still have the originals after you delete them from your memory card. Follow this procedure every time you upload photos.

Importing Photos

You're ready to import photos.

1   Start the Lphoto program.

2   Click on the **Import** tab (one of the tabs circled in Figure 8-13).

3   Click the **Rescan** button on the lower left. This will look for attached USB storage and find your card reader. The lower left will show the icon of a camera, with the label **Generic STORAGE DEVICE**.

The camera icon is actually a button that will start the import of the image files from the card reader. (You could also import the files from the copies you made on disk, which will be faster than reading from USB. But if you do a second upload in the same month, you'll lose track of what's been imported and what hasn't. It's foolproof just to grab them all from the cardreader both times).

4   The current version of Lphoto only supports pictures in JPG format. Support for the high-end TIFF format is on Linspire's list of things to do. As the pictures are imported, thumbnails of each image appear on the main window of Lphoto.

5   When the importing has completed, a window offers the choice of deleting all the images from the card reader. Since you are maintaining a separate backup copy of the pictures, it's quite safe to click on **Yes**, delete the images.

6   After the deletion finishes, right-click on the icon representing the card reader, and select **Unmount** to flush the filesystem changes to the card. A message will tell you **It is safe to remove your device or media**.

7   Gently unplug the card reader from the USB port.

8   Retrieve the storage card from the card reader. Make sure your camera is powered off, then put the card back in your camera.

Organizing Your Pictures with Lphoto

Lphoto uses the metaphor of photo albums to store and organize your pictures. Under the covers, albums are really just folders. The list of albums is displayed in the panel at the top left of LPhoto. Since you haven't created any yet, only the three you get by default are shown: the Photo Library (a holding area for anything you haven't yet put into an album), the Latest Import (the latest set of pictures you uploaded or imported), and the Trash (deleted pictures).

Exchangeable Image File data—EXIF

All but the most basic digital cameras and scanners save some EXIF data into their image files. The EXIF data records the settings that were used to take the picture: camera shutter speed, aperture diameter, and so on. EXIF is metadata for the image data.

In the days before digital photography, obsessively keen photographers used to record the EXIF information by hand. Now your camera records it for you. Lphoto 1.0.61 does not have any way to display the EXIF data, but it's planned for a future version. People who just want pictures without knowing the difference between an F-stop and a bus stop will be fine without EXIF data. Others can use EXIF data to compare more successful pictures with others and gradually build up technical photographic expertise. View EXIF using the plug-in for the GIMP found at http://registry.gimp.org/plugin?id=4153.

There's an EXIF tag for recording latitude, longitude, and altitude. There aren't any regular cameras yet that have built-in GPS and an altimeter, although high-end Nikon cameras have IP addresses and wifi networking. Add Bluetooth (low-power low-speed wifi) to that and cameras will be able to read their position from any nearby GPS systems.

Cellphone cameras can fill out the location data today. They use the wireless towers to triangulate on the cell phone's signal. More and more pictures will include EXIF location data, and I'm confident that it will eventually be searchable at Google. Type in a location, and Google will return web pages containing pictures taken in the vicinity. Amazon already has something like this at the site http://www.amazon.com/gp/yp. *Search on a business near a place you know. See if there's a picture. Go up and down the street. Apple's Tiger release of MacOS X already includes EXIF metadata when you search your PC.*

Viewing and Deleting Photos

1 Switch to the **Organize** tab. Your window should look similar to Figure 8-15.

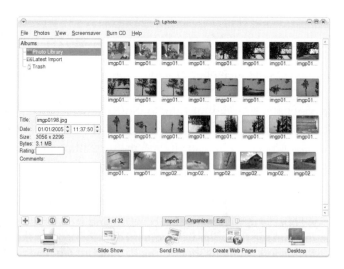

Figure 8-15   Organizing your newly imported pictures in the photo library

After importing a new set of photos, you typically examine them all individually, delete the dud shots, and make sure they are all oriented correctly.

2 Hold your mouse over a picture to see a larger version (Figure 8-16).

Figure 8-16   Expanding a picture in the LPhoto photo library

3 Often expanding the picture this way is enough to decide if the picture is good enough to keep or not.

• If not, you can double-click on a picture to open it in the Edit tab and really get a good look at it. Switch back to the Organize tab when you are done.

• Delete an individual picture by right-clicking and choosing **Move to Trash**.

Figure 8-16 contains a photo of the historic Agnew railroad station outside the HQ of Sun Microsystems in Santa Clara, California. The picture is too dark, but I'll leave it undeleted because I may be able to enhance it during editing. Weed out your poor pictures ruthlessly. You have the original backups if you need them.

Selecting Multiple Pictures

You can select multiple photos in Lphoto by clicking the photo at one end of the sequence, then shift-clicking the photo at the other end of the sequence. The endpoint photos and all the photos between them will be selected. (Multiple selections by click-dragging a rubberbanded box was not implemented in Lphoto version 1.0.61 used in this chapter. Choose **Help** > **About Lphoto** to see the version number.)

You can toggle the selected/unselected status of an individual photo, without affecting any other pictures, by holding down the control key as you click on the photo.

When you carry out a command like delete, duplicate, print, email, export, or rotate, it will be done on every picture in the selection.

Rotating Pictures

Some of the pictures may be portrait shots rather than landscape. You can rotate an image 90 degrees clockwise by clicking on its thumbnail image to highlight it, then clicking the rotate icon. Rotating counterclockwise is an entry on the Photos menu item.

Using Icon Controls

The mysterious little icon buttons in Figure 8-17 look as out of place in Lphoto as they are in Apple's iPhoto.

Figure 8-17   Icon buttons in Lphoto

From left to right, these buttons have the following effects.

- Add album – This creates a new empty album in the top left Lphoto window.

- Start slideshow – This displays a window that sets options for a slideshow of your pictures. It duplicates the Slide Show button along the bottom edge of Lphoto. Press the **Escape** key to end a slideshow.

- Toggle info – This shows or hides the panel of picture metadata (date taken, size, comments, etc.) which can be seen above this row of buttons in Figure 8-15. You can add your own annotation to any picture by typing in the field marked **Comments**.

- Rotate picture – This rotates a picture 90 degrees clockwise. It would be nice to have a control that let you set the angle of rotation—everyone occasionally takes pictures that are slightly skewed.

Improving Your Pictures with Lphoto

After cutting your pictures down to just the ones worth saving, you can start improving them, removing red eye and so on. If you just need to do a small amount of enhancement or cropping, Lphoto will do the job. You can only look at and edit one picture at a time in Lphoto. If you need to compare two pictures with both on the screen at once, or do more involved image editing, use the GIMP. You can still organize your photos with Lphoto.

Lphoto is still under active development. I mention several limitations of the application in the next few sections. These may well have been addressed by the time you read these words. It's worth testing a limitation, to see if it is still there.

Removing Red-Eye

1   Click on a thumbnail that contains red eye in the **Organize** tab, then click on the **Edit** tab. The main view window will display a large copy of that photo.

2   Zoom in on the eye portion of the picture by rotating the mouse scroll wheel (a difference from Apple iPhoto and a mistake in the Lphoto interface, this should scroll the image up or down), or by moving the slider underneath the picture.

3   Click slightly to the left and above the eye, and drag the mouse slightly right and below the other eye to draw a box around the eyes, as in Figure 8-18.

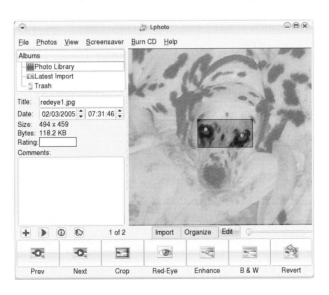

Figure 8-18   Selecting the red-eye area

4   Click the **Red-eye** button at the bottom center of the Lphoto window. It will filter some of the red out of that area. Repeat the steps for more filtering. If you don't like the change, click the **Revert** button.

5   Revert undoes all changes, and puts you back to the original picture as it was imported. For this reason, you might wish to choose **Photos > Duplicate a picture** at each stage of editing, so that you can revert each edit individually.

When you have finished the sequence of edits, delete the unwanted intermediate steps.

What is that red eye in photos, anyway?

In a word (or three), it's coaxial retinal reflection. Red eye shows up particularly in photos taken in dim light. The pupils of your eyes dilate (grow bigger) in dim light to let more light fall on the retina (the part of the eye with the light-sensing rods and cones). The pupils can open up wide enough that the camera flash lights up the blood vessels in the retina at the back of the eye.

The red-eye reduction feature takes advantage of the eye's adaptation to ambient light. A couple of preliminary flashes make the human iris shrink before the picture is taken, reducing reflection.

Retinal reflection shows up particularly in cats and dogs (and other animals such as deer) because their retinas have a reflective layer that is not present in the human eye. Depending on the camera angle, animals sometimes have white eye, as in Figure 8-19.

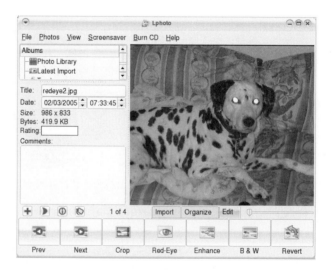

Figure 8-19   For white-eye, use GIMP

When I take pet pictures with a flash, I extend my arm out to the side and click my fingers to make the pet look away from the camera lens. Reflection off the retina thus bounces somewhere other than into the lens. Works for kids, too.

The Red-Eye button does nothing for the white-eye seen in Dickens in Figure 8-19. You can use the GIMP image editor to fill in white eye. There is a good tutorial on the GIMP, and the eye touch-up part of it is located at the web site http://www.gimp.org/tutorials/Red_Eye_Removal. The dogs are not allowed on the sofa, so please don't mention this picture to my wife.

Cropping Pictures

You can crop your pictures so that extraneous junk around the edges is removed. You have to apply artistic judgment about what goes and what stays. Occasionally it is obvious, as in Figure 8-20: lose the telephone wires.

Figure 8-20   Selecting the area of the photo you want to keep

1   Highlight an area of the picture (just as with red-eye reduction), then click the **Crop** button. The area outside the box is trimmed off, and the remaining image, resized in the main window, as shown in Figure 8-21. The blurring seen here is an artifact of the original image, which was not taken with the help of a tripod.

2   Notice the information panel of Figure 8-20. It tells us that the full image is 3.1MB in size. After cropping off the unwanted portions, Figure 8-21 shows that the size has changed and the picture now only takes 460 KB.

Figure 8-21   After cropping

3   Cropping a picture usually makes it display larger in the main window, as LPhoto will try to use the space to maximum effect. You can also zoom in and out of a picture by using your mouse scroll wheel or the slider under the right corner of the picture.

Digital photography—megapixels versus zoom

Let's settle a long-running digital camera debate. Which camera will get you better pictures, one with more megapixels, or with more optical zoom? Only consider optical zoom; digital zoom is a worthless feature in a still camera.

The better camera (other things being equal) is the one that gets the most pixels on the subject. Assume that at a given zoom, all cameras have the same cone of view. The formula is as follows:

$$comparison\ factor = megapixels \times (optical\ zoom)^2$$

Consider, for example, these two contemporary cameras:

- *Nikon Coolpix 8800 with 8 Mpixels and 10x zoom*

- *Panasonic DMC-FZ20 with 5 Mpixels and 12x zoom*

The Nikon "comparison factor" is $8 \times 10^2 = 800$.

The Panasonic "comparison factor" is $5 \times 12^2 = 720$.

Since 800 is larger than 720, the Nikon will get more pixels on the subject and hence produce the better picture when both cameras are at maximum zoom, even though the Nikon has less zoom.

There are plenty of other factors to consider in a camera: size, ease of use, lens quality (the Panasonic uses a lens from the highly regarded Leica company), price, and so on. But the resolution you get on an image is critical. Both of these cameras come with image stabilization, which would make a big positive difference if just one of them had it.

The conclusion is that pixels are a multiplier, but zoom is exponential; it takes a lot of pixels to be worth even a little zoom.

Enhancing Pictures

Lphoto has a one-button Enhance control. The Enhance button cannot put blurry pictures back in focus. To prevent focus problems, wait for image stabilization to migrate from the high end into all digital cameras. I'm not going to win any prizes for this picture, which was a target of opportunity while I was photographing something else. However, Enhance does a good job of brightening dull photos.

Display the picture in the **Edit** tab view, and click the **Enhance** button in the bottom row of Lphoto.

Figure 8-21 on page 276 is the "before Enhance" and Figure 8-22 is the "after". In the window, I can now see the undercarriage, for example, and the colors are bright enough that I can recognize the livery of Southwest Airlines.

But what is Enhance doing exactly? By studying the Lphoto source code, I see that the Lphoto enhance button runs the Convert command line image editor with arguments that tell it to boost the contrast a bit to span the full range of color values. Convert is bundled with Lphoto. It is just one of several tools in the ImageMagick suite, which can be downloaded from CNR and is described in http://www.linuxfocus.org/English/July2001/article211.shtml.

That is much less sophisticated than Apple's iPhoto Enhance. Apple never says exactly what their enhance does, presumably because they don't want other companies to pinch their good ideas. But Apple's enhance does some image normalization, and some hue and saturation adjustment. It does this on super-samples (regions of the image) not per-pixel. Apple's approach usually gives a superior result.

As with any do everything adjustment, undo (the **Revert** button) is your friend. Lphoto currently does not have any explicit controls to change the brightness or contrast. These are eagerly anticipated.

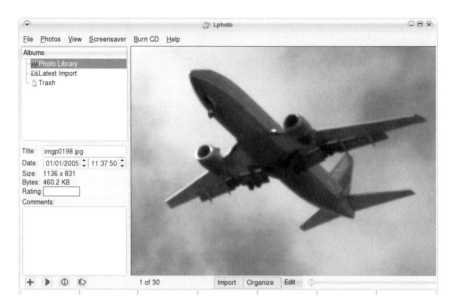

Figure 8-22   After enhancing

Putting Pictures in Albums

When you have finished editing all your pictures, move them into an album. Create a new album by pressing the + icon button. An icon for the album will appear in the album panel. Highlight the name and change it from Album 1 to something more meaningful, like train pictures.

- To display thumbnails of the pictures you were most recently working on, click on the **Latest Import** album. Fill the newly created album, or a pre-existing one, by dragging thumbnails from the main window onto the album.

- To use an album as images for a screensaver, highlight the album, then choose **Screensaver > Set Screensaver Album**.

- To play a slideshow of an album, click the **Slide Show** button (the right-facing crescent, near bottom left of Lphoto). There is not currently a way to play music to accompany the slideshow, other than by starting and stopping Lsongs independently. Albums can nest inside other albums, just as folders can contain other folders.

Exporting Your Pictures from Lphoto

Besides convenient tools to import, re-touch, manage, and share digital photos quickly and easily, the latest version of Lphoto includes advanced features like burn-album-to-CD and burn-album-to-DVD along with options to create MP3 soundtracks on custom DVD slide shows. So you can create a DVD slideshow that includes music but you can't (yet) run a slideshow in Lphoto and include music.

Desktop background

*Figure 8-23 on page 280 indicates the use of the Desktop button in Lphoto. If you highlight an individual thumbnail on the Organize page, you can click the **Desktop** button (Lphoto, bottom right) and that photo will become your window manager background. In Figure 8-23, I have chosen the thumbnail on the far right.*

Exporting Pictures to Web Pages

One of the Lphoto features I really love is its ability to generate web pages of pictures that you can import into Nvu to fine-tune the HTML (if you wish) and then upload to your web site.

1 Click on the **Organize** tab in Lphoto. Click the button labeled **Create Web Pages** to open the Create Web Pages window, as shown in Figure 8-23.

2 By default, Lphoto will put the generated web page at

/root/My Documents/My Photos/Lphoto Library/web pages/albumname

and that is a horrible place. First, it's buried six levels deep (seven levels for an ordinary user). Worse than that, every component of the pathname except first and last has a space in it, and no operating system handles spaces in pathnames gracefully. Users frequently hit an unnecessary roadblock when they download something into My Documents, and the script that builds it can't cope with spaces.

Correcting this isn't seen as a priority at Linspire because it mostly impacts command line users and they're supposed to be able to handle problems like that (by quoting the entire pathname).

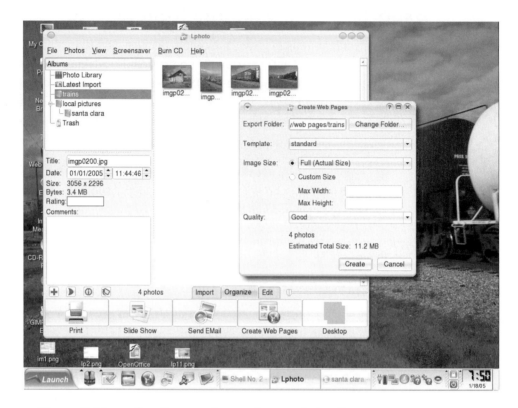

Figure 8-23   Creating a web page from a photo album

3   Outside Lphoto use the command line or the File Manager to create a folder
`~/Desktop/web/albumname` to hold your generated web pages. Then, back on the
Create Web Pages window, click **Change Folder** to use the folder you just
created.

4   Select a size from the **Image Size** list. Files direct from current digital
cameras are several megabytes in size—too large to be convenient for many
web surfers. Medium or Large is generally right.

5   Keep an eye on the **Estimated Total Size** for each choice of image size—are
you comfortable asking web readers to download that much? Select **Best** or
Original quality levels—there is little point to putting poor quality photos on
display.

6   When you have done all this, click the **Create** button, and a progress scrollbar
will appear next, followed by a browser window showing your newly created
web page, including photo thumbnails, shown in Figure 8-24.

Figure 8-24   A web page from a photo album

If a reader clicks on one of the photos, it's shown in the size you chose.

7   To put the page on your web site, tar or zip everything in the web albumname directory. Lphoto creates a couple of subdirectories. You can use the Ark utility or these two commands to zip files.

```
cd ~/Desktop/web

zip trains.zip trains
```

8   Move the zip file to your web site using ftp, or upload individual pages using Nvu.

If you use Nvu, you have to manually upload every HTML file in your web albumname directory. In other words, the pages with full size images do not get uploaded automatically, merely because the thumbnail page links to them. This is not what users expect, and I filed bug #158 with Linspire to ask them to address it.

Emailing Pictures

There is an "email these pictures" feature in Lphoto. It's the middle button on the Organize view.

Lphoto requires that email clients are able to create an new email from the command line with multiple attachments, since you can select multiple images.

Not many email clients support this, so LPhoto is hardwired to use the Mozilla email client, which definitely works. Or will do, once you carry out the Mozilla mail initial configuration.

Follow these steps.

1   Put the photos you want to send in an album, and choose **File** > **Export Album to Folder**. That pops up a window that gives you a chance to change the image size. It should be no more than medium for files you intend to mail.

2   As with web pages, create a folder on your Desktop to hold the files. The default directory to which Lphoto will export is buried umpteen levels deep in the filesystem.

3   Open your normal email application, and attach the files manually.

4   If you want to do anything with files in Lphoto directly, the files are kept in the following location:

~/My Documents/My Photos/LPhoto Library/*year*/*number*/*number*.

Resizing Pictures

You can easily use Lphoto to resize images.

1   Go into edit mode on the picture.

2   Choose **File** > **Export Selection to Folder** > **Custom size**.

3   Fill in numbers for one or both of **Max height** and **Width**.

4   Click **Export**.

The photo will be exported with the maximum stated dimensions. There are two great things about the resize on export feature:

•   The aspect ratio of the picture will not be changed. If you specify a maximum height of 500 pixels, the width will be scaled so the proportions of the picture remain undistorted. If you specify maximums for both height and width, the picture will be scaled so that it fits inside a rectangle of that size and still retains its original proportions.

•   You can apply the resizing to a number of photos at once, not merely one, and they will all be properly scaled.

The programmer of Lphoto, Will, has done a great job in bringing us this software. At the 2005 Linux Desktop Summit (a developer conference for Linspire), I asked Will about his experience implementing Lphoto. It's written in the Python language. Will explained that he had worked in C++ many years, and originally preferred it for most software development. After using Python for Lphoto, Will swore off C++ altogether, and Python is now the language he feels he can be most productive in. Linspire has done the Open Source Community a great service in sharing Lphoto with all. SuSE has already picked it up for their distro.

Burning a Picture CD

You can also burn your pictures onto a CD. You can store them as either unchanged data files, or in the VCD format.

Making a Backup Copy of Pictures

The data format is useful for keeping a backup copy of your pictures, for moving some albums to another PC, or for mailing to friends and family. Burn the pictures in data format by choosing **Burn CD** > **Copy Album To CD**.

Putting a Finished Slideshow on CD

The VCD (Video CD) format is for putting a finished slideshow on CD. It can be played back on other PCs and most DVD players, often just by loading the VCD. The data is stored as an MPEG stream, which is capable of holding video clickable menus. Lphoto isn't currently able to put that kind of content on a VCD.

1   Choose **Burn CD** > **Burn Album To Video CD** to display the window shown in Figure 8-25.

Figure 8-25   Burning a VCD

2 Click the button enigmatically marked **...** to select an MP3 soundtrack for the VCD. Make any other changes you want (VCD for compatibility with most players, Super VCD for better quality but less compatibility).

3 Place a blank CD in your drive and click **Burn VCD**.

Legends and lore of Linux—The beer license

I've mentioned that Linux and much other open source software is distributed under the terms of the GNU Public License. There are plenty of other licenses that programmers apply to their volunteer work, ranging from the officious to the whimsical. Firmly in the latter category is the Postcardware license.

Postcardware is software distributed on condition that if you like the program, you send the developer a postcard. It's fun for developers to increase karma around the world and get postcards back in return. Then there's the Artistic License under which much Perl software has been issued. The Artistic License is the one with the thoughtful clarification "'You' is you" in the definition section.

There's another whimsical software license: the beerware license. Beerware is software for which the purchase price is to buy the developer a beer if you ever meet him. Other versions have it as drinking a beer in the developer's name when you use the software. At first, I suspected beerware was somebody's hoax, as I'd never seen it in many years of software development. Then I discovered it's used in software integrated with Mozilla.

```
/*

* ----------------------------------------------------------------

* "THE BEER-WARE LICENSE" (Revision 42):

* phk@freeBSD wrote this file.  As long as you retain this notice you

* can do whatever you want with this stuff. If we meet some day, and you think

* this stuff is worth it, you can buy me a beer in return.   Poul-Henning Kamp

* ----------------------------------------------------------------

*

*/
```

Yep, there's beerware-licensed software in a program that is on practically every Linux system! You can see for yourself. Mozilla source code is online at the site http://lxr.mozilla.org/mozilla/source/nsprpub/pr/src/malloc/prmalloc.c

Poul-Henning created the original beerware license in 1994, partly to register his dissatisfaction with excessively lengthy legal clauses in other popular software licenses. As he points out, by open sourcing his spare-time software, employers know his capabilities, and he gets a lot of interesting work because of it. Beerware was also a subtle dig at the GPL, which is traditionally described as "Free as in speech, not free as in beer." That slogan has always been a muddled way of expressing "You might or might not have to pay for the software, but you can change it, add to it, and sell it yourself if you want." Poul-Henning's concept was more along the lines "It's free, take it, but don't forget who wrote it."

The denouement came when Poul-Henning presented a paper at the 2002 BSD Europe Conference. The organizers of the conference ambushed him with fifty mugs of beer in gratitude for his software (see Figure 8-26).

Figure 8-26   The creator of the Beerware license (left) gets his reward

But no beer for me; I'm off to develop some software released under my revolutionary new "chocolateware" license.

## CHAPTER 9

Filesystems and Optical Storage (CDs and DVDs)

Getting Started

This chapter tells you all about using CDs and DVDs—how to play them, how to rip them, as well as how to burn data, music, and video files on Linux.

CDs and DVDs are written (or "burned") and read using a laser. Lasers produce beams of light; hence CDs and DVDs are known as optical storage devices, in contrast to magnetic storage devices, like floppies, hard disks, and Zip drives.

Files of music can be read from a music CD, and encoded into the space-saving MP3 format to store on your PC. Copying files off a CD and shrinking them is known as "ripping".

Filesystems and How to Mount Them

The information in this chapter is easier to follow once you know how files are organized into a filesystem and how Linux deals with filesystems. It's possible to jump ahead to the "how do I burn" instructions, but you'll miss out on a deeper understanding. I'll start with the basics of filesystems.

Fun with Filesystems

A collection of files and folders is called a filesystem. A filesystem is not just the data held in files; it also includes all the information that lets you access the files go from a pathname to the data in a file. This information is called *metadata*. The term means "data about data."

The data in files belongs to you. Most of the metadata (things like pointers from a file allocation table to files, file permissions, and creation timestamps) belongs to the filesystem, and most of the time you never see it. You see your data in a filesystem, not the metadata holding it together.

A filesystem isn't just for hard disks; every device that has files keeps them organized in some kind of filesystem. The storage card that holds your digital photos in a digital camera keeps the images in a filesystem. This filesystem is usually Microsoft's FAT32 filesystem.

Folders in the Linux Root Folder

There are three decades of history dictating the contents of the Unix and hence Linux filesystem. In the beginning the folders in the root directory, /, had a simple organization:

/dev   Special files representing physical devices

/tmp   Temporary files

/bin   Application binaries

/etc   The system administration and configuration files

/man   Manuals

/usr   Home directories for users

Administrators often wanted to put the user home directories on a separate disk. When you add a disk drive, it has to show up in the filesystem as a separate directory, and /usr was the obvious place. Experts like short names, so it was called /usr not /users-home-directories (see Figure 9-1). Some people think /usr is an abbreviation for Unix System Resources. That isn't mentioned in the first Unix manual (1971), so it's a backronym. The point of /usr is that it contains resources for users, not the system.

Often there were program binaries and manuals that were intended for users, and that should go on the /usr disk. To keep things organized, /usr was given a set of folders with the same names as those in the root folder, so we got /usr/bin and /usr/etc and /usr/man for user programs, configuration files, and manuals respectively.

Then SunOS (a very influential Unix version) introduced the concept that system files could be divided into those that don't change often and those that are written to all the time. If the changeable files were moved onto a different disk, the system disk could effectively became read-only. Thus the variable system files including /tmp were put into /var.

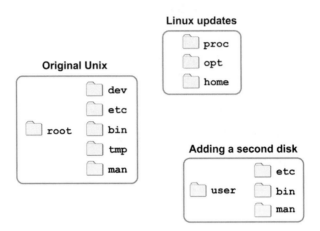

Figure 9-1 The Unix filesystem evolved over three decades

Several new directories were added to better organize the system:

- /mnt – A place for mounting additional storage devices. Standard Linux uses the /media directory as the starting point for all removable disks.

- /opt – Optional (not required for system operation) applications.

- /home – The new standard place for users home directories.

- /boot – Files used in the boot process. Often a separate partition.

The /proc filesystem is particularly interesting. It looks like a read-only file system, but it is actually a clever and standard way for the kernel to provide information about the system hardware, processes, and device modules to programs and system administrators. What look like files are really access points to kernel routines. These provide the data on demand when you read the file.

For example, you can use the /proc filesystem later to get details of the CD drives on the system. The "file" /proc/pci is a list of the cards plugged into your PC's PCI bus. There's a lot of detail even to the level of identifying the key chips on the cards. This often helps when you need to find a device driver.

The "file" /proc/version provides details on the kernel version and compiler used to build it. The cat (concatenate) command types out one or more files.

Type out the file with this command:

```
cat /proc/version
```

Linux version 2.6.10 (root@khrystal) (gcc version 3.3.5 (Debian 1:3.3.5-3)) #1 Wed Mar 2 22:37:07 PST 2005

Some information provided in /proc is dynamic—it changes moment by moment. For example, there is a folder in /proc for each process. The folder name is the numeric process ID. You can use cd to go to /proc/1 and see a dozen or so files that represent the status of process ID 1, which is the first process started by a system as it boots up. All of this data is calculated dynamically when someone asks for it. By presenting it in the form of text files, it's easy for scripts and people to read it.

In a way, /proc is like the Windows registry—a special-purpose filesystem that contains metadata about the system. But since /proc is maintained by the kernel and cannot be modified by people or applications, it is much more robust and reliable than the Windows registry.

Different Filesystems

The filesystems implementations are part of the kernel, and the Linux interface has been designed to allow comparatively easy addition of support for new filesystems. The user never sees any of the implementation, but you do see the effects of differences between filesystems. Different filesystems have different limits and capabilities. Let's look at the ISO-9960 filesystem used on CDs and review how it has improved over time. CD filesystems can be puzzling until you understand that they were designed to match the characteristics of optical storage devices.

The High Sierra Filesystem

A CD filesystem is quite different from any hard disk filesystems. It is laid out differently on the storage media, it uses different data structures to organize the data, it has different capacity limits, and there are different rules for the characters that are permitted in a file name.

Most CDs are written with a filesystem called ISO-9660, named after the international standard that describes it. It's also called the *High Sierra filesystem* after the High Sierra Hotel and Casino in Reno, Nevada where the specification was agreed on back in 1985.

In basic ISO-9660, file names are a maximum of eight characters with a three-character extension, and can only use the letters A–Z and digits 0–9. Lowercase letters and spaces are not allowed in file names.

Rock Ridge and Joliet Extensions

Eight-character, uppercase-only file names are unacceptably limited. As soon as CDs started to be used on computers, OS vendors came up with sets of extensions. The Rock Ridge extension (named after the town in the *Blazing Saddles* movie because it's also part of the Old West) supports Unix-like semantics. The Joliet CD extension means that you can burn a CD and later copy it onto Windows and still have all the long file names. All Linux distros support both Rock Ridge and Joliet extensions to ISO 9660.

Other Filesystems

As well as specifying the range of permissible characters in file names, each kind of filesystem defines other qualities such as the maximum size of an individual file, the maximum size of the overall filesystem (known as the volume size), and the kind of ownership data stored to control access to files. Table 9-1 compares some of the popular filesystems in use today.

Table 9-1   Filesystem comparison

Name	First used in	Max. volume size	Max. file size	Max. length of pathname	Max. length of file name	Characters allowed in file names
FAT32	Windows 95 Release 2	up to 2 TB	4 GB	260 bytes	255 bytes	Space and printable characters except / \ : ? * " > <
NTFS	Windows NT	16 EB	16 EB	32767 bytes	255 bytes	Same as FAT32
ext3	Linux	2 TB	16 GB	No limit	255 bytes	Any except / or null
ReiserFS	Linux	8 TB	16 TB	No limit	4032 bytes	Any except / or null
ISO-9660	CD-ROMs	15 TB	2 GB	255 bytes	11 bytes	0 to 9, A to Z, underscore

The main thing to appreciate from Table 9-1 is that there are different filesystems, and there are significant differences among them.

Note – Some of the filesystem limits depend on block and cluster sizes, chosen when generating the filesystem. Some Microsoft software, including the Windows XP installer, won't allow creation of FAT32 partitions larger than 32 GB. That forces you to use NTFS, which doesn't interoperate the way FAT does.

Megabytes and more

- *A megabyte (MB) is about one million bytes—enough to hold 35 pages of a phone directory.*

- *A gigabyte (GB) is 1000 MB. Computer disks are measured in GB, and the largest common size is about 250 GB at this time (2005). 1 GB can hold about 30 phone directories. A typical DVD movie takes 4 GB of storage.*

- *A terabyte (TB) is 1000 GB. 1 TB of raw disk costs only $500, but to use it effectively and reliably, you need some very costly administration software. A TB can store about 250 movies. The inventory of a typical video rental store can be put on 8 TB of storage.*

- *A petabyte (PB) is 1000 TB. Back in 2001, Google reported that it was using over 1 PB of storage to index 1.25 billion web pages. In 2004 it was indexing more than 8 billion web pages, using presumably about 6 PB of disk. Google does this on thousands of PCs all running Linux.*

- *An exabyte (EB) is 1000 PB. No storage array this large has yet been assembled as far as we know. Forbes Magazine reported that the world generated 5 EB of information in 2002. Beyond EB lies zettabyte (ZB), which is 1000 EB.*

To expand on some of the entries in Table 9-1, here are the characteristics of four filesystems that you will encounter in Linux and Windows. There are plenty of other filesystem types, and the technology remains an active area of research.

- FAT32 – Named after its key data structure (the 32-bit File Allocation Table), this Microsoft filesystem evolved from a long line of earlier FAT filesystems with less capacity. Just about every operating system can access and write a FAT32 filesystem.

  Think of FAT32 as being the lowest common denominator of filesystems. Don't use it unless you are forced to, for compatibility reasons.

- NTFS – The NT filesystem is a modern, Unix-like filesystem. Now that the Windows 9x code base has been unified with the NT product to form Windows XP, NTFS is the filesystem Microsoft would prefer you to use.

Microsoft keeps the specification of NTFS secret to hinder interoperability with other operating systems.

Linux has read access to NTFS files and there is some experimental code that provides write access, but nothing of production quality. So as of 2005, your Linux programs can read local files in NTFS but not write them. You can read and write NTFS files on a different PC using Samba, as described in Chapter 10, "Sharing on Your Local Network," on page 347.

If you have a dual boot system (both Windows and Linspire on the disk, and you are able to boot up in either), your XP C:\ drive files show up in directory under /mnt, typically /mnt/hda1.

- Ext3 – The third extended filesystem for Linux is in widespread use. It replaced the ext2, or second extended, filesystem, which had been part of Linux since almost the beginning. The main advantage of ext3 is that it adds a feature called journalling to ext2, in a very convenient and backward-compatible manner. Journalling is described in *Journalling filesystems*.

- ReiserFS – Developed by a team under the leadership of Hans Reiser, this filesystem offers high reliability, and it is also a journalled filesystem. ReiserFS gives better performance than ext3 for directories with large numbers of small files.

  ReiserFS is not backward compatible with ext2, but because of its advantages many Linux distributions (e.g., Linspire, SuSE, and Xandros) have made it their default filesystem. Development continues and Reiser4 is gradually being introduced.

- The most advanced filesystem in the world runs on Unix. It's the Zetta File System (ZFS), created by world-class engineers at Sun Microsystems, and available only for Solaris 10. ZFS uses 64-bit addressing and avoids the low or arbitrary limits of all other filesystems. ZFS is safe, fast, and secure. It actually detects and repairs disk corruption as it runs. It would be great to see ZFS become an industry standard.

Partitioning a Disk

You'll learn more about this in Chapter 12, "Installation and Boot," but there's actually a two-step process to laying down a filesystem on most storage devices.

- Partitioning the disk – The first step, partitioning the disk, divides the raw storage into one or more partitions.

If a storage device is like a building, a partition is like a room within that building. It holds a fraction of the whole, and it can be filled or emptied without affecting other rooms. With a small disk, under 20 GB say, it's best to devote the whole thing to one partition. Partitioning a disk creates a "partition table" at the start of the disk saying where each partition starts, and how big it is. A partition is never supposed to interfere with another partition. But if you make a mistake when creating partitions and somehow let two overlap, they will overwrite each other with disastrous results for both.

- Formatting the partition – The second step is to create an empty filesystem on each partition, a process known as formatting the partition. Each partition holds exactly one filesystem (ignoring a minor exception that I'll get to later). Many tools blur the distinction between dividing up the disk into partitions and putting an empty filesystem on each partition, but they are two different things. If you later expand the size of the partition, it does not magically expand the size of the filesystem contained within it.

It's common to split larger disks into several partitions that you will use for different purposes. One popular arrangement is to set up a disk with the following:

- An NTFS or FAT32 partition of at least 5 to 10 GB for Windows.

- A similar-sized ReiserFS or ext3 partition for Linux.

- The rest of the space for a FAT32 partition that is writable by both Windows and Linux. You will keep most of your data in this partition. Chapter 12, "Installation and Boot," has more detail on partitioning and how to do it.

CDs Aren't Partitioned in Advance

Filesystems for CDs are a special case. Because of the physical hardware and difficulties with precise positioning of the laser, you get exactly one chance to write each byte during a burn. It's not possible to lay down an empty ISO 9660 filesystem on a CD, and then go back later and burn new files within the filesystem.

There is a technology to add files to a CD, making what is called a multi-session CD. It relies on recording a new lead-in and lead-out, consuming 20 MB for each new burning session. The UDF filesystem, commonly used on DVDs, was developed to address the limitations of CD hardware.

By far the easiest way to cope with CD media limitations is to create the entire ISO 9660 filesystem and all the files and data within it, in one go. The mkisofs command does exactly this, producing an .iso file. The complete bundle of filesystem metadata and data can then be burned onto the CD in one pass. You used to have to create an ISO filesystem manually when you burned a data CD. Modern burning programs still do this, but they hide the process from you to make it appear simpler. CDs can have several partitions, just like disks, but there is usually only one partition on a CD.

Journalling filesystems

I mentioned the journalling feature of filesystems. This is a modern filesystem development, intended to improve the integrity of a filesystem. Many of the system crashes of Windows 9x were caused by corruption in the FAT32 filesystem. Journalling eliminates this.

Before writing to a file, a journalled filesystem writes a record of the intended changes. Then it makes those changes to the filesystem. After the changes are successfully made, it discards that journal entry. If there is an unscheduled system interruption caused by a power failure or other problem, the journal of pending changes can be "replayed" to quickly bring the filesystem to a consistent state. If the problem occurs while the journal is being written, the incomplete log entry is ignored. There is no need for lengthy integrity checks or risky filesystem repairs. Disk writes are either fully complete or are not started, so the filesystem is always consistent.

NTFS, ext3, and ReiserFS are all journalling filesystems.

The Filesystem "Tree"

Essentially all modern filesystems are organized as trees as shown in Figure 9-2.

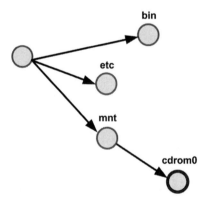

Figure 9-2   In a tree, each file is in exactly one folder, and each folder has exactly one parent folder

OK, it's the part of a tree that's above ground, and it's lying on its side with the trunk to the left. The arrows represent the branches of a real tree. The circles represent folders and files of a filesystem tree. Branches connect folders with the files they contain. A file is like a leaf in a real tree—it doesn't have any further branches coming out of it.

You can see why the complete name of a file is called a pathname—the complete name is made up of the path you travel from the root end of the tree to the leaf end. The point is that all files have a unique pathname in a tree. Nothing loops back on itself; a file isn't in two folders at once.

Windows and Linux take different approaches to access the filesystems on devices. Windows gives each partition a drive letter. The first partition on the first hard disk is typically the C: drive, dating from the days before PCs had hard disk drives. (In 1981 all PCs came with either one or two floppy drives, the A: and B: devices.)

Linux doesn't use drive letters, but fits all storage devices into one big unified file system. The Linux way of naming filesystems means that it is very easy to do some operation on all filesystems. For example, you can easily search everywhere for a file with a certain name or content. You don't need to specify a long list of places to look: on the CD, both disks, on the floppy, etc.

The kernel uses a file-based interface to each device. The kernel keeps track of all hardware devices by giving them a pathname that starts in the /dev directory. (You might recall reading about /dev/modem in Chapter 4.)

You never directly use or change any file in /dev; each file there is a pointer to the device driver for some piece of hardware. By calling routines in the device driver, the kernel makes stuff happen on the device.

More About Mount

A storage device can be connected to the system physically but not be visible in the file system. To make it accessible, you first tell the operating system what kind of filesystem is on the storage device (FAT32, ext3, etc.), and where in the filesystem tree you would like those files to appear. This is called mounting a filesystem.

On Windows, all storage media are mounted automatically for you. This happens with Linspire too, but is not true for all Linux distros. The hard disk that you booted from is always mounted automatically, but other media might require an extra manual step.

When it mounts the filesystem on a CD (or floppy disk or other device), Linux takes the file system on the CD and grafts it into the main disk file system. The directory where you want the device filesystem grafted on is called the mount point—in Figure 9-3 the mount point for the CD is /mnt/cdrom0.

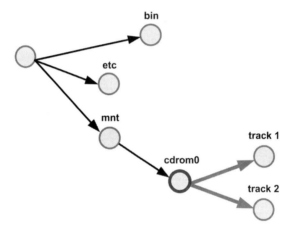

Figure 9-3   The CD filesystem is grafted onto the filesystem at the mount point

If you want to start using the files on the CD, look for them in the mount point directory, /mnt/cdrom0. Other distros use the folder /media to hold directories that are mount points for removable storage. There will be a directory in /mnt or /media for each individual device, such as /mnt/cdrom0 and /mnt/floppy0. Any directory can be used as a mount point. If you have some files in a mount point directory, after you mount some storage device on it, the directory contents will be unavailable until you unmount the filesystem.

The mount command lets you mount filesystems manually and determine where to put them. From reading the man page, it looks like it takes lots of arguments, but there are really only three important ones:

- The /dev pathname to the device with the filesystem
- The filesystem the device holds (FAT32, NTFS, ReiserFS, ISO-9660, etc.)
- Where you want it to appear in the main filesystem

The file /etc/fstab holds a list of all the filesystems to be mounted when Linux boots up. You can edit entries in this file to change what happens by default.

Mounting your Windows partition for ordinary users

When you install Linux, you can set things up so that your Windows partition remains on the disk. You will then have read access to the files on it. Unfortunately, the default options used to mount the Windows partition deny access to ordinary users. Only the administrator (root user) can access the Windows partition.

You can easily correct this manually. Log on as the root user, unmount the Windows partition, then mount it again with the correct option. Your Windows partition will typically be hda1, but if it is something else, use that in place of hda1 in the commands below:

```
umount /mnt/hda1
```

```
mount -o umask=022 /dev/hda1 /mnt/hda1
```

This will mount the Windows partition with permissions allowing a non-root user to read and execute files. To make the change permanent, make a backup copy then edit the file /etc/fstab. Look for the line containing /mnt/hda1 and add umask=22 *to the other options, like this:*

Before:

```
/dev/hda1 /mnt/hda1 ntfs noatime,user,exec,dev,suid  0 0
```

After:

```
/dev/hda1 /mnt/hda1 ntfs noatime,user,exec,dev,suid,umask=22  0 0
```

Links and Filesystems

The description of a filesystem presented previously ("a file isn't in two folders at once") is slightly simplified. I'm going to take back a little bit of that information by telling you about links. You don't have to know about links. But if you don't, you're missing out on some of the power of Linux.

Hard Links and Soft Links

There are two kinds of links in Unix, hard links and soft links, and their purpose is to provide alternative pathnames for files. For example, you can use a link to provide a simpler name for a file, or to make a path to a file from a different directory. Links have the same effect as shortcuts in the Windows world.

But a Windows shortcut is just a regular file, not part of the filesystem. That means that a Windows program that might encounter a shortcut to a file has to know to follow it. Otherwise it will process the shortcut file instead of the file it points to. In Linux, the filesystem automatically follows a link and delivers the real file at the end. Programs never take special steps to deal with links.

When you look at the disk filesystem implementation, it turns out that files aren't actually "in" folders at all. A folder has a table of entries. Each entry contains the name of a file, some file metadata, and a pointer to the file contents. A hard link is simply an additional directory entry (in the same or another directory) pointing to the same file contents. You can only hard link to a file, not a directory, and hard links are not allowed to point into some other filesystem partition.

Soft links were developed later, to get around these limitations. Soft links, also known as *symlinks* or symbolic links, are a sort of file indirection. A new file is created whose contents point to the original file. A symbolic link can point to any directory or file even across partitions. It can even point to a file that doesn't exist (this is a broken symlink).

When you have a symlink, deleting the original file will cause the file to be erased and the symlinks pointing to it to become broken. When you delete a hard link, the file's link count is decremented. The link count is one of the pieces of metadata for a file. The file is not removed until its link count reaches zero, because that means there are no other directory entries pointing to it. The right way to think about hard links is that the creation of a file creates the first link to it. Any entry in a directory is just a hard link to a file.

Symbolic links have no permissions or status of their own. Instead, they use the permissions of the file they point to, though the permissions field of the link will show lrwxrwxrwx (read/write/execute for everybody, and the l at the beginning tips you off that it's a link). Hard links can be given a different permission from the original file. Links are a little bit subtle. Most of the time you want the convenience and flexibility of symlinks.

Microsoft's FAT32 filesystem doesn't support any kind of link. If you try to create a link on a FAT32 partition from Linux, you'll get an error that boils down to "Operation not permitted".

To end with a concrete example, as I was writing this book, I kept the chapters several levels deep in my home directory, in folders with names like:

`/home/peter/books/book.linux/chapters/ch01/`

So that I could quickly go from my home directory to numbered chapters, I created symlinks like this:

ln -s /home/peter/books/book.linux/chapters/ch01/ /home/peter/ch01

Then from my home directory, I need to type only:

cd ch01

to go to the folder containing the first chapter. If you have a dual boot system, you might create a link from your desktop to your Windows files so you can read them more easily.

ln -s /mnt/hda1/Documents\ and\ Settings/peter /home/peter/winxp

Link to a Folder

Another use for a link is to put an icon on your desktop that represents one of your other folders. It's easy to create a link using KDE.

1   Right-click on an unused part of the desktop and choose **Create New** > **File** > **Link to Location (URL)**.

2   In the **File name** field, type the name you want this link to have on your desktop, and in the **Enter link to location (URL)** field, the pathname to the file or folder (see Figure 9-4).

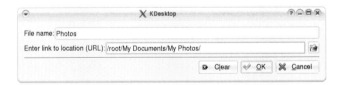

Figure 9-4   Creating a link to another folder

3   Click **OK** and a new icon link will appear on your desktop, labeled with the file name you gave it.

When you double-click on the icon, a File Manager window will open and show that directory.

4   Change the icon by right-clicking on it and choosing **Properties**. In the Properties window, select the **General** tab. Click on the icon's image immediately under the General tab. That brings up a window that lets you browse for and select a system icon or another kind of icon.

Enough about filesystems, mounts, and links. Let us go on with the details of CDs and DVDs.

Reading Data CDs and Creating Device Icons

This section covers reading data CDs and making desktop icons for your CD drive or other devices.

Reading Data CDs

1 To read a data CD, place the CD in the drive.

2 The CD platter will spin up, and the disk will be mounted, meaning the filesystem on the disk will be attached to the operating system's file structure.

3 The Konqueror file manager will open a window showing the contents of the CD (see Figure 9-5).

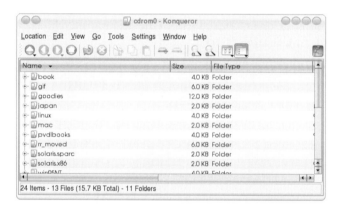

Figure 9-5   The file manager window for removable media

Some distros and past versions of Linspire required you to mount CDs manually, by right-clicking on an icon that represented the drive to display a menu with Mount and Eject as two of the choices.

Making Icons for Devices

You can have desktop icons representing various devices, like floppy and CD drives.

1 Right-click on any unused part of the desktop, and choose **Configure Desktop**.

2 That will bring up the window shown in Figure 9-6. Click on the **Behavior** icon, then the **Device Icons** tab.

3 Select any icons for devices that you would like to see on the desktop, then click **OK**.

It's a good idea to have icons for most of the mounted devices. That means when those devices are active you can easily read their contents. Your hard disk is active all the time, and you don't need an icon on the desktop for that.

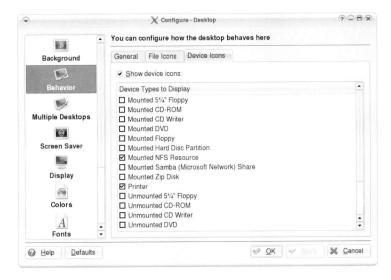

Figure 9-6   Device Icons tab

Burning Data CDs

This section covers using the K3b application to make data and music CDs and DVDs.

*   To burn a CD, start with *Starting the K3b Application* on page 304, then continue through *Burning the CD* on page 308.

*   To copy a CD, see *Copying a CD* on page 309.

*   To erase a CD or DVD, see *Erasing a CD-RW or DVD-RW* on page 309.

About K3b

K3b is just a slick GUI layer that provides convenient burning defaults. K3b works by calling several command line utilities including mkisofs, cdrecord (lately renamed as cdrtools), and cdrdao. If you are troubleshooting a CD burn, you might want to try these underlying utilities directly—see *Burner Problems* on page 341.

K3b is actively maintained, and has a home page at http://www.k3b.org where you can read (a very little) more about the program, report bugs, and get the latest version.

The K3b help button in Linspire 5 just dumps you into the K3b handbook, which can be helpful. For more help, go to that K3b web site or do a web search in Google Groups for answers.

Starting the K3b Application

Linspire uses the K3b application to burn CDs.

1 Start the application by clicking **Launch > Run Programs > Audio and MP3 > CD and DVD Burning (K3b)**.

2 The first time you do this, K3b will ask you about the fastest speed of your CD burner, as shown in Figure 9-7. The factor you select here (1x, 4x, 10x and so on) is used as the highest value in the list of choices when you set a burn speed manually. But the kind of CD media you use also affects the maximum burn speed. Most people select **Auto** for the burn speed and let the drive figure it out.

Just put a high factor in here. No need to go nuts trying to dig out the fine print of the specification for your drive.

Figure 9-7 The K3b application

3 The main application window opens.

K3b optical burner

K3b was written by Sebastien Trueg, who still maintains it along with a number of volunteers. I asked Sebastian what's behind the name. Seb explained that he originally created K3b as a small utility intended just for himself. Since he was going to be the only user, he felt that the cliché "Burn, baby burn"was a good enough name.

But there was already a CD-burning application called "Burn, baby burn". (The name comes from a 1974 pop hit by two ex-Strawbs members, which once heard, lodges in the recesses of your brain forever.) Since someone had been beaten Seb to "Burn, baby burn", he just took the three Bs and prefixed them with the standard KDE letter K to get "K3b".

Choosing the Kind of CD to Create

The first step in burning is to select the kind of CD you want to create:

- **An audio CD** that will play in a car stereo or a boom box, as well as on a PC. This is the format that commercial music CDs come in.

- **A data CD** that contains any kind of files and folders, and which is intended to be stored or read by application programs, rather than played. A CD can hold around 700 MB of data.

- **A data DVD** that contains any kind of files and folders, and intended to be read by application programs, rather than played. The most common DVD available to consumers in 2005 holds about 4400 MB (4.4 GB) of data. Sony is working on its Blu-ray media, and Toshiba on a rival HD-DVD project, both hoping to create the next-generation DVD with up to 30 GB capacity.

Specifying the CD Contents

K3b expects you to create a project that is a list of the files and folders that you want on the CD/DVD. You will create an audio project, a data project, or a DVD data project corresponding to the type of format you want to burn.

1   Click on one of the icons shown in the lower part of Figure 9-8.

Or you can select one of the other half dozen possibilities by choosing **File > New Project**. The three most common choices are a CD data project, DVD data project, or copying a CD. If you want to burn an audio CD, it can be quicker and easier to use the Lsongs application, described in *Burning and Using MP3s* on page 322.

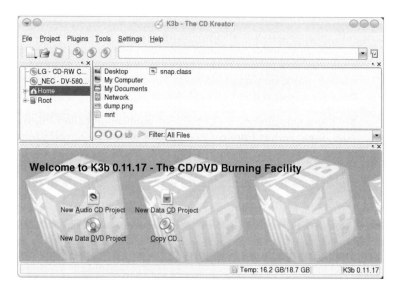

Figure 9-8   Choosing a CD or DVD data project in the main K3b window

2   When you select the project type, the lower half of the K3b window changes into the form shown in Figure 9-9.

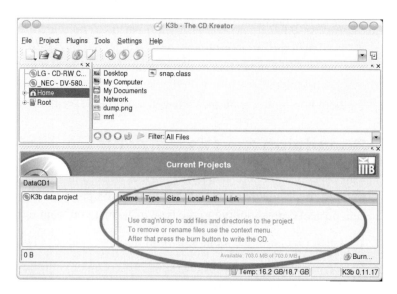

Figure 9-9   Lower panel for project files and folders

3   Drag the files and/or folders that you want on the CD into the lower window.

4   You can remove a file or folder from this lower window by right-clicking on it and choosing **Remove**.

Burn Settings

1   When you have selected all the files and folders for your data CD/DVD, click the **Burn** icon in the lower right of the K3b window (it's also on the icon bar).

2   This will bring up a Data Project window that allows you to select from about thirty different options. Figure 9-10 shows an example of the Writing tab in that window.

To get the most reliable results, burn on the slowest supported speed in the **Speed** list.

Figure 9-10   Burning a CD using K3b

3   The first time you use K3b, it's worth looking through all the choices available on all five tabs: Writing, Settings, Volume Desc, Filesystem, Advanced. The default settings are almost always acceptable. The Volume tab lets you give a name to the CD (naming it for the date you burned it can be helpful for back up CDs).

4   The Filesystem tab lets you select the Rock Ridge and Joliet extensions, which make file names more compatible with other operating systems.

You always want to select **Rock Ridge**. You only need Joliet if the CD will be used on Windows.

5   On the Writing tab, the **Writing Mode** list has the following entries:

- Auto – The software will select the writing mode (usually the best approach).

- DAO (Disk At Once) – The platter is written in one continuous stream from beginning to end. If you're having trouble burning, try selecting DAO.

- TAO (Track At Once) – The laser is turned off between adjacent tracks (files), introducing a two-second gap between tracks. (A CD track can be any length and is quite different from a hard disk track that has a fixed size).

  TAO is particularly used in combination with multi-session audio CDs, where you burn each audio track at different times. Since CDs now cost just a few cents a platter, there is no reason to endure the complexities of multi-session CDs, and you should not usually bother with TAO.

- Raw – Raw mode copies the input files directly and bit-for-bit identically onto the CD without applying any data checking or correction algorithms. This is typically not what you want. You'd use it when you are cloning a CD that implements copy protection through sectors that are deliberately written incorrectly.

Burning the CD

1   After making any setting changes, usually none, click the button labeled **Burn**. A new window will show the progress of the burn, as in Figure 9-11.

This window keeps you advised of progress, and will report any errors encountered.

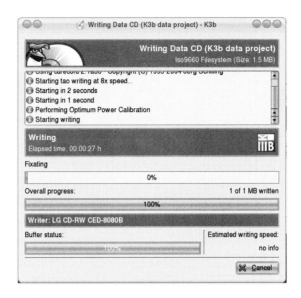

Figure 9-11   CD burn progress status

2   A bugle sounds *Assembly Call* when the burn has completed. Some people like an audible notification so they can do something else while a CD is burning.

If you don't like it, turn it off by choosing **Settings** > **Configure K3b** > **Notifications**.

Copying a CD

1   The Tools menu also has an entry allowing you to copy a CD; choose **Tools** > **CD** > **Copy CD**. See Figure 9-12.

2   Follow the instructions onscreen.

Erasing a CD-RW or DVD-RW

1   To erase a rewritable CD/DVD, choose **Tools** > **CD** > **Erase CD-RW** or **Tools** > **DVD** > **Erase DVD**. See Figure 9-12.

Figure 9-12   Using the Tools menu in K3b to copy, erase, or burn an image

2   Follow the instructions onscreen.

Burning an Image or ISO File

An ISO file, also known as an image file, is an exact binary copy of a CD or a hard disk. It holds not just the files and folders on the CD, but is a duplicate of every bit written on the CD including the boot sector, the file allocation tables, and all the other metadata. It's called an ISO file because it contains an ISO 9660 filesystem. As it holds a complete filesystem, you can do to it all the things that you can do with any filesystem, such as mount it and then read from it.

An ISO image is a handy way to pass around or download a complete CD filesystem in a single file, and later burn it to get a duplicate of the original CD. They are the most common form in which a Linux distro is distributed. You need to know about ISO files so you can write a CD that will be bootable. Part of the ISO image is a boot sector that is not accessible through the filesystem. You can't get that with a zip archive because that only holds files and folders, not raw disk sectors in special places.

The boot sector is described in more detail in Chapter 12. It is typically the first sector on a disk, and it holds software run during the last stages of booting up. It manages the transition from running code in the BIOS, to running code in the operating system on disk. It's difficult (but not impossible) to make the boot sector a file within the filesystem. You need to access the boot sector before any operating system is running, hence you don't yet have filesystem capabilities.

Burning an ISO file on non-Linux systems

If you haven't installed Linux yet, then you can't use Linux to burn an ISO Linux installation CD. Here's how you burn an ISO CD on other operating systems. Almost all CD burning software has a way to burn an ISO CD. It's just a matter of looking for the right menu entry in the GUI.

- *MacOS 10.x – In the Finder, go to the folder Applications\Utilities. Double-click to start the program called Disk Utility. Move your ISO image on your desktop, so you will have a visible icon for it. Drag the icon into the left-hand tab of disk utility, and click on it. Put a blank CD into the drive and click the **Burn** icon at top left of the Disk Utility tool bar. That's all! Disk Utility automatically burns an ISO image.*

- *Windows – If you don't have or don't like the existing CD burning program, there are a couple of freeware downloads that will burn ISOs. Visit* http://www.snapfiles.com/freeware/gmm/fwcdburn.html *and download the DeepBurner software for Windows. Other people like the CD-Mate software found at* http://www.cd-mate.com/downloads.php. *There's also the ISO recorder at* http://isorecorder.alexfeinman.com/isorecorder.htm.

El Torito Spec for Bootable CDs

You might have heard the phrase *El Torito*. This is the specification for formatting a CD so that you can boot from it. A few years ago, many PCs were not able to boot from CD. Today, such limited PCs are no longer manufactured, and El Torito compliant CDs are the norm.

You might be amused to hear that El Torito works by faking out the BIOS to make a file on the CD appear to be the floppy disk drive. That file will contain the image of a bootable floppy disk. This is why you can't use the first floppy and the CD drive together during the boot process. This was a quick hack to get bootable CDs working, and it worked so well no one saw any need to change it.

Linux distributions, including Linspire, are often published as one or more .iso files. You download the .iso files (each one will take up to about 700 MB, the capacity of a CD) and burn a CD of each. However, you should not burn the file containing an ISO image as an ordinary data CD. If you burn it as an ordinary file, you get a data CD that is not El Torito compliant, and which contains a single file that contains the image of a CD. What you want is a bootable CD that is a bit-for-bit duplicate of the contents of the image file, with its multiple directories.

All common CD-writing programs on all operating systems support burning a bootable ISO image. However, because most people do it rarely, the correct menu item or setting is often unknown to them.

1   In K3b, choose **Tools > CD > Burn CD Image** as shown in Figure 9-12.

2   That brings up the Burn CD Image window shown in Figure 9-13.

Figure 9-13   Burning an ISO image in K3b

3   You give K3b the pathname to the image file by typing it in the circled text
        field at the top of Figure 9-13. Or you can click the **open folder** icon next to
        the text field, to select the file by browsing the filesystem.

MD5 Checksums for Files

Notice the lower circle in Figure 9-13. Some of the files in an ISO image (or files
anywhere) may have a checksum, so that you can easily tell if the file has been
corrupted. The ISO images that Linspire issues have checksums for half a dozen
files, and the checksums are stored in a file called md5sums.dat in the image. Md5
means "message digest 5"—it was the fifth in a series of algorithms for
constructing a fingerprint or checksum of a file.

When you get an ISO image (or any file with a checksum), you can find its md5
checksum with the command:

md5sum filename.iso

On MacOS, the command is md5; on Windows, download and use the program at
http://www.toast442.org/md5/ or from http://www.fastsum.com.

If the current checksum matches the original checksum given by the person who created the file, then the file is very probably a good copy. If the old and current checksums do not match, the file was probably corrupted during the download, and you need to download it again. It's a complete waste of time to burn a CD from an .iso file with a bad checksum.

K3b calculates and checks the MD5 sums automatically when it sees an md5sums.dat file. It reports a matching result with a check mark shown in the lower circled text in Figure 9-13.

Start the ISO Burn

1 Click the **Start** button in K3b to start the burn, bringing up the status window shown in Figure 9-14.

2 When the burn is complete, remove the CD and it's ready for use.

Figure 9-14   Starting an ISO burn

Looking at files inside an ISO image

You can review the content of an ISO image file before burning it if you mount it. You can then, for instance, examine the operating system installation scripts before installing. You won't be able to change anything because this kind of ISO image is read-only.

Here are the commands for mounting an ISO image file.

```
mkdir /mnt/iso
mount file.iso  /mnt/iso/ -t iso9660 -o loop=/dev/loop0
```

The loop=/dev/loop0 *option introduced by the* -o *option flag says "do this mount using loopback device zero". The loopback device (there are eight of them by default,* loop0 *to* loop7*) is a kernel contrivance that allows an ordinary file to be accessed as though it were a disk device. This is the "minor exception" to the rule that each partition contains one filesystem. Mounting a file with loopback causes the kernel to retrieve the contents of the file, then "loop back" into the kernel to reinterpret those bytes as if they were raw data coming from the CD. You might do this if you're involved in preparing Linux releases.*

The file file.iso *represents your ISO file. You can now type* cd /mnt/iso *and look through the directories in the image. When you are finished, type* cd *to get out of there and issue this command:*

```
umount /mnt/iso
```

Note the command is umount, *not* unmount.

Playing Music CDs

Playing a music CD is a breeze. Just insert the CD and sit back. Lsongs will play commercial audio CDs and the music CDs that you create.

Playing a CD with Lsongs

KDE recognizes music CDs and automatically starts the Lsongs music application shown in Figure 9-15. Click on a track or just click the triangular **play button** at the lower left of the Lsongs window.

Notice the CD icon on the column labeled **Source** (circled in Figure 9-15). It represents the CD you have put in the drive. If you select something in the Source column, its content will be displayed on the right.

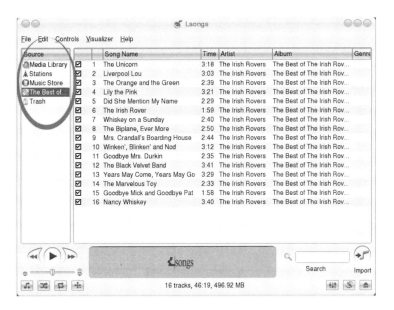

Figure 9-15   The Lsongs CD player

Lsongs (and its digital photo companion, Lphoto) is an application written by Linspire and open sourced for the benefit of all Linux distributions. Lsongs and Lphoto support many of the features pioneered by Apple's iTunes and iPhoto applications. Lsongs and Lphoto are written in the Python programming language, and Linspire ships their source code.

If you want to take a look at some Python code, or even modify these programs, look in the following location for the folders Lsongs and Lphoto:

/usr/lib/python2.3/site-packages/

Sound support in Linux: ALSA and JACK

You normally don't need to know this, but it gives you the vocabulary for sound in Linspire. The 2.6 Linux kernel uses the Advanced Linux Sound Architecture (ALSA) device drivers and tools for sound cards. ALSA supports a great many sound devices. You can find a complete list at the following location: http://www.alsa-project.org/alsa-doc/index.php?vendor=All#matrix.

In Linspire 5.0, ALSA works with a user-level sound server called JACK. JACK is a replacement for the older ARTS software. ALSA lets one process at a time push a sound through the sound chipset. But real world systems often have multiple processes wanting to make multiple sounds: you're playing an MP3, while burning a CD, when mail comes in.

All three of those might want to make a noise at once. The JACK software layer is there to manage and multiplex this correctly.

JACK is a core component of KDE and manages sound from multiple simultaneous sources. KDE tells Jack the noises it wants, Jack multiplexes that with other sound sources and tells ALSA. ALSA drives the sound card. There are some settings that might improve sound performance under **Launch** > **Control Center** > **Sound and Multimedia**. *They amount to allocating a larger buffer.*

Playing a CD with the Older Kscd CD Player

Linux distros that have not yet bundled Lsongs will automatically start Kscd or one of the other, older CD player utilities instead. The **s** in Kscd stands for simple, which is always a good attribute of a program. The Kscd player doesn't use menus. Instead, it uses icons very similar to the icons on a physical CD player to represent play/pause, loop, next track, and so on (see Figure 9-16).

Figure 9-16   The Kscd interface CD player window

Click on the icon to get that function. If you don't recognize an icon, let your mouse rest on it for a couple of seconds and a tooltip will appear giving a few words of description.

There's an eject button to the left of the track name, but very old CD-ROM drives might not support software eject. The hammer and screwdriver button in the center (not usually seen on a physical CD player) brings up a configuration window for Kscd. You can configure colors and a few play options.

If the CD doesn't have track and title information, Kscd tries to display it by querying the database at www.freedb.org. You can enable or disable this from the freedb icon on the configuration panel (click the hammer and screwdriver icon). There is a complete handbook for Kscd at the KDE documentation site http://docs.kde.org/en/3.1/kdemultimedia/kscd if you need more information.

Rip, Mix, Burn—Creating Music CDs!

As the Apple slogan memorably pointed out, a lot of the enjoyment people get from digital music is in the "Rip, Mix, Burn".

Rip Music CDs

Just to be clear, "ripping" a CD means copying all the data files off it, and converting the copies to more convenient formats. You can then store the copies on your PC or download them onto a portable music player (often an MP3 player).

Ripping a CD is nothing to do with the phrase "rip off" meaning theft, no matter what the Recording Industry Association of America would like everyone to believe. It just lets you play the music you bought on your player of choice.

1   The main window of Lsongs displays the tracks of a music CD that you just inserted (see to Figure 9-15). Note the check marks to the left of the numbers.

2   Unmark the checkbox for each of the album tracks you don't want.

3   Click the **Import** icon at the bottom right of Lsongs; see Figure 9-17.

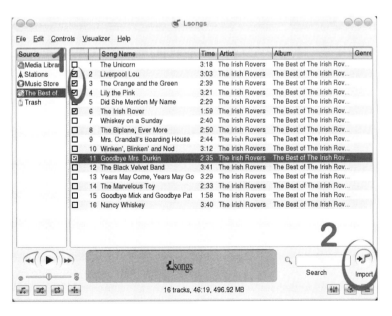

Figure 9-17   Unchecking the tracks you don't want, then clicking Import

4   That starts importing the selected tracks. It might take 45 minutes or more to rip a 500 MB CD. It depends on the speed of your drive. Lsongs uses cdda2wav as the default ripper.

5   If you have some scratched or hard-to-read CDs, choose **File** > **Preferences** > **CD** > **Use error correction**, which will invoke the slower but sturdier CD Paranoia ripper.

Ripping problems

You might find that one particular disk won't rip, while all your others rip just fine. Try gently washing the disk with mild soapy water. Rinse thoroughly and dry it well with a soft lint-free cloth. This gets rid of greasy fingerprints, which obscure the platter from the laser.

If the disk still won't rip, check if it shows the official compact disc logo on the CD or the case. If not, the disc probably has an anti-copying technology, such as Cactus Datashield or SafeAudio. Since you are legally entitled to copy the CD for personal use and play the songs on your MP3 player, the best thing to do here is to return the CD to the store. Explain that it won't play in some of your players. This will encourage the Music Industry to stop fighting legal and common uses of music CDs that you have bought.

Lsongs takes the audio files you selected, converts them into the much smaller MP3 format, and writes those MP3 files to Lsongs' media library. The Lsongs media library is organized by recording artist, and by album name for each artist.

Changing Lsong's Default Action

1   You can change Lsongs' default action when a music CD is placed in the drive. Choose **File** > **Preferences** > **CD**, then look at the **On CD Insert** list.

2   The entries like Begin Playing are self-explanatory. One choice is **Import Songs and Eject**. This is to help you rip a pile of CDs. Each song is copied to hard disk, and then the lengthy encoding into MP3 format is done in the background, allowing the CD to be ejected immediately and the next one to be processed.

CD formats: audio CD vs. MP3 vs. Ogg Vorbis

Just as you can store the same words and pictures in a web page, or in a word-processing document, there are several formats for storing music on a CD. A word-processing document typically has very fine control over layout and presentation, but it takes up more space than a web page. There are similar space versus quality tradeoffs between the audio CD format and the MP3 format for music files.

The format for tracks on an audio CD was laid down in 1980 by Philips and Sony in the colorfully named Red Book specification. It says that audio CDs will contain 44,100 samples per second, each of which is a stereo pair of 16-bit signals. (The odd sample frequency came from the desire to work well with television video signals). That rate adds up to about 10.5 MB needed for each minute of song (or silence, or the audience shuffling its feet, or the conductor clearing his throat, etc.). The CD data is typically stored in files in Audio Interchange File Format—a very flexible format invented by Apple Computer.

The most popular format used for ripped audio CDs comes from the digital movie world, where it is known as MPEG-1, audio layer 3, or MP3 for short. MP3 files discard the frequencies the human ear can't hear, and compress the rest. The impetus for MP3 was the surge of music downloading and file sharing corresponding to the rise of Napster. To make that work well, people needed to pass smaller files around. MP3 lets you squeeze about 1 minute of music into about 1 MB of storage, and often the signal degradation is imperceptible.

There are plenty of other formats for digital music, too, some of them better than MP3. For iTunes, Apple uses a format called Advanced Audio Coding or AAC. AAC works in tandem with Apple's FairPlay copy restriction scheme.

For CD quality, Microsoft uses WAVEform audio format (.wav files) which is a close relative of Apple's Audio Interchange File Format (AIFF). Windows Media Audio (.wma or .asf) is Microsoft's equivalent to MP3, but with copy restriction enforcement. Lsongs does not play .wma files, but utilities such as lame, madplay, and mpg321 will convert .wma to .mp3 format, and some of these remove the digital rights restrictions too.

Vorbis is the open source response to the 1998 announcement by the German company that invented MP3 compression that they were going to start charging licensing fees. Linspire has promised that future versions of Lsongs will work with Vorbis. Open source and Linux fans should support Vorbis where possible by choosing Vorbis-capable hardware like the iRiver, Rio Karma, and Cowon players. Vorbis data is frequently put in a file that meets the Ogg specification. It is then called "Ogg Vorbis". Ogg stands for "Operation Good Guys"—the title of a much-loved British spoof documentary. There is a rich lore of whimsical names in computer science.

Importing MP3 Files into Lsongs

You might already have a large collection of already-ripped MP3 files that you'd like to bring into Lsongs. If you have a dual-boot installation (see Chapter 12, "Installation and Boot"), your Windows C:\ partition is probably under /mnt/hda1.

Your MP3 files will thus be under /mnt/hda1/Documents and Settings/username/My Documents/My Music.

If your MP3 files are on another PC, either burn them to CD, or transfer them using the local networking features described in Chapter 10, "Sharing on Your Local Network."

1   Once the files are accessible to your Linspire PC, choose **File** > **Add Folder to Media Library**.

2   That brings up a browsing window in which you can select the folder with the music files. You can also add an individual file to Lsongs if you wish. Figure 9-18 shows the menu for both choices.

Some people like to keep their music in a network-shared folder that they can access from all their computers. Be aware that, unlike some Windows jukebox software, Lsongs does not currently scan for new music files that are added to a folder. The user needs to manually import the music to Lsongs.

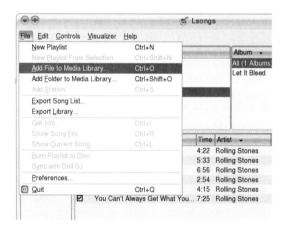

Figure 9-18   Importing MP3 files or folders into Lsongs

Mixing Music CDs

Once their music is in Lsongs, many people then create playlists, which are lists of 10 or 20 tracks they think belong nicely together. This is called mixing. Mixing is where you apply your artistic judgment to combine music and artists. When you have created a playlist, you can play it in Lsongs or you can burn it to a CD.

1   Choose **File** > **New Playlist**.

2   That will create an entry called **Untitled play_list** in the leftmost column of Lsongs.

Give it a more descriptive name by highlighting the name, then right-click and choose **Rename Playlist**. Figure 9-19 shows how to rename a playlist.

Figure 9-19   Renaming a new playlist

3   After creating and naming an empty playlist, drag tracks from the media library (or other source in the Source column of Lsongs) to the playlist icon in the **Source** column.

4   Highlight the source of the tracks. Often this will be the Lsongs Media Library, but it could be a CD you haven't ripped yet, or another playlist.

5   Drill down in the list of artists and their albums until you can see a track you want. Highlight the tracks you want to add to your playlist, as in Figure 9-20.

6   You can select multiple tracks at once by highlighting one track, then holding down the shift key, and clicking on a second track to highlight it. All the tracks positioned between the two mouse clicks will be highlighted. When you have a range of consecutive tracks highlighted, you can add or remove individual tracks by holding down the control key and clicking on a track to toggle whether it is selected or not. When you drag the mouse over and release the left button while over the playlist, all those highlighted tracks will be moved to the playlist.

Note in Figure 9-20 that Lsongs shows you the total size of the playlist as you add to it. If you go over about 680 MB, it won't fit on a CD. The size is displayed at the bottom center of the Lsongs window.

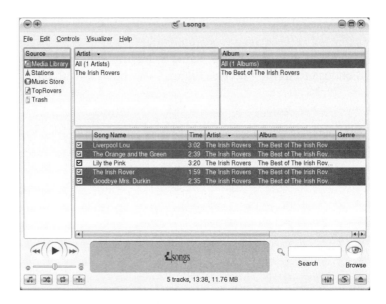

Figure 9-20   Highlighting the tracks you want to add to your new playlist

7   To remove a track from a playlist, display the playlist (double-click on the playlist in the Source window), right-click on the track, and choose **Remove from Playlist**.

Burning and Using MP3s

This section covers using Lsongs to burn a CD of MP3s, as well as topics related to IPods and more.

Burning a Playlist of MP3s

Once your playlist is complete, you can play it in Lsongs or burn it on a CD. To burn the tracks, first select the format for the CD: do you want this to be an audio CD or an MP3 CD? An MP3 CD can hold many more tracks, but it might not play in older CD players, and the quality will be lower than an audio CD. If you're playing the CD in a poor listening environment like a car, you probably won't notice the difference.

1   Choose **File > Preferences > CD tab > Burn Disc Format**. Figure 9-21 shows this window.

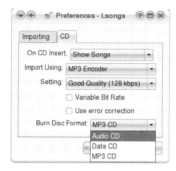

Figure 9-21   Choosing audio, MP3, or data format

2   Click on the playlist in the source column if it is not already highlighted. When there is a playlist open, the Lsongs window will display a Burn button prominently at the bottom right. Insert a recordable CD in the drive, and click the **Burn** button.

3   The bottom of the Lsongs window changes to display the burn status. If you asked for an audio CD format, Lsongs will first convert all the tracks from MP3 to AIFF format, which takes a little longer than just burning the MP3s directly. See Figure 9-22 for an example window just after starting to burn an audio CD.

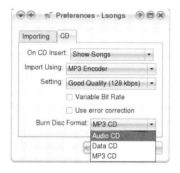

Figure 9-22   Burning a playlist

Burning an audio format CD from Lsongs won't magically reacquire the CD audio quality that was lost when the tunes were automatically converted to MP3 as you imported them into Lsongs. If you want high-quality mixed CDs, you should rip, copy, and assemble the original AIFF or WAV files manually, not pass them through Lsongs on the way!

The Apple iPod and Linux

Many people also like to transfer their music files to an MP3 player, and by far the most popular one is Apple's iPod product. The iPod is essentially an elementary PDA with a miniaturized FireWire disk drive and some music playing hardware and software. Good as Lsongs is, many people would like to see iTunes ported to Linux so they can load their iPod from Linux. Apple would certainly find it easier to port iTunes from one version of Unix (MacOS X) to another (Linux) than it was to port it to Windows.

Porting iTunes to Linux doesn't serve a strategic purpose for Apple. So it probably won't happen any time soon, but there other avenues. Alan Donovan has a web site at http://people.csail.mit.edu/people/adonovan/hacks/ipod.html explaining how to access the iPod disk from Linux using a PCMCIA card and the GtkPod software. Apple doesn't, and doesn't want to, make it easy to use the iPod with Linux, and you might want to look for MP3 players that are more Linux-friendly.

The CodeWeavers organization sells a $40 product called Crossover Office that lets you run some Windows applications on Linux. Crossover Office is based on the open source Wine Windows emulator. Wine is not a layer on top of Windows, and you don't need a copy of Windows at all to use Wine or Crossover Office.

CodeWeavers supports iTunes at their bronze level, meaning you can install iTunes and access some of its fundamental features. Some users report difficulty with it, though. You can visit CodeWeavers at http://www.codeweavers.com.

More About Lsongs

Linspire intends that Lsongs will match most features of Apple's iTunes. Most features are working in Lsongs now, and some are placeholders for future releases.

One piece that works today is radio-over-the-Internet streaming. Many radio stations stream a data feed of their broadcasts over the Internet for anyone who wants to listen. Often there is a both a high-bandwidth and a low-bandwidth version of these feeds.

Figure 9-23 illustrates the way you listen to Internet radio stations via Lsongs. Select Stations on the source, then scroll down to use the search field to find a particular station or artist of interest.

Figure 9-23   Lsongs can play streaming radio stations

Figure 9-23 also shows the results of a search for Imus, the radio interviewer and brash New York disk jockey Don Imus. As well as finding several stations carrying Imus' show, the search also highlights other stations that match the string such as Radio Kimmimusic from Italy.

Scroll down the Lsongs page of results, and click on the **Tune in** button for the station that interests you.

The radio station feature in Lsongs is a front end for the Shoutcast streaming audio services from Nullsoft.

LSongs Music Store

From the late 1990s up to its first demise in mid 2001, the success of Napster demonstrated the huge consumer demand for online music. Unfortunately the record industry, correctly recognizing that the Internet threatened its monopoly on music distribution and incorrectly citing piracy, did everything it could to frustrate digital music. Take a look at Courtney Love's web page if you want to see an artist's perspective on record companies: http://www.therecordindustry.com/courtney_artist_rights.htm.

The recording industry was quick to blame Internet piracy for a drop in CD sales from the year 2000, but in August 2002 Forrester Research refuted that claim. Forrester showed that the recession and increased competition from video games and DVDs had caused the two-year 15% drop in music sales. Forrester further predicted that digital music revenues would rise to $2 billion if record labels embraced online sales without monthly fees.

It wasn't until April 2003 that Steve Jobs, CEO of Apple, was able to line up record industry support for Apple's iTunes music store. ITunes allows customers to sample 30 seconds of any track, and buy individual tracks at 99 cents each. The track is immediately downloaded to the purchaser's computer. It can be stored on up to five computers at a time, and you can't burn a playlist more than seven times without making a change to it. Naturally iTunes and the iPod work smoothly together to deliver superior digital music on the desktop and on the road.

Lsongs has an icon for Music Store in the Source part of the window. The Lsongs Music Store passes you through to http://mp3tunes.com. Customers can browse the catalog there, listen to previews, purchase, and download. The browser interface lets users purchase music without requiring Lsongs.

In contrast to all the other music stores selling online music, Linspire will deliver MP3 files untainted by software rights restrictions. The downside is that the catalog is smaller, and consists mostly of independent artists and smaller labels. Mainstream record companies are still fighting to retain their distribution monopoly and won't participate without software restrictions. See the web site http://www.virtualrecordings.com/mp3.htm for background information on the saga.

Playing Movie DVDs

Linspire uses the gmplayer application to play video DVDs, as in Figure 9-24. Gmplayer is the GUI version of the popular command line mplayer software, which has its web site at http://www.mplayerhq.hu. To play a copy-protected DVD (most Hollywood movies), you need more software, available in CNR. I'll explain how to download equivalent software for free from another site.

Figure 9-24   The mplayer application plays movie DVDs

Gmplayer has a coder/decoder (codec) for almost every audio and video format and can play nearly everything. It even plays Microsoft-proprietary .wmv files— Linspire licenses the necessary codec source code from Microsoft.

Starting the mplayer DVD Player from the Command Line

If you want to invoke mplayer from the command line to play a DVD, the command is as follows:

```
mplayer dvd://1
```

The URL-like thing is the device-independent way of telling mplayer to find the DVD on the system.

Full-Screen DVD Playing

When gmplayer starts, it is usually in a configuration of 720 by 480 pixels. To use full screen mode, you need a video card that has direct rendering. Direct rendering means that software can write bytes representing individual pixels directly to frame buffer memory. This is a direct hardware interface, and far faster than graphics cards which only support a software interface through the device driver.

To check if your video card supports direct rendering, type the command:

```
glxinfo | grep direct
```

Output that includes

```
direct rendering: Yes
```

means that you can expand gmplayer to the full screen. If you don't see that output, then you either need a better graphics card or a better graphics driver.

To see if a better driver will solve it, right-click on gmplayer interface, then select **Preferences**. In the video tab, change the video driver from X11 to xv, which supports direct rendering. Then right-click again and choose **Preferences** > **Full screen**.

Encrypted DVDs

To play encrypted DVD movies (most commercial movies) with a player approved by the DVD Copy Control Association, you will need the DVD Player from CNR. It costs a few dollars. The charge covers the licensing cost of the software to decrypt the files on the DVD. Linspire doesn't bundle it, because that would burden everyone with the cost, including those who do not have a DVD player on their PC. Only when DVD players are as universal as CD drives now are, will it make sense to bundle the player software.

The topic of encrypted movie DVDs has been a contentious one in the past few years. Movie studios are terrified of getting Napstered and having their products distributed for free across the Internet. As a result they have successfully lobbied for legislation to extend the copyright period, and to make it a criminal offence to use your own decryption software to play your own DVD movies. The copyright period in the USA is now an astonishing 120 years from the date of creation of a commercial work.

Many people believe the laws have gone too far, unfairly gifting extra rights to the movie studios by taking away some well-established consumer rights, such as the right to run whatever software you see fit on your own PC, and the right to make a personal backup copy of a DVD you have purchased.

If you live in a part of the world that is not beholden to the Motion Picture Association of America, you can obtain a free open source library that will decrypt DVD movies so you can play them in mplayer. Add this line to the /etc/apt/sources.list file:

```
deb ftp://ftp.nerim.net/debian-marillat/ unstable main
```

Save the file and type these commands:

```
apt-get update
apt-get install libdvdcss2
```

The mplayer application is well-designed, and will automatically use the decryption library if it is there.

Alternatively, you can get a very good DVD player called vlc from the web site http://www.videolan.org. All of these players are threatened by the use of software patents. All important multimedia techniques and formats are covered by broad and trivial patents. Software patents have the bad effect of preventing competition, without the good original intent of patents—to reduce trade secrets, thereby encouraging competition. Don't get me started on software patents. There's a great explanation of the issues in the document titled *Why can't I patent my movie?*" at http://www.ffii.se/dokument/filmpatent_eng.html

Making a Backup Copy of a Movie DVD

This section describes how to make a backup copy of a DVD that contains a movie. This might be a professionally produced movie of a wedding in your family, some video that you shot yourself, or some other video. As long as the DVD files follow the standard format, you'll be able to make a backup copy by following this procedure.

The DVD video standard format uses a folder called VIDEO_TS at the top level on the DVD, containing .VOB and .IFO files.

- The .VOB files hold the MPEG2 video and Dolby audio signal and are split so that each is 1 GB or less in size.

- The .IFO files store the formatting information telling the DVD player the aspect ratio, subtitles, languages, and menus for the corresponding .VOB file.

You will need a DVD drive that can burn DVDs (not just CDs). The two most popular kinds of DVD burner are DVD+RW and DVD-RW. Either will work, but you cannot use one type of media in the other type of drive.

You can also use K3b to back up some kinds of DVD to your hard disk and to encode to an MPEG-4 compliant AVI file. As with CD burning, K3B is only a GUI interface to underlying command line tools. In the case of DVDs, K3b is the front end to that Swiss army knife of Linux tools, the transcode program.

This section presents a longer, but more general way of backing up a wider range of DVDs without using K3b. You need to install several new programs and libraries on your system, and a summary of the process is:

1   Update the sources.list file to say where to find the software. See *Update the sources.list File*.

2   Get the Debian-packaged software using apt-get, and get the compiler tools if you didn't already. See *Get the Debian-Packaged Software* on page 332.

3   Get the unpackaged software by downloading another two programs manually, then build and install them. See *Get the Unpackaged Software* on page 333.

4   Edit the configuration file. See *Edit the Configuration File* on page 335.

5   You can then make all the DVD backups you want. See *Make a DVD Backup* on page 335.

Update the sources.list File

The section *Using Debian's Advanced Packaging Tool* on page 216 described software packaging in the Debian distro (Linspire is based on Debian). You might want to briefly review that.

Sarge Sid Woody reporting for duty

Any software that is under active development will exist in several versions. The Debian distro of Linux is no exception. It has three variants which currently have the code names woody, sid, and sarge. The Debian code names are all characters from the movie Toy Story.

- The build currently shipping is called the stable build. This build doesn't change except in rare circumstances, such as fixing security holes. In the Debian distro, this is currently the Debian GNU/Linux 3.0 release made in July 2002, code-named woody. A previous release, Debian 2.2, was called potato.

- The next release under active development is constantly changing and hence known as the unstable build. State of the art build might be a better name. This build will never get officially released, but packages can be downloaded for use at your own risk. Packages from the unstable build will propagate into the testing build and the testing build will eventually be blessed as a real release. In the Debian distro, the current unstable build is code-named sid. Linspire 5.0 is based on a snapshot of sid from January 2005, extensively tested/updated for stability.

- *Between stable and unstable builds, there is a testing build. This will eventually be the next major release after woody, probably numbered Debian GNU/Linux 3.1. The Debian testing build is code-named sarge. The release date for sarge is driven by content, not date. Sarge will use gcc 3.3 as the default compiler, and many other components will be brought up-to-date too. When the features is in place and working, sarge will replace woody as the current release.*

Tell the apt utilities about a new server it should search for the software you want. To do so, make sure these three lines are in the following file:

```
/etc/apt/sources.list
deb ftp://ftp.us.debian.org/debian/ sid main  contrib  non-free
deb http://non-us.debian.org/debian-non-US sid/non-US main contrib non-free
deb ftp://ftp.nerim.net/debian-marillat/ unstable main
```

The first two lines may be in the file already, but are commented out by a # at the start of the line. If so, remove the # character after checking that the rest of the line matches what is written here. You might see the word sid instead of the word unstable; they are synonyms in this context and indicate the Debian release that is currently under development.

After making the changes, save the file and exit the editor, then run this command to tell apt about the new places to look for software:

```
apt-get update
```

You might get output similar to this, or you might not if your system is up to date.

```
Get:1 ftp://ftp.us.debian.org sid/main Packages [3385kB]
Get:2 ftp://non-us.debian.org sid/non-US/main Packages [5116B]
Get:3 ftp://ftp.nerim.net unstable/main Packages [16.9kB]
Get:4 ftp://non-us.debian.org sid/non-US/main Release [89B]
Get:5 ftp://ftp.nerim.net unstable/main Release [112B]
Get:6 ftp://non-us.debian.org sid/non-US/contrib Packages [20B]
Get:7 ftp://non-us.debian.org sid/non-US/contrib Release [92B]
Get:8 ftp://non-us.debian.org sid/non-US/non-free Packages [1440B]
Get:9 ftp://non-us.debian.org sid/non-US/non-free Release [93B]
Get:10 ftp://ftp.us.debian.org sid/main Release [82B]
Get:11 ftp://ftp.us.debian.org sid/contrib Packages [74.5kB]
Get:12 ftp://ftp.us.debian.org sid/contrib Release [85B]
Get:13 ftp://ftp.us.debian.org sid/non-free Packages [68.8kB]
```

```
Get:14 ftp://ftp.us.debian.org sid/non-free Release [86B]
Fetched 3553kB in 27s (129kB/s)
Reading Package Lists... Done
```

That completes the first step.

Get the Debian-Packaged Software

Download the libraries and software that have been packaged in the Debian format. If you didn't already install the compiler tools, do so now with these two commands.

If you're not sure whether you did it or not, do it again and apt-get will tell you if they are already installed.

```
apt-get install g++
apt-get install make
```

Next, download three packages with the commands below:

```
apt-get install dvdauthor
apt-get install libdvdread3-dev
apt-get install libdvdcss2
```

The first package shows an example of software dependency. You will see that it also installs three libraries that dvdauthor depends on (needs in order to run).

The output for all three apt-gets is similar. The first one looks like this:

```
# apt-get install dvdauthor
Reading Package Lists... Done
Building Dependency Tree... Done
The following extra packages will be installed:
  libdvdread3 libfribidi0 libmagick6
The following NEW packages will be installed:
  dvdauthor libdvdread3 libfribidi0 libmagick6
0 upgraded, 4 newly installed, 0 to remove and 110 not upgraded.
Need to get 1428kB of archives.
After unpacking 4661kB of additional disk space will be used.
Do you want to continue? [Y/n]
```

Note that you need to type Y to answer the continue? question.

Get the Unpackaged Software

Download the libraries and software that have not been packaged in the debian format. Some developers prefer to package their software for one particular distro, such as Red Hat (.rpm files) or Debian (.deb files). That's more work for the developer and restricts the package to a specific distro.

Other developers provide the source code, and let you compile for whatever distro you are using.

Get Streamdvd

You need to download and install the streamdvd application. Go to the web page http://www.badabum.de/streamdvd.html and click on the link for the latest over time. If streamdvd is not found on that site, then do a web search for it, and also check the web site for this book http://afu.com/linux.

Right-click on the link and choose **Save link target as**. I like to save to the desktop, so I can find downloads easily. The streamdvd file is only 20 KB in size. Unpack it with:

```
tar -xvzf streamdvd-0.4.tar.gz
```

You can also use the Ark GUI to unpack the file. Click **Launch** > **Programs** > **Utilities** > **Archiving Tool**.

The tar file is well behaved and unpacks into a folder of its own, rather than dumping the many files into the folder where you unpack it. Type cd to move into that directory and build and install the software with the commands. Use the pathname and version number that apply to your system, not mine.

```
cd StreamDVD-0.4
make
make install
```

When I compiled the program, I got a number of compiler warnings like these:

```
# make
g++ -g -Wall -ldvdread -lm -o streamdvd -I. -Implex streamdvd.c requant.c mplex/*.c mplex/*.cpp
streamdvd.c: In function `void get_av_delay()':
streamdvd.c:176: warning: converting to `int' from `double'
requant.c: In function `int slice_init(int)':
```

requant.c:1434: warning: comparison between signed and unsigned integer
expressions

requant.c: In function `void mpeg2_slice(int)':

mplex/zalphastrm_in.cpp:307: warning: int format, different type arg (arg 4)

None of these are significant, and when I finish this manuscript I will send the fixes for them to the developer responsible for streamdvd. That's the way open source works.

The make install puts a copy of the streamdvd executable in directory /usr/local/bin. So you either need to add that directory to your execution search path or use the simpler approach of copying the streamdvd executable to the /usr/bin directory:

cp streamdvd /usr/bin/

Get lxdvdrip

You'll now carry out the same steps to get and install the lxdvdrip program. Web page http://developer.berlios.de/projects/lxdvdrip/ is the home of lxdvdrip (January 2005), but do a web search if it is not there.

The download links are at the foot of the web page. Click on the latest stable one, which was 1.43 in mid-2005 but is probably higher now. The click will take you to another web page.

Select the source .gz (gzipped tar file of source code) for the latest stable version, and download to your desktop. The file is about 0.5 MB in size.

Unpack it with tar or the Ark GUI tool.

tar -xvzf lxdvdrip-1.41-2.tgz

Then use cd to get into the lxdvdrip directory and use the make and make install commands as shown:

cd ~/Desktop/lxdvdrip
make
make install
cp lxdvdrip /usr/bin

The lxdvdrip program puts a configuration file in /etc/lxdvdrip.conf and the following section *Edit the Configuration File* explains how to adjust that for Linspire.

Edit the Configuration File

As always, before changing a configuration file, make a backup copy:

```
cd /etc
cp lxdvdrip.conf lxdvdrip.conf.bak
```

Using your favorite editor, open the configuration file /etc/lxdvdrip.conf. It's a file of about 200 lines, but most of those are comments. The bad news is most of the comments are in German! Change these lines in the file to what is shown here, and leave the other lines alone. Check the book web site for other updates.

```
audio=2
dvdleser=/dev/hdc
dvdbrenner=/dev/hdc
language=en
speed=1
```

The pathname /dev/hdc is the DVD reader device and also the DVD burner device on my system, and probably yours too. You can confirm this by reading *Learning About Your CD/DVD Drives* on page 340. If you have two DVD drives, you can use one for reading and one for writing; dvdleser is the reading drive, while dvdbrenner is the burning drive. Linspire 4.5 used the Linux 2.4 kernel, and the DVD device was referred to as 0,0,0 or something similar. This was the old SCSI-style addressing of target, bus, and logical unit.

That completes the one-time setup work. You're now ready to back up a DVD.

Make a DVD Backup

All the foregoing steps are part of the one-time setup. When you've completed that, you only need a single command to make a backup copy of a DVD.

The Burning Process

Put the DVD you want to back up into the drive, and issue the following command:

```
lxdvdrip
```

Assuming you completed all the setup correctly, the program prints out a list of the configuration choices and goes to work.

It might take two or three hours to make a backup copy of a DVD—there's a huge amount of data on it. And you might need 8–12 GB of free disk space. The program shows a status line saying something like STAT: VOBU 2646 at 639 MB, 1 PGCS. As those numbers go up, you can see that the program is still at work.

top Command

You can also check on lxdvdrip or any program by running the top command. top shows you the busiest 20 or so processes on your PC and gives information about how long each has been running and how much memory each is using.

After lxdvdrip has copied all the data from the DVD and compressed it to fit on a consumer DVD-RW or +RW, it will display the files it has created like this:

```
INFO: dvdauthor creating table of contents
INFO: Scanning /tmp/film-dvd/VIDEO_TS/VTS_01_0.IFO
eject /dev/hdc
Files in Video-Directory:
ls -C -s -h /tmp/film-dvd/VIDEO_TS/*
8.0K /tmp/film-dvd/VIDEO_TS/VIDEO_TS.BUP
8.0K /tmp/film-dvd/VIDEO_TS/VIDEO_TS.IFO
76K /tmp/film-dvd/VIDEO_TS/VTS_01_0.BUP
76K /tmp/film-dvd/VIDEO_TS/VTS_01_0.IFO
1.1G /tmp/film-dvd/VIDEO_TS/VTS_01_1.VOB
1.1G /tmp/film-dvd/VIDEO_TS/VTS_01_2.VOB
1.1G /tmp/film-dvd/VIDEO_TS/VTS_01_3.VOB
654M /tmp/film-dvd/VIDEO_TS/VTS_01_4.VOB
To start preview with mplayer, please press Enter (C=Cancel):
```

It will eject the DVD, allowing you to insert a recordable DVD. It doesn't matter whether you respond with ENTER or C to the question about previewing with mplayer—the version of lxdvdrip that I tested started mplayer regardless (a bug).

Exit mplayer as usual by clicking on the x icon at the top right of its window.

Once you've killed mplayer, the program will start the transfer of the file backup to the DVD+RW. It can take 30 minutes or an hour to burn the DVD, depending on how much data you are backing up. The DVD drive will eject the platter when it has finished, and you should make sure the finished results give you what you expected.

Sound and Burner Troubleshooting

There are two kinds of problems that you might run into with sounds and CDs.

First, if you have a notebook PC, it's quite possible that the sound system (rarely a selling point of a notebook) won't work well, or won't work at all.

Second, you might find that—in spite of carefully following all the steps in this chapter—you can't burn a DVD. One problem here is the novelty of DVD burners. At this time (early 2005) DVD burners are not ubiquitous. Therefore there are still a few corner cases and pathological problems to work out in the software. This is equally true for DVD burners under Windows, too.

Sound Advice

Let's deal with sound hardware that doesn't work under Linux, but works under Windows. First, check that your speakers are not muted, and turn the volume way up. Any remaining issue is almost always the same old problem: PC manufacturers try to cut costs, so they use the cheapest sound chipset they can find. If someone offers them a different sound chipset, almost as good and 10 cents cheaper, they'll switch to it immediately.

Your PC ends up with a proprietary sound chipset that needs a one-off special device driver. That chipset won't work with any of the standard sound device drivers that come with Linux or Windows. The vendor gets sound working under Windows by preinstalling a special driver, but Linux users are left hanging. My recently purchased, high-end, expensive HP Pavilion zx5070 laptop has this issue.

The problem will diminish as vendors increasingly see they lose sales when they disadvantage Linux customers. Vendors will still use the cheapest possible hardware, but they'll make Linux drivers available too. nVidia already provides Linux drivers for their video cards, and other vendors are getting the message.

Hunting for the Right Sound Driver

The first resort for balky sound devices is to make sure you have a device driver for the sound hardware. Going this route is for experts only.

1   Find out exactly what sound hardware you have.

The sound hardware typically plugs into the PCI bus, so list the hardware on the PCI bus using the command lspci, and use the command grep to just print the lines with the string audio as follows.

```
lspci | grep audio
```

```
0000:00:07.5 Multimedia audio controller: Yamaha OPL3-SA3 AC97 Audio Controller
```

So this PC has a sound system based on the OPL3-SA3 chip set from Yamaha.

2 Find a driver for that sound hardware.

Take a look at this directory; use the correct kernel version number for your installation.

```
# find /lib/modules/2.6.10/kernel/sound/drivers -name \*.\*o -print
```

```
mpu401.ko snd-aloop.ko snd-portman2x4.ko    snd-virmidi.ko snd-opl3-lib.ko
```

That directory and its subdirectories contain the sound drivers that are bundled with Linspire. Does one of these drivers have the same or similar name as the sound device on your PC? Why, yes! The opl3-sa3 chip closely matches the snd-opl3-lib.ko driver. That suggests that you have a device driver for this sound device, and so the problem lies elsewhere.

If there was no match, then search the web to locate a Linux driver for that chipset, and compile it yourself. Then put the .ko file in the sound/drivers directory.

3 Install the driver on your Linux PC.

Assume that you have located the driver, which will be an .o or .ko file. Follow the instructions that come with the driver to compile and install it. Typical instructions are make; make install. Load the driver into the kernel manually by typing (use the name of the module for your own chipset, not opl3 as here, and omit the .o or .ko suffix):

```
# modprobe snd-opl3-lib
```

You can check that the driver loaded correctly by typing this command and checking that the driver now appears in the output.

```
# lsmod | grep snd
```

If this all went smoothly, and sound now works, add the name of the driver module to the configuration file /etc/modules. Again, omit the .o or .ko suffix. That file contains a list of modules that are loaded automatically on each boot. Make sure the line you add comes ahead of any other lines containing snd, so that your driver will be the one preferred by the kernel.

If you can't make this work for you, the last resort could be the suggestion in the following section *Use a New Sound Device*.

Use a New Sound Device

Another possible workaround for the lack of a sound device driver is to fit sound hardware that does have a Linux driver. One such device is the Sound Blaster MP3+ USB adapter available for $35–45. This is an external box that plugs into a USB port. You then plug external speakers into the box.

These devices are supported by the Advanced Linux Sound Architecture (ALSA) used in the Linspire distro. ALSA has a home page at http://www.alsa-project.org if you want to check on support for some other vendor or chipset. If you attach a Soundblaster MP3+ and speakers, you need to tell the kernel to use this instead of any other sound devices you have. Restart your PC using the Redetect option on the boot screen. This will scan for new hardware that requires a device driver.

Next, you will edit the kernel configuration file /etc/modules. Make the usual back-up copy before you change this or any system file. The /etc/modules file contains a list of device drivers to be loaded at boot time (other device drivers are linked in with the kernel or loaded when you need them).

The file is only one or two dozen lines long, and each line containing snd-represents a device driver for a sound device. Whichever sound driver is listed first in /etc/modules will get loaded first, and the hardware it controls will become the sound device that all programs default to using.

If the line

```
snd-usb-audio
```

is not in the file, add it. Make sure that line appears before any other lines that have snd- in the name. Save the file and quit the editor.

This will ensure that the USB sound driver comes before any other sound drivers. Now reboot the computer and play a CD to confirm it works. Before you buy one of these Soundblaster MP3+ boxes, check the Linspire forums or the book web site at http://afu.com/linux for new information.

Learning About Your CD/DVD Drives

To learn more details of your CD and DVD drives, use the command cat. All files in the /proc filesystem contain information about some aspect of the system.

```
cat /proc/sys/dev/cdrom/info
CD-ROM information, Id: cdrom.c 3.20 2003/12/17
```

	hdd	hdc
drive name:	hdd	hdc
drive speed:	32	20
drive # of slots:	1	1
Can close tray:	1	1
Can open tray:	1	1
Can lock tray:	1	1
Can change speed:	1	1
Can select disk:	0	0
Can read multisession:	1	1
Can read MCN:	1	1
Reports media changed:	1	1
Can play audio:	1	1
Can write CD-R:	1	0
Can write CD-RW:	**1**	**0**
Can read DVD:	**0**	**1**
Can write DVD-R:	0	0
Can write DVD-RAM:	0	0
Can read MRW:	1	1
Can write MRW:	1	1
Can write RAM:	1	1

If you have two or more drives you get one column for each drive, as in this example. A 1 in a column means yes, a 0 means no. So for example, the two rows in larger font in the previous list say that the /dev/hdd device can write CD-RW platters, and the /dev/hdc device can read DVDs.

Under Linspire 4.5 and older Linuxes, the equivalent command to get information on the CD drives is cdrecord -scanbus.

Burner Problems

If you are having problems burning, follow these steps in this order

1   Make certain you are using media appropriate to the drive. It is easy to overlook the difference between DVD+R (with a +) and DVD-R (with a -) but the two media types are not interchangeable. After the media has been written it can be read in any type of DVD drive.

2   Use a new pack of Verbatim CD-Rs (among the best CD-R media you can buy). If you can't get Verbatim, try to get media from whoever made the drive, such as Sony. If you can't match the drive, get platters from another high quality vendor like Memorex, Fuji, or HP. Any computer product that advertises itself with a name like "Great Quality" isn't.

3   If the problem is a platter stuck in the CD drive, unfold a paper clip and gently insert it in the paper-clip-wire sized hole at the front of the tray. All CD drives are built with this emergency release, which connects to the mechanical tray eject arm.

4   Burn at the slowest speed your drive supports. I have burned so many coasters (dud CDs and DVDs) on so many operating systems, that I now prefer the slowest possible setting. It invariably gives less wasteful results.

5   Thoroughly search the web sites of both the PC vendor and the driver vendor to see if there is a firmware update or a Linux driver update for this drive.

6   Consider using the strace debugging aide, described in Appendix F, "Troubleshooting with Strace," on page 573.

7   If you have a dual-boot system (see Chapter 12, "Installation and Boot," for the definition of dual-boot), find out whether you can burn this kind of CD using this drive under Windows.

8   Find out whether you can burn this kind of CD using this drive under another distro of Linux, such as Klaus Knopper's excellent Knoppix distribution, at http://www.knoppix.net/ which is also Debian based.

9   Write down any error messages that you get from using cdrecord to burn from the command line. Use these commands to do a test burn:

```
mkisofs -R -r -l -J -o mydata.iso folder-name
cdrecord -v -pad speed=1 dev=/dev/hdc mydata.iso
```

The folder name is the folder that contains the files you want to put on CD. Use the correct drive name for your CD device in place of /dev/hdc.

To see the CD drive name, use this command:

`cat /proc/sys/dev/cdrom/info`

10 Do a web and newsgroup search for any error message that you see in the previous step. Email someone who mentions it and ask how he or she solved the problem.

Legends of Linux—The Windows trademark

The Linspire company did not always have that name. The company started under the name Lindows, to suggest the blend of Linux quality coupled with a window-based operating system. Things went fine for the first couple of years, but as Linux matured into a highly acceptable Windows replacement, Microsoft got concerned about the growing popularity of Linux.

Microsoft surreptitiously funded the SCO group, a failing Utah-based software company that was trying to charge royalties on Linux. SCO claimed that IBM and others had tainted Linux by contributing code to which SCO had rights. SCO has never given details of what that code might be, and when details have slipped out, SCO has been shown to be mistaken.

Microsoft funded SCO with $30M directly in the guise of license fees and introduced them to venture capital backers who came through with another $50M. The Microsoft puppet show was revealed when an email leaked from the venture capitalist who brokered the deal. Microsoft and SCO made red-faced denials, but were unable to refute the email or provide an alternative explanation.

The Microsoft war chest allowed SCO to hire top legal talent in its campaign to force Linux vendors to pay royalties. By mid-2005 SCO's treasure chest had almost run out, without convincing a single judge or Linux vendor that SCO was entitled to a dime. You can read more about this disgraceful episode at the site http://www.groklaw.net.

Some industry watchers think that Microsoft's next sneaky attempt to subvert Linux will come in the form of patent infringement claims. Issuing patents for software is a controversial new U.S. policy, which benefits a few big companies at the expense of the public and smaller companies. The EU is about to make the same disastrous policy mistake of granting patents on software. Software patents form a topic that deserves a chapter of its own. Only it can't have one.

In early 2005, IBM announced free use by open source developers of 500 of its software patents. Many people interpreted IBM's action as a warning to Microsoft that IBM wouldn't stand for attempts to tie Linux up in spurious patent litigation. IBM, one of the most-established computer companies, makes extensive use of Linux in its products and is a huge supporter of Linux software.

Around this time Microsoft launched a trademark infringement suit against Lindows, as the company was then called. In Microsoft's view, Lindows was close enough to the Windows trademark that customers may get confused over what they were getting.

Trademarks are protected from unauthorized use in proportion to how distinctive they are. A made-up word like Kodak or Velcro is tightly protected. Dictionary words that aren't connected to the line of business, like Apple for computers or Eagle for pencils, are also fully protected.

Descriptive terms are one notch lower in the hierarchy of tradenames. Descriptive terms are words that apply to the business in some way, such as Holiday Inn or Burger King. It is only fair to give less protection to descriptive terms. Otherwise a business could trademark several common descriptions for its products and lock out competitors from ever using those words.

On the other hand, after five years in use a descriptive term is held to have acquired secondary meaning as a brand name. It can be registered and protected like other trademarks. But a lawsuit over a purely descriptive term is unpredictable and might be decided in favor of either party.

At the bottom of the pile are generic term trademarks. These don't describe the product; they actually are the common name for the product, such as shoe or beer. You don't see many names like this as trademarks because anyone can use them. They are not registrable and can't be infringed.

In a nasty surprise for Microsoft, Lindows based its defense case on the validity or otherwise of the trademark on Windows. Lindows argued in court that the name Windows was a generic term, and therefore not even eligible for trademark protection.

Microsoft countered Lindow's defense by pointing out that no one who wanted to buy a computer operating system would go into a software store and say I'm looking for a windows. They'd say "I'm looking for an operating system." They might even say, "I'm looking for a windows-based operating system," using the term adjectivally to describe the frames of a GUI. But, said Microsoft's lawyer, in no sense is "windows" the common word the public uses for "operating system." Microsoft acknowledged that, in this context, Windows is a descriptive term, but they invoked the five year rule, and claimed it was now a protectable brand name.

Clever, but not quite clever enough. Linspire responded in the obvious way. The Lindows legal team said that it doesn't matter what the part of speech is. An adjective can be a generic term just as well as a noun can. They said that Microsoft used the term Windows simply as a short form of windows-based operating system, which is, itself, a generic term for a specific type of operating system.

The Federal judge in Seattle showed signs of accepting Lindows' argument. He noted that people have used "windows" to describe a GUI before, during, and after the launch of Microsoft's current operating system. He pointed out that a dictionary definition of "windows" matched the way Lindows used the term. And he denied Microsoft's request for a preliminary injunction preventing Lindows from using its trademark.

Realizing that things were going badly, Microsoft looked for another strategy to roll over Lindows. They found one. Lindows sells a lot of its product overseas. Microsoft started bringing individual trademark cases in many European countries. Suddenly Lindows wasn't fighting one case in the U.S. It was fighting ten cases in ten different countries, needing to hire local attorneys in each place. A common legal strategy is to try to exhaust the financial resources of a less well-funded adversary.

The European judges started making preliminary rulings that Lindows could not use the mark, as it was too similar to "windows". Obviously "windows" is not a generic dictionary word in Belgium, Holland, etc. So the "generic word" defense might not be available to Lindows. To Belgian eyes, all you have is two made-up words that rhyme with each other.

But Lindows was bolstered by the legal doctrine known as "foreign equivalents". It says when a term is descriptive or generic in its own language, then using it overseas will not make it any stronger or entitle it to greater trademark protection. However, not every country recognizes this; and the protection of trademarks is on a country-by-country basis. All Microsoft had to do was cherry-pick the venues that didn't recognize foreign equivalents. It looked like Lindows was all set to lose these cases, and the company briefly had to stop shipping products in Belgium.

Lindows asked the judge in the United States to order Microsoft to stop the European actions, pending the result of the U.S. case. The judge refused that request, but he did something just as good. He intimated that, while he wouldn't order Microsoft to hold the European cases, Microsoft could either proceed with the overseas cases, or with the case in his court, but not both. It's not clear why he reached this decision. Maybe he thought the Belgians needed a reminder to lay off the lace-and-foamy-beer, and get with the "foreign equivalents" program.

Microsoft intended the case to be about whether Lindows was too similar to Windows. But it turned out to be about whether Windows is a generic word or a descriptive word in the United States. Microsoft didn't want that kind of debate at all. Microsoft has been unwise in choosing generic names for many brands: Windows for the windows-based operating system, Office for the office application suite, Project for the project tracking software, Pocket PC for the PC that fits in your pocket, and so on. The prospect of losing the Windows brand name was too awful for them to contemplate, but it was one possible outcome.

Weighing the risks against the benefits, Microsoft immediately offered to drop the case. The Lindows guys said "Wait a minute, you sued us! In umpteen different countries!" The negotiators got to work, and reached agreement. All the terms of the settlement were kept secret, but here's what happened. Lindows changed its name to Linspire. Microsoft forked over $20M to Linspire. Linspire used the settlement to pay for the creation of Linspire 5.0. And everyone was happy. Or, at least, relieved.

## CHAPTER 10

Sharing on Your Local Network

Introduction to Workgroup Networking

This chapter assumes that all of the following are true:

- You have two or more PCs at home.

- They are connected on some form of local area network, either wired or wireless, of the kind shown in Figure 10-1 on page 351.

- You want to share files or a printer on one PC with another PC.

If any of those prerequisites are not true, you might want to skip this chapter and return as the need arises.

Two Approaches to Networking

The Apple Mac, Linspire, and Windows XP all include software that lets PCs on the same network share files and printers. If you only have one PC, or you don't have a network connecting your PCs, you might be unaware of this Microsoft Windows Workgroup Networking feature. I'll briefly review it here, and then look at how Linspire fits in with it.

Microsoft has two approaches to networking Windows PCs:

- The **workgroup network**. As the name unfortunately doesn't suggest, this is a very simple kind of network intended for use within a home, not a business environment. Microsoft also calls this peer-to-peer networking.

  A workgroup network is set up and turned on for you when you run the XP wizard to set up an Internet connection between a host on your network and your ISP. A Microsoft workgroup network has very little security.

- The **domain network**. This kind of Microsoft network is intended for commercial and business environments. It supports the fine-grained network and security policies that an organization may want to impose.

  Domain networks are a heavyweight approach intended for networks with more than three or four computers. A system administrator is needed to set up a domain network and keep one running. PCs running Windows XP Home Edition cannot be part of a domain network.

This chapter describes Windows XP workgroup networking, the low-overhead local file-sharing approach that you get by default. If you're in a domain network in a business environment, ask your network administrator how to use the network to share files and printers with Linux.

Network Security Warning!

The features described in this chapter rely on Microsoft's workgroup file sharing protocol, which was not designed with security as a consideration.

Some network worms explicitly target and exploit Microsoft file sharing. Almost as bad, the Windows file sharing has some quirky bugs, and occasionally just doesn't work, for no readily apparent reason. I found the Windows implementation a bit fragile in some places. Sometimes I had to do something twice to get it to work. When in doubt, reboot. But in the end it always came around, and it will for you too. File sharing performance can be glacially slow— hangs of 20–30 seconds to make a connection are common.

I don't recommend file sharing with Windows 9x/Me (in fact I don't recommend Windows 9x/ME at all). If you decide to use Windows file sharing between Linux and Windows, make sure that you have the latest security patches from Microsoft, and that you are up-to-date with the latest antivirus software for Windows.

In spite of these real drawbacks, Windows file sharing is popular because it is easy to use. If you do decide to use it, take these precautions:

- Have strong passwords.

- Use read-only access where appropriate.

- Use a router or other firewall on your ISP connection before it reaches your PC.

- If you are using a wireless connections, run WEP encryption and MAC address filtering (see Chapter 4, "Onto the Net," for details).

Shortcut: Sharing Files Without a Network

Even if you don't have a computer network at home, you can use the file sharing capabilities described in this chapter to move files between two unnetworked PCs. This tip is also a great way to get your data off your old PC when you buy a new one. This works for moving data between *any* two computers that have a wired Ethernet connection: Mac, Linux, Windows, etc. You can also do it with wifi, but I'll focus on the simpler case.

Pick out the PC that has the data and the PC to which you want to transfer the data. Connect them with a length of Ethernet CAT-5 crossover cable plugged into each PC's Ethernet port. Cat-5 cable costs about a dollar per foot in short lengths, and you must use crossover cable, not regular cable.

Make sure both PCs are not connected to any other network, such as your ISP. Configure a fake network between the two PCs by assigning each a static IP address. Give one of them the address 192.168.1.1 and the other 192.168.1.2. These IP addresses are in a range of non-routable addresses reserved for uses like this. Chapter 4, "Onto the Net," on page 93 explains how to give a Linux host a static IP address.

Give a Windows XP system a static IP address following these steps.

1   In **Control Panel**, open **Network Connections**.

2   Right-click on the **Local Area Connection** icon and select **Properties**.

3   In the Local Area Connection Properties window, select **Internet Protocol** in the scrolling list, and click **Properties**.

4   That brings up a window titled Internet Protocol (TCP/IP) Properties where you can click on **Use the Following IP Address** and then enter the IP address you want to use.

From this point, the two PCs behave like any two hosts on a larger network, with one exception. The DNS service isn't running, so you'll need to do everything in terms of IP addresses, not host names. Move files by using ftp commands. The G-FTP software in the CNR warehouse provides an easy-to-use wrapper for ftp.

Setting Up Windows Workgroup Networking

In a typical home network, you're likely to have computers running different operating systems as shown in Figure 10-1.

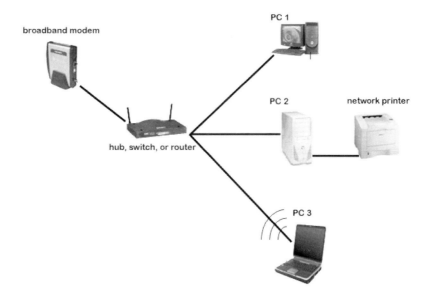

Figure 10-1 A typical home network

Some of your PCs may be running Linux, some running Windows, and some may be Apple computers running MacOS X (which, like Linux, is just a dialect of Unix).

Here are the steps in this section.

- *Setting Your Windows Host and Workgroup Names*

- *Putting All Your Windows PCs in the Same Workgroup*

- *Deciding What to Share*

- *Looking at Your Windows Network Places*

Setting Your Windows Host and Workgroup Names

You'll make things a lot easier for yourself if, before embarking on the adventure of file sharing, you give all your home Windows PCs easily recognizable host names. Instead of calling your desktop system ZZZ, set the host name to something that represents the hardware (like HP-laptop), or give it a description that says where it is in the house, or some other identifying remarks.

1　In Windows XP, click **Start**, right-click **My Computer > Properties**.

2　When the System Properties window opens, click the **Computer Name** tab.

3　In the text field, enter a computer description (such as kitchen computer). (Always give your Windows XP PC and its workgroup simple, clear names.) You will also use this window on all of your Windows PCs to put them into the same named workgroup.

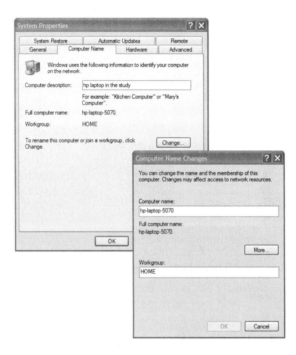

Figure 10-2　System Properties and Computer Name Changes windows

You can also click the **Change** button to bring up the Computer Name Changes window shown in Figure 10-2.

Putting All Your Windows PCs in the Same Workgroup

You can read and set the host name and the workgroup name in Windows XP. These names can be up to 15 characters. Hyphens are allowed but no spaces. A good name for a home workgroup is HOME. Go through all your Windows PCs to give them simple clear names and put them in the same workgroup.

Microsoft host names aren't really host names

What Microsoft calls the host name is not really the host name used in long-established Internet standards employed throughout the entire computer industry. It is a Microsoft-specific NetBEUI name.

NetBEUI—the NetBIOS Extended User Interface—is a set of services and extensions that Microsoft piled on top of the NetBIOS software they got from IBM in the 1980s. The only thing worth knowing about NetBEUI is that it is still used in Microsoft networking for file and print sharing.

Since the Windows host name you set isn't a real host name, it won't show up in any Internet tools (like ssh, ping, or ftp). You have to use IP addresses. However, true host names as used on your Linux computers are recognized by Microsoft software, even the file sharing software.

Deciding What to Share

If you're not sure about how widely to share files with different users, the default should be to share nothing. If you're sharing access among several PCs where you're the only user, open up all access to everything everywhere. Your own situation will be somewhere between these two extremes. You might designate one folder to hold all the files you want to share with other PCs.

The Windows folder C:\Documents and Settings\All Users\Shared Documents whose contents are visible to all users on a single PC, is a good default choice for the first folder you share across the local net. That folder also contains two folders, Shared Pictures and Shared Music, giving you some ready-made organization.

Creating an Account on Windows XP

You don't have to take this step, but it might save you unnecessary frustration. Set up a Windows account for each person on each Windows PC where you want them to have shared access. Give each individual the same Windows account name and password on each PC.

For instance, Fred should be user fred on PC1, PC2, and PC3. Sally should be user sally on all the PCs.

You set up a user account and password on Windows XP by choosing **Control Panel** > **User Accounts**. Click through a very simple wizard (series of panes each asking one question). The wizard captures information like user name and password.

Creating an Account on Older Windows Systems

You set up a user account and password on Windows 2000 by clicking on **Control Panel** > **Users and Passwords**, then click on **Users must enter.** Click through a wizard that captures information like user name and password.

On Windows 9x and Me you need to manually enable **File and Print Sharing** from the **Control Panel**.

Looking at Your Windows Network Places

1 On Windows XP, you can click on **Start** > **My Network Places** to bring up a window showing all the Windows PCs that are in the same workgroup on your local network. (This is why the first step is making sure that all your PCs had the same workgroup name, and sensible host names.) On older versions of Windows, the icon may be labeled Network Neighborhood and be on the desktop, not under the Start button.

2 Click on the icon on the left side of the window labeled **View workgroup computers**.

Figure 10-3 shows a typical display in the My Network Places window. This view will only show Windows PCs, not Linux or Apple computers.

Tip – The same Windows PC that you are using to look at the other computers in the workgroup, also shows up as one of My Network Places. Many people find that confusing.

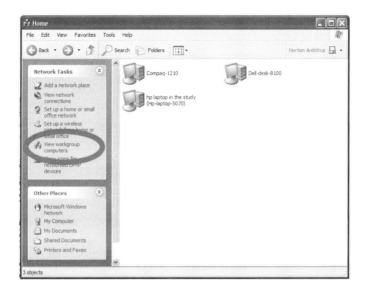

Figure 10-3   Clicking **View workgroup computers** shows the computers in this workgroup

Tip – The XP tab My Network Places remembers data about other hosts it has seen on your local net, even when they are not currently on the net. If you have any PCs that can boot in more than one operating system, and you reboot from XP to Linux, you'll get an impressive and lengthy display of inaccurate information about your local net.

There isn't any way to flush the junk from the XP tab and tell it take another look and report what's on the net now. It's a severe human interface error in Windows to have a window that displays dynamic data inaccurately, and have no way for the user to bring it up to date. The F5 refresh key just refreshes the screen; it does not go out and check the network again.

Setting Up Windows Clients

Here are the steps involved in setting up Windows clients.

* *Windows Client Accesses Files on Windows Server*
* *Windows XP Client Accesses Files on Linux Server*

Windows Client Accesses Files on Windows Server

Once you can see other computers in your workgroup in Windows, you have done nearly all the work needed to share files!

In other words, Windows starts the file sharing service automatically. All that's left for you to do is designate which folders you want to make visible to other PCs on your local network.

Sharing a Windows Folder

To make a folder (always a folder, never an individual file) on a Windows box visible on other PCs locally, follow these steps.

1   Right-click on the folder you want to share and select **Sharing and Security**. That brings up the window shown in Figure 10-4.

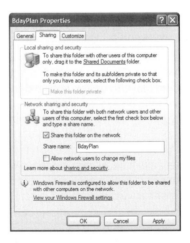

Figure 10-4   How to share a folder in Windows

2   The three choices you can make on this window are:

♦   To share or stop sharing the folder on the network

♦   To provide an alternative name for the shared folder that remote users will see

♦   To make the shared folder read-only, or to allow users to change the contents

Make your choices, then click **Apply** or **OK**. (In case you are wondering, this will automatically make the necessary change in your Windows firewall to allow file/printer sharing packets through.)

Notice from Figure 10-5 that the icon for a Windows folder changes slightly when you share it: a small hand cups the folder from underneath.

BdayPlan   BdayPlan

Unshared   Shared

Figure 10-5   Changes in the Windows folder icon when shared

That's a visible caution that whatever you put in that folder, someone else might have their hand in it too.

Reaching a Windows Shared Folder

1 Go to some other Windows PC on your local network, not the one where you created the shared folder.

2 Choose **My Computer** > **My Network Places**. There are a couple of easy alternatives for finding shared folders using the My Network Places window.

3 When the My Network Places window appears, it may have a number of icons representing Windows PCs with shared folders displayed in it already. You can click on an icon to display the folders shared from that host. Then open a folder and use the contents the same way you use local files.

You can also search for remote PCs that host some shared folders. Click on the Search icon in the icon bar in My Network Places. That brings up a search text field. You can enter a PC name here using Microsoft's Universal Naming Convention (UNC). That is a double backslash followed by an IP address or a Microsoft host name. Figure 10-6 illustrates both alternatives.

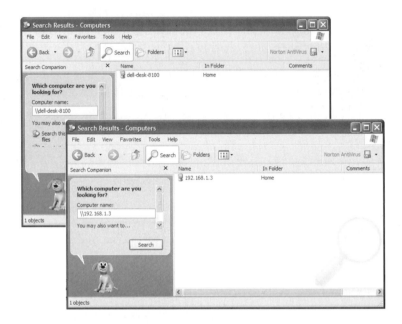

Figure 10-6   Reaching a shared folder on Windows

Microsoft's universal naming convention

Microsoft's Universal Naming Convention references a remote PC by prefixing its NetBEUI or Internet host name or its IP address with two backslashes. As an example, these names can be used on Windows (only) to refer to one of my Linux PCs:

```
\\dell-desk-8100
```

```
\\192.168.1.3
```

UNC is universally not used outside Microsoft software.

4   Click on the **host icon** (the tiny blue PC window displayed under Name in the right part of the window in Figure 10-6) to drill down to the shared folders on that PC.

5   If the shared folders are password protected, a window will pop up to accept the user name and password.

6   You will see icons representing various things that can be shared out from that host: printers, modems, faxes, and any shared folders (see Figure 10-7). What you see depends on what has actually been made available for sharing.

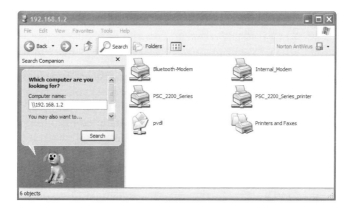

Figure 10-7   Clicking on the host icon shows the shared resources

7   Once you can see the icon for a shared file, you can do anything with it (subject to the sharing permissions) just as though it were a local file.

Microsoft Windows XP supports two types of file sharing:

- **Simple file sharing** – Files are shared to everyone in the same workgroup. This is the only kind of sharing supported in XP Home edition.

- **Standard file sharing** – File sharing permissions can be specified to the level of individual users. XP Pro can do either simple or standard file sharing. Once you are part of a domain, only standard file sharing is available.

Under XP Pro, if you are not part of a network domain, then WinXP Pro enables simple file sharing by default. It uses a default workgroup name of MSHOME (older versions have a default workgroup of WORKGROUP).

If you want the stricter security of standard file sharing with user names and passwords, then you have to turn off simple file sharing. Select any folder and choose **Tools** > **Folder Options** > **View** to see the correct radio button. None of this applies to XP Home Edition.

Microsoft security holes

Microsoft got network connections very badly wrong in Windows 9x and ME. When customers turned on File and Print Sharing for their local network, Windows 9x and ME also shared the files to the entire Internet.

Anyone who could guess your IP address (or hunt for it in a range of addresses issued to your ISP) could access your data and store their own files onto your system. The problem was made worse by other Microsoft bugs, like the one that made it easy for crackers to compromise password-protected shared folders (see http://www.microsoft.com/technet/security/bulletin/MS00-072.mspx). *Microsoft clearly didn't give enough consideration to the security and privacy of their customers.*

File and printer sharing was for years one of the most dangerous and easily exploited Windows 9X/ME security holes. It is common for novice users to end up with their entire hard drive shared to the Internet without realizing it. Industry commentator Steve Gibson wrote a detailed web page on this unhappy saga. You can find it at http://grc.com/su-bondage.htm.

Microsoft still doesn't have this right in Windows XP. After Service Pack 2, Microsoft issued a support bulletin, warning that an administrator-privileged guest account combined with printer sharing allows any user who can access your computer over the network [to] administer your computer. See the site http://support.microsoft.com/?kbid=870903.

That's great, but most Windows users will never hear that warning. It's only people (like me) who read the Microsoft support bulletins who will find out about it. And the crackers, of course. They always know. Everyone else will see the effects when their systems are penetrated.

Windows XP Client Accesses Files on Linux Server

Before you first try accessing a Linux shared folder from Windows, do a basic sanity test. Use the ping command to confirm that you have basic network connectivity between the Linux PC and the Windows PC. Review IP addresses in Chapter 4 if necessary. Get the Linux PC's IP address by typing the command ifconfig. Get the Linux PC's host name by typing the command hostname. Get the Window PC's IP address by typing the command ipconfig. Write your results in Figure 10-1.

Table 10-1   Recording information from ping test

Command	Example output	Output from running this command on your Linux PC
hostname	cloud	
ifconfig	Several lines of output including an IP address with this general form: 192.168.1.3	

Then on the Windows PC from which you wish to access a Linux file, type the command

ping -c 5 192.168.1.3

using the actual IP address of the Linux PC instead of 192.168.1.3. You should get back a few lines reporting the replies received and the speed statistics. If instead you get a timeout or other error, then you don't have basic network connectivity, and no filesharing will work. Consult *Troubleshoot the Wired Connection* on page 102 for the network troubleshooting process.

Next, repeat the ping command, but using the Linux host name instead of the IP address. You need to see a similar result about replies received and some statistics. This tells you that the Domain Name Service is working on Windows and is able to resolve host names into IP addresses. If everything is working OK, proceed to do a network share. If not, double-check that you followed all the procedures here to the letter, check the book web site at http://afu.com/linux for any updates, then use the Linspire customer forums (described in Chapter 2, "Running the Linux Live CD," on page 25). Make sure you have a clear description of what you did, what you saw, and what failed.

The Samba Jive

Linux shares files with Microsoft's proprietary networking using an open source program, called Samba. The name Samba is a riff on the data structure that Microsoft uses to share files among Windows systems. This data structure is called the Server Message Block (SMB). Samba makes Linux appear as another Windows box to a Windows PC asking for a shared folder.

Samba comes preinstalled and ready to share files on the Linspire distro. If you are using another Debian-based distro, you can install Samba by using these commands:

```
apt-get update
apt-get install samba
```

The installation process will ask a few questions, such as if you want to run it as a daemon (background process, and you do want this), your workgroup name, and so on. Samba will automatically start after installation, and will also start automatically on subsequent reboots.

About Samba

The Samba software was written by a small group of talented programmers at the Australian National University in Canberra, Australia, led by Andrew "Tridge" Tridgell. He reverse-engineered the Microsoft protocol by looking at the Ethernet packets sent for each request. Then he designed and wrote Samba to "speak the same language".

I bumped into Tridge at a Linux conference in San Jose, California several years ago, and asked him whether he'd ever been able to get any help from Microsoft. From what Tridge told me, I concluded that Microsoft actively works to undermine software that allows other operating systems to interoperate with Windows. Microsoft does this by not publishing details of the protocol, and by changing it without warning.

Client/Server Terminology

Whenever you share a resource like a printer or files over a network, the (one) computer that physically hosts the resource is called the server. The (possibly many) computers that make requests to the server are called clients.

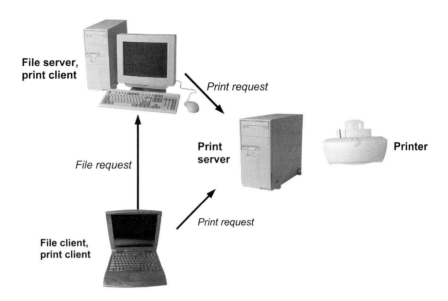

Figure 10-8   A server manages a shared resource and serves it out to clients

Figure 10-8 illustrates client/server resource sharing. One PC can be both a client and a server. Two PCs can be both a client and a server to each other for different resources. For example, each may be sharing a different folder to the other.

Setting up file sharing between Linspire and any other operating system is just a matter of deciding which end is the server and which end is the client, and then doing the appropriate operating system-specific configuration to export a share and to search for a share respectively.

Starting Samba File Sharing on Linux

As a preliminary step to sharing a folder located on a Linux server, start Samba.

Setting the Basic Samba Configuration

1 Click **Launch > Settings > Control Panel > Network > Samba Configuration**, then click the **Base Settings** tab shown in Figure 10-9.

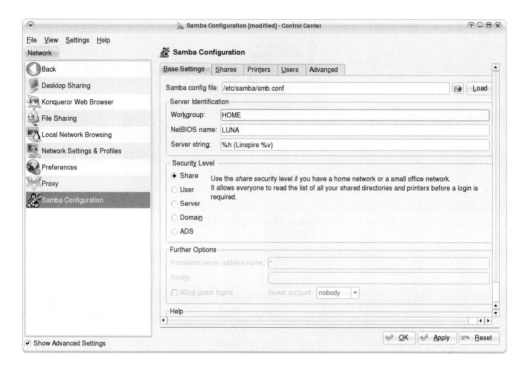

Figure 10-9   Setting the basic Samba configuration

2 Fill in the **workgroup name** of HOME or whatever you used on Windows. Set the security level to **Share**. You can make this more stringent later, to require password challenges, by setting it to **User**.

3 Click **Apply**.

Samba has a great many other custom settings, but these two will be enough to get you started.

Turning on Samba Sharing

1 Click **Launch > Settings > Control Panel > Network > File Sharing**.

2 Click the **Settings** tab shown in Figure 10-10.

3 Click **Enable local network file sharing**, then **Simple sharing**.

4 Click **OK**.

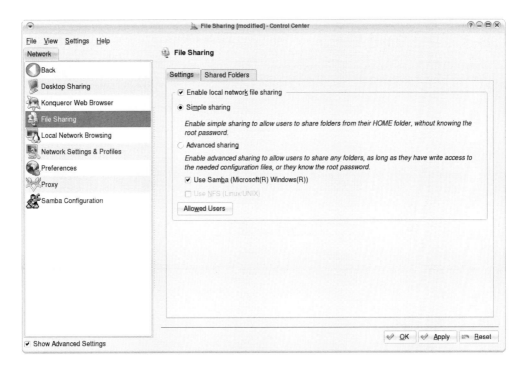

Figure 10-10   Starting file sharing from Linux

Sharing a Linux Folder

Now designate some Linux folder as one that will be shared.

1   Find an **icon representing the folder**, either on the desktop or in the File Manager.

2   Right-click on it and select **Share**.

3   That will bring up a window that looks like Figure 10-11.

Note – Clicking on **Share** dismisses the menu containing Share as it brings up the Properties menu, so you won't see the menu and the properties tabs both in the window at once as in the figure.

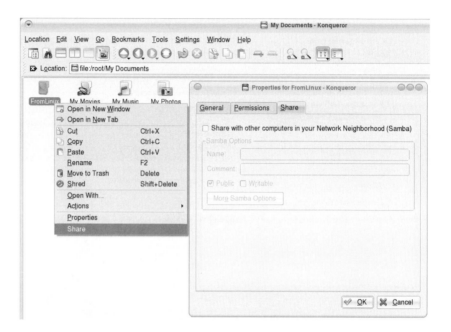

Figure 10-11 Sharing a folder in Linux

You can see that Samba and Windows are broadly similar by comparing Windows Figure 10-4 with Samba's window shown in Figure 10-11. They both collect the same information, because they both talk the same SMB language.

4   Click on the **Share with other computers in your Network Neighborhood (Samba)** checkbox. If you wish the folder to be known by another name (an alias) on sharing clients, type that name into the field. You might want to provide a shorter name, or a name that includes the host it comes from, to keep things well-organized.

5   Leave the **Configure File Sharing** button alone. You already completed that.

Don't click **OK** to close the window yet. You need it for the next step.

6   Set the correct permission on the shared Linux folder. Click on the **Permissions** tab of the Properties window. You will see the window change to look like Figure 10-12.

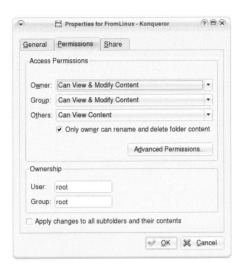

Figure 10-12   Setting the access permissions for the folder

7   If you want others to be able to change the content of files in the folder, you need to grant that permission here. Click **OK** to dismiss the window.

Note from Figure 10-13 that the icon for a Linux folder changes slightly when you share it: an electrical cord appears, implying that the folder is plugged into the net.

Figure 10-13   Linux folders: unshared (left), and shared (right)

That takes care of setting up everything on the Linux PC. Now walk over to the Windows PC and access the Linux folder you just shared.

Accessing Linux Files from the Windows PC

You will now be able to access the files in the Linux folder you shared, from your Windows PC. Your Linspire PC will share files almost exactly like a Windows XP host, but Linux hosts are not always automatically discovered by Windows— you might have to specify them explicitly.

1   From Windows, you reach Linux PCs by clicking **Start** > **My Network Places**. That brings up a My Network Places window.

2   Click on **Search**, and in the search field that appears, type \\ followed by the Linux PC's host name or IP address (your choice). The \\ is Microsoft's non-standard UNC notation for a remote host. You'll see later a better notation that looks more like a URL for a web browser. That will update the display to look like Figure 10-14.

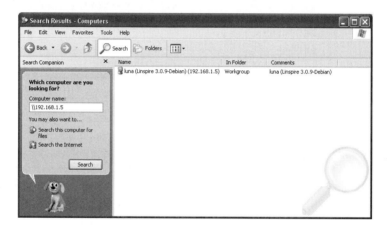

Figure 10-14   Windows finds the Linux PC

3   Now you can click down on the **hostname icon** on the right part of the Search Results window to see the folders shared from the Linux PC. The luna hostname icon is shown in Figure 10-14. If you had used a password to protect access, you would be challenged for a password at this point on the Windows PC.

4   Double-click on a **folder name** to look at the folder contents, as seen in Figure 10-15. It's a folder with an image file of an old wrecked car. The Rolls factory has a special term for a car in this state: *bedeviled*. Not that I'm insinuating anything about workgroup networking.

Figure 10-15   This folder is being served to a Windows client from a Linux PC

Now you can work with the files, and (as long as you granted write access on Linux) add to the Linux folder, delete files, etc., just as if they were local Windows files.

5   If you omitted the Samba server setup on the Linux PC, Windows will give you an error dialog box like that shown in Figure 10-16. This error means that the remote Linux PC doesn't have Samba configured.

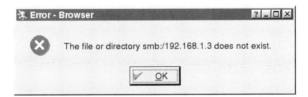

Figure 10-16   Message indicating the remote Linux PC doesn't have Samba configured

If you want to share files between two Linux systems, Samba will get something running quickly. But the right way to do it when using Linux exclusively, is to use Unix's native file sharing protocol known as NFS. NFS benchmarks up to ten times faster than Samba, and is a lot more secure as well. You can get information about NFS by searching the Linspire forums.

Setting Up Linux Clients

This section covers how to set up Linux clients to access files on Windows or Linux servers.

- *Linux Client Accesses Files on a Windows Server*

- *Linux Client Accesses Files on a Linux Server*

- *A Mac Client Accesses Files on a Linux Server*

Linux Client Accesses Files on a Windows Server

Using a Linux PC to access files on a Windows PC is straightforward, once the naming convention used on Linux is described. In this case, the Windows PC is the server, and the Linux PC is the client.

Setting Up Sharing

1   Share your folder on the Windows PC as described *Sharing a Windows Folder* on page 356. Then go to your Linux PC to set up the client side of Samba networking and see the shared folder.

2   On Linux, click **Launch > Settings > Control Panel > Network > Local Network Browsing** to open the window shown in Figure 10-17.

3   Fill in the **user name** and **password** that match those on the Windows PC serving the folder. You can quickly check what user names are in use on an XP system by clicking **Start > Log Off > Switch User**. The default user name if you haven't set any up is user.

4   Fill in the **workgroup name**, such as HOME.

5   Click **OK**.

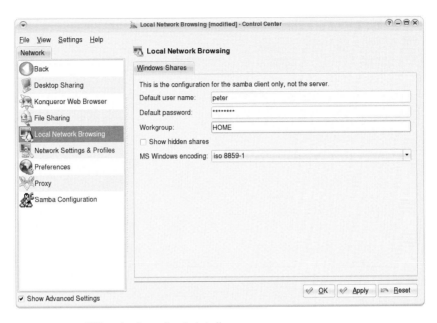

Figure 10-17   Filling in the client details

6 Back on Linux, double-click on the **Network Share Manager** icon on the desktop. This brings up the window shown in Figure 10-18.

7 When the Network Browser window appears, expand the tree labeled **Entire Network**, to go down into your workgroup and into all computers in that workgroup. Clicking on an **individual computer name** will open the tree to display all the shared folders on that server.

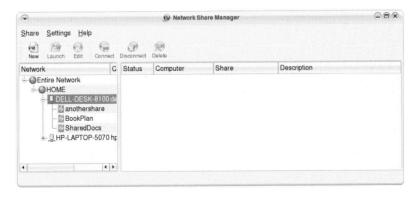

Figure 10-18   Opening the Network Share Manager

8 Click on **any folder** to open it, and see the icons representing the files.

Making a Windows Folder Automatically Shared on Reboot

If you're working on a Windows folder frequently, you might want to set it up so that your Linux client automatically mounts the folder (i.e., makes it available as a share) after booting.

1 Bring up the **Network Share Manager**, shown in Figure 10-18.

2 Expand the tree until it is displaying the individual folder that you want to automatically connect to each time you start Linux.

3 Right-click on that folder in the right-hand part of the Network Share Manager Window and select **Edit**. You'll see the window in Figure 10-19.

Figure 10-19   Making the share reconnect automatically on reboot

4 Check the **Automatically reconnect at start-up** option if you always want this folder to be available on this client.

Linux Client Accesses Files on a Linux Server

It should be no great surprise to learn that you can carry out Linux-to-Linux file sharing simply by combining the appropriate portions of the previous sections.

1 Decide which system is exporting the folder, and complete the Linux server part in *Linux Client Accesses Files on a Linux Server* on page 372.

2 Then go to the system that you want to access the remote folder and complete the Linux client part described in *Linux Client Accesses Files on a Windows Server* on page 370.

Linux Client Accesses Files on a Mac Server

It should be no surprise at all to learn that you can share files with an Apple Mac, too. The MacOS X environment is, like Linux, just another flavor of Unix, but with a particularly excellent GUI. MacOS X 10.2 or later supports Windows file sharing using SMB, which means it also supports access from Linux.

To help interoperability with the Windows world, Apple actually integrates the Samba software into MacOS X (just as Linspire does with Linux), so you don't have anything to install. Samba works equally well talking from a Mac server to a Linux system, as it does between Windows systems. It crashes the Mac Finder when running as a client (as at MacOS 10.3.9).

Using a Mac as a Samba Server

Serving a Folder from the Mac

1   Click on the **Apple** (top left of screen) and choose **System Preferences** > **Sharing** to bring up the window shown in Figure 10-20.

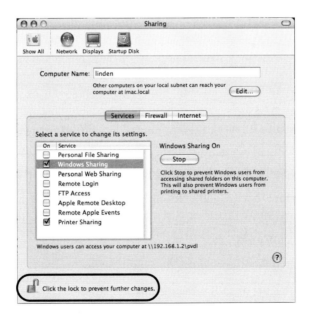

Figure 10-20   Making a Mac share files to Linux, Windows, and Macs using Samba

2   Click on the **padlock icon** (circled in Figure 10-20) and enter your administrator password in the dialog box that pops up. You are then free to select Windows sharing.

3   Notice that when you turn on Windows sharing the Mac displays its UNC address under the column of checkboxes. It reads Windows users can access your computer at \\192.168.1.2\pvdl (the entire home directory of the Mac user is shared; you cannot designate folders individually). A Linux PC will reference the folder as smb://192.168.1.2/pvdl.

Adding or Changing MacOS X Username/Passwords

1   Click on the **apple** at top left of the screen and choose **System Preferences > Show All > Accounts**.

2   In the Accounts window, click the **padlock** to authenticate as an Administrator user.

3   Change an existing user by highlighting the **user name** in the list, then clicking one of the four tabs in the window: **Password**, **Picture**, **Security**, or **Limitations**. Enter the new details.

4   Add a new user by clicking on the **small + sign** directly above the padlock, and entering at least the name and password details.

5   Click the **lock icon** to prevent further changes, and quit **System Preferences**.

Set the Windows Workgroup Name in MacOS X

1   Use the **Finder** to go to the /Applications/Utilities folder, and double-click on the **Directory Access** program. That brings up the window shown in Figure 10-21.

2   Click the **padlock** to authenticate as an Administrator user.

3   Ensure there is a **checkmark** next to **SMB** in the Services list. (It's very easy to overlook this.)

4   Click **Configure**.

5   Select the **name of the desired workgroup** (e.g., home), or type it.

6   Leave the **WINS server** blank.

7   Click **OK**.

8   Click **Apply**.

9   Click the **lock** to prevent further changes, and quit **Directory Access**.

10 To make the change take effect immediately, turn off **Windows Sharing** and then turn it on again (described at the beginning of this section).

Figure 10-21   Setting the workgroup name using the Directory Access utility

A Mac Client Accesses Files on a Linux Server

This procedure takes you through the procedure using the GUI. Using the GUI fails in the current release of MacOS and the current release of Samba at the time this book was written. If you'd like to try the command line approach, which does work with the current release, see page 377.

Access a shared folder from a Mac client as follows.

1 Click on the **desktop background** to bring the **Finder menu** to the top of the screen. (In a disastrously bad design decision, Mac menus are attached to the top of the screen, not to the top of individual windows, so you can only see one program's menu bar at a time.)

2 Click on the Finder **Go** menu and choose **Connect to server** to bring up the window shown in Figure 10-22.

Figure 10-22   Connect to Server window

3   Type the server address in the **Server Address** field. This uses the same type of URL as Linux uses in Samba, e.g., smb://192.168.1.3. Use the IP address of your Windows or Linux PC.

You might be challenged for a **password**, as shown in Figure 10-23. It wants your MacOS X user name/password, not that of the file owner on the server.

Figure 10-23   A password challenge to a Mac client of a network share

4   Unfortunately, there's a hiccup here. The Finder program crashes in MacOS X 10.3.9, and so the share never completes, as shown in Figure 10-24.

Figure 10-24   Finder crashes while trying to reach a Samba server

From looking at the crash log, I can see that it choked on a null pointer while it was trying to keep track of some glyphs (not a critical feature).

But all is not lost! I was able to mount a directory shared from a Windows XP system using the MacOS X command line.

```
$ mount -t smbfs //192.168.1.5/from-xp ~/mnt
```

Password:

Using a similar command I was also able to mount a shared folder from a Linux server onto a Mac client, though it failed a couple of times before it succeeded.

Bugs in the protocol

The problems that the Mac hit while running as a Samba client are not necessarily bugs in the Mac software. In the early 1980s, when TCP/IP computer networking was still pretty new, there was a lot of rivalry between different vendors. One customer had a lab full of networked DEC computers (DEC was eventually swallowed up by Compaq, which in turn was consumed by HP).

The DEC computers all worked fine together, until a Sun Microsystems workstation was added to the net. The DECs immediately started having network problems, with high packet collision rates leading to kernel crashes and hangs.

The normal rule of troubleshooting says that the last thing you changed caused the problem so the DEC salespeople were quick to claim that Sun was causing the problem, suggesting that Sun was not following the Ethernet standard. DEC even briefed its other salespeople on how to use this issue to shut Sun out of accounts.

As usual, it took a few weeks for this issue to propagate back into Sun's development labs, where an intensive and urgent investigation concluded that the Sun equipment followed the standard perfectly. In particular, Sun workstations respected the 9.6 microsecond interframe gap specified by the IEEE 802.3 Ethernet standard, and Sun was actually slowing down its Ethernet transmissions to stay on the right side of the limit. The investigation also found the cause of the problems at the customer site: the DEC systems were not able to accept packets that came that close together, even though the Ethernet standard required it.

The DEC salespeople all went uncharacteristically quiet for a few weeks, while it was Sun's turn to make hay. The lesson is that a problem might be at either end of a two-party protocol; it is not necessarily at the end that shows the symptom.

For more information on Samba, see *Working with Samba* on page 545.

You'll finish with the *Setting Up Print Servers* and *Remote Desktop Sharing* sections.

Setting Up Print Servers

This section covers how to set up clients for print servers.

- *Linux Client of a Windows Print Server*
- *Windows Client of a Linux Print Server*
- *Linux Client of a Linux Print Server*

Linux Client of a Windows Print Server

To permit remote access to your Windows printer that has already been installed and is working, you must first share the printer at the Windows end.

Setting Up a Windows Print Server

1   Click **Start** > **Printers and Faxes**.

2   Right-click the **printer** that you want to share and select **Sharing**. This will bring up the Properties window for the printer, displaying the Sharing tab shown in Figure 10-25.

Figure 10-25   Using the Sharing tab to advertise a Windows printer over the network

3   On the Sharing tab, select **Share this printer**.

4   Type a brief name (no spaces) in the **Share name** field, and click **OK**. This is the name by which the printer will be identified on the network.

Setting Up a Linux Client of a Shared Printer

Follow these steps on the Linspire system where you want to use the remote printer.

1   Double-click the **Printers** icon on the Desktop to bring up the Configure Printers window shown in Figure 10-26.

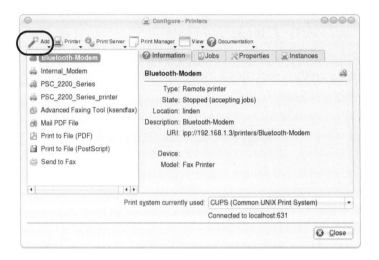

Figure 10-26   Configure Printers window

2   In the Configure Printers window, click on the **Add** icon circled at the top of Figure 10-26 and select **Add PrinterClass**.

3   The Add Printer Wizard appears. Click **Next** to get past the introductory window.

4   In the window shown in Figure 10-27, select the **SMB Shared Printer (Windows)** radio button.

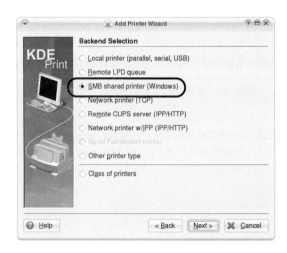

Figure 10-27   Add Printer wizard, Backend Selection window

5   Click **Next**; the window in Figure 10-28 will appear. Fill in the **name** and **password** of the Windows user. Don't use the anonymous or Guest accounts (Microsoft warns you about the security problems if you access Windows print sharing this way).

Figure 10-28   Add Printer Wizard, User Identification window

6   Click **Next;** the window in Figure 10-29 will open.

7   Click on the **Scan** button to see what systems Samba will find in this workgroup. Click on the **plus sign** to show your chosen system. As shown in Figure 10-29, Samba has found one other host in this workgroup.

Figure 10-29   Add Printer Wizard, SMB Printer Settings window

8 If the host or printer doesn't show up there, it is not yet visible to Samba. In that case, specify the **IP address** for the MS Windows computer that is acting as a print server, and explicitly type the **Printer name** in the text field.

9 Click **Next**. The Printer Model Selection window will appear.

10 The window in Figure 10-30 has a list of many contemporary printers. If your printer is not there, often a similar model number from the same vendor will work. The other button lets you browse for the driver files. You'll use this if you've done a web search and downloaded the right driver.

Select the **Manufacturer** from the left list box and the specific **Model** of your printer from the right list box. Your window will now look similar to Figure 10-30.

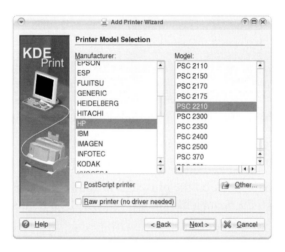

Figure 10-30   Add Printer Wizard, Printer Model Selection window

The choice at the bottom of the panel between Postscript printer and Raw printer needs a bit of explaining. **Printers in the Common Unix Printing System** can use a Postscript Printer Description (PPD) filter. This is a file with the extension .ppd that helps translate a print request into something a specific printer can cope with. You will generally get better results by choosing a postscript printer and specifying the model number.

11 Click **Next**.

12 The subsequent wizard window will give you the chance to print a test page; click **Test** to do so. After the page finishes printing, click **OK**.

13 Click **Next** to continue with the wizard.

14 In the next two or three wizard windows you can set up options that nobody uses on home computers: options like a banner page, page quotas, and so on. Click **Next** through these, giving a **name** and **description** to the printer when prompted. That name is how you will refer to the printer in Linux, so select something simple and meaningful.

15 When you reach the final wizard page, shown in Figure 10-31, click **Finish** to exit the wizard.

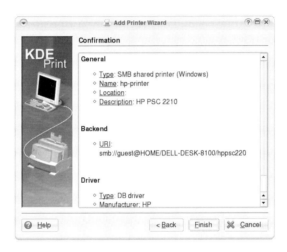

Figure 10-31   Add Printer Wizard, Confirmation window

If this doesn't work immediately for you, and it is not because of a missing printer driver, then do the usual Samba troubleshooting. ping both ways between PCs, using IP address and then host names. Check that the Windows printer works locally, is not out of paper, and so on.

Windows Client of a Linux Print Server

First make sure your Linux printer works when printing locally. If you have an older, balky printer, or there is some other problem in making a local printer work with Linux, your first resource is the web site http://www.linuxprinting.org.

The odds are about 90% that you will be able to coax an arbitrary printer to work with Linux, based on statistics from that site. If you have not already configured your printer with Linux, follow these instructions.

Configuring a Local Linux Printer

Configuring a local (directly attached to this PC) Linux printer is straightforward these days. Everything can be done using a wizard. The wizard collects information to give to CUPS—the Common Unix Printing System used by Linspire, MacOS X, Red Hat Linux, and many others. Follow these steps.

1   Double-click the **Printers** icon on the Desktop, to bring up the Add Printer window (shown in Figure 10-30 on page 382).

2   In the Add Printer window, click on the **Add icon** at the top left and select **Add Printer/Class** to start the Add Printer wizard.

3   Click **Next** to get past the introductory window.

4   Select **local printer** and answer the rest of the questions in the wizard.

5   You'll be asked to select a valid detected port, shown in Figure 10-32. You need to select the port by which your printer connects to the PC: **Parallel**, **Serial**, or **USB** according to which type of connector your printer is using to attach to your PC.

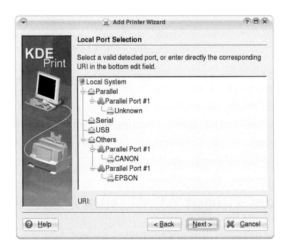

Figure 10-32   Select the port by which your printer connects to the PC

If you're not sure you can recognize these three kinds of connections, refer to your printer manual. A parallel cable is the one that connects to what Microsoft calls the LPT1 port. It's a fat 25-pin D-shaped plug.

Very old computers might use a serial cable connected to what Microsoft calls the COM port (the rest of the world calls it by the standard name RS232 or serial port). You're supposed to power down your PC before plugging in or removing a parallel or serial cable. Most modern computers (say, everything sold since 2002) use a USB port for printing. USB cables are hot pluggable, meaning you don't have to power the PC off to plug or unplug the cable to the device.

6 Print a test page when the wizard offers you the chance.

7 Finish the wizard when prompted.

8 Once the printer wizard has completed, right-click on that **printer name** in the Printers—KDE Control Module window, click on the **Instances** tab and select **Set As Default**.

9 Close the window.

Once Linux printing works locally, it is equally straightforward to share the printer to a Windows (or other) system on your local network.

Using the Web Interface to a Linux Printer

You can also administer any CUPS printer using the web interface in your browser. On the computer to which the printer is attached, browse the URL http://127.0.0.1:631 to bring up the display shown in Figure 10-33.

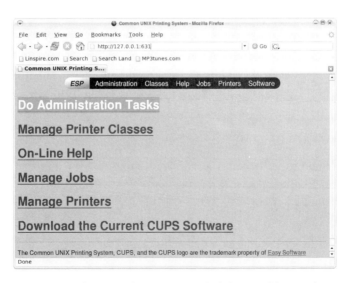

Figure 10-33   Using your browser to administer a Linux printer

You click on a link to carry out the corresponding task. You might be prompted for the root password when you want to change something. The web interface is so easy to use that some people prefer it to the wizards.

Making a Linux Printer Available to Other PCs

If you decide to allow other PCs on your local network to print on the printer attached to your Linux system, you need to turn on file and printer sharing on Linux.

1   Printer sharing is based on file sharing. Follow the process outlined in the section *Starting Samba File Sharing on Linux* on page 363.

2   Then go to each client and follow the appropriate process to make it use a remote printer. Use either *Setting Up a Linux Client of a Shared Printer* on page 379 or *Setting Up a Windows Client of a Shared Linux Printer* on page 386.

Setting Up a Windows Client of a Shared Linux Printer

To access your printer connected to a Linspire PC from Microsoft Windows, do the following:

1   On Windows, click **Start** > **Control Panel** > **Printers and Faxes**.

2   In the Printers and Faxes window, choose **File** > **Add Printer**. That brings up the Windows Add Printer wizard.

3   Select **A Network Printer**.

4   Click **Next** to continue through the wizard.

5   Still in the Add Printer wizard, select **Connect to this printer** and enter the **IP address** of the Linux print server in UNC form.

    \\192.168.1.3\local-hp

    Use your Linux PC's IP address and printer name.

6   Windows will display a message stating that it's important to be certain that the computer sharing this printer is trustworthy. Since both PCs belong to you, click **Yes**.

7   Now Windows will need to install the device driver for this printer locally. put the driver CD that you got with the printer in the PC and click **OK** in the dialog box to search for the driver.

There isn't much to installing a printer driver—just have the CD available and direct the wizard to use it. If you don't have the CD, select the **no CD** approach and select the most similar other model from the same vendor. When this is complete, click **Finish** in the wizard.

You might wonder why Windows needs to install a device driver when the device is not attached to it. Printer sharing is completely implemented in terms of file sharing. In fact, you get printer sharing practically for free when you implement file sharing. To print remotely, first print to a local file. Then ship that local file to a remote system.

You need to install the printer device driver locally so that Windows can execute the local print to file command. That file is then shipped across the network to the system with the printer, which is where the print file command will be run.

8   Right-click on the newly created printer icon in the Printers and Faxes window, and open the **Properties** menu item. Click the **Print Test Page** button and confirm the test page prints OK.

9   Click **Cancel** in the Properties window.

Note – My printer icon in Microsoft Windows' Printers and Faxes window has a small note next to it reading "Access denied, unable to conn..." However, despite this message, remote printing functions perfectly.

Linux Client of a Linux Print Server

To print remotely from Linux to Linux, set up a Linux print server as described in *Windows Client of a Linux Print Server* and set up a Linux Samba print client to use it, as described in *Linux Client of a Windows Print Server*. That's all! You can also use the Common User Printing Service (CUPS), which is integrated with the Linspire distro.

Remote Desktop Sharing

This chapter wouldn't be complete without describing another network sharing feature that Linspire calls Desktop Sharing. This feature replicates the display of one desktop on another PC located anywhere on the Internet. You can even control the first PC from the second one. Desktop Sharing is really an application called VNC, but remote desktop sharing is a more descriptive term. You might use VNC across the Internet to access your uncle's PC and fix some configuration issue. Or a salesman might use it at a client site to demonstrate some software installed on the PC back in his office.

VNC—the name means "Virtual Network Computing—was developed in a research lab in England, and made available to everyone under the GNU Public License. VNC works in two parts. One part runs on the system that is making its desktop available to someone else. It is serving an image of the desktop, so it is called the server. The other part of VNC runs on the system that will be getting the image of the remote desktop. This end is called the client, even though it controls the actions of the other system.

You make your desktop available for someone else to see and operate by clicking **Launch > Run Programs > Utilities > Desktop Sharing > Share This Desktop**. That brings up a panel allowing you to issue an invitation by email or display the information needed to connect. It is not secure to issue an invitation by email, unless you are using encrypted email. So instead, use the **Create Personal Invitation** option.

1   Click **Create Personal Invitation** to bring up a window similar to the one shown in Figure 10-34.

To help you see which of the two systems is displaying what, let's assume Uncle Josh wants to share his desktop out to Peter.

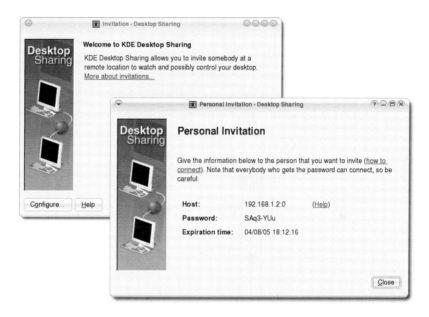

Figure 10-34   Uncle Josh generates the data Peter needs to connect to his desktop

Note that this tells you the IP address and password that Peter will need to connect to Uncle Josh's desktop. Pass the data by phone, or other secure means. The IP address has :0 appended to it. This is the convention for display number 0. Josh might have several monitors connected to his PC.

2   On Peter's system, click **Launch** > **Run Programs** > **Utilities** > **Desktop Sharing** > **Connect to Remote Desktop**. That brings up a panel allowing Peter to enter Josh's IP address and display number, shown in Figure 10-35.

Figure 10-35   Peter wants to connect to Uncle Josh's remote desktop

3   Click **Connect**. That will cause Peter's system to try to connect to the remote system.

4   You'll get another dialog box here asking if you have a fast or slow network connection. If the system is anywhere other than in the same building, specify that you have a **slow connection**.

5   The remote system (Josh's system) displays a message saying a connection is being requested and giving Peter's IP address (so you can check that the connection request is from who you think it is). See Figure 10-36.

Figure 10-36   Josh's system notices the connection request from Peter

6   Josh clicks **Accept Connection**.

7   Peter's system will challenge him for the password that Josh supplied. See Figure 10-37.

Figure 10-37   Peter's system challenges him for the password that Josh told him

8   Peter will enter the **password**. As soon as Josh's system authenticates it, Josh's system will start serving its display image out over the network to the VNC application running on Peter's computer. Peter's computer will display Josh's display in a big window, similar to that of Figure 10-38.

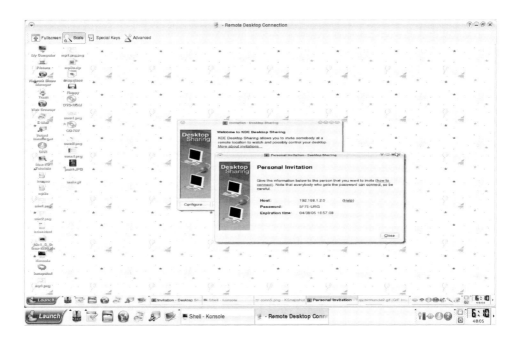

Figure 10-38   Peter's system now shows Josh's display

Notice that there are two KDE Kicker panels in Figure 10-38. The lower one is the Kicker panel for Peter's PC. The Kicker running above that is the Kicker panel from Josh's display. And the whole rest of the screen is Josh's display. It's a window that can be moved to one side, if Peter wants to reach his own desktop.

Josh's desktop is still displaying his part of the VNC application (the invitation generator). Josh's desktop appears slightly stretched on Peter's monitor because the two PCs have screens with different resolutions. Josh's screen is 1600 by 1200, and it has to be squeezed onto Peter's 1280 by 800 LCD.

The great thing about VNC is that Peter can now operate Josh's desktop, just as though he were in the same room with it. Peter's mouse will drive the mouse on Josh's screen, and Peter can do many system administration tasks remotely for Josh. Since VNC is an ordinary application, it requires the operating system to run, so Peter can't do anything too fancy like install a new operating system or reboot the system.

If there is a firewall between the two systems, you have to configure the firewall to allow traffic through on ports 5900, 5901, and 5902 on the PC that is running the VNC server.

To avoid reconfiguring the router, I simply get Uncle Josh to plug his PC Ethernet cable directly into the broadband modem for the duration of the remote session. Don't do that if the host is a Windows PC!

Remote desktop sharing requires quite a bit of bandwidth, and it will not run over a dial-up connection. VNC software is available for all operating systems. It's a really winning piece of software. Uncle Josh swears by it.

The lore of Linux—Playing the Linux game on Microsoft's XBox

Microsoft makes a couple of hardware products: a variety of mice, some wireless accessories, and the game box known as XBox. The XBox is sold as a console game system but it's actually a general-purpose PC, partially disabled to prevent you getting general-purpose use from it.

The first generation XBox contains a 733MHz Pentium III, 64 MB memory, 10 GB disk, nVidia GeForce graphics, a DVD-ROM, four USB ports, an Ethernet adapter, and a modem. It runs a modified version of Windows 2000. This was a pretty good hardware configuration when the XBox was launched in 2001, and it's still adequate today.

Microsoft sells XBox on the same principle that made King Gillette so wealthy: sell the hardware cheap, and make the money on the recurring expenditures, razor blades and game software, respectively. XBox retails at $150, but Microsoft sells them for less than the manufacturing cost, and loses an estimated $160 on every sale. Microsoft hopes to make this up by extracting a royalty on all games.

You buy and own the XBox hardware, but Microsoft has to approve (and get a cut of) all XBox software that you want to run. Microsoft enforces its software restriction through public key cryptography, of the same type described in Chapter 11, "Keeping Your Data Private." The XBox hardware won't execute any programs that Microsoft has not signed with its 2048 bit private key. Microsoft charges game publishers $5–$10 for every copy of an XBox game sold. And wouldn't Microsoft love to extend that model to the PC world, if they could get away with it. By an amazing coincidence, the Palladium digital rights restrictions being introduced with the next release of Windows, coupled with another new and incompatible filesystem, present two such opportunities. So keep your eyes open.

Noticing the cheap hardware, courtesy of the subsidy from Microsoft, hackers at once started work to create a new game for the XBox, but a game not blessed by Microsoft. The game would be called "let's run the Linux kernel". It would somehow circumvent the crypto protection, turning the XBox into the world's cheapest Linux PC! As an additional incentive, a mysterious and anonymous benefactor put up a multi-thousand dollar prize for the first person who found a way to run Linux on an Xbox without modifying the hardware.

It's easy enough to modify the XBox hardware to remove the restrictions. People even sell install-yourself kits and already-modified systems. Web search for "xbox mod chip" to see a long list of suppliers. Hardware changes are beyond the expertise of many people, but everyone knows how to run programs.

It took 18 months to find an ingenious software hack. The encryption stood up against all attacks. Then in 2003, a hacker with the pen name of Habibi discovered that the "007; Agent Under Fire" game from Electronic Arts had a buffer overrun bug in the "load a saved game" feature. It could be exploited so that it would load an arbitrary, unsigned program, including a version of Linux.

It was later found that Microsoft's own MechAssault game could be exploited the same way. More exploits were found, in the font library, in in the audio subsystem, and in disk handling. You can find a step-by-step guide at the site http://www.xbox-linux.org. *Microsoft rushes to plug the holes as fast as they are found and will even remotely remove files from your XBox disk when you connect to a network. That's a remarkable contrast with Sony, who sells kits transforming PlayStation 2 into a Linux box.*

Unlike most financial hacking challenges, this anonymous benefactor made good on his pledge and paid out a $70,000 bounty. Mentioning it probably won't win me any new friends in San Diego (so if anyone asks, you didn't hear it from me), but the benefactor who put up the XBox Linux prize turned out to be none other than Michael Robertson, chairman of Linspire!

Today, Linux owns the XBox, and if you want a very cheap Linux PC, you know where to go and who to thank. The hardware is no longer as competitive as it once was, but the price is right. Some people are even building clusters of XBoxes. The second generation XBox 360 is expected in late 2005. Let the Linux modding commence!

## CHAPTER 11

Keeping Your Data Private

Why This Information Is Important

One of the qualities that distinguishes Linux from competitors is its superior support for your privacy and security. Some people and organizations quite rightly want to protect their data files and email from snooping eyes. They keep the files in coded form, a practice known as encryption. To make an informed decision about keeping your data private, you have to know that the choice exists. That's the reason I show you how to use encryption.

Keeping your data and email truly private is an increasingly important skill in these times. Privacy through encryption is apparently important enough that the governments of France, Britain, and Iran want to deny it to their citizens. In the USA, the First Amendment to the Constitution inhibits the government from denying freedom of speech to its citizens. Or at least makes it more probable that such denial will eventually be overturned in the courts. Freedom of speech has been interpreted by the courts to include freedom of dance, of song, of cinema, and it includes the freedom to write down whatever random numbers you like.

Linux encryption software is not as polished as it should be. That's a too-frequent limitation of software produced by volunteers. However, most of the hurdles lie in the one-time set up part, not in daily use. When I wrote this chapter, I debated about whether to omit the encryption material entirely (as all other introductory Linux texts do) or to exile it to an appendix. In the end, I decided to present the knowledge in the main text and let you make the decision about when to try it. It's here when you're ready for it.

Who Me, Do Encryption?

Don't think encryption is only for spies, or computer gurus with ponytails down to the waist and witty tshirts from www.thinkgeek.com. Putting an ordinary file on a PC is like leaving a letter face up on a desk. It's in plain view for anyone who passes by. Encryption is practical for ordinary people who want to keep their data private when they put it on a PC. It effectively puts that letter into a strong sealed envelope. You can do it, and it's an important ability to have.

Before You Begin

This chapter demonstrate how to use the gpg encryption software that you downloaded, compiled and installed in *Building from Source: GNU Privacy Guard Application* on page 237. If you didn't do that, no problem, just do the one-click install of gnupg from the Click-N-Run warehouse now, so you can follow along with the examples.

Introducing GNU Privacy Guard

The terms gnupg and gpg refer to the same thing, the GNU Privacy Guard program. Gpg is the file name of the executable, and gnupg is used in some of the documentation. The name is a deliberate spoof on a very similar program called Pretty Good Privacy or PGP. PGP used to be an open source program but later versions went commercial, so the Linux community reimplemented a free version and named it accordingly.

What the Software Does

GNU Privacy Guard or gpg is software that will scramble and unscramble files or email on command. The purpose of scrambling (i.e., encrypting) a file is to keep its contents private from those who do not have the key.

If an unauthorized person somehow gets hold of an encrypted file, they will not be able to make sense of the contents. The contents of an encrypted file are fundamentally changed, not merely mixed up. It is extremely difficult to retrieve the original contents from the scrambled version unless you have the secret key.

If the information is important enough, governments or rich organizations may be able to do it by exhaustive searching using many powerful computers. The average consumer or company does not have the resources to break gpg encryption.

Terminology

For reasons relating to mathematical definitions, we refer to encryption algorithms, encrypting, and decrypting, where non-mathematicians would say codes, encoding, and decoding. To the ordinary user, these three pairs of terms correspond to each other. The meanings of "code" in source code, and the code used to encrypt a file, were originally similar in philosophy, but there's no useful overlap so separate them in your mind.

Check that you have installed gpg correctly by running the program with the -help option. Bring up a command line window (click **Launch** > **Run Command** and type **xterm**). In the xterminal window, type this command:

```
# gpg --help
```

You should see about 120 lines of (not terrifically helpful) help information flash by, ending in a line like this:

```
Please report bugs to <gnupg-bugs@gnu.org>.
```

If the program doesn't start, or doesn't produce that help information, there is a problem with your gpg installation that needs to be fixed before you can move forward. To the Linspire customer forums with you, and bring with you a full description of what you did and saw.

Basics of Public Key Encryption

For hundreds of years, conventional codes have relied on using a single key. The key is a secret number or phrase that is used in the transformation of plaintext into the coded message. The recipient of the message uses the same key to reverse the procedure and recover the plaintext. Figure 11-1 depicts the classic approach to cryptography: a single key for both coding and decoding.

Lock   Dual-purpose key

Figure 11-1   Traditional cryptography—one key encrypts and decrypts

People have added very clever refinements, such as changing the letter substitution with every letter in the message (the German Enigma code machine did this). But the basic approach has a single secret key used by both coder and decoder. Managing shared secret keys is very expensive and a source of considerable insecurity. It requires you to send a secret message (the key) secretly before you can send a secret message.

Gpg uses two keys: one public, one private. GNU Privacy Guard uses a different encryption technique called public key encryption (PKE), invented comparatively recently. Each user of Public Key Encryption has two keys. The two keys are very long numbers (thousands of digits long) that are related mathematically and form a pair that work together. No two people should ever have the same numbers. Your two numbers have a mathematical relationship between them, but knowing one number doesn't provide any practical way to learn the second number.

One key is used to encrypt messages for a specific user, and (amazingly) this key is published to the world. Hence it is called a *public key*. If the world wants to send Biff a secret message, the world will use Biff's public key to encrypt it so no one else can make sense of it.

The other key of the matched pair is employed by the user to decrypt the messages that were encrypted by someone using his public key. This decrypting key has to be kept secret. Hence it is called a *private key*.

Anyone who wants to send you an encrypted message looks up your public key (on your web page, or from a floppy disk you sent them, or from a PKE server). The encryption program crunches the secret message with your public key, to produce an encrypted message. This encrypted message is just a string of random-looking text. It is not possible for just anyone to decrypt it, even when they know your public key.

The only practical way to decrypt a message encrypted with your public key is with your private key. The two numbers were generated as a matched pair to ensure that they would have this "one encodes, the other decodes" quality. The gpg program does some intensive processing to convert the encrypted message plus your private key, back into the original text. You must keep your private key well guarded, as anyone who has your private key will be able to decrypt any secret files intended only for you.

You might think it would be clearer if your public and private key were called a locking key and an unlocking key, respectively. There's a good reason why those terms aren't used, which I'll discuss at the end of the chapter.

The public key converts plain text into random-looking encoded text. Only the corresponding private key can unlock the meaning—neither your public key nor anybody else's public or private key will recover the original text.

Figure 11-2 portrays public key cryptography. As shown, a public key is used to encrypt a file. The corresponding private key is used to decrypt the file.

Locking key

Unlocking key

Lock

Figure 11-2   Public key cryptography—one key encrypts and the other decrypts

You have already used public and private keys whenever you send your credit card details to an online store in a browser. The browser encrypts the details using the store's public key before sending them across the Internet. This is part of the "secure http" protocol, also known as https.

The mathematical qualities that PKE relies on have a beautiful symmetry to them, and PKE rocked the worlds of computer science and encryption when it appeared in the 1970s. Government scientists in Britain's GCHQ eavesdropping and phone-tapping center later claimed that they had invented the technique some years earlier, but kept it secret! Indeed, they did uncover some of the theory, but it was clear that the GCHQ guys hadn't grasped its practical significance.

Before PKE, secret communications relied on the sender and receiver having the same key and keeping it secret. This was a real weakness. The big advance of PKE is that you no longer have to send someone a secret message (key) before you can send them a secret message. With PKE, the recipient openly publishes something that allows anyone to send him a secret message.

Creating Your Own GPG Key demonstrates the one-time setup to get your pair of keys for use with gpg.

Creating Your Own GPG Key

You need a key pair of your own to be able to encrypt and decrypt. There are a number of commercial organizations that will sell you a key pair, and provide varying assurances that your key really belongs to you, and not to some imposter. They call the key pair plus the assurance, a *certificate* and it exists in the form of a computer file.

Most people encoding and decoding for personal use don't need that level of trustability by the outside world. They create their own key using the gpg utility. There is a way to boost confidence in personally created keys by getting your friends to vouch for them electronically.

gnupg is still evolving

The gnupg program is under active development, and the team makes several new releases a year. This chapter was developed with gpg version 1.4.1. You might find that you are working with a later version of gpg, and that the output does not precisely match the prompts or output shown here.

That's fine. Make the small adjustments to map between the text and the gpg program. The fundamentals won't change.

Use gpg to Generate Your Pair of Keys

In this section, you'll create a pair of keys: one to publish, and one to keep highly secret.

1   Create the pair by running the gpg program, with the command line option
    `--gen-key`.

2   Launch a command line window by choosing **Launch** > **Run Command** >
    xterm.

3   In the window, type gpg --gen-key which means generate keys.

4   The gpg program runs interactively and asks us a few questions. The characters in larger bold text in the following example are the ones you enter. It's fine to accept the default suggestions made by gpg.

```
# gpg --gen-key
gpg (GnuPG) 1.4.1; Copyright (C) 2005 Free Software Foundation, Inc.

This program comes with ABSOLUTELY NO WARRANTY.
This is free software, and you are welcome to redistribute it
under certain conditions. See the file COPYING for details.

Please select what kind of key you want:
   (1) DSA and Elgamal (default)
   (2) DSA (sign only)
   (5) RSA (sign only)
Your selection? 1

DSA keypair will have 1024 bits.
ELG-E keys may be between 1024 and 4096 bits long.

What keysize do you want? (2048)
Requested keysize is 2048 bits

Please specify how long the key should be valid.
     0 = key does not expire
      = key expires in n days
    w = key expires in n weeks
    m = key expires in n months
    y = key expires in n years

Key is valid for? (0) 5

Key expires at Thu 07 Apr 2005 05:11:17 PM PDT
Is this correct? (y/N) Y

You need a user ID to identify your key; the software constructs the user ID
from the Real Name, Comment and Email Address in this form:
   "Heinrich Heine (Der Dichter) "

Real name: Peter van der Linden
Email address: peter@gmail.com
Comment: working on Linux

You selected this USER-ID:
   "Peter van der Linden (working on Linux) "
```

Change (N)ame, (C)omment, (E)mail or (O)kay/(Q)uit? **O**

You need a Passphrase to protect your secret key.
Enter passphrase: **Secret phrase entered here**
Repeat passphrase: **Secret phrase entered here**

We need to generate a lot of random bytes. It is a good idea to perform
some other action (type on the keyboard, move the mouse, utilize the
disks) during the prime generation; this gives the random number
generator a better chance to gain enough entropy.

```
.+++++++++..+++++++++++++++++++++++++++++++++++++++++++++++++++++++++
+++++++..+++++.++++++++++++++++.++++++++++++++++..+++++..++++++++
++.++++++++++++++++>.+++++.+++++>+++++..............<+++++>.+++++...<+++
++.................>+++++..<.+++++>+++++..................................................
..+++++
```

We need to generate a lot of random bytes. It is a good idea to perform
some other action (type on the keyboard, move the mouse, utilize the
disks) during the prime generation; this gives the random number
generator a better chance to gain enough entropy.

```
+++++++++++++++...+++++.+++++.+++++..+++++.++++++++++++++++++++
++++++++++.+++++..+++++.++++++++++..+++++.+++++.++++++++++.+++++
.+++++++++++++++++++++++++++++++++++>.+++++++++++>.+++++>+++++
...............<.+++++>...+++++.<+++++..........>.+++++...........................................
...............<+++++............................>.+++++.....................................+++++^^^
```

gpg: /root/.gnupg/trustdb.gpg: trustdb created
gpg: key 6C7C81B2 marked as ultimately trusted
public and secret key created and signed.
gpg: checking the trustdb
gpg: 3 marginal(s) needed, 1 complete(s) needed, PGP trust model
gpg: depth: 0 valid: 1 signed: 0 trust: 0-, 0q, 0n, 0m, 0f, 1u
gpg: next trustdb check due at 2005-04-08
pub   1024D/6C7C81B2 2005-04-03 [expires: 2005-04-08]

Key fingerprint = C2A9 6818 3158 C13B 457A 1409 11ED 2943 6C7C 81B2

uid Peter van der Linden (working on Linux)

sub   2048g/68F3472B 2005-04-03 [expires: 2005-04-08]

As you might surmise, the gpg program was created by programmers who are
more skilled at cryptography than at human interface design. The program
takes just a few seconds to run, and you get back three things from it:

5   A pair of very big numbers (the public and private keys) is created for you and stored in binary form in files in directory ~/.gnupg. These files are given permissions that prevent other users from reading or writing them. Burn a copy of that directory to CD now, and lock the CD safely away. This allows you to restore your key regardless of future disk or system failure.

You are given a fingerprint, also called a key ID, which is a 40-byte-long checksum of your newly created public key. You can use the fingerprint (or even the last 8 digits of it, 6C7C 81B2 here) when talking to gnupg as a short-cut for your public key, and it will retrieve and use the key for you.

The email address and the passphrase you gave are associated with the keys and the fingerprint, and these are also used to identify and authenticate you.

They call it a passphrase rather than a password to emphasize that it needs to be lengthy and secure. It's pointless to use gpg with a weak passphrase like dog. If you can't remember a brief phrase, pick any short sentence from any book and outline it with yellow highlighter so you can always find it again.

You must give the passphrase when you need to access the secret key to decrypt something. If you forget your passphrase, practically speaking, the files you encrypted can never be decrypted.

Understanding Levels of Trust in Keys

The gpg program has the concept of levels of trust in keys. A key that someone leaves on a CD on your desk has a lower level of trust. Perhaps someone switched or copied the CD. A key that you yourself generated a moment ago can be trusted absolutely. You might notice that the output described previously includes the text key marked as ultimately trusted.

Convey the level of assurance with the following --edit-keys option to gpg. The bold larger font indicates the part I typed. Make sure you use your email address, not mine.

```
# gpg  --edit-key   peter@gmail.com
 a few lines of output, ignored
Command> trust

Your decision? 4
 a couple of lines of output, ignored
Command> save
#
```

The levels of trust run from 1 to 5 with these meanings:

1 I don't know, or don't want to specify, what trust I place in this key

2 I do not trust this key

3 I trust this key marginally

4 I trust this key fully

5 I place ultimate trust in this key

By typing this sequence once, you avoid unnecessary reminders from gpg saying that it is not certain that the key belongs to the person named in the user ID.

Encrypting Files demonstrates how to encrypt and decrypt files using gpg.

Encrypting Files

Now you're ready to encrypt a file.

Encrypting a File

Create a text file to work on. Open an editor by clicking **Launch > Programs > Software Development > Advanced Text Editor** and create a file called myinfo.txt containing some highly secret text. You can equally well create the file with the following command.

```
# echo "Parmesan cheese smells funny" > myinfo.txt
```

Looking at the contents of any file

It's quite helpful when learning about gpg to be able to look at the contents of any file. Normally you can't type out the contents of a binary file, like an executable or an encrypted file. The bytes that don't contain printable ASCII codes are interpreted as terminal control characters. If the file happens to contain the wrong values, it can cause the terminal to freeze or behave strangely.

You can use a couple of handy utilities to avoid the terminal going wild and output any file in printable form.

- *You can use the od utility to dump out the bytes of a file. It is a very simple command that is already installed on your system. The command takes several different options to format the output. To see the file as printable representation of bytes, use od -c filename.*

- *If you'd rather see the file contents in a GUI, get KHexEdit from Click-N-Run. When you use CNR to install it, It will show up on your Programs menu, under Utilities. Important: Do not use apt-get to install khexedit as this is one of the programs whose installation will overwrite Linspire-specific libraries. You can also search for the khexedit tarball source and build it for practice if so inclined.*

Here is the od (octal dump) output for our file of secret information.

```
# od -c myinfo.txt
0000000   P   a   r   m   e   s   a   n       c   h   e   e   s   e
0000020   s   m   e   l   l   s       f   u   n   n   y  \n
0000035
```

Compare this with the encrypted file.

You can create an encrypted version of this file that no one can read without your secret key, with this command:

```
# gpg    --recipient peter@gmail.com    --encrypt  myinfo.txt
```

Notes

- Use your own identifying email address where I have put peter@gmail.com. It will be the email address you gave when generating the keys.

- You provide the name of the file you want encrypted. The output will go in a file of the same name but with .gpg appended. The encrypted file in this example will be called myinfo.txt.gpg. Although the input file contained readable text, the output file contains binary data.

- You can encrypt any kind of file this way, not just files of ASCII text. You can encrypt applications, images, spreadsheets, documents, and so on.

- The unencrypted file myinfo.txt is not changed by this operation, so if you truly want the information to be secret, you must delete that file and any other files that contain the information in the clear.

  Don't use an ordinary old delete, but a secure delete that repeatedly overwrites the bits in the deleted file on disk. If you intend a really secure system, do a web search for "secure delete Linux" to locate some free tools to help with this.

Here are the results of running od on the encrypted file. The encrypted file is longer than the plaintext file because gpg puts some extra housekeeping data in there (like the program version number) to assist when decrypting.

```
#  od -c myinfo.txt.gpg
0000000 205 001 016 003 332 027   o   _ 202 331 252   7 020 003 375 033
0000020   w   @ 244 333 245 024   P 271   ! 337  \n 333   t 205 200  \0
0000040   1 202 331 306 266 024 034 204  \0   ^ 375   "   (   u 032 255
0000060 327 263 263 225   M 216   , 314 207 340 023 222   ? 207 203 337
0000100   i 205 006 200   Q 266   m   4 177   ~ 257   ;  \a   5   W 205
0000120   i   k 034   \ 367   5 230 334   f 330 355   M   &   n   .   `
0000140 356   W 272 254   @   q 334   r 237 345 255  \f 003   y 272 343
0000160 032   t   0   z 265 371 261 334 274 247 350 247 271 342 324 001
0000200 325 352   %   v 024 240 362 027 353   ~  \0 227 364  \n 273 003
0000220 377   s 304   :   T   e 367  \f   )   3   .   Z 215   ! 361   D
0000240   `   r 262   h   @   { 216   ?   u 001   ' 221   v   d 235 332
0000260 337 030   6 215 030 363   g 235   }   = 030   C 321 326 337 312
0000300 272 027   Y 225 311 264   q   v 337 210 257   2 213   L 346   \
0000320 347 370 027  \f 355 250 234 027 340   i 242   5 036 242 241 302
0000340   8 311   g   4 235   b 220 207 367   d   H   z   7   N 221 213
0000360   9 276 005 220   D   R 320   1 211 247   : 374 233 305   =   B
0000400 203 337 206   R   $   .   { 210   P 027 307   (   v   r   " 345
0000420 030 322   V 001 315 027 262 345   c   ' 361   |   ?  \a   1 212
0000440 212 320 374 004 210 242 361   g 376   8 364 335 242 312 314   z
0000460   q 371 261   {   ! 211 345   G 031 260 335 016   ] 203   G 330
0000500   d   ( 244 227 320 024 263 353 301  \r   j   e   z 302   j 307
0000520 301 301   *   I 362 367  \n 220   x 307 276   8 027  \0 205   2
0000540 211   \ 332 213   x 234   9   s   >
0000551
```

As you can see, the encrypted file is a binary file. If you prefer an encrypted file expressed in the form of printable characters (perhaps you want to email it, or view it in an editor), you can use the -a option for gpg. That ensures that the encrypted output is expressed in short lines of printable ASCII characters.

The command is as follows:

```
# gpg   -a   --recipient peter@gmail.com   --encrypt  myinfo.txt
```

The new output file will be the input file name plus the extension .asc. A printable ASCII output file might be 50% bigger than the corresponding binary output file. Dump the encrypted ASCII file so that you can compare the contents with the binary version. You will see the following:

```
# od -c myinfo.txt.asc
0000000   -   -   -   -   -   B   E   G   I   N       P   G   P       M
0000020   E   S   S   A   G   E   -   -   -   -   -  \n   V   e   r   s
0000040   i   o   n   :       G   n   u   P   G       v   1   .   2   .
0000060   6       (   G   N   U   /   L   i   n   u   x   )  \n  \n   h
0000100   Q   E   O   A   7   X   F   U   y   1   w   s   Q   8   y   E
0000120   A   P   +   K   /   i   8   H   p   X   U   x   K   e   O   W
0000140   7   5   o   1   3   Q   U   q   Z   L   Q   g   R   e   N   f
0000160   a   X   J   N   K   O   4   D   0   5   r   k   T   0   h  \n
0000200   9   M   M   s   o   C   E   u   S   q   I   4   T   7   i   m
0000220   b   q   Z   d   y   U   8   w   I   d   E   m   L   x   V   d
0000240   2   n   N   t   T   V   y   z   H   L   3   y   c   q   H   u
0000260   m   B   X   F   8   X   O   5   F   n   m   k   I   x   q   Y
0000300  \n   x   x   N   O   K   9   s   5   F   r   A   R   r   6   A
0000320   Y   U   P   Q   w   1   w   j   I   5   +   z   N   D   4   F
0000340   w   C   V   R   7   5   Z   M   t   g   3   E   Y   P   8   V
0000360   h   1   J   P   a   A   f   7   a   8   6   7   Z   y   G   8
0000400   D  \n   /   2   0   j   1   b   o   c   J   8   i   B   N   n
0000420   4   1   7   0   X   2   e   x   Y   n   Z   i   U   N   y   O
0000440   i   2   E   h   Y   X   9   O   T   Z   I   V   M   u   4   n
0000460   d   Q   M   t   Y   1   Z   v   a   t   1   1   0   X   p   G
0000500   a   4  \n   E   T   n   7   /   X   Y   1   d   k   2   B   1
0000520   2   T   C   f   H   G   i   Y   c   z   g   w   V   c   r   8
0000540   8   8   L   b   G   q   c   n   p   y   +   6   T   G   v   M
0000560   q   8   w   1   D   L   N   O   c   O   J   q   U   /   s   a
0000600   N   6   x  \n   D   A   a   u   1   6   w   I   /   S   Q
0000620   u   5   Y   d   3   A   y   2   Q   g   m   2   1   5   k   p
```

```
0000640    4    d    r    A    p    0    t    G    9    8    s    l    y    C    g    t
0000660    0    l    g    B    /    Q    x    7    9    s    H    b    W    Q    q    m
0000700    k    8    I    B   \n    G    x    0    M    E    L    7    M    7    M    z
0000720    V    u    q    4    W    k    f    l    j    6    Z    f    4    F    c    m
0000740    n    3    8    1    d    9    i    G    M    H    /    e    x    k    5    t
0000760    /    4    s    q    z    H    3    A    E    s    d    P    t    N    k    D
0001000    3    /    f    4    I   \n    x    E    U    K    5    X    9    u    x    J
0001020    s    D    a    p    j    J    T    U    E    y    2    t    y    0    y    P
0001040    j    k    2    0    9    k    N    l    U    X   \n    =    d    w    1    4
0001060   \n    -    -    -    -    -    E    N    D         P    G    P         M    E
0001100    S    S    A    G    E    -    -    -    -    -   \n
0001113
```

That file represents my secret information that Parmesan cheese smells funny, but you'll never know that unless you have my private key. Or unless you've been in the same room with Parmesan cheese.

One message to five people, needs five coded messages, each to one person

Remember that you encrypt a message using a specific public key. Only the one person with the private key that corresponds to that public key can decrypt that message.

If you need to send the same coded message to all five of your henchmen, you have to turn it into five different coded messages. Each henchman can only decrypt the message encoded with his public key. He can run the decryption using his key on a message intended for someone else. It will only yield random junk, not the original message. Except you should never send the same or a similar plaintext message twice, because it gives too much help to people trying to break the code.

You could let all the henchmen use the same one key-pair. If you do that, you can no longer send them individual messages that are secret from the other henchmen. So you can't prevent them from banding together and overthrowing your secret Arctic stronghold.

The encrypted message is all in ASCII with short line lengths, so it can be sent in email without loss. Never edit an encrypted file or change it in any way. If you do, the private key will not be able to transform it back into the original, readable file.

Encrypting Many Files

Sometimes you want to encrypt many files at once, such as an entire directory. To encrypt many files, first bundle up all the files into one archive file. You can do this using the ark GUI utility, or from the command line. This command will create a single compressed tarball containing the contents of your My Documents folder. You need to be in the parent directory of My Documents or you need to give the complete path to My Documents.

```
# tar -cvzf mydocs.tar.gz  My\ Documents
```

A tar.gz file is like a zip file under Windows—it's a compressed archive containing several files. It is traditional to give a gzipped tar file that you create in this way the extension .tar.gz or .tgz so everyone can recognize what it is, and hence how to unpack it. Use a backslash or quotes around My Documents to stop the space in the file name causing problems. (Without them it looks like two file names, My and Documents.)

Doing so will create a single archive file, containing the files in the folder called My Documents. Then encrypt that single archive file in the usual way:

```
# gpg   --recipient peter@gmail.com   --encrypt mydocs.tar.gz
```

The encrypted output file will be mydocs.tar.gz.gpg. Read on to learn how to decrypt an encrypted file to get your information in clear form.

Decrypting a File

To decrypt a file, you have to know the secret key that goes with the public key that was used to encrypt it. You might well have several key pairs for your different types of correspondence. You tell gpg which secret key to use by specifying the public key owner. Since this often occurs in the context of messages, the owner is called a recipient.

Gpg will use the secret key for the recipient that you name. But first gpg will challenge you to provide the corresponding passphrase. Successfully meeting that challenge tells gpg that you are entitled to use that secret key. You give the options first, including the -o *somefilename* argument to specify the name of the output file. The action to take, namely --decrypt *somefilename*, has to come last on the command line.

Here is an example of the command line.

```
# gpg --recipient peter@gmail.com -o plaintext.txt --decrypt myinfo.txt.gpg
```

```
You need a passphrase to unlock the secret key for
user: "Peter van der Linden (working on Linux) "
2048-bit ELG-E key, ID 68F3472B, created 2005-04-03 (main key ID 6C7C81B2)
type your passphrase here
gpg: encrypted with 2048-bit ELG-E key, ID 68F3472B, created 2005-04-03
      "Peter van der Linden (working on Linux) "
```

```
luna:~# cat plaintext.txt
Parmesan cheese smells funny
```

That command recovers the file into plaintext.txt. You should confirm this by running the commands and examining the files.

```
 # ls -l
-rw-r--r--  1 root root        29 2005-04-02 17:29 myinfo.txt
-rw-r--r--  1 root root       949 2005-04-02 17:40 myinfo.txt.asc
-rw-r--r--  1 root root       629 2005-04-02 17:34 myinfo.txt.gpg
-rw-r--r--  1 root root        29 2005-04-02 18:32 plaintext.txt
# cat plaintext.txt
Parmesan cheese smells funny
```

You can probably guess how you decrypt a file you get from someone else. They need to have encoded it with your public key before sending it to you. Then you decode it with your private key just as though it were a file that you encrypted in the first place. Your correspondents have to get your public key from a place that you can both trust. If it's from a web page, it needs to be a web page that cannot be changed by someone who is trying to learn your secret information or trying to sabotage your communications.

Decrypting an Archive of Files

If you have an encrypted archive file, such as the one created in the previous section, you can decrypt it as shown in that section. You can give the output file from the decryption any name, but it's good practice to use file names consistently and to use the extension to indicate the file type.

Here's how you would get back the unencrypted files.

1   First, decrypt the archive file.

```
gpg    --recipient peter@gmail.com  -o  mydocs.tgz  --decrypt
mydocs.tar.gz.gpg
```

a couple of lines of output, ignored

2   Enter your passphrase. You'll see this:

```
Enter passphrase: type your passphrase here
```

a couple of lines of output, ignored

3   Then use tar or ark to unpack the archive. You can start ark (the archive processing utility) by clicking **Launch** > **Programs** > **Utilities** > **Archiving tool**. Alternatively, the tar command is

```
tar -xzvf mydocs.tgz
```

That will unpack (into a folder called My Documents in your current directory) all the files that were originally put into the mydocs archive. You might want to create a temporary directory first and move the archive there before unpacking it. That way you won't accidentally overwrite a newer file with an older version from the archive.

Using Key Management

There's no security-related reason not to publish your public key widely. The more widely published the better, because it will allow more people to send you confidential files.

The gpg framework includes a number of searchable databases of public keys maintained by public-spirited organizations. You can load your key into one of these databases without charge, making it widely available.

Managing Your Private Key

The vital thing you need to do with your private key is to keep it out of unauthorized hands. That's not quite as easy as it may seem. To be really secure, the system that holds your private data, such as your private key file and the passphrase used to access it, should not be connected to any network. This was the mistake that Massachusetts-based bulk retailer BJ's Wholesale Club made in March 2004, when they suffered a network security breach. More than 40,000 customers had their credit card numbers compromised when attackers infiltrated BJ's network. Those credit card numbers should never have been stored on a server reachable from the Internet, nor should BJ's have been running unsecured wireless networks.

Make one backup copy of the ~/.gnupg folder onto a CD and store it somewhere completely trustworthy. You should not include anything confidential in your regular system backups. Either keep your files encrypted all the time, and only decrypt a file when you actually need to look at the contents; or don't allow system backups, and do your own backups of your confidential data. Overlooking this simple point was the downfall of Oliver North.

Throughout 1986, working from his White House office, North waged a secret war in Central America financed by illegal arms shipments to Iran. When a Middle Eastern newspaper exposed the arms shipments in November 1986, North deleted the email record of his activities. But the email was recovered from the weekly backups, and North was convicted of aiding and abetting the obstruction of a congressional inquiry and destruction of documents. The conviction was later overturned on a technicality.

Sharing Public Keys

You will want to pull a copy of your public key out of the gnupg folder, so that you can publish it to other people. You can do that with this command. The -o argument directs output into the file name that appears after it.

```
gpg --export --armor -o ~/Desktop/my-public-key.asc
```

That creates what is called an armored public key file. The term armor doesn't mean that the file has any magical protective properties. It just means that the file holds your public key in short lines of ASCII, not binary data.

Some mail programs used to fail if you included non-ASCII data in the message, so the armor option safeguards messages sent by mail. The options --armor and -a are interchangeable.

Arguments to commands

The optional arguments to many Linux programs are single letters introduced by a hyphen. You can get a directory listing with the command ls. *If you add the* -l *option so the complete command is* ls -l *(ls with the letter el), you get a long listing that shows the permissions on each file. The letter* l *stands for* long. *There are plenty of other options for* ls, *too. You can string them together; an example is* ls -alt. *That means list all files, including hidden files, make it a long listing, and present it in timestamp order.*

A few years ago, the GNU folks decided to introduce complete words as options to new programs. To distinguish a word option from several single letter options, use double hyphens before a keyword option. A few commands (gpg is one of them) accept both kinds of options.

So

gpg -a *and* gpg --armor

have exactly the same effect (to produce the gpg output in ASCII form).

Here are the contents of the my-public-key.asc file.

```
-----BEGIN PGP PUBLIC KEY BLOCK-----
Version: GnuPG v1.2.6 (GNU/Linux)
```

```
mQGiBEGGx/8RBACri2RSuN0NIzYjlF7yqXXqBIQOJWtXfPnoKjV/GDW6lOAlcx+F
HtmTC/60lY/+WQl4Qk4uIP47/nKg3cGWI+6E3Pps/FknoxEfGMVF2sCKT8cTXcWb
2sXRSSIv32SaygrGToPV3tR68XweBNIiOKmMaa8Ezkfczy4ObUReAP5jEwCgxvUp
ikabuHHo5MS7OHXycbPzOp8EAImgLyfTAf2sttrI4VAGGg2HYjTuNORLTV08muRJ
Z0OvKEYjSv8NbgTisCddSZW3fGyK16KU4HntiZrFEe6ZVlA9pkpQLf3AQ1iSpWEM
N/jKc+6hoBviwzESXzJSQZilzEajwl215Bc9+Ih3QTqyAO0CAFg4q0LqUUZzqzCv
C4hHA/9F022k4lYpgH9/qqDmRyFYMQWpMrSGPTgdfOwuX8ehX5+2VSGwhAc30bZ+
zUlP/j2hD37JxgTYvRbaZ2BIEKrsFwp2PCL+4gyP1lwN2wIrKHB3y+P9k4bOyuCs
2cWbddb7Jz9jvFnDjBTBszgK4ffr/38eKJC8PscliVNix353B7Q3UGV0ZXIgdmFu
IGRlciBMaW5kZW4gKHHdvcmtpbmcgb24gTGludXggpIDxwZXRlckBhZnUZ29tPohe
BBMRAgAeBQJBhsf/AhsDBgsJCAcDAgMVAgMDFgIBAh4BAheAAAoJECYgSs7nbRXV
LbcAoLxwvfQFiMuCk60jbpnIfTO7eHzyAJ0UZZwXL1oad5dRIZ6WIIONj6YZzLkB
```

```
DQRBhsgCEAQA3xi6cTWumCylHpoNkzW8FHJQiCvoEAOHbRqt2mx+zA7zD9wj1r9D
vQk6n6+aBdo31LerL/eVvnKlkmAe9H88G++qFzeqlH9RsRxqVwytkzNtPrTCztG/
3mZ/uNhUsi1yQ6wvenhe1PITbcJD7ENHo4a9tA1Ut7FZoRblauo5KdsAAwUD/2Px
HVe+SAAMMG+D9H1nCSnsq4qbo3VhX1Jq121yQXV0/HOw9Wn86WgWbceHaxZYmWAX
+sUzvYKHSQCWyRwKOBMzMx3XfIcO4oWrm6qHgg5/+St/3Gpc3jyhbsQepTakTt4n
pXqkJZlUrJ14qeai5hyICs8tAnBpGbOlPUiuEBBwiEkEGBECAAkFAkGGyAICGwwA
CgkQJiBKzudtFdV75QCgi0LtN4P34WdP0S1bDglmccgKE2YAn2Glcvp8OLM/aNxh
OfiYt5AMnd+4
=tucQ
-----END PGP PUBLIC KEY BLOCK-----
```

Tip – When you use the --armor option to force the output to be in ASCII with short lines, the convention is to give the output file the extension .asc as in this example.

```
# gpg   --armor  --recipient peter@gmail.com  --encrypt  mysecret.txt
```

This command will put the encrypted output into file mysecret.txt.asc.

Give people a copy of your my_public_key.asc file (perhaps on a CD) and they can use your public key to send you encrypted mail. You can also place your public key on one of the servers that a number of public-spirited organizations run, and retrieve others' keys from the servers.

Getting Other People's Public Keys

If you want to send alice@yahoo.com an encrypted message, you first need to make her public key known to your gpg library. Perhaps you copied Alice's public key from her web site. It's not secure for Alice to email you her armored key. How can you be sure that mail really came from her or was not changed by someone else on the way?

The best way is to get Alice's public key on a CD from her in person. Put Alice's key in a file called something like alice-public-key.asc. Then type this command:

```
# gpg   --import   alice-public-key.asc
```

Alice's key will now be available to gpg on your PC, and you can send her encrypted files. Gpg stores the keys in a series of files that it collectively calls a keyring.

Another way to bring someone's public key onto your machine is to search the keyservers, stating the key ID you are interested in. The host pgp.mit.edu is a keyserver located at the Massachusetts Institute of Technology. There are other keyservers and most of them regularly exchange data with each other so that recipients can often obtain a public key by asking a different server than the one the key was originally sent to.

```
# gpg   --keyserver pgp.mit.edu   --recv-key  0F3BB819
```

That will import one of my public keys onto your PC. The key ID identifies the key to import. Some people have more than one email address associated with a key. You can look at the email addresses by listing the keys, described in *Listing the Keys on Your Keyring*.

Listing the Keys on Your Keyring

After you have added a few keys, you will find it useful to be able to list them. Use this option to gpg:

```
# gpg   --list-keys
```

You will see a series of lines, two lines per key, showing the public keys that gpg has stored locally, and the email address associated with each. Here's an example of output from the command:

```
# gpg   --list-keys
/root/.gnupg/pubring.gpg
------------------------
pub   1024D/6C7C81B2 2005-04-03 [expires: 2005-04-08]
uid               Peter van der Linden (working on Linux)
sub   2048g/68F3472B 2005-04-03 [expires: 2005-04-08]


pub   1024D/09AC0A6A 1998-07-14
uid               Alice Smith <alice@yahoo.com>
sub   2048g/81451634 1998-07-14


pub  1024D/C94AEC02 2000-02-22
UID               Harry Jones <harry@hmft.com>
sub  2048g/DAB1F6A4 2000-02-22
```

As you can see, the first line of each entry reads something like the following:

```
pub 1024D/xxxxxxxx
```

This means "public key that is 1024 digits long". The characters after the `pub 1024D/` are the last eight characters of the fingerprint, also called the key ID.

Limitations of Encryption

Although public key cryptography is one of the most secure code systems known, some factors make it less than perfect in practice. First, gpg relies on a passphrase, and passphrases can be stolen, or overheard. Accounts can be broken into. Passphrases do not protect against physical access to the data. If an adversary can get access to your PC, they can often get to the data.

You should never use gnupg on a remote system because it is too easy to snoop on what you type as it travels over the network.

The key length that you select determines how break-resistant your encrypted data is. A key length of 1024 digits is good enough for most purposes now, but in some years time, it may easily be broken by supercomputers. A few years after that, it may be broken by desktop PCs.

Although the core gpg system is secure, everything going into it and coming out of it needs to be very carefully considered. When you get a public key from Alice, how sure can you be that it really came from her, and that it was not really from Bob who administers Alice's mail server? Bob could then intercept all your secret mail to Alice, read it, and reencode it with her true key before sending it on to her. This is known as a "man in the middle" attack.

You might have noticed that during the key creation process, you just had to assert who you were. But anyone could create a public/private key pair and say that it belonged to Peter van der Linden , and there's nothing anyone can do about it. The imposter could even publish that key on the MIT key server and use coded messages and pretend to be me.

You can guard against this with *certificates* and *signatures*.

- A certificate is a guarantee for a public key, ideally from a trusted authority. You can go to a company like Thwaite or Verisign and persuade them of your identity (with a passport or driver's license) and give them some money. They will give you a certificate in digital form that is bundled with your public key.

  The meaning of the certificate is "*Verisign believes this key belongs to some- one who has a lot of identity documents belonging to Peter van der Linden.*" If Verisign is doing their job, imposters cannot get such a certificate on a fraud- ulent key generated using someone else's name and address.

- Most people who use encryption for personal files don't bother with this. To protect against impersonation, you talk to some of your friends and ask them to sign your key after they verify that it belongs to you. Those *signatures* move around with your public key. So after I've verified that the key I got from MIT really does belong to you (with a phone call, say, just in case someone has hijacked your email and is faking the whole conversation), I sign it. If a third friend picks up your key, she can see that I've vouched for the fact that it's really your key, and maybe to her, my word is as good as Verisign's. A chain of trust is thus built.

It's not enough to delete the file containing the original unencrypted data. Deleted files can be recovered with enough effort. You need to securely delete the file, which means overwriting its blocks multiple times with random data. Even this is not good enough for national secrets—government standards call for the physical destruction of storage media when a PC with secret data is removed from a secure location, typically at the end of its useful life.

Encryption is a fascinating topic, and it sometimes raises passions. Up to the late 1990s, encryption software (like gpg) was restricted by the U.S. government under the International Traffic in Arms Regulations. It was illegal for people in the United States to send such software overseas, just the way we cannot mail machine guns or artillery pieces to our nephews.

The gpg software was implemented outside the United States precisely to avoid breaking this U.S. restriction. Even today, some countries such as France have made it illegal for their citizens to use cryptography. Recently in Britain a regulation was written (but not yet put into effect) making it a criminal offence to refuse to give up encryption keys or plaintext versions of encrypted data. I don't know how they expect to enforce that for people who keep their collections of random numbers, wink wink, in disk files.

Summary of Common gpg Commands

Here are some common commands for key management, encryption, and decryption.

Key Management

`gpg --help`

> Print lengthy but not terrifically helpful help message.

`gpg --gen-key`

> Generate pair of keys for a user.

`gpg --list-keys`

> List the keys that have been imported by the user who runs the command.

`gpg --fingerprint peter@gmail.com`

> List the key fingerprint (shorthand) for this user.

`gpg --export --armor -o ~/Desktop/my-public-key.asc`

> Put this user's key in an ASCII file.

`gpg --import alice-public-key.asc`

> Import a key from this ASCII file.

`gpg --keyserver pgp.mit.edu --recv-key 0x9369CDF3`

> Import the key with this fingerprint from this keyserver.

`gpg --keyserver pgp.mit.edu --send-key peter@gmail.com`

> Put Peter's key onto the MIT keyserver.

`gpg --keyserver pgp.mit.edu --list-keys bill@yahoo.com`

> List any key for bill@yahoo.com on the MIT keyserver.

`gpg --edit-key bill@yahoo.com`

> Edit the key for bill@yahoo.com, e.g. to change the level of trust you have in it.

Encryption

`gpg --recipient peter@gmail.com  --encrypt myinfo.txt`

Encrypt an individual file into binary for peter@gmail.com; don't forget to securely wipe the clear text file. Encrypted file is input-filename.gpg.

`gpg -a --recipient peter@gmail.com  --encrypt myinfo.txt`

Encrypt an individual file into emailable ASCII for peter@gmail.com. Don't forget to securely wipe the clear text file. Encrypted file is input-filename.asc.

`tar -cvzf mydocs.tar.gz "My Documents"`

`gpg --recipient peter@gmail.com  --encrypt mydocs.tar.gz`

Encrypt an entire directory. Don't forget to securely wipe all the clear text files. Encrypted file is input-filename.gpg.

Decryption

`gpg --recipient peter@gmail.com  -o myinfo.clear.txt  --decrypt myinfo.txt.gpg`

Decrypt an individual file using Peter's key (it will ask for a passphrase).

`gpg  --recipient peter@gmail.com  -o mydocs.tar.gz  --decrypt mydocs.tar.gz.gpg`

`tar -xvzf mydocs.tar.gz`

Decrypt and restore a directory archive (it will ask for a passphrase).

Encrypting Email

This section describes how to use gpg for encrypting your private email before sending it to a friend, and how to automatically decrypt any incoming encrypted email. Gpg provides the encryption library, and you also need to install a couple of other libraries to interface your mail program to the encryption routines.

I mentioned earlier that my favorite email client is the Thunderbird program, which is based on just the email part of the all-in-one Mozilla program.

I'll demonstrate how to add these two small libraries to the Mozilla or Thunderbird mail clients to provide seamless support for encryption.

There is also a browser called Firefox based on just the browser part of Mozilla. All three programs, Mozilla, Thunderbird, and Firefox, are closely related, and a great many add-ons and plug-ins are available for them.

You can find a list of the available extensions at the web site http://extensionroom.mozdev.org. There is a brief description of each extension.

Here are the steps for encrypting email covered in this section.

- *Downloading and Installing Enigmail*
- *Sending Encrypted Mail*
- *Receiving Encrypted Mail*
- *Signing Email and Files*

Downloading and Installing Enigmail

Enigmail is the software that handles the Thunderbird/Mozilla mail end of the interface to gpg encryption. You're going to find the Enigmail software, download it, and install it to the Thunderbird mail client.

The name Enigmail relates to the German Enigma encryption device used in WWII, which was cracked by a brilliant Polish mathematician, and exploited by the British to track and sink Nazi U-Boats. Enigmail provides secure communication by scrambling email so only the intended recipient can read it.

You'll complete the following steps:

- *Get the Mailer Version Number*
- *Download the Mailer Extension*
- *Install Enigmail into Thunderbird Email*
- *Complete the Thunderbird Mail Interface to gpg*
- *Verify That You Installed the Right Enigmail Version*

Get the Mailer Version Number

You need to find out the version number of Mozilla or Thunderbird that you are using. There are different Enigmail versions for the different Mozilla versions, and the wrong one will fail with a mysterious and unhelpful error message.

- In Mozilla email, choose **Help** > **About Internet Suite** and find the Internet Suite version number. It will likely be 1.5, 1.6, or 2.1. Make a note of it.
- In Thunderbird, choose **Help** > **About Mozilla Thunderbird**, and check the version number. The number will be 0.9 or something greater.

Download the Mailer Extension

Now that you know the mailer version number, browse to the Enigmail download page at http://Enigmail.mozdev.org/download.html.

If you scroll down the page, you'll find several versions of the downloads for different operating systems and different mail clients. Make sure that you are on the part of the page that shows Downloads for Linux x86-32.

You are going to download and install an Enigmail module. If you're still using Mozilla mail, the installation will be slightly different, and you might also need to download an Enigmime module.

1 Find the Enigmail module that matches your operating system and mailer application version. The web page has improved a lot recently, but can still be confusing. See Figure 11-3.

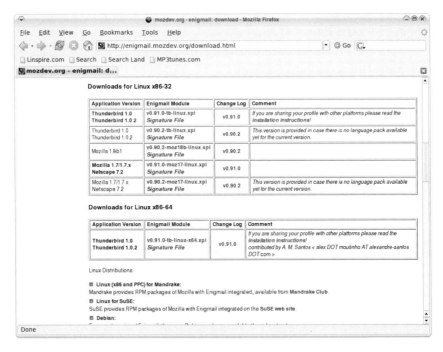

Figure 11-3   Enigmail download page

2 Make sure you are looking at the Linux part of the web site, not the Windows part. Double-check the version numbers before proceeding.

Note – It is very easy to download the wrong versions of the two files. If you do, the mailer will not be able to handle encryption, and you will not get any sensible error messages. If things aren't working, this is the first thing to double-check.

---

3   Right-click on the link for that Enigmail module and select **Save Link As**. Save the linked file to your desktop so it is easy to find again.

The downloaded file will have a name like `enigmail-0.91.0-tb-linux.xpi`. An .xpi file is a Mozilla format for mailer and browser add-ons. It's a ZIP archive that contains several Javascript files with a bunch of instructions that tell the Mozilla application how to add new menu items, and what programs to run when the new menu items are clicked.

Install Enigmail into Thunderbird Email

You're ready to install the downloaded Enigmail file (and Enigmime if necessary).

1   Start Thunderbird, then choose **Tools** > **Extensions** > **Install**.

2   Browse for the Enigmail .xpi file you just downloaded and install it, as shown in Figure 11-4.

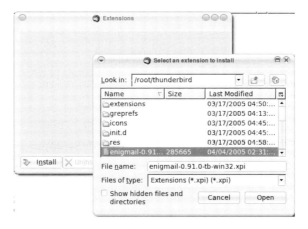

Figure 11-4   Installing the Enigmail library

3   Now completely exit and restart Thunderbird to make Enigmail available.

Complete the Thunderbird Mail Interface to gpg

1   Start Thunderbird mail. Note that there is a new menu item, Enigmail. Figure 11-5 shows the entries on the Enigmail menu item.

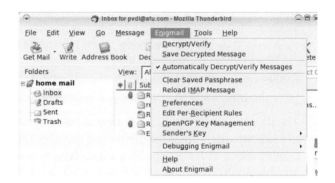

Figure 11-5   Thunderbird menus after installing Enigmail

2   You need to complete a very small amount of configuration to be able to process encrypted mail. Choose **Enigmail** > **Preferences** to bring up the window shown in Figure 11-6.

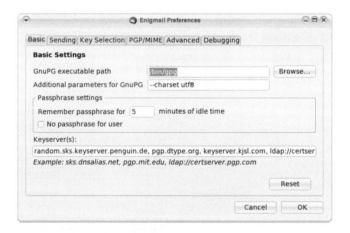

Figure 11-6   Thunderbird's Enigmail preferences

3   Enter the path to the program in the **GnuPG executable path** field and click **OK**.

If you can't recall where it is, in Konqueror choose **Tools** > **Find File** to search for it by name.

The Thunderbird Enigmail Preferences panel seen in Figure 11-6 has six different tabs. Explore them and see if there are other settings you would like to change, such as **Timeout before requesting a pass phrase**, or the option to add a keyserver such as pgp.mit.edu.

Verify That You Installed the Right Enigmail Version

1   Bring up the Thunderbird Enigmail Preferences panel in Figure 11-6 again.

2   Click the **Debugging** tab shown in Figure 11-7.

3   Fill in your own email address in the **Test email** field, and click the **Test** button. You will be prompted for your gpg passphrase.

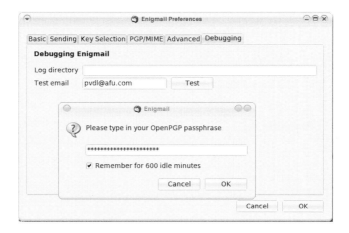

Figure 11-7   Testing gpg with Thunderbird

The test button doesn't actually send mail (so it is a bug to label the button "test email") but it goes through the motions of making sure that Thunderbird can talk to gpg.

4   What happens next depends on if everything is working.

   ◆   If everything is working together, you will see a dialog box like the one shown in Figure 11-8. Just click **OK**.

Figure 11-8   This message means the mailer and gpg are talking to each other

   ◆   If the mailer can't make contact with the Enigmail library, it will pop up the dialog shown in Figure 11-9.

Figure 11-9   This message suggests you installed the wrong Enigmail module

This error dialog almost certainly means you installed an Enigmail or Enigmime module that doesn't match your email client. That's really easy to do, and really hard to notice. Uninstall Enigmail by choosing **Tools > Extensions > Uninstall** button, and try again.

Sending Encrypted Mail

The last part of configuring Thunderbird for encrypted mail is to tell Thunderbird what your gpg identity is. The easiest way to do that is to compose an email, ask for encryption, and let it prompt you for the information it needs.

1   In Thunderbird, hold down the **Shift key** and click **Write** to compose a new mail message. The shift key turns off HTML formatting for the email. When you're encrypting a message, you don't want all kinds of HTML markup littered throughout it.

You can turn off the use of HTML in mail for good, by choosing **Edit > Account Settings > Composition & Addressing > Compose messages in HTML format**.

2   In the new empty email window, fill in the fields **To**, **Subject**, and **Body**,.

3   Click **OpenPGP**.

4   The message in Figure 11-10 will appear. Click **Yes**.

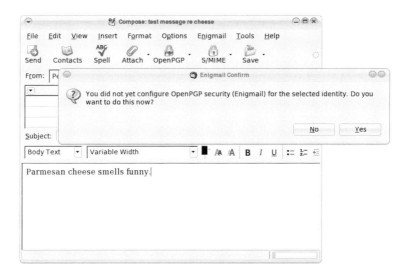

Figure 11-10   Thunderbird prompts you to configure security

5 The window shown in Figure 11-11 will appear.

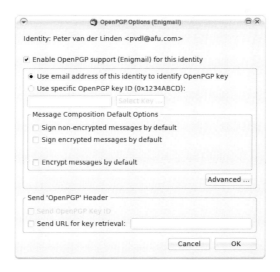

Figure 11-11   Telling Thunderbird which gpg key ID is you

If the email identity you are using in Thunderbird matches the email identity that you used when you set up your gpg key, select **Enable OpenPGP support (Enigmail) for this identity**.

If the mail addresses are not the same, select **Use specific OpenPGP key ID.**
Then click **Select Key** and select the appropriate key ID from the list that
appears.

6   When you have made those settings, click **OK**.

7   The configuration screens will disappear, leaving your compose window and
a small dialog window offering you several choices, including Encrypt
Message. See Figure 11-12. Make your selection, then click **OK**.

Figure 11-12   Encrypting or signing the message

8   Finally, click **Send** to send the mail.

Please don't send me email to test this. I am several months behind in my
email and falling further behind every day. Send the first message to yourself
to show how it works.

Only the body and attachments of the email will be encrypted, so don't give
your secret plans away in the subject line.

9   If Enigmail can't find the public key for the recipient, it will display the
OpenPGP Key Selection window, seen in Figure 11-13. The window allows
you to highlight the public key that you want used to encrypt the message.

You can also click **Download missing keys** and specify a keyserver from
which to retrieve a key.

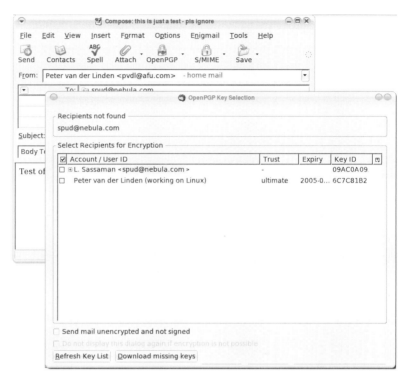

Figure 11-13   Select the public key corresponding to the message recipient

Receiving Encrypted Mail

As an email is sent across the Internet to its addressee, anyone who administers any host that it passes through can take a copy of the mail. If the email is encrypted, this copy will look something like the mail shown in the following example. It is effectively immune to eavesdropping efforts.

An encrypted email as seen by an eavesdropper

```
From pvdl@gmail.com Mon Apr  4 23:41:12 2005 +0000
Message-ID: <4251D097.70701@gmail.com>
Date: Mon, 04 Apr 2005 16:41:11 -0700
From: Peter van der Linden
User-Agent: Mozilla Thunderbird 1.0.2 (X11/20050317)
X-Accept-Language: en-us, en
MIME-Version: 1.0
```

```
To: Peter van der Linden
Subject: test message re cheese
X-Enigmail-Version: 0.91.0.0
Content-Type: text/plain; charset=ISO-8859-1
Content-Transfer-Encoding: 7bit
Status: RO
X-Status:
X-Keywords:
X-UID: 71
-----BEGIN PGP MESSAGE-----
Charset: ISO-8859-1
Version: GnuPG v1.4.1 (GNU/Linux)
Comment: Using GnuPG with Thunderbird - http://enigmail.mozdev.org
hQEOA7XFUy1wsQ8yEAQAsh+0abSkGnGZV2DiLESQ9Wl5pwGx1ApDUh2bMCHjwWw9
FGzT3keACkmFUJfo+eSMpcdX6zDMzeG0N/eGjuHACYbQZjBDBDUd/+o2pP6GuGmA
D6ZwnNXi8NDWDXlyqHefPDKDCFuX3D8ZDkzmowepzJTCtsFvpGB6aMkAIx75OQgD
/RX8FvYd6v+clYGOzS+FwyncwHRjRw5uyKXwb/PGZd4yZ2wyVkNTIxqlS2gtTdx9
vKUZJ/GNABhvo2ACdbEvpoQqsjcfyVZ41w05SO8SRh5cJg1/oS5W63/kI61X+vzM
42yT7iSpUloOZdbZqeyOVylDnKFDhbIPkACtzWr74uLfhQIOAxSOslBo80crEAf+
NOdFkg47W0GCJHt00QxZA4pDlIMQoS+mBIHBJrIDo/U+Lguvj7qb4Ox8/1PwiIHW
KAEXwGu0fmQyQakroLhlocfdPNb9jy/SsV0uUL9P/qKtRdwy9VLwCFByA462HbiM
2qqgKB+Hcys+8fNKe+mSOeZCQVzJvX97kGdhUzXSE57tZxEiNhYvnO8rdjUMmbCw
HzsdilHxO0kvG2199duYZy0Kbdd0tQEkgpSMfCN+l0nAtGx3pWWyrR9nWud0yW3a
+TaOGSilIwMJJIiDVVFP5znP9W3u9fZJ4GQ2ANh61KWKlWG55ErtuKJHFBIfQoWf
xWCaz9YRwvWUR/0dIrxXFAf/S5yscIpM0e/vVYxDNrBjQCVM9OaXkSA6CCchIsQR
OaZJl0PMcezJcYQQ3wn00MTnTzOsTt0wbo1VjVOnZ/LjPLxRzcmVNIsXdM2LNCUe
EK6Krqk9aMHinfuPKp8NRbGcf9oUPiZbSCDG6qIYTGHT63ulicsdgBjfb6m8ISje
abKz6jOZsnR+bZBYNNEpfZEPlBkX9+VX8f11tfbzQarWpXM9aLPHZHiuXXC0kxNW
HUUtHugMHKLm4P3Hsonw+VL8T58t/iMsEZrH2KrFJRRxKl1G39OSpNK/LFw75P5F
avImA1MzAAder3ztkBvNdfscBLambGz3fMFcAPOGn29qJ9JaAfn5bdrAsXuQSoHR
dspVhd8OGJt16DEugL0XRqasBfr30p3Ed1wy7SQ31RT4XnV7oCPMMiOpkDhDzy9O
SOLqcy6cGM3eFkWzsMsPGN3sG2zh/31Y9CbHyHO1
=fj8m
-----END PGP MESSAGE-----
```

When the mail comes into your own system, Thunderbird and Enigmail work together to decrypt it automatically. Thunderbird tells Enigmail "Hey, I have an encrypted mail here." Enigmail looks to see if it was encoded with the public key of the user who is reading the email. If so, it decodes it with the private key, and hands the result back to Mozilla. The resulting clear text is in Figure 11-14.

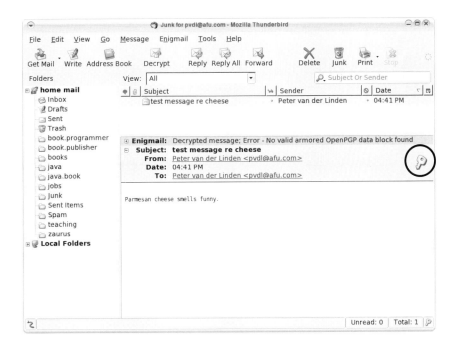

Figure 11-14   Incoming encrypted mail is decrypted automatically

Note the key symbol circled in Figure 11-14. If Enigmail doesn't have the private key to decode the mail, that key icon will be displayed in two broken pieces.

Signing Email and Files

Encryption can be used to guarantee email authenticity, as well as to conceal messages. Just as you sign a bank check or a letter written on paper to guarantee that it was issued by you, you can sign an email message to assure readers that it came from you. You can sign arbitrary files (programs, operating system patches, word processor files) to assure readers that they came from you.

The system is designed so that public key and private key are symmetric. You can use either one to encode and use the other to decode. If someone encrypts a file with his private key, anyone can decode it using the sender's public key. The only key that will decode the file correctly is the sender's public key, so you know that the file really did come from the sender (or someone with access to the sender's private key).

Signing email

Encryption can be applied to email another way. Encryption can be used to show that email (or any file) came from a specific sender, and that the content has not been modified somewhere in transmission. This is called signing the email.

In other words, encryption can raise confidence that the email is authentic. It can thus reliably be used where the stakes are high: in monetary transactions, in legal evidence, in matters of personal commitment, and so on. Because it is so easily forged, ordinary email is unsuitable for all of these.

Encryption falls short of an absolute guarantee of authenticity because codes can be broken, people bribed, keyboards tapped, etc. But you can put a lot more trust in the authenticity of signed email compared with unsigned.

For convenience of readers, you might send the email in plain text, with an attachment containing the encrypted version. The recipient can read the plaintext immediately, and check that it is accurate by decrypting the attachment and comparing it to the plaintext.

You don't even have to encrypt the plaintext. It's enough to get a checksum summary of the plaintext (known as a *message digest*) and encrypt that. For email, the message digest is typically in two pieces added before and after the body of the email. With non-email files, the message digest is typically kept in a separate file, but with a name that relates it to the file for which it is a summary.

When a file has been signed, the recipient has an easy way to check if the file contents have been altered at all after the signing. Calculate the digest of the message that was received. There are several popular digest programs: SHA1, SHA2, and MD5. Use the sender's public key to decrypt the digest that was received. Calculate the checksum using the same checksum program that the sender used. If the message has been altered, the decrypted message digest will not exactly match the calculated message digest.

Signing is the reason we don't refer to a public key as a locking key, nor to a private key as an unlocking key. Depending on whether you are encrypting or signing, you will process the message with the recipient's public key or your private key. When I want to send Alice a confidential message, I use her public key to encrypt the message.

But if Alice wants to sign a reply to me, she will use her private key to encrypt it. If she wants to encrypt a reply to me, she will use my public key to encrypt the message. Both public and private keys can be used for locking and unlocking. Whichever key you used for locking, you use the other key for unlocking.

Enigmail gives an option to sign email as well as encrypting it. You can also sign files with gpg commands. If you have a file called contract.txt containing this text:

```
Jim, I accept your offer of $4,500 for my BMW motorbike.
```

you can sign it with this command:

```
gpg --armor --clearsign  contract.txt
```

That will leave the original file unchanged, and create a new file contract.txt.asc that contains the old file plus the signature information. (You can use the --detach-sign option to create a signature in a separate file.)

```
 -----BEGIN PGP SIGNED MESSAGE-----
Hash: SHA1


Jim, I accept your offer of $4500 for my BMW motorbike.
-----BEGIN PGP SIGNATURE-----
Version: GnuPG v1.2.4 (GNU/Linux)


iD8DBQFBoma2i6dDdQ87uBkRAg+EAJ9mIbtcW+nYInTRchqTcouLoIAeFACggkaS
y+udY7E8v/G9A/Henuxo1cE=
=1IhY
-----END PGP SIGNATURE-----
```

When Jim gets that contract.txt.asc file from me, he can verify that he is reading the same thing that I signed by running this command:

```
gpg --verify contract.txt.asc
```

If indeed it does match, the output will be:

```
gpg: Signature made Mon Nov 22 17:22:46 2004 EST using DSA key ID 0F3BB819
gpg: Good signature from "Peter van der Linden (Master of the Bookshelf) "
```

On the other hand, say dishonest Dick intercepts my message, and changes the text. He does not have my secret key, so he cannot generate a new signature that will be recognized as mine. But he might change the message to this:

```
-----BEGIN PGP SIGNED MESSAGE-----
Hash: SHA1


Jim, I do NOT accept your offer of $4500 for my BMW motorbike.
-----BEGIN PGP SIGNATURE-----
Version: GnuPG v1.2.4 (GNU/Linux)


iD8DBQFBoma2i6dDdQ87uBkRAg+EAJ9mIbtcW+nYInTRchqTcouLoIAeFACggkaS
y+udY7E8v/G9A/Henuxo1cE=
=1IhY
-----END PGP SIGNATURE-----
```

When Jim runs the gpg verification on the changed message, he will get this result:

```
gpg: Signature made Mon Nov 22 17:22:46 2004 EST using DSA key ID 0F3BB819
gpg: BAD signature from "Peter van der Linden (Master of the Bookshelf) "
```

Widespread use of cryptographically signed mail would go a long way to solving the spam problem. In many jurisdictions, sending spam is illegal and spammers thus conceal their identities by forging the origin of the mail.

If all your contacts signed their email with a signature certified by a trusted third party, you could simply discard unsigned email or mail where the signature did not match the source. Spammers would be unable to sign their email because it would identify them. They would be reduced to spamming through identity theft which is time consuming and risky.

People often sign files or email that they encrypt. That way, only the intended recipient can read it, and the recipient knows that you are definitely the person who sent it, too. Computerized signatures based on encryption are far more reliable than written signatures that are forged on a daily basis by people with criminal intent. But computerized signatures are only as good as the encryption scheme and key length you use. For gpg, that's a pretty good assurance, until you start to look at all the interfaces outside gpg that can be subverted.

Gpg is the strongest part of a system that has some quite weak parts where humans are involved. Rather than encrypting individual files, the kernel should be transparently encrypting entire filesystems at block level. Some products do this, but they are not in widespread use. One is http://sourceforge.net/projects/loop-aes.

References

You might have found gpg somewhat hard to use. That's a common reaction. In practice the inconvenience of gpg is enough that the program is not in use by the majority of Linux users. It's quite rare to get encrypted mail. A program called seahorse (in CNR, and on the web at http://seahorse.sourceforge.net) is a GUI for gpg key management. It's good as far as it goes, which isn't far.

The lack of a good, simple user interface for gpg is definitely holding back widespread adoption of public key encryption. Maybe gpg is not the right starting point, when looking for easy-to-use encryption. Or perhaps the right way to look at it is that you endure the one-time pain of gpg setup, and then Thunderbird makes mail encryption easy.

This chapter contains all the information that you need to use gpg. There are additional features too. A central configuration file called ~/.gnupg/gnupg.conf (it may be ~/.gnupg/options on Red Hat Linux) can store certain command options, such as your favorite key server, so you do not have to specify them in commands. You can find out about features like these by reading the references I list later.

You should be careful looking at the Mozilla mail documentation for encryption, as it can be misleading. Because Mozilla is an everything-at-once combined email client, news reader, HTML editor, and browser, the documentation that you reference from the email help menu may actually take you to a file that was intended for the web browser help!

This happens in Mozilla 1.5 if you search for encryption. You get some totally inapplicable material talking about certificates. That really relates to how the browser deals with the https secure protocol. It's nothing to do with email encryption. This is yet another reason why three or four small fast applications with shared libraries are usually better than one big multi-function application.

Here are some links to further sources of information.

- The GNU Privacy Guard home page at http://www.gnupg.org has the latest software for download, and also a section on documentation. It includes the GNU Privacy Handbook, which is, frankly, more of a reference manual than an introductory handbook.

- The newsgroup accessible through google.com called comp.security.pgp.discuss. Many of the issues and questions about PGP (the commercial product) apply equally to gpg (the freeware re-implementation).

- http://lrcressy.com/linux/mozilla.pdf has a fuller tutorial on using gpg with email on Linux. This is one of the better web tutorials on the subject.

- Bruce Schneier's *Applied Cryptography* is a very readable guide to the whole field of cryptography, although it is intended for practitioners, not laypersons. The book is published by Wiley and the ISBN is 0471117099.

- David Kahn's *The Codebreakers* is an excellent, very readable review of codes and code breaking through the ages, down to the present day. It is published by Scribner with an ISBN of 0684831309. Although the list price is $70, you can sometimes find used copies on Amazon for $20.

The lore of Linux—Beowulf clusters

As Linux gained traction in the 1990s, researchers latched onto it in a big way. Not only did Linux have a big price advantage (free), but the open source model made it accessible and easily customized.

When researchers create a new computer design today, they frequently decide to run it under Linux. Once they have adapted Linux to run on their new system (a process known as "porting" the kernel), they have a world of existing Linux applications that only need be recompiled to work on the new hardware.

So it was no surprise when NASA engineer Donald Becker chose Linux as the operating system for his experimental high-performance computer built in 1994 using dozens of cheap PCs. This kind of system is called a cluster. All the PCs are connected with very fast Ethernet. A control PC parcels out pieces of the workload to each of the worker-bee PCs and coordinates the results.

Clusters run best when given tasks that can easily be split into multiple pieces. In keeping with the topic of this chapter, "breaking encrypted messages" is an application ideally suited for running on a cluster. The total hardware cost for Don's 24-node Beowulf cluster was $57,000. It could run some jobs with a speed comparable to commercial supercomputers costing several million dollars.

The Linux-based super computer was named Beowulf, after the hero in the epic English poem from the year 1000. Beowulf was said to have "thirty men's heft of grasp in the gripe of his hand," so it's a pretty good name for a multi-processor computer system.

A number of distros are now specialized for the task of running nodes in a Beowulf cluster. Don Becker oversees one of them, the Scyld distro. Scyld is another character from Beowulf, and the Scyld company has written a great deal of software to make it easy to set up and operate a Beowulf cluster.

One of the most interesting developments in Linux clustering is the use of live CDs that boot up and dynamically self-configure into a cluster. If you can borrow 100 PCs for a day, you can string them all on an Ethernet, boot them from a live clustering CD, and voila: instant supercomputer!

Linux owns the supercomputer cluster space; Microsoft has no product for this market at all. The entire computer special effects sector in the film industry is now on Linux clusters or trying to get there as soon as possible. The movies Titanic and Lord of the Rings were both rendered (drawn) on Linux supercomputers. So the next time you're watching spectacular effects on the big screen, you can thank the small screens of a Linux cluster for bringing it to you.

Installation and Boot

Getting Started

Call me overly logical, but it strikes me as a bad idea when Linux books put installation in one of the first chapters. Normal people install an operating system only a few times in their life. Those books lead with the topic that is least familiar and that presents the biggest challenges for new users.

With the advent of live CDs, there is no reason to force readers through installation before getting to the good stuff of using Linux day-to-day. Sure, you need to know a little about booting to use a live CD, but there's a lot of low level "use once" material that can be deferred. Installation is the last topic, after you have familiarized yourself with the look and feel of Linux. As I point out at the beginning, you can always jump ahead to this chapter at any time.

I'll explain installation in terms of what you are trying to achieve with the underlying pieces, and also suggest some ways to sidestep the tough parts. Before writing this text, I spent six months working full time on Linux support forums, actively solving users' problems. That experience translates to a practical chapter that takes the "stall" out of installation.

Linux with Zero Effort: Buying Linux Preinstalled

If the process of installation seems offputting to you, take the royal road. Get your Linux system the same way you get Windows: preinstalled. Walmart, CompUSA, Microtelpc.com and Staples all sell PCs with Linux preinstalled from their web sites. The Linspire web site has a longer list of retailers. If there is one in your area, select a mom-and-pop PC supplier, since they will provide better service and ongoing support.

In June 2004, Fry's, a large U.S. electronics retailer, was offering a PC with 128 MB memory, a 40 GB hard disk, a CD drive, modem, and Linspire preinstalled. The price was $149—less than the retail cost of Windows by itself. Linux PCs are a lot cheaper than Windows PCs because you don't have to pay the Microsoft tax. The PC might even be cheap enough to buy just as a Linux evaluation. Buying a preinstalled Linux system guarantees all the right device drivers are present.

If you select this option, you're done with this chapter!

Installation Checklist

For the hands-on approach, there are three basic approaches:

- You can install Linux right over your current Windows operating system.

- You can buy an extra disk with Linux on it, and fit it on your Windows computer.

- You can set up a Linux/Windows dual boot on your current Windows computer.

This list takes you through the process of selecting which approach to use, preparing for each, and implementing each one.

1 Make sure you have the Linux operating system software. See *Downloading Your Linux Distro and Burning It to CD* on page 442.

2 Read the short description of what an installation is like. See *What Happens During an Installation* on page 444.

3 You'll need to understand partitions to help you decide how to do the installation. Review the section on disk partitions to remind yourself how a disk drive can be split into smaller self-contained units. See *More About Disk Partitions* on page 445.

4 Now that you understand the installation and partitions, you're ready to decide how you're going to do the installation. Consider whether you want to preserve your existing Windows installation or not. Preserving an existing Windows installation is a little extra work, but it results in a flexible system that can boot up in either Windows or Linux.

Read *Choosing Whether to Dual Boot* on page 447, which briefly describes the options of overwriting Windows, keeping Windows and installing Linux on another disk, as well as choosing to set up a dual boot.

5 After deciding whether to preserve Windows and whether to go with a dual-boot installation or not, read about the type of installation you decided on and complete the preparatory steps described in the section for your installation.

- *Choice A—Wiping Out Windows* on page 448 means you'll just install Linux right over Windows.

- ◆ *Choice B—Putting Linux on a Separate Disk* on page 448 preserves Windows. You'll buy a separate disk, fit it to your computer, and install Linux on it; or you'll buy a disk with Linux preinstalled and fit that to your computer. If you buy the preinstalled disk, this is your last step.

- ◆ *Choice C—Advanced Installation for Dual Boot* on page 453 preserves Windows. You'll set up partitions, then install Linux on a partition where Windows isn't installed.

6 To know what's really going on in the installation process, you need to know what happens when a PC boots up. Read the section titled *What Happens During a Boot* on page 458.

7 Install your Linux distro.

- ◆ If you're installing a distro other than Linspire, review *What You Need to Have Done by This Point* on page 461. Then follow the instructions for your distro.

- ◆ If you're installing Linspire, do the *Linspire Installation* on page 461.

8 For troubleshooting, see *Troubleshooting After Installation* on page 482. Also remember you can get help. See *Linux with Zero Effort: Buying Linux Preinstalled* on page 440.

9 For any additional system administration tasks, see *System Administration Know-How* on page 484.

> **A little help from your LUG—Tap into your local Linux Users' Group**
>
> *Your local Linux Users' Group is an excellent resource. Find your local group by doing a web search on the name of your nearest university or metro area plus "Linux user group". Many Linux user groups hold monthly "installfests" where they help people with installation or other issues.*

Downloading Your Linux Distro and Burning It to CD

You now need to get a Linux installation CD whose contents can be installed to your hard disk. You can't use the live CD that came with this book for your permanent installation; it doesn't have the scripts that will install to a hard disk. Some other live CDs, like the popular Knoppix distro, can be installed, but not this one.

Linspire is the Linux distro used throughout this book. It is a Debian-based distro, so it has the best software packaging by far of any distro. Debian favors stability over leading-edge novelty, which is also good for new users.

Linspire is the easiest of all Linux distros for new users to learn. It comes ready to play more media types, like MP3 or Flash files, than any other distro.

Table 12-1 shows you where to download Linspire and one of the free alternatives, Fedora (a desktop spin-off of Red Hat server Linux). The Linux costs compare very favorably to the $850 retail cost of Windows XP Pro ($299) plus Office 2003 ($499) plus an antivirus package and subscription ($52).

Table 12-1   Linux distro reference

Distro	Download site	Price and benefit
Linspire	http://www.linspire.com/lindows_storefront.php	$50 $90 with CNR membership Customer support, prepackaged applications, ease-of-use, localizations, online forums, and FAQs
Red Hat Fedora	http://fedora.redhat.com/download	Free

You can install Linspire, or Fedora, or Knoppix, or Mepis, Xandros, or any of the other Linux distros. The web site http://distrowatch.com has the facts and figures on more than 100 Linux distros.

You'll have an easier time and better support with Linspire. Generally, the distros that charge are the ones that offer the best support to new users; the price covers the cost of providing support. Each reader needs to make the tradeoff of handholding versus cost for themselves.

Most distros encourage you to download the installation ISO file, either from their web site, from a load-sharing duplicate web site called a mirror server, or using the BitTorrent P2P network. These methods of distributing the installation image are cheaper and quicker than paying someone to mail you a physical CD. If you insist on that, try the online fulfillment house http://cheapbytes.com, which has $5–$10 CDs for many distros. In Britain, http://www.cheeplinux.co.uk fills the same role. There isn't any legal way to get the Linspire installable distro without paying for it, either for access to the .iso file download or for a CD.

Dial-up is problematic for downloading Linux. Even the fastest phone modem would take more than 30 hours, far longer than you can go without some line noise and hence file corruption. If you're stuck without broadband at home, go to a school, library, workplace, cafe, or friend with broadband, or buy the CD.

The download will consist of one or more ISO image files. When you have downloaded all of them, check the MD5 checksum then burn them onto CDs using the special technique for an ISO image described in Chapter 9, "Filesystems and Optical Storage (CDs and DVDs)," on page 287. Recent ISO files are approaching 700 MB in size. Make sure you use blank media that is big enough to hold the image.

Beyond this point, you'll need to have your installation CD on hand.

What Happens During an Installation

All Linux installations share the same four basic steps:

1   The user decides which disk partition to use and selects other configuration details. If your partition choice requires disk partition changes, the changes might be made as the first step in installation, or you might need to make them as a separate pre-installation step (Linspire 5.0 takes this approach).

2   The user restarts the system causing it to boot from the installation CD. When the system comes up, it starts running installation scripts to collect configuration details from the user. This part looks like a Windows Installshield wizard. When the wizard has collected enough information about the user's choices, it proceeds to the next step to put them into effect.

3   The files that make up the operating system are copied from CD onto the disk partition that you chose, and then updated with the configuration information that you provided.

4   The system reboots itself. In the process it detects all the hardware it recognizes on your PC and configures itself accordingly. The new operating system has completed installation at this point.

In addition, you might need to do some post-installation setup, provide more information, and review online license terms and tutorials.

There are really only two stumbling blocks; one that might crop up before installation and one that can rear its ugly head after installation:

- Disk partitions: what are they, and how do I get them?

- What do I do when some hardware—sound, screen, modem, etc.—doesn't work correctly after installation?

The question of disk partitioning is a critical one, and the following section titled *More About Disk Partitions* covers it. I'll cover non-functioning devices in *Troubleshooting After Installation* on page 482.

More About Disk Partitions

Disk partitioning was explained in Chapter 9, "Filesystems and Optical Storage (CDs and DVDs)." Partitions allow you to treat a large disk as though it were several smaller disks. That helps you organize your files, and can simplify data backups.

Windows typically covers the entire disk with a single partition containing a filesystem for Windows and your data. As a result, partitions are not part of the Windows user experience and many users have never seen anything about them.

Let's take a look at partitions again before continuing to the installation. A good way to understand anything hidden, like a disk partition, is to make it visible. To familiarize yourself with disk partitions, you can look at them in Windows. Under Windows XP (both Home and Pro editions), the Computer Management window will display your disk partitions.

1 In your **Control Panel** (using the Classic View), double-click **Administrative Tools** to bring up the **Computer Management** window; see Figure 12-1.

2 Select **Computer Management**, then select **Disk Management** from the tree in the left column.

Earlier versions of Windows have the fdisk command line utility that provides similar information in text form.

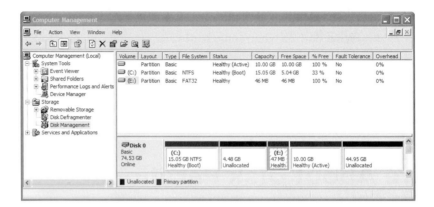

Figure 12-1   Using the Computer Management window in Microsoft Windows to look at partitions

The **Disk Management** choice in the Computer Management window shows you all mounted hard drives and all partitions on those disks. There is only one disk in this system, called disk 0 by Windows.

Stretching the truth—elastic disk sizes

Windows says this disk has a capacity of 74.53 GB. The manufacturer rates the disk capacity at 80 GB.

The difference arises because the manufacturer is using units of 10^9 (a billion bytes), while Windows is using more natural units of 2^{30} (a Gigabyte). Since 10^9 is smaller than 2^{30}, it has the effect of slightly inflating GB disk sizes from the manufacturer. All disk manufacturers are quick to take advantage of this.

In 1998, the International Electrotechnical Commission (a Swiss-based industry group) issued a standard acknowledging the different numbers, and urging different names for powers-of-two values: kibibyte, mebibyte, and gibibyte. Although it involves a change to established terminology, it would put the disk manufacturers in the clear, should it ever catch on.

There was a similar situation a few years ago with monitors. Vendors were advertising monitor sizes by measuring to the very edge of the glass, rather than to the edge that the CRT gun can actually light up. Some sharp lawyers seized on it and brought a class action lawsuit. The deceived monitor owners got something like a coupon for 10 cents off a dust cloth, while the sharp lawyers made out like bandits.

The "elastic" disk capacity is not quite as egregious as the case of monitors, but it is worth knowing when you are calculating your storage requirements finely.

The upper window in Figure 12-1 lists only the three partitions. The lower bar graph display in Figure 12-1 gives a more accurate picture of what's on the disk, because it includes the free space:

- The 14 GB C: partition, formatted as NTFS

- A 4.4 GB unallocated gap of free space

- The 46 MB E: partition, formatted as FAT32, which is empty

- The 10 GB unrecognized partition (Linux)

- 44.94 GB more unallocated space

Many Windows PCs are shipped with just one partition on the disk, and no unallocated space. Sometimes Windows recovery files are put into a second partition on the same disk, called the D: drive. The D: drive letter might alternatively be assigned to an additional storage device like a CD drive or second disk.

Windows always uses drive letters to refer to *individual partitions*. It's easy to overlook that "drive letter equals partition" because the most common case is an entire drive containing just one Windows partition. It (wrongly) looks like the letter refers to the drive. People talk about "the C: drive" when they really mean "the C: partition". In any event, if you have a hidden D: recovery partition, be careful not to overwrite it unless you're junking Windows altogether.

Choosing Whether to Dual Boot

Your PC probably runs Windows at present. You need to make an informed decision about whether to preserve the ability to run Windows, in addition to installing and running Linux. If your copy of Windows is any older than Windows 2000, frankly, it's not worth keeping. (Unless you're chained to some critical app that is only available on Windows, poor you.)

With antique versions of Windows, back up your Windows data. Then install Linux over the top of Windows, telling Linux to take over the entire disk.

On the other hand, if you want to retain your PC's ability to boot into its existing Windows installation, you must provide a separate space to install Linux. That separate space can be on a second disk, or on a new partition on the existing disk. There are some minor organizational advantages to putting Linux on a second disk: mostly, it prevents Windows from interfering with it.

So it comes down to three choices:

A   Wipe out Windows completely by installing Linux over the top.

B   Get a second disk and install Linux there (or buy a second disk with Linux on it already), and fit that disk to your computer. This approach doesn't affect your Windows installation on the first disk.

C   Create a partition for Linux on your Windows disk, without affecting your Windows installation on the first partition.

The first and second choices are called a "takeover disk" installation. The third option is the one chosen by most people, and Linspire calls it an "advanced installation". It's not really "advanced"; they just don't want to scare users by using unfamiliar terms like "partition" and "dual boot".

Choice A—Wiping Out Windows

The simplest approach is just to go ahead and overwrite Windows. If you honestly don't care about heroic measures to keep Windows viable on your PC, you can skip over the next several pages all the way to *What Happens During a Boot* on page 458. Then follow the instructions for the takeover disk installation in *Linspire Installation* on page 461.

Choice B—Putting Linux on a Separate Disk

The most flexible approach is to get an additional disk and use that for Linux. That lets you keep Windows. It lets you use the simplicity of the takeover disk installation, but keep the flexibility of having both Windows and Linux available on your PC.

This section describes different ways to get a PC with both a Linux and a Windows disk available. Not many people decide to go with this path (it involves buying and fitting a new disk), but flexibility can be important, so here goes.

The following steps are involved:

*   *Choosing the Additional Disk*

*   *Fitting the Additional Disk*

Choosing the Additional Disk

Find a good disk and the installation will go more smoothly.

Where to Find a Disk

The web site http://www.pricewatch.com offers all kinds of computer hardware for the budget conscious. You don't have to get a new disk. You can pick up used but working disks for about two-thirds the price you'd pay for new ones (check out eBay or www.craigslist.org).

Factors That Affect Disk Life

Several factors affect the life of used disks, include hours of operation, number of duty cycles, and environmental conditions, but most brands of IDE disk fail once they age much past three years. However all desktop drives made by Seagate since July 2004 come with a five-year warranty. So disks from Seagate are always preferred, and disks over three years old are a very poor choice.

You can determine how much use a disk has had and whether it's about to fail by running the SMART tools from http://smartmontools.sourceforge.net. There are versions for Linux, MaxOS X, BSD, and Windows.

Getting the Right Kind of Disk

When buying an additional disk, keep in mind that almost all PCs use IDE disks internally. A few high-end systems use SCSI or fibre channel disks. SCSI and Fiber disks are regarded as server technologies, and aren't supported by the Linspire distro.

IDE disks at the time of writing in 2005 are making a transition from parallel ATA to the much faster serial ATA (SATA) interfaces. One reason that SATA is faster is that it requires a controller for each disk. You can't chain several devices the way you can with SCSI, or have two devices (master and slave) connected to a PCI controller the way you can with IDE. The illustration at right shows a 40-pin IDE ribbon cable.

40-pin IDE cable

SATA uses slimmer connectors, with just seven wires. It's not plug compatible with motherboards designed for older parallel ATA drives with a wide ribbon cable. Make sure that any new disk you buy is the same type as your current disk, IDE or new SATA. The illustration at right shows a seven-pin SATA cable.

You can install a bigger capacity disk on modern PCs without problem, although sometimes there is an overall limit set by the BIOS, a disk controller, or a bus controller. I have a PC that can address only 128 GB of disk, even if a bigger disk is fitted.

Seven-pin SATA cable

Choosing Whether to Buy a Disk with Linux Preinstalled

If you want to install Linux yourself or you have found a good price on a disk without Linux, that's a perfectly reasonable way to go.

If you want to skip a step, find a disk with Linux preinstalled. Linux retailer Sub300 offers a disk drive with Linspire preinstalled on it at a reasonable price. Their web site is at http://www.sub300.com. Sub300 has a range of great Linux-friendly products.

Note – Just because Linux is preinstalled on the disk, it doesn't mean that it will include device drivers for all the peripherals on your PC.

This is slightly different than buying an entire PC with Linux preinstalled. It's cheaper, but you also need to fit the disk inside your PC yourself.

Fitting the Additional Disk

Now that you've got your disk that you'll run Linux on, you need to connect it to your PC. Again, you get to select your approach from a few different options.

- Option 1: Fit the second internal disk to your PC. See *Option 1: Replace the Windows Disk with a Linux Disk* on page 451.

  If there is room, you can leave the second disk permanently installed. There is not enough room in a laptop to add a second disk, so you'll have to physically exchange the Windows disk and the Linux disk according to what you want to boot.

- Option 2: Get an additional disk and a couple of rack trays. Fit your current Windows disk in one tray and the new disk to the other. Install Linux on the new disk. When the system is powered off, you can easily slide either the Windows tray or the Linux tray into one of the front bays of the computer, without opening the PC case. See *Option 2: Supplement the Windows Disk with a Linux Disk* on page 452.

  People like this approach because there is nothing either operating system can do to adversely affect the other.

- Option 3: If you have a modern PC that has the ability to boot from external USB or FireWire storage, this is the easiest solution. USB 1 storage is numbingly slow, but may be acceptable for an evaluation. If you're not sure whether your PC has this boot capability, review the vendor web site, or call the manufacturer support line and ask. See *Option 3: Use Linux on an External Drive* on page 452.

Option 1: Replace the Windows Disk with a Linux Disk

It is very easy to swap the disks in most notebook PCs (first check if this affects your warranty). Almost every vendor puts a disk access panel underneath the notebook, held on by one or two screws. The disk will be under that, fastened to L-shaped brackets called rails.

The screws in the disk rails might have *torx* heads—instead of a straight slot or a cross for Phillips head, the holes at the top of the screws are star-shaped. You'll need a special screwdriver for these screws, of course; buy a set of torx screwdrivers in your local hardware store or on eBay for $5. You want sizes T5 to T9.

Torx-head screw

Make sure any jumpers on your new disk are place identically to those on your old disk. Write Windows disk on the old disk with a permanent marker so you can tell them apart. The first time you replace a laptop disk it will take you fifteen minutes. Soon you'll be exchanging disks with the flair of a tire crew at the Indianapolis 500.

It takes a little longer to remove the covers from a desktop PC and swap out the hard drive, but the technique works equally well. The big advantage of swapping a drive, rather than fitting a second one, is that you don't have to connect any new cables for data and power. The cables and rails to support a second drive might already be there, or they might not. Replacing one hard drive by another is easier than adding a second drive.

Option 2: Supplement the Windows Disk with a Linux Disk

On a desktop computer you do have the choice of permanently installing a second drive, perhaps in place of a floppy drive or CD. Most current floppy, CD, DVD and disk drives use the same 40 pin ribbon cable and power connectors. Second drive installation in a desktop is beyond our scope here, as it involves opening the case, connecting power cables, and possibly changing jumpers on the second drive. None of this is rocket science, but it's a lot easier to have someone show you the first time.

The web site http://www.pcbuyerbeware.co.uk/IDE.htm has some information on this, and your local Linux group will almost certainly have someone who can help.

CompUSA and other suppliers sell a removable *disk tray* that allows IDE drives to be quickly swapped in any PC with an available 5.25 inch drive bay without opening the computer. Ask the store if they can help you fit it. They retail at around $20. Slick!

Using removable disk trays can be better than leaving a second disk permanently installed, as long as you handle and store the disks carefully. The disk is not in use all the time, for one thing. There is no chance of corruption in the event of a power surge for another.

Removable trays also provide a very straightforward path to reliable and flexible system backups. Is maintaining duplicate disks costly? It depends what you compare it with. How much is your data worth to you?

Option 3: Use Linux on an External Drive

Bootable attached storage is a comparatively recent development in the PC world, although Apple has featured it with FireWire drives for years. Booting from USB or FireWire is a very welcome development, as you can put a Linux image such as the one from http://damnsmalllinux.org or http://featherlinux.berlios.de on a 64MB USB jump drive (rather than a hard drive), and boot from that. This means can effectively carry your PC identity with you on your key chain! Plug the drive into any PC, boot from it, and you have your entire environment with you.

It's common to buy an external disk bundled with the container box that has the USB/Firewire connector. However, if you acquire the disk and external container separately and put them together yourself, all that stuff in *Choosing the Additional Disk* on page 449 applies here too.

If you decide to follow one of the suggestions in this section, and do a takeover disk installation, then skip ahead to *What Happens During a Boot* on page 458.

Choice C—Advanced Installation for Dual Boot

The alternative to takeover disk installation is to create an additional partition to hold Linux. The user can then decide on each reboot whether to bring up Windows or Linux. This arrangement is called a dual boot system. You don't have to stop at two operating systems. You can keep several extra partitions for test copies of new OS releases or for experimenting with other distros.

The big decision for you is whether you want a dual boot system and thus need to learn how to do disk partitioning. If you haven't completed your Linux evaluation yet, you really should retain some way to boot Windows. That may be a dual boot installation, or one of the additional-disk alternatives in the previous section.

Dual boot systems work just fine on Linspire, and a large proportion of all Linux users have a dual boot system. As a company, Linspire does not support dual boot systems because they see their main customer base as people who are buying the system preinstalled, or who do a Full Takeover installation and use Linspire as their primary OS.

It's fine to go ahead and create a dual boot Linspire installation, if that suits your needs. All the information you need is in this chapter and Appendix E, "Disk Basics and Partitioning," on page 553. If you need additional interactive help, people in the Linspire forums are knowledgeable enough to resolve problems.

Partition Prep

You can only create partitions from contiguous free space on your disk. If you need more free space, you can shrink or delete a partition. The drawback is that the tools for manipulating partitions are all really abysmal, particularly the commercial ones like Symantec's Norton Partition Magic. The software looks terrible, is hard to use, the documentation is a bad joke, and it's costly too. I'll demonstrate how to use some open source partition-changing software in Appendix E. First you need to get a clear idea of what partitions you need.

Choosing Your Partitions

You will need a 4 GB minimum size partition for Linux. You can get the necessary disk space by reducing the size of your Windows partition. If you have a very small disk, say less than 8 GB, it is only adequate for one operating system; make a single partition dedicated to Linux.

With disks larger than 8 GB, you should look at how much room your current Windows partition is occupying and how much you can shrink it. You'll need at least 4 GB for Linux. You also need to allocate however much room you need for your data. Your data can be kept on the same partition as the Linux operating system (for simplicity, as Windows does) or in a separate partition (for ease of managing backups and sharing).

Data Portability Factors

The second factor for choosing the number and size of partitions is data portability. Some people like to dedicate a separate partition to hold their home directory and hence all their data files and settings. This is easy to archive using "partition at a time" tools.

If you choose a dual boot system (or you fit a second disk), it's convenient for both Linux and Windows to be able to write files that the other can see. For example, suppose you sometimes write letters using Linux, and you later want to work on those letters while running Windows and then give the results back to Linux. You can do this by emailing the file back and forth to yourself, but it's easier to keep it in a partition that both operating systems can read and write.

Because there is not yet a production-quality solution for writing NTFS from Linux, the easiest way for Linux to write files that Windows can see is to use a partition formatted with the FAT32 filesystem. FAT32 is the "lowest common denominator" of filesystems, and can be read and written by both Linux and Windows.

Summary of Partition Needs

- A partition is a software concept for dividing a disk into independent chunks, each of which acts like an independent disk.

- All the space on a disk is either part of some partition, or is unallocated free space waiting to be turned into a partition.

- A partition either contains a filesystem or has not yet been formatted (called a "raw" partition).

You need the following partitions:

- A partition for Linux – This has to be at least 4 GB in size, plus however much space you want to allow for the data you will generate and keep with Linux.

- Optional – If you want a dual-boot system, and your disk is big enough, the Linux partition can be in addition to the Windows partition. Otherwise, plan to get rid of Windows and install Linux in its place.

- Optional – To make it easy to backup and restore your data in one large chunk, and to keep it from intermingling with system files, you might make an additional partition to contain all your personal files (for instance, your home directory). If you're making a dual boot system, for maximum data interoperability with Windows, format this as a FAT32 partition. If you're not sharing data with Windows, format the partition with one of the Linux filesystems, such as Reiser4. Dedicating a partition to the /home directory has another significant benefit: you will be able to upgrade or reinstall Linux without affecting your data.

- Optional for some distros, required in others – Some other distros also want you to create an additional partition for "swap space". Linux (like Windows) uses virtual memory, meaning that the (fast) main memory is used as a cache to hold processes that are running or ready to run.

  Other processes are temporarily saved on (slow) disk. The swap partition is the area of disk used to hold these processes.

When you choose to do an advanced install, Linspire uses a swap file within the regular filesystem for holding processes that won't fit in main memory, so you don't need to create a separate swap partition. The Linspire swap file is /boot/linux-swap.swp.

If you choose a takeover disk install, Linspire will make a swap partition. In both kinds of install, Linspire automatically takes care of swap needs and the size of swap. You don't need to do anything. In other distros, you might need to create swap space yourself.

Swappiness and you

After installation, there's a file in /proc *that lets you adjust the swapping behavior of your system. You might find that you can micro-optimize to get better performance for your specific workload. The file is* /proc/sys/vm/ swappiness *and it holds a value between 0 (try to never page out processes) and 100 (aggressively write out process pages to disk).*

You can set the swappiness value with a command such as:

echo 40 > /proc/sys/vm/swappiness

The system will resize kernel buffers and caches in an attempt to follow your wishes. This might or might not improve performance, but you'll have fun experimenting.

As an example of partition choices, one of my PCs runs a dual boot system. There are three partitions on the disk: a very small FAT32 one needed by Partition Magic, a 14 GB NTFS partition for Windows, and a 10 GB partition for Linux. I have read-only access to my Windows NTFS C:\ data from Linux (it's in folder /mnt/hda1) and that's enough to work on files that I created using Windows. If I need a file to reappear back in Windows, I mail it to myself from Linux, and read the mail while booted in Windows. I keep the rest of the disk free, ready to add space where it is needed, or to create an additional test partition.

Partitions and device names

Just as in Windows, in Linux each partition on a disk gets its own device name. The first IDE disk in a system is /dev/hda. *That refers to the entire disk. The partitions on it are* /dev/hda1, /dev/hda2, /dev/hda3, *and so on.*

The second IDE disk is /dev/hdb. *Its partitions are* /dev/hdb1, /dev/hdb2 *and so on. This naming scheme only covers IDE disks and partitions; unallocated space on a disk doesn't show up with a name at all. The first USB mass storage device is* /dev/sda.

Backing up Your Windows Data

Backing up Windows can be problematic because of Microsoft's licensing restrictions. You cannot copy a Windows partition or drive to a second disk and then boot that second disk in a new system (if the original PC failed, for example). Windows XP records the motherboard and other characteristics and will refuse to boot the image on a different PC. Corporate Volume License Keys are frequently leaked on the Internet, and you can find software that generates a license key not requiring activation. Not only is that a violation of Microsoft's license, but how can you trust such a program you download from an arbitrary source?

Windows Backup Steps in XP Pro

If you have XP Pro, you can use its built-in backup software.

1 Log in to XP Pro with Administrator privileges.

2 Choose **Start** > **All Programs** > **Accessories** > **System Tools** > **Backup**.

3 Proceed through the dialog boxes and follow all directions. When you get to the What to Back Up dialog box, select **All information on this computer**.

This will create a floppy disk that you can later use to boot your PC and to restore the backup after data loss. Unfortunately, Microsoft decided to remove the backup utility from Windows XP Home Edition. It is only installed with XP Pro, although it is on the Home Edition CD.

You should probably back up your Windows data folders separately from the Windows OS. Your data is everything under C:\Documents and Settings plus anything you created outside this folder.

Restoring Windows from Backup

Restoring Windows from backup often means reinstalling Windows, the PC vendor's drivers, the Windows patches and service packs, all your applications, and finally restoring your data on top of that. Because your Windows partition is visible in Linux, you can back it up from Linux. Some methods to back up Windows or Linux are given in *Making Backups* on page 484.

Partitioning Your Disk

Now decide and write down the characteristics of the two or three partitions you will change or create. At a minimum, you will need two partitions for a multiboot system. As an example, splitting an 80 GB disk, your partitions might look like this:

- Partition 1, existing Windows C:\ partition, shrink it to 35 GB
- Partition 2, new Linux partition, create with size 45 GB

Or you might do something like this:

- Partition 1, existing Windows C:\ partition, shrink it to 10 GB
- Partition 2, new Linux partition, create with size 30 GB
- Partition 3, new shared data partition, formatted as FAT32 with size 5 GB
- Unallocated, unpartitioned free space, remainder of disk

It all depends on how big your disk is, how much space Windows is using now, and how much data space you want for Linux. On a disk that's large (compared to your data needs), it's fine to leave some space unallocated. It gives you the flexibility to add a new partition later, or resize an existing partition as needed (not always easy, but can be done).

Notice from Figure 12-1 that Windows tells you how much free space there is on a partition, and thus how much is available to grab for some other partition. Before you do anything whatsoever to any partition, follow the golden rule: back up all data that you don't want to risk losing. In particular, back up your Windows partition before adjusting your disk partitions.

Appendix E, "Disk Basics and Partitioning," on page 553 shows how to use QtParted for disk partitioning. Follow the instructions in Appendix E to partition your disk, then come back here and start *What Happens During a Boot*.

What Happens During a Boot

To understand what's really going on in the installation process, you need to know what happens when a PC boots up. The same sequence of steps happens whether you are booting into Linux or into Windows.

Booting Step-by-Step

The purpose of booting is to find an operating system, load it into memory, and transfer control to it. Booting plays an important part during installation. Two reboots take place during a successful Linux installation. When you understand the steps involved in booting, the terminology of the partitioning and installation process (like MBR) will make sense.

The term boot comes from the phrase "pulling yourself up by your own boot-straps". While that's physically impossible, it refers to each step in the boot process having just enough power to set up and start the next, more complicated, step.

Figure 12-2 illustrates the steps in the boot process.

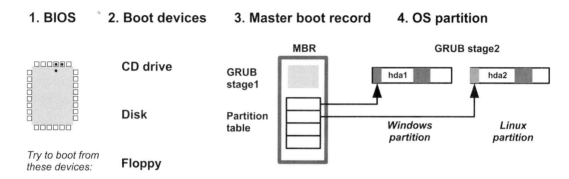

Figure 12-2   Booting involves several steps of increasing sophistication

When you power on (a cold boot), or choose to restart the operating system without power cycling (a warm boot), the CPU starts executing a routine at a predefined address in read-only memory. Some BIOS code is kept in ROM there. After some checking and initialization, the BIOS starts looking for an operating system to boot.

The BIOS has a list of peripherals it should try to boot from, and it starts going down that boot list in order. You can change the devices on the boot list, and the order in which they occur. A typical boot list is "CD, floppy drive, hard disk".

As it goes down the boot list, the BIOS retrieves the first 512 bytes stored on a device (it doesn't look for any filesystem, just says "give me the 512 bytes starting at address 0). The BIOS is looking for a valid Master Boot Record (MBR), and it stops going down the boot list as soon as it finds one.

An MBR has three parts.

- The first part is a block of code.

- The second part of an MBR on disk is a partition table giving the disk address of up to four primary partitions.

- The third part of an MBR is the hex value AA55 marking its end.

When the BIOS finds an MBR pointing to an active partition, it starts executing the block of code in the MBR. This code in the MBR is an attractive target for virus-writers. It is run each time you boot, and isn't in the regular filesystem so it can't be reached by most tools.

The code in the MBR is the first part of the operating system boot loader. Linspire uses a boot loader called GRUB; there are older ones in use, such as LILO. The part of GRUB that lives in the disk MBR is called stage1.

Because the MBR also has to hold the partition table and end signature, stage1 can be no more than 428 bytes in length. Luckily its job is very simple. It has to find stage1_5 (a longer and more complicated program), bring that code into memory, and start executing it.

Stage1_5 in turn loads GRUB's stage2. If you're quick, you might see stage1_5 flash briefly on the monitor during a boot, quickly followed by stage2. That indicates progress through the boot. If you don't see these, it's a clue about where you're getting stuck.

Stage2 reads the file /boot/grub/menu.lst and displays the menu of operating system choices found there. The usual procedure is that you select a menu item using your cursor keys, then press **Enter** on the keyboard. GRUB stage2 boots up that operating system.

However, by pressing **c** at the GRUB menu, you can enter the GRUB command shell and change some boot-related configuration. Alternatively, press **e** to enter a little cursor-based line-editor that lets you add or change the kernel boot parameters—for example, to specify some settings for the graphics adapter, like screen resolution or number of colors. Most people never need to do either of these.

Init Runs Linux's Startup Scripts as the Last Step in Boot

This step is not shown in Figure 12-2. As the last step of the boot sequence, the Linux kernel starts a process called, appropriately enough, init. The init process directly or indirectly starts all other processes running on Linux. The init process keeps running after boot so that it can restart anything essential that dies. You can see init when you run the pstree command.

The init process now runs the shell scripts that are kept in directory /etc/rcS.d/ The file names of these scripts all start with S and a number, and they are run in order. As an example, after the S40 scripts have completed, all the local filesystems are mounted and networking is available. You can add your own scripts to be run at boot time. Color me whimsical, but I like my computers to say the HAL-9000 line from the film 2001 when they boot up: "*I'm completely operational and all my circuits are functioning perfectly.*" Sure it's cheesy, but if you like cheese, you can find many such .wav files at http://www.palantir.net/2001/sounds.html.

Run Levels

Linux has half a dozen "run-levels" that define what services are started. The run level is set in file /etc/inittab on the line starting id:. By default your system boots to run level 2, which Linspire defines as multi-user mode with X Window started.

Run level 1, also called single-user mode, is a system with no network services or X Window system running and only root log in allowed. Boot into run level 1 when you plan to archive the root filesystem. This minimizes changes to the filesystem as you are backing it up. You can enter run level 1 by typing the command init 1.

Linspire Installation

If you're installing some other distro than Linspire, it's a good idea to review the prerequisites in this section anyway, and read the installation process as well. Then install your distro according to the instructions included with it. Come back to this book for troubleshooting.

What You Need to Have Done by This Point

Before you start this section, you must have:

- Created or obtained the installation CD (not the live CD that accompanies this book). See *Downloading Your Linux Distro and Burning It to CD* on page 442.

- Decided how you will install Linspire. See *Choosing Whether to Dual Boot* on page 447.

- Completed any changes to your disk partitions. See *Partitioning Your Disk* on page 457.

Also refer to *Installation Checklist* on page 441.

Hardware Requirements

Be sure to follow both the requirements and the notes for what not to do.

Hardware "Must Haves"

The hardware requirements for Linspire 5 are:

- PC with 800 MHz or higher processor.

- 256 MB of RAM.

- 4 GB hard drive free space.

- 1024 x 768 or higher resolution graphics card and monitor.

- CD or DVD drive.

- Hardware phone modem (many Winmodems won't work) or broadband modem. Broadband will give you a much better experience.

The system will work with less capable hardware, but it might be slower and the Linspire support team will not be able to answer questions about it.

Hardware "Do Nots"

Please take a moment to review this checklist of "do nots". You must avoid these for successful installation.

- Linspire 5.0 does not support SCSI or fibre channel disk.

- Linspire 5.0 does not support RAID hardware.

- Linspire 5.0 does not support multiprocessor CPUs.

- Linspire 5.0 does not support overclocking (artificially speeding up the CPU by installing a faster clock chip). Put the system clock back to standard while you install. You can always speed up again after a successful installation.

- Linspire 5.0 supports 64-bit CPU chips, but it is a separate download, not the mainstream install image.

- Remove, if possible, anything that makes your PC substantially different from the mainstream. Things like customized BIOS chips, highly specialized hardware cards, one-of-a-kind monitors, etc. Linspire is built to support the ordinary and the usual, not the special cases.

- If your BIOS supports several speed settings for your video card (typically 2x, 4x, and 8x for an Advanced Graphics Processor), select the slowest setting for the installation. You can always go back and speed it up later. You can check whether you have this setting by reviewing your BIOS hardware configuration screens.

- Disable any boot sector virus checking that you have on your PC. If this feature is present on your computer, it is an option in the BIOS. Part of installation requires writing to the boot sector (MBR).

- Make sure that your system BIOS is set to boot from CD. *Troubleshooting BIOS* on page 508 provides more information about this BIOS setting.

When you have checked off these prerequisites, you are ready to proceed with installation.

Installing

Installation takes only 10 to 15 minutes. The key to a smooth installation lies in completing all the preparation. Then follow these steps to install.

1   Put the installation CD in your CD drive, and restart your PC. It will boot up and display the three choices shown in Figure 12-3.

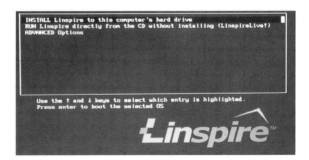

Figure 12-3   Booting from the installation CD

2   Press **Enter** to select **Install Linspire**.

3   You might briefly see a few lines of text on the screen, then the screen will go dark, then it will put up a progress bar on a Linspire splash screen, as it reads from the CD.

4   You might get a brief display of random garbage on the screen, as the X Window System starts. Then you'll see a screen with a cursor, and finally the welcome window shown in Figure 12-4.

Figure 12-4   The first window after booting from the install CD

5   Click **Next** on the welcome window to continue.

6   The window after Welcome (not pictured here) allows you to select the keyboard layout, such as United States, Spanish, or Japanese. Highlight the list entry that most closely matches the keyboard you are using. Click **Next** to continue.

That brings you to the Installation or Update window shown in Figure 12-5.

7   If the installer sees a Reiser filesystem on your disk, it will offer you the chance to update what it assumes is an older installation or to carry out a full install. Select **Install**, shown in Figure 12-5. The update option is used to upgrade an existing Linspire installation with a later version.

The installer may notice a Reiser filesystem if you formatted the partition with reiserfs when you created it, and offer the upgrade for this reason.

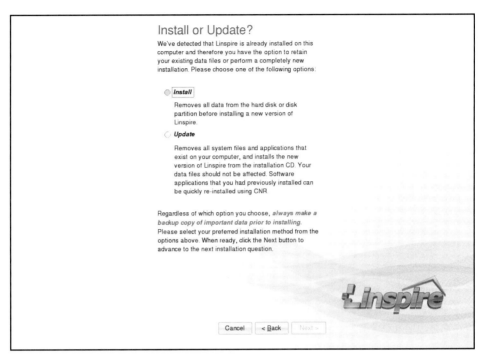

Figure 12-5   Select **Install** for a new installation

8   Click **Next** to continue.

9   The Installation Method window appears (Figure 12-6). Choose whether you want the install to take over the entire disk or a specific partition from all those on the disk.

Linspire refers to the specific partition choice as an advanced install. Select **Advanced Install** if you created a new partition for Linspire.

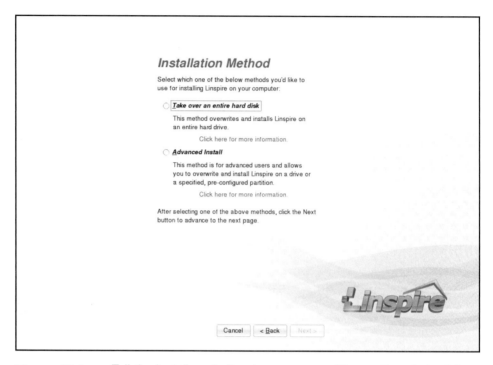

Figure 12-6   Tell the installer whether to use one partition or the whole disk

10 Make your choice, and click **Next** to continue. If you chose the entire disk, continue at step 14.

11 Assuming you chose the Advanced Install to an individual partition, a window similar to the one shown in Figure 12-7 will now appear. This figure shows just one partition on the disk; usually, you will have several partitions, including the one you just created for Linux.

Figure 12-7   Click on the partition you want to install onto

12 The installer displays your disks and disk partitions to you. Highlight the
partition on which you want to install. Note that the installer will show all
disks that are attached to your PC, including external drives. Your computer
BIOS might not support booting from external drives, so don't install there
unless you know you can boot from there. Some versions of Linspire allow
sophisticated users to set the filesystem to Reiser4 by clicking in the **Filesystem** column on this window.

13 Notice the **Write a new Master Boot Record** checkbox. The *Booting Step-
by-step* section described a Master Boot Record (MBR) at length. Normally
you will leave that selected—you do want a new master boot record to be set
up for you. A new MBR will lead to the choice of operating systems to use
when you reboot. You would install a new MBR if you're an advanced user
who already has some other preferred boot loader. Make your choice, and
click **Next** to continue.

14 The Computer Name window allows you to set the host name and root
password (see Figure 12-8).

The computer name is how your PC will be identified on your network, so enter something meaningful, like hp-in-study. The name can only contain letters, numbers and hyphens, and you'll be cut off at twenty characters.

15 Type the administrator (root account) password twice. Although this is optional, you should set a password.

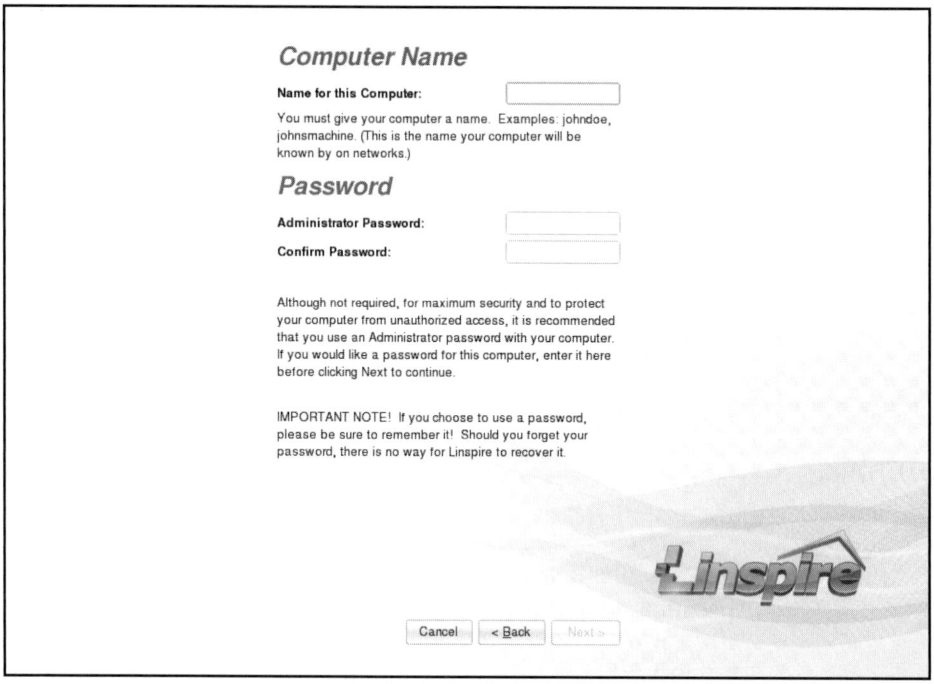

Figure 12-8   Enter host name and root account password

The window cautions "Should you forget your password, there is no way for Linspire to recover it." That's true, but I'll show you a way to reset a forgotten password in *Resetting a Password* on page 492.

16 Click **Next** to continue. The window after Computer Name is a setup confirmation, shown in Figure 12-9.

Figure 12-9   Confirm your choices

17 Review the data that is presented, particularly your choice of partition or disk. Be careful about this: the installation will wipe out whatever was there before.

18 Click **Back** if you need to revisit your choice, or **Finish** to continue.

19 A second dialog will appear, asking in effect, are you really, really, really sure? Of course you're sure! Click **Yes I'm sure**. (Don't bother clicking on Finish a second time, as that button doesn't do anything at this point, and it's a mistake to leave it visible to users).

20 The installation proper now starts. A series of screens appear giving information about Linspire features. All the screens have a progress bar at the bottom. You can see an example in Figure 12-10.

Figure 12-10   Installation happens

21 It takes about 10 minutes to complete installation from this point. There is no further interaction, so you can safely take a break. Or watch the monitor and read about the Linspire highlights.

If you have one, you will see the "in use" LED on the CD light up repeatedly during installation, as the data is copied off the CD, decompressed, and written to disk. When this task is complete, a second dialog will appear, shown in Figure 12-11.

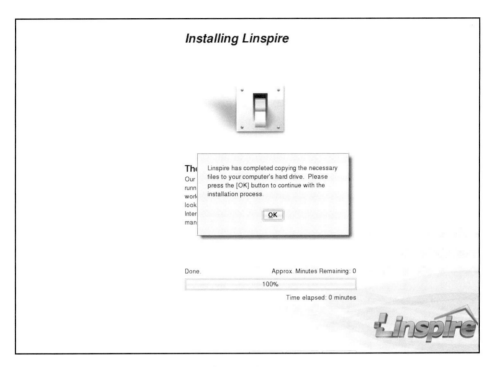

Installing Linspire

Th| Linspire has completed copying the necessary
Our| files to your computer's hard drive. Please
runn| press the [OK] button to continue with the
work| installation process.
look|
Inter|
man|

OK

Done.   Approx. Minutes Remaining: 0
                              100%
                              Time elapsed: 0 minutes

Figure 12-11   Installation is complete

22 Click the **OK** button. After a few seconds, your CD will eject. Remove the CD and press the **Enter** key to continue.

Installation is now complete, and you had to provide only five or six obvious pieces of information. There are a couple of post-installation actions to carry out; these are described in the following section, *Post-Installation Setup*.

Post-Installation Setup

When your computer reboots immediately after installation, it might ask which operating system to boot into. This confirms that the MBR has been updated with GRUB stage 1. If this is now a multi-boot system, it will provide the choices similar to the ones shown in Figure 12-12 on subsequent reboots. (The precise version numbers will vary.)

Booting the Computer After Setup

To complete installation, select **Linspire**. The Diagnostics choice will print out more messages about what is happening at boot time. This can be useful if you run into some problem when booting. The additional messages will help you or others pinpoint what the system is trying to do at the time it goes awry. Use the Redetect option when you want the OS to probe all the hardware and look for new or changed devices, for example after installing a different video card. On some versions of Linspire, Redetect will leave you at Linspire's run level 1.

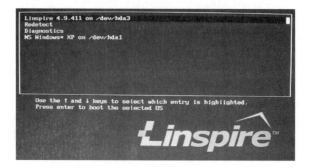

Figure 12-12   The GRUB menu lets you select what and how to boot

So that a boot doesn't get stuck forever waiting for input, it counts down and will go ahead with the default after thirty seconds. The boot screen inaccurately labels any and every version of Windows as "Windows XP" (refer to Figure 12-12). See the end of Appendix E for information on changing GRUB defaults like the Windows name, the timeout length, or which OS is booted by default.

1   After you have chosen Linspire your PC will start to boot up. You might see a quick progression of a blank screen, a screen with a progress bar, a garbled video screen, another blank screen, and then either a login window or a Welcome to Linspire window.

2   If you get the login window, log in using a user name of root and the password you set on the window shown in Figure 12-8 on page 468. The click-through license window shown in Figure 12-13 appears.

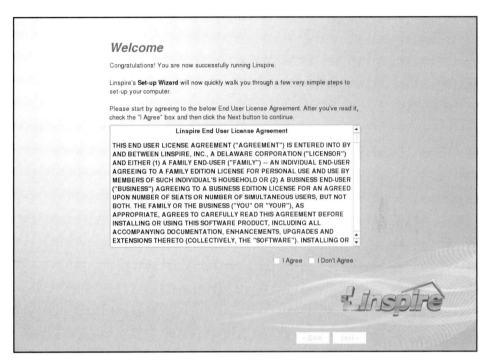

Figure 12-13   The Linspire click-through user license

3   You need to select **I Agree** before you can click **Next** to continue. You can also read the license at http://www.linspire.com/lindows_products_OSEULA.php if you want to study it in detail. A pretty cool feature is that one license (that is, one purchase) covers all PCs in your household.

4   The Sound Volume window appears, shown in Figure 12-14. Move the slider to the left or right until you hear music playing at a comfortable level. In some rare cases, you might hear nothing even with the slider all the way to the right. In that case, you'll have to do some troubleshooting to get sound on this system, but move the slider all the way right.

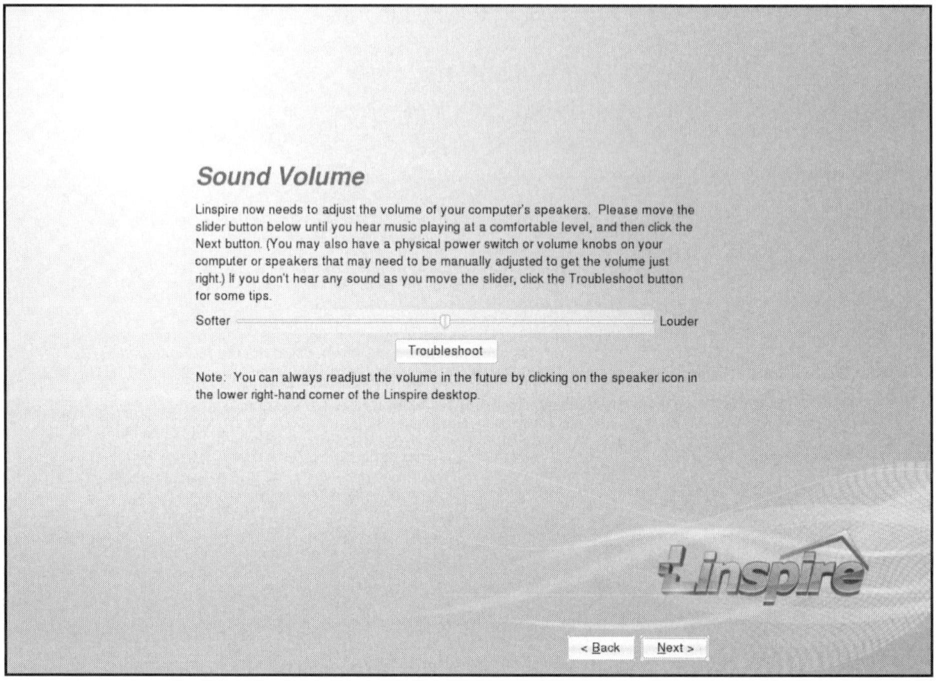

Figure 12-14   Adjust the sound volume

The Troubleshoot button doesn't *really* troubleshoot. It just pops up a dialog to remind you that you need sound hardware and speakers that are plugged in, powered, turned on, and given reasonable volume.

5   When you are ready, click **Next** to continue.

6   You are now given an opportunity to set your time and time zone with the window shown in Figure 12-15. The Linspire HQ is in San Diego, California, within the Pacific Standard Timezone. However, they always set the default timezone to Eastern Standard Time to make it easier to find time-related bugs.

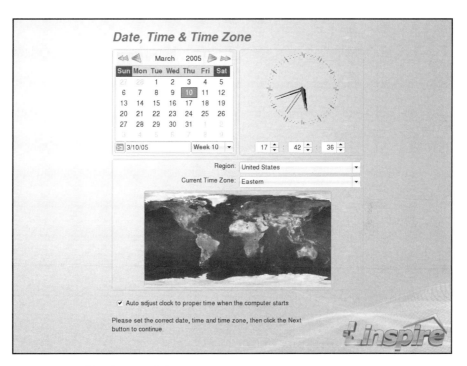

Figure 12-15   Set time and timezone

7 Click on your approximate location on the map to set the timezone. Or you can use the drop-down lists of region and timezone. Then, click on the calendar to select the current date, and the numbers under the clock to set the time. (Leave the Auto adjust clock checkbox selected. This will keep your PC time more accurate by checking a time server on the network each time you reboot). When you are ready, click **Next**.

8 If you later need to change the date, time, or timezone, right-click on the clock shown at the right end of the system tray. That brings up a menu with entries for adjusting all date/time related settings.

9 The Advanced Settings window appears, shown in Figure 12-16.

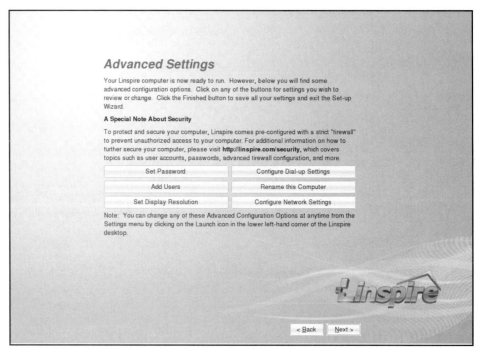

Figure 12-16   Check your network settings

This window offers you the chance to:

+ Set your password, or add a user account

+ Rename the computer

+ Change the display resolution

+ Configure network or modem settings

If you are sharing this system among several family members, set up an account for each of them now by clicking **Add Users**. You'll walk through the process in *Adding User Accounts* on page 479. This goes against the accepted wisdom, but if this will be a single-user PC, it is not necessary to set up a user account for yourself immediately. You can keep using the root account.

When you select **Configure Network Settings** or **Configure Dial-up Settings**, you get the same windows that you do when you select them within the control center.

10 As usual, click **Next** to continue.

11 Don't be alarmed if you see the window shown in Figure 12-17.

Figure 12-17   If you wait too long, you'll get the X screen saver

This is the X Window default screen saver. It means you delayed responding to some screen long enough for the automatic screen saver to come up.

Press the **space bar** to dismiss the screen saver.

12 You'll be reminded that (if you have one) you can load the Linspire Extras CD after installation. The window is shown in Figure 12-18.

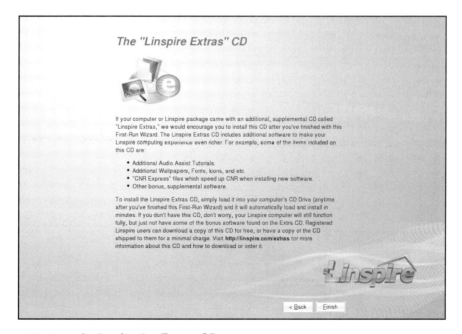

Figure 12-18   A plug for the Extras CD

13 Click **Finish** to complete the post-installation process.

14 You will briefly see the standard desktop, then a Shockwave Flash tutorial will start and take over the whole screen. You can also watch these tutorials offline by browsing http://support.linspire.com/support_tutorials.php. The Tutorial window is shown in Figure 12-19.

Figure 12-19   The tutorials

15 When finished with the tutorials, click **Exit Tutorials**. You have now completed the post-installation setup, and your window will show the standard Linspire desktop (see Figure 12-20).

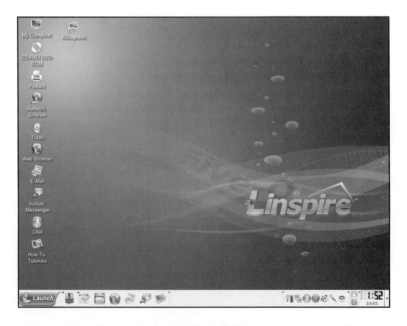

Figure 12-20   Linspire desktop: post-installation steps are complete

Adding User Accounts

All Linux installations create a user account called root. Notice that the home directory for root is /root pronounced "slash root". And the name given to the / directory is also "root"—don't let the name triplication throw you. The root user is also called the superuser and he or she has the privileges needed to do system administration.

Setting Up Users

As you saw in Figure 12-13, the post-installation setup process gives you a chance to add more users. You can also add users at any time, using KUser Manager.

1 Start the KUser Manager by clicking **Launch** > **Settings** > **Additional Options** > **User Manager**.

2 When the tool starts, click the green + button at the left end of its toolbar. A small text field will appear, prompting for the user account name.

3 Provide one, and click **OK**. That will display the User Properties – KUser window shown in Figure 12-21.

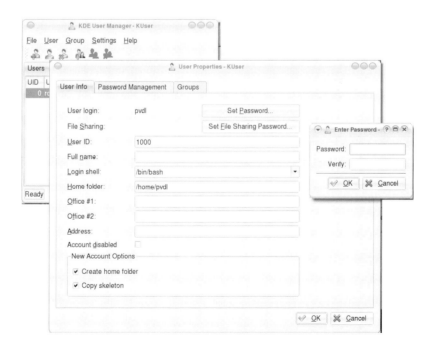

Figure 12-21   Adding a user account

4   Appropriate defaults are set for everything, but you should click the **Set Password** button to bring up the Enter Password window.

5   Enter a password for the user, and click **OK**. Some of the text fields are empty, and you can fill them with information or not as you wish. The user ID is incremented automatically for each user you add, starting at 1000. The user ID must be a different number for every user on the system.

The Password Management tab on the User Properties window lets you set all kinds of policies relating to password expiry. The defaults are fine for most home users. If you're sharing the computer in a business setting, you might want to require new passwords regularly for security reasons. You can do so using this window.

The Groups tab on the User Properties window lets you put the user into one or more groups. The purpose of groups is to provide more flexible access to files than just "owner" and "everyone else". Every file belongs to exactly one group. Every user belongs to one or more groups. If a user belongs to the same group as a file, he or she has access to the file as specified in the file's group permission, not the file's "everyone else" permission.

Groups are widely used in Linspire, and by default, a user belongs to about a dozen groups including audio, CD-ROM, cnr, dialout, and desktop. All of these give a user certain file (and hence program) access privileges he or she would not otherwise have. The default groups that users are put into by default are fine. As an example of group use, you'll need to add a user to the group 106 "camera" for that user to import pictures directly from a camera in Lphoto.

Root Versus User Accounts

Unix has the concept of a root user, also known as the superuser. On Windows, this account is called the administrative user or system administrator. The superuser can do anything on a Unix system, regardless of what file permissions are set.

It has long been established practice in the Unix world that you do not generally run as superuser. Instead you create and use a user account, reserving the superuser account solely for administrative work that requires superuser privileges. The justification has always been that, as a user, your mistakes should only affect your own files and not affect anybody else on the system.

Some other distros force you to create at least one user account as the last post-installation step. Of course, they can't force you to actually use a non-root account. Linspire makes it easy to create user accounts, but it does not force you to. It's easy for the user to continue running as root under any distro, including Linspire.

On the other hand, Linspire has made user improvements that are yet to be adopted in other distros: floppy disks, CDs, and USB drives can be accessed in Linspire by ordinary users. In some distros, superuser privileges are needed to handle removable media.

Root Access and Security

One justification for the "don't run as root" advice is that all Windows XP home, Windows Me, and earlier editions run as root. These systems are plagued by program viruses, document viruses, and spyware. Linux solves that problem in other ways, by being more secure, by not running email attachments automatically, and by not having virus-propagation software like Internet Explorer and Outlook. (Remember the prophetic words of the Magic-8 Ball: "*Outlook not so good.*")

Consider the reasons behind the "don't run as root" advice. Ask yourself what an attacker cannot do if he takes over your user account, as opposed to your root account, on a single user PC. The attacker cannot change certain system files. However, he can install and run programs as you and delete or change your files. That's enough to do all the things attackers want to do, namely send spam mail, install a keylogger or zombie remote control, and store their files on your system. Running as root does not make the consequences of a system penetration any worse on a single user PC.

Your Data Is More Important Than System Data

The case against root use dates from the days when all Unix systems were server systems. On a server, you don't want users to administer the system or to interfere with other users. But neither of these cases apply to a single user PC. I'd like to present a contrarian viewpoint and suggest that it's fine for you to run as root on a single user PC behind a router firewall if you want to.

Then there's the argument that you might inadvertently remove or adjust vital system files. On a single user PC, your most valuable resource is not the system files. It's your data. In 15 minutes you can completely reinstall the system, but if the only copy of your data is lost, it's gone forever.

In conclusion, the trend toward Linux/Unix on single-user PCs behind a router firewall requires a critical re-think of the security paradigms that apply to Unix on server systems. There isn't a compelling reason to avoid running as root on a single user Linux PC. It doesn't make it any easier or harder to get hacked, and it does make system administration more convenient for you. Running as a user doesn't prevent an attacker from doing the things he wants to do when he gets in. Go ahead and run as root with a clear conscience, as long as you back up your data regularly.

This advice may change as Linux gains more features. SELinux (Security-Enhanced Linux, from the U.S. Government's National Security Agency) is a proof-of-concept that implements capability-based security. Current Linux/Unix security is coarse-grained, based on per-process privileges. SELinux uses a finer-grained approach, where programs are temporarily given specific rights to do things, and only for the duration needed. The result is better security without the limitations of the current Unix model. The Linspire OS team has SELinux under consideration for the next major release, but it involves a large amount of work.

Troubleshooting After Installation

> *"The trouble with troubleshooting is that trouble shoots back."*
>
> ~ *Quip found in the Linspire bugzilla database*

The most common problem encountered after installation is a balky device—some peripheral device that refuses to be driven by Linux. First check your non-working devices against the Linspire Hardware Compatibility List at http://www.linspire.com/hcl. That will tell you if the device is supposed to be supported, or if it has not been tested before.

The basic approach here is to find out exactly what kind of hardware your PC uses in the balky device, and then find out what kind of support Linux has for that hardware. You might be able to download a device driver that will solve the problem.

Devices to Check

Table 12-2 shows you the devices that are most likely to give you problems and chapters that provide troubleshooting.

Table 12-2   Troubleshooting reference

Device	More information
Modem	Chapter 2, Chapter 4
Graphics	Chapter 3
Sound	Chapter 2, Chapter 9
CD, DVD burner	Chapter 9
Ethernet and wireless networking	Chapter 2, Chapter 4
Printer	Chapter 3

Getting Informative Error Messages

Boot in diagnostic mode, and look at any errors. If the PC hangs, look at the last few lines of output before it stops. If you have been able to complete an installation, run the `dmesg` command.

The error messages you get from these suggestions probably won't give you enough information to solve the problem on your own. But it will tell the people in the support forums where it is getting stuck, and possibly why. Also check the Linspire web page at `http://info.linspire.com/installhelp`.

Top Two Troubleshooting Tips

If you encounter problems while installing, most of the time there isn't much you can do to help yourself except go to the forums. But there are a couple of troubleshooting tips that are quick and easy to try.

If you think Linux might have a problem driving your graphics card, first see if the problem is too little video memory. Some PCs, particularly laptops, have a BIOS setting allowing you to increase the amount of memory allocated to graphics. The factory setting might be as low as 1 or 2 MB. Appendix B explains how to make adjustments in the BIOS. If your screen is staying dark early in the boot process, look for this BIOS setting and increase it to 8 MB.

The second possibility is to tell Linux to use basic VESA graphics. Follow these steps:

1   Boot from the install CD.

2   When the GRUB menu of boot choices appears, press **E** (for "edit").

3   Use the cursor up/down keys to scroll to the line starting with kernel (when installing) or with initrd (when using the live CD). Then press **E** again.

4   Use the cursor right key to go all the way to the end of the line. Add a kernel boot parameter saying xdriver=vesa.

5   Press the Escape key to exit from editing mode, then press the **B** key to start booting.

After you install, you will have to set the parameter again to boot at the end of installation. Then go to the control center under **Peripherals** > **Display** and set your video driver to Vesa.

If this makes no difference, then the problem is probably not related to the graphics driver.

System Administration Know-How

This section has information on system administration tasks that you will probably need to do at some point. Linux system uptime is frequently measured in years, so there isn't too much to do, but I'll show you how to address a couple of common issues.

Making Backups

At last—the guilty secret of PC ownership. Almost no one actually does backups. How can they? It's difficult, and no one explains how. They just spout the advice, and if you don't do it, anything that happens is your own fault. There's a better way with Linux. Backups are easy, and I'll show you exactly how.

How Frequently Should I Back Up My Data?

"Backups are for wimps. Real men upload their data to an FTP site and have everyone else mirror it."

~ *Linus Torvalds*

Linus was just kidding about using public mirrors for backup—that's how the Linux source code is distributed. The truth is there are two kinds of people in the world: those who have already experienced a hard disk crash, and those who will do so. How much computer work, email, and MP3 files are you willing to irretrievably lose at a time? A day's worth? A week's worth? A month?

Whatever your answer is, that determines the frequency with which you need carry out backups. You also need to make decisions on these issues:

- How much to back up at a time (individual files, a complete filesystem, or a bootable partition)

- What medium you will write the backup to (external disk, CD/DVD, or network server)

There are different tradeoffs for the different choices. One tradeoff is speed of the different media, shown in Figure 12-22. This graph raises several interesting points. These are bus speeds, not device speeds, so theoretical not practical. First, USB 1 is so slow as to almost be off the chart. Second, even the fastest FireWire, FireWire 800, is 25% slower than a modern IDE disk. And third, how soon can I get that future SATA disk?

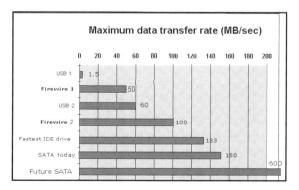

Figure 12-22   Speeds of different backup devices

A 10 GB backup that can be done in two minutes with FireWire 800 will take more than two hours using USB 1. So set your expectations accordingly when backing up filesystems.

Alternative 1: Back Up Partition to External Drive

One approach for regular backups is to use a separate external disk onto which you transfer one or more entire partitions. This is a good approach when you have more than a few tens of GB of data. External disk is a costly medium for backups, but it has three clear advantages:

- You can equally well archive a Linux partition or a Windows partition.

- You can restore individual files from the archived copy or restore the entire partition.

- You can start the backup running and then leave it to complete unattended.

For example, I use a 120 GB Weibetech external USB drive. This external disk is recognized as /dev/sda when I plug it into my notebook system. I formatted the disk with the command:

```
mkreiserfs  -f  /dev/sda
```

The external disk needs to be big enough to hold your Linspire partition. You can then backup the entire Linspire partition to the external disk with this one command:

```
dd  if=/dev/hda3  of=/dev/sda1
```

The if option is an abbreviation for input file, of is for output file. Use whatever your device and partition names actually are, not necessarily the hda3 and sda1 shown here. If you have a minimal 5 GB installation, it will take at least an hour to write the data over USB.

You can use this backup method to make a copy of your entire Windows partition to external disk. This copied partition can later be restored to the same computer. If you restore the Windows partition to a different computer, the Windows licensing will prevent it from booting.

If you select this approach to back up, you might like to look at the site http://www.partimage.org. Partition Image is a utility that saves partitions to an image file. Partition Image will only copy data from the used portions of the partition. Unlike the dd command, empty blocks are not written to the image file.

The dd command is one of the oldest commands in Unix. It is an abbreviation of Data Definition, and was brought into the first implementation of Unix in the late 1960s as a copy of the equally revolting IBM job control language dd feature. As a result of its origin, practically nothing is intuitive or obvious about dd. Its arguments are formed very differently to just about every other command in Unix. Use the man pages to review the arguments for dd.

Restore Partition

You can restore by mounting the external disk and copying individual files. Or you can blast the entire partition back in (thereby overwriting whatever was on the hard disk partition) by using:

```
dd  if=/dev/sda1   of=/dev/hda3
```

With all of the commands, you must use your actual partition and pathnames, which are not necessarily the same as the example ones shown here. Type the command mount to see a list of your mounted filesystems and the corresponding device names. If you like seeing it all lined up nicely in columns, pipe the output of mount into the column command. Here's an example of the command and output:

```
# mount |column -t
/dev/hda3                                on /            type reiserfs (rw)
none                                     on /dev         type devfs (rw)
proc                                     on /proc        type proc (rw)
sysf                                     on /sys         type sysfs (rw)
tmpfs                                    on /dev/shm     type tmpfs (rw)
usbfs                                    on /proc/bus/usb type usbfs (rw)
none                                     on /dev/sh      type tmpfs (rw)
/dev/ide/host0/bus0/target0/lun0/part1   on /mnt/hda1    type ntfs (rw,noatime)
/dev/ide/host0/bus0/target0/lun0/part2   on /mnt/hda2    type reiser4 (rw,noatime)
/dev/ide/host0/bus0/target0/lun0/part5   on /mnt/hda5    type vfat (rw,noatime)
/dev/ide/host0/bus0/target0/lun0/part6   on /mnt/hda6    type vfat (rw,noatime)
```

The lines that start with /dev are filesystems on true hardware devices. The other filesystems, like tmpfs, are operating system concepts for organizing data by making it look like it is a file system.

SCSI, ATAPI, IDE—Where will it all end?

Linux gives the names /dev/sda, sdb, sdc and so on to hard disks that are accessed using the SCSI software protocol, rather than the ATA Packet Interface (ATAPI) protocol. Don't confuse the use of the SCSI software command set with SCSI hardware—they are two different things. ATA is just another name for IDE—both refer to disk drives packaged with the disk controller in the disk case.

The SCSI protocol supports queues of commands with multiple outstanding requests. ATA does not support this. This makes the SCSI command set very suitable for accessing mixes of fast (internal) and slow (external) devices on the same bus.

Caution – While you back up a partition, the filesystem should not be in use at all, and ideally not even mounted. You must restore a partition to the same partition on the disk (e.g., hda3) and you must not change the size of the partition (e.g., you cannot shrink the disk partition and then restore to it).

Alternative 2: Back Up to Multiple CDs or DVDs

If you don't have an external disk, you can back up a filesystem or part of a filesystem to a series of DVDs or CDs. This kind of backup is less convenient to create and to restore, because you are backing up to a series of files and you need to keep track of the pieces yourself. But it is less costly in backup media (DVD platters instead of disk). To restore the root filesystem from this kind of backup, you will need to have two CD or DVD drives.

Backing Up Files

In this kind of backup, you specify how much data to put on the platter, so this will continue to work well when high-capacity DVD platters become widespread.

Again, with all of these commands, you must use your actual partition and pathnames, not necessarily the example ones shown here. Type mount to see a list of mounted partitions and the corresponding device names.

The process works as follows: go through an entire filesystem copying a CD-sized chunk, then write that chunk to CD before proceeding to the next one. There's some one-time preparation to create a directory called /partial to hold each tar file before burning to CD or DVD. Here's the command:

mkdir /partial

You'll use the tar (tape archive) command to create the backup archive. Although originally intended to work with tape drives, tar can read and write from any device.

Next, create an exclusion file that tells tar not to back up certain files. One of these is the 1 GB swap file. The swap file holds the memory for processes that have started running but are not able to run at this precise moment. It doesn't make any sense to archive something transient like that.

Another file you do not want to write in the tar archive is the output file tar is itself creating. (In other words, don't include the tar output file in the input to tar.) Use your favorite text editor to create the file /dont-backup-list.txt with these lines in it.

```
/partial/backup.tar
/boot/linux-swap.swp
/tmp
```

Add lines giving the pathnames of other big files you don't want to back up, if there are any. Alternatively, if you put the /partial directory on another partition, you don't have to exclude it from the backup. The --one-file-system option will cause other partitions (like anything under /mnt or /proc) to be excluded from the backup, too.

Then you can create a series of tar files with the following command. You can use a different pathname instead of /. For instance, use /root to back up the /root directory and everything underneath it.

```
tar --one-file-system --absolute-names -M -L number -cvf /partial/backup.tar / -X /
dont-backup-list.txt
```

I've had to break the line here to print it in a book, but you will type it on one line.

You should have no other programs running when you do this backup, or when you do the corresponding restore. You should disconnect from the net so that no Ethernet traffic comes in or goes out. You should not have a mail program open, nor use your browser. This is to avoid changes to the filesystem while you are backing it up. (If it's too much to remember to halt all these programs, put the system in Linspire's run level 1 mentioned previously).

If backing up to DVD, use 4000000 for *number* .
If backing up to CD, use 650000 for *number* .

You need to specify something less than the full capacity of the media to leave some room for metadata.

The -L option instructs tar to pause after every *number* KBs written, allowing you to burn the file /partial/backup.tar to a data DVD using K3b as described in *Burning Data CDs* on page 303. After the file has been written to DVD, press **Enter** and tar will continue.

Caution – tar will start writing again at the beginning of output file /partial/backup.tar, so if you failed to save that off to DVD when tar paused, you have now lost it for good and you need to restart the backup.

Repeat until tar completes. Write on the DVD labels the date, the backup directory, and the order in which each was written.

Backing up just your home directory

As I've stressed several times, the most important files on your PC are your own data files, not the files that make up the operating system. You might therefore wish to back up just your home directory. It is straightforward to do. You no longer need an exclude file—the whole point is to back up everything you own.

Backing up your home directory

Use this command to create a series of 600 MB tar files that together form an archive of the home directory of user peter *and everything underneath it. You should be logged in as root when you back up a user directory, not as the user.*

tar -M -L 650000 -cvf /backup.tar /home/peter

After creating the first /backup.tar *file, the tar program will pause and output the message:*

Prepare volume #2 for '/backup.tar' and press Return:

That's your cue to start the K3b program by clicking **Launch** > **Run Programs** > **Audio and MP3** > **CD and DVD Burning (K3b)**. *Then create a data project, and burn the single file* /backup.tar *to it. When the CD has completed burning, remove it from the drive, and label it with a permanent marker; something like* /home/peter backup.tar, *March 3, 2005, file #1.*

Now go back to the command line window, and press **Return** *to allow tar to continue. If you allow tar to continue prematurely (before the K3b burn to CD has completed), you will overwrite with new data a file that is still being written to CD.*

In other words, you have to carefully alternate between creating a file with tar, and writing that same file to CD with K3b. The same one file name is used repeatedly as the output of tar, so you can't generate five tar files one after the other, and then write them all to CD one after the other. Be ready to load and burn each new blank CD as many times as needed.

Restoring your home directory

Later the root user can restore the user's entire home directory with these commands.

cd /

tar -Mxvf /mnt/cdrom0/backup.tar

After reading the first /backup.tar file from the CD, the tar program will pause and output the message:

Prepare volume #2 for '/mnt/cdrom0/backup.tar' and press Return:

That's your cue to eject the first CD, and put the second one in the drive, then tap return. Keep watching tar and loading each subsequent CD in the correct order as tar prompts, until tar finishes. At that point the home directory will be fully restored from backup.

Note: *You must be logged in as root when you archive and restore a user home directory as described here. If you want to archive or restore the root directory, you must boot into single-user mode and archive or restore it without X Window running.*

Restoring from tar Files

You can restore an individual file to your home directory in an active partition, but it is unwise to restore the entire / partition when the filesystem is in use. This is because it is not safe to archive or restore files that are actually in use, such as the Desktop directory of the logged-in user. The problem is that you will overwrite the disk copy of binaries that are in the course of execution, the caches of various system processes, the dynamic program loader, and so on.

You need two CD or DVD drives to restore an entire filesystem from this kind of backup. In one CD drive, you'll boot from a live CD, and mount the hard disk partition you want to restore. You'll use the second drive to read the CD or DVDs with the tar files. Alternatively, if your system supports it, you could boot from an external disk drive. You will restore by putting the tar DVDs or CDs in the drive, one after the other.

When the first disk is in the drive, use this command:

```
tar --absolute-names -Mxvf /mnt/cdrom0/backup.tar  /
```

It will stop after each tar file is read, allowing you to put the next platter in the drive. The pathname, / in the previous example, needs to be the pathname you used on writing the archive. For example, if you wrote out /root, that is the path you will restore. You might also give the pathname of any individual files or folders contained in the archive if you wish to restore less than the entire archive. If you wrote out /, you can restore just the file /home/peter/taxes.sxc for example.

Alternative 3: Use a Commercial Backup Product

Some people will always be happier using a commercial backup product with a GUI and with some user support. There are several alternatives for Linux.

One popular commercial Linux backup product, currently free for consumer use, is the Storix product. Details are available at http://www.storix.com/product.html

Resetting a Password

The root user can set or reset a user password by running the KDE User Manager. But what if it is the root user password that has been forgotten? If you don't have the superuser password, you won't be able to log in as the superuser to run the KDE User Manager.

Resetting a Forgotten Root Password

In this case, boot from a live CD, and edit the the file /etc/shadow on the hard disk. It will have a pathname like /mnt/hda3/etc/shadow, where hda3 is the partition that contains your Linux filesystem.

As always, make a backup copy of any system file before you edit it. To maintain system security, change the file mode of this backup copy so that it can only be read by root.

```
cd /mnt/hda3/etc
mv shadow shadow.orig
cp shadow.orig shadow
chmod 400 shadow.orig
```

Make the backup copy by renaming the original, then copying it back to the original name, because it leaves the duplicate of the original with the timestamp of the original file. The file /etc/shadow contains a list of user names matched with their encrypted passwords. Find the entry for the root user, which is usually the first line in the file.

The fields in this file are separated by colons. The first field is the user name, the second field is the 13-character encrypted password, and all the other fields keep track of number of days relating to passwords: "number of days (since January 1, 1970) since the password was last changed"; "The number of days before password may be changed (0 indicates it may be changed at any time)"; "The number of days after which the password must be changed (99999 indicates user can keep his or her password unchanged for many, many years)"; and so on.

On my system the first few lines of /etc/shadow look like this:

```
root:$1$IVEyJhjt$9LNFHdFdN4fhtyqkXXCFW.:12812:0:99999:7:::
daemon:*:12812:0:99999:7:::
bin:*:12812:0:99999:7:::
sys:*:12812:0:99999:7:::
```

Change the password field for the root user so that it's blank, by deleting everything between the first pair of colons. A blank entry (such as ::) indicates that a password is not required to log in. A * entry (such as :*:) indicates the account has been disabled, preventing that user from logging in. The daemon account exists for certain system processes, like maintaining the line printer queue. It is not intended that anyone ever log in as daemon, hence logins are disabled.

By the way, the 1 at the beginning of the password is an indicator that the password was encrypted with our old friend from Chapter 9, "Filesystems and Optical Storage (CDs and DVDs)," Message Digest 5, MD5. This is stronger than the Data Encryption Standard algorithm used by older Linuxes, but weaker than OpenBSD's Blowfish algorithm. The password that the user types is not stored anywhere in plaintext on the system, only its encrypted form.

Be very careful that you make the correct change. After giving root an empty password, the first few lines of the file now look like this:

```
root::12812:0:99999:7:::
daemon:*:12812:0:99999:7:::
bin:*:12812:0:99999:7:::
sys:*:12812:0:99999:7:::
```

You can now reboot from disk, log in as root, and re-establish a root password with the command:

```
passwd
```

Setting a Password Using the KDE User Manager

You can also use the KDE User Manager to set a password. Choose **Settings** > **Additional Options** > **User Manager (KUser)**. You can also start it by typing kuser on the command line. Figure 12-21 on page 479 shows KUser in action.

The End, and the Beginning: Going Forward With Linux

That brings us to the end of this text. But my hope is that you are now beginning a long, productive, and enjoyable relationship with Linux.

Send me an email if you liked this book, or want to make a suggestion: pvdl@afu.com. Look for me on the Linux forums and newsgroups, and I'll keep an eye out for you too.

Linux is one of the best developments in software ever, in terms of both the results and the cooperative process. We all share in it freely. It's the way things ought to be. It's the way of the future. Linux belongs to you.

Malicious Windows Software

Windows Viruses Are Getting More Dangerous

The goal of this appendix is to explain the pathology of the Windows viruses that are common today. For the first few years, Windows viruses were mostly just a novelty and a nuisance. They played a tune, or displayed an animated graphic, or taunted you, or rebooted your system. In recent years viruses have become both more numerous and more serious, to the point today where some viruses endanger your financial security.

Three trends have come together in recent years to move current Windows viruses well beyond the nuisance category.

- Virus writers have learned how to install a virus directly onto other people's computers, without any action from the user. Like Netsky-P, some viruses can install themselves even if you never click on any email attachment. The installation often relies on flaws in specific versions of Microsoft software that change over time, but such viruses can spread rapidly.

  The Sasser worm of May 2004 was self-installing, and infected hundreds of thousands of computers. The Blaster worm that penetrated millions of Windows PCs in August 2003 was self-installing.

- Some viruses now disable virus-checking software. They look for products from the major Internet security companies, and stop them from running. The disabling is not immediately apparent to users. That leaves the PC open to further attacks, and the owner with a false sense of security.

  The Gibe-F virus (also called "Swen") of September 2003 was spread by an email that falsely claimed to be from Microsoft and invited users to download a patch. When users did that, it installed the virus. The first action of the virus was to terminate many different kinds of security and antivirus software on the computer.

- Many viruses now include "backdoor" capabilities. Instead of noticeable disruption, the virus secretly installs a backdoor program on your system. Backdoor software (also known as a Trojan horse, or a Remote Access Trojan) gives the virus writer control over your computer from anywhere on the Internet.

Backdoor software can give the virus writer more power over your PC than you yourself have. Backdoor software can keep a record of the keys you press on your keyboard ("keylogging"), and display a copy of your screen on the virus writer's monitor.

The Damaru-A virus of August 2003 installed a backdoor onto computers it infected. The Backdoor-CGT virus of July 2004 installed backdoor software.

Unfortunately, it is not rare for computer viruses to incorporate all three of these techniques: self-installing viruses that disable security software and give backdoor control of your system to someone else. The Badtrans virus from April 2001 used all three techniques. So did the Bugbear-B virus from September 2002. So did the Bobax virus of May 2004.

According to Internet security company Sophos, Inc., more than 900 new Windows viruses were released in one month, May 2004. Viruses are out of control in the Windows world. By switching to Linux you will reduce virus attacks from a raging full flood torrent down to a very slow and occasional drip.

More About Backdoors

You might wonder why anyone would bother gaining remote control of your PC. Your PC individually might or might not have a lot of value to "black-hat" hackers, depending on how much of your financial data you keep there. But backdoor attacks are mounted in the millions, and PCs are taken over in the thousands with each new virus.

Virus writers want a pool of compliant PCs for three purposes, and they are all malicious.

To Send Spam Mail

Legitimate avenues for sending junk email are gradually being closed off by laws and by better server security. Junk mail fraudsters are responding by using mail servers in third-world countries, and by paying virus writers to deliver a pool of backdoored PCs that can be remotely controlled to send out spam mail. These captive PCs are known as "zombie spambots".

To Attack and Steal from You

If a criminal can access your PC, they can upload all your private files. Do you use your PC to complete your tax returns? Do you have a spreadsheet with details of your savings accounts? Do you reconcile bank statements or keep medical, financial or personal information on your PC? Do you keep them encrypted? All of these are valuable and vulnerable data.

Unlike the loss of a wallet or purse, access to your PC can let a criminal steal money from your accounts before you are aware of it. The money will quickly be transferred to somewhere like China or Eastern Europe where Western-style banking laws are not honored. Your personal details may be sold to others who will use them to obtain and misuse credit under your name—identity theft.

In July 2003, a 25-year-old New York City resident named JuJu Jiang pleaded guilty to computer fraud. He had secretly installed keyboard logging hardware on PCs used by the public in Kinko's copy shops around Manhattan. (A keyboard logger records every key pressed on the keyboard, and can replay them on demand to yield passwords and credit card numbers you have typed.) He could just as easily have sent a keyboard logger in a Windows virus, or installed the logger in libraries, schools, or workplaces he had access to. Over a two-year period, Jiang collected over 450 online banking user IDs and passwords. He stole money from most of these accounts and also sold personal details to other thieves.

To Attack and Steal from Others

The most common form of attack by a group of zombie PCs is the Distributed Denial Of Service or DDOS attack. The attacker coordinates all the captured PCs to access a target web site simultaneously. There can easily be hundreds or thousands of simultaneous requests, and just about any web site will be overwhelmed and left unable to respond to browser requests for web pages.

The DDOS attack may be purely malicious to drive the site off the web for a few hours. In February 2000, independent DDOS attacks knocked the Yahoo, eBay, Amazon.com, and CNN web sites off the net. In October 2002, there was a DDOS attack on Network Solutions, Inc., the company that runs the servers directing traffic across the backbone of the Internet. The attack lasted an hour and took down 9 of the 13 critical servers. If the attack had been sustained longer, it would have completely shut down large parts of the Internet.

Google was significantly impacted in July 2004, in the crucial weeks before its stock market public offering, by a denial of service attack from the Mydoom.O Windows virus.

Some Denial Of Service attacks are aimed at Internet sites working against spammers. Anti-spam organization Spamhaus maintains lists of spam sources and works with law enforcement worldwide to identify and reduce illegal spam. The Sobig virus of July 2003 created tens of thousands of backdoored Windows systems that were used to bombard Spamhaus.org with high volume web requests over a two month period. Spam senders have clearly added some virus writers to their payroll.

The third kind of DDOS attack is linked to an extortion demand. The attacker demands money to refrain from blocking the web site. This is a modern version of the old style protection racket. Organized crime syndicates actually hire virus writers to acquire the backdoored PCs and then make the attacks. In July 2004, police arrested three gang leaders in St. Petersburg, Russia. The gang had allegedly extorted hundreds of thousands of dollars from several online betting services.

The www.auctionstealer.com web site was driven off the web for two days in May 2003 after refusing to pay an extortion demand. In April 2004, the e-commerce firm 2Checkout based in Columbus, Ohio, was hit with a week-long DDOS attack after it rebuffed an extortion attempt. It's a serious criminal matter when Windows PCs belonging to you and hundreds of others are used for extortion.

The backdoor attacks on Windows PCs are particularly worrying. Although such attacks don't yet have a high profile, they are a totally unacceptable risk to Windows users. If your system has been compromised by a backdoor attack, it's a powerful incentive to switch to an operating system that is less vulnerable.

In June 2005, a security architect with Computer Associates described a commodity market for backdoored PCs. Spammers and criminals pay virus writers five cents per machine for compromised Windows PCs. High-profile viruses striking millions of systems are being replaced by low-profile stealth viruses that take over a few thousand PCs and then stop. The pool of compromised systems is then sold, and the next virus released for the next customer.

Windows Web Servers Penetrated Worldwide

The final straw with Windows (for me) came in early June 2004 when Russian hackers figured out how to use defects in Microsoft's IIS 5.0 web server program. They broke into hundreds of top-tier web sites worldwide and made hidden changes to web pages.

When a user browsed one of those hacked web sites with Microsoft Internet Explorer on Windows 2000 or XP, the browser ran a script. The script told Internet Explorer to download a backdoor program from a server belonging to the E-Neverland Network Company in Moscow, Russia.

The attack was named Download.Ject (also called Scob). More than six hundred high-volume banking, financial, and commercial web sites were infiltrated, each with thousands to hundreds of thousands of users. Millions of users were at risk.

Network security company McAfee rated this the most serious threat of the year 2004, and a McAfee spokesman commented "Once it got into networks, the impact was huge." Cyveillance Inc., a provider of online risk monitoring software, announced that 641 sites were still infected with the Download.Ject virus as of June 27, 2004.

The Download.Ject attack was very worrying in two new ways: many users were familiar with email as an avenue for viruses, but getting a backdoor program just by visiting a familiar and trusted web site is something new. Second, Microsoft was unable to provide a timely fix for the Internet Explorer bug that allowed the backdoor exploit.

An alert web site quietly informed security professionals about the penetration and the network security industry went into action. Symantec published a technical analysis of the attack. Internet Service Providers and law enforcement officials got the Russian server taken off the network on June 24, 2004. According to the Pittsburgh Post Gazette, the attack affected several auction sites and fifty of the world's largest banks. However, no public warning was issued, and only one of the penetrated web sites (Kelley Blue Book, www.kbb.com) chose to identify itself.

Why Weren't Users Warned of Download.Ject?

Shamefully, very few of the top-tier web sites publicly admitted they had spread virus software to their users. The failure to widely disclose the June 2004 Download.Ject attack meant many home users remained unaware of the backdoor installed on their Windows PC. There is a discussion of this topic by Infoworld columnist Ed Foster at http://weblog.infoworld.com/foster/2004/07/17.html.

Companies find it very cheap to conduct business on the web. They don't want to do anything that will undermine online business, even if it means covering up problems. So the burden falls wholly on you, the user, to secure your system from Windows viruses spread from sites you trust.

You can check whether your Windows PC was compromised by Download.Ject. Search for a file called kk32.dll.

1 Click **Start** > **Search** > **All Files and Folders**.

2 Enter kk32.dll under **...the file name**.

3 Click on more advanced options. Select **Search hidden files and folders** and click **Search**. If you have the file, you have the Download.Ject backdoor.

U.S. Government Warns "Don't Use Internet Explorer"

The situation with Windows viruses brings to mind the story of the frog in the pot. If a frog is dropped into a pot of very hot water, it immediately feels the heat and leaps out. But if the frog is dropped in a pot of room temperature water, and the water gradually raised to boiling point, the frog won't recognize how uncomfortable things are getting until too late. Windows viruses have increased in the last few years to the point where we are all in very hot water. But not everyone has noticed yet.

Microsoft issued a series of fixes to partially repair the security holes in IIS and Internet Explorer. Some of their workarounds broke other applications. Worse still, security researchers soon pointed out inadequacies in the fixes. Fully patched versions of Internet Explorer could still stealthily download dangerous software onto your PC. They eventually got a patch out in August 2004. The patch also included fixes for two other completely unrelated but critical security weaknesses.

Microsoft's design for Internet Explorer is fundamentally flawed, and it cannot be made secure in any short timeframe. Internet Explorer classifies web pages into zones and assigns different levels of trust to a zone representing a file on your PC versus a zone representing a web page from an untrusted site. Many exploits work by fooling Internet Explorer about which zone they are in. Windows users run a continuing risk of future Download.Ject-style attacks.

Microsoft's bugs had spread a computer virus using popular and trusted web sites as virus transmitters. The infection was designed to take control of the PCs and steal personal information from web users visiting those sites. Microsoft could not come up with a fix. Because of this and related security problems, in June 2004 the U.S. Government's Computer Emergency Response Team (a government computer security clearing house) had to advise users to stop using Microsoft's Internet Explorer.

Why Does Microsoft Software Have So Many Security Problems?

Microsoft claims that their products suffer from security problems because they have the largest share of the market. That is self-serving marketing spin.

Consider some software where Microsoft does not dominate the market: web servers. Microsoft is just a small though important vendor in that market, but Microsoft's IIS web server is still plagued by far more vulnerabilities and security penetrations than all other web server software. A study at George Mason University in 2001 concluded that:

- Apache (the leading web server, with twice the market share of IIS) is clearly more secure than Microsoft's IIS.

- This result is consistent with another study showing that Windows has far more security problems than Linux.

- Microsoft products may be attacked more because they are more widespread. But they are penetrated more because they are badly designed, badly implemented, and come with poorly chosen default settings.

- In its Knowledge Base Article 228985, Microsoft provides a list of its own games that need administrator authority to play. (The system administrator has more privileges than ordinary users, and can change operating system files. Most ordinary users should not use the administrator account and should not have administrator privileges.)

Why should you need operating system privileges to play Flight Simulator, for goodness sake? Worse still, every Windows home user is given administrator privileges. These practices are a powerful statement about Microsoft's lack of true commitment to security. (The system privileges are needed to access the graphics hardware directly, for performance in this game, by the way.)

Although Outlook now blocks most executable attachments, it's still possible to override those protections. Historically, Microsoft saw security as far less important than ease-of-use. The Internet requires everyone to rethink those priorities, but it is next to impossible to retrofit security into software products.

Some Microsoft software was designed so that it tied users to other Microsoft software and strengthened the monopoly. Internet Explorer was converted from an application into part of the operating system and the change undermines security. Microsoft ignored the security part of the mail attachments (known as MIME) specification. Years later, they still won't revert to something more secure. If Windows were a car, the government would have stepped in years ago to order a mandatory recall to fix the problems.

Microsoft started a Trustworthy Computing Initiative in January 2002, but incredibly, did not publish concrete goals such as "Within two years we will reduce by 50% the viruses that affect more than one million Windows customers." The initiative has achieved some positive things, like Windows Updates over the network. But Windows Update is only available to PCs that Microsoft can confirm are currently licensed, and the update depends on ActiveX scripting that US-CERT recommends you turn off.

According to an October 2003 report at News.com, Microsoft finally conceded that its strategy of patching Windows holes as they emerge doesn't work. People are too busy to download and install Microsoft's "bug fix of the week".

"It's just hard," (for users to keep patching Windows) explained Microsoft sales chief Orlando Ayala, while declining to describe what Microsoft would do to address this. It's even harder for non-technical people to make informed judgments when important information about Windows virus attacks (like Download.Ject) is kept from them.

All this is not to say that Linux is magically immune to viruses. You will still have to follow good security practices. You must still avoid running random executables that you download or get by email, and you will still have to use a firewall (explained later) and install patches from time to time. It just won't be a weekly event.

It is very easy to download the wrong versions of the two files. If you do, the mailer will not be able to handle encryption, and you will not get any sensible error messages. If things aren't working, this is the first thing to double-check.

Making Your Hardware Obey You—BIOS and Device Drivers

Troubleshooting BIOS

The boot process for a PC uses an assembly language program called the "BIOS" or Basic Input-Output System. There's some version of the BIOS on every PC.

The BIOS (a pun on the Greek word "bios" meaning "life") is a program, permanently kept in read-only memory, that brings your computer to life when you turn the power on. It's just an x86 program like any other application, except it runs on a bare machine before the operating system has started. Originally, the BIOS had four major components:

- The power-on self test (POST) routines that initialize hardware and run quick basic sanity checks.

- A bootstrap loader to start loading the operating system from a drive.

- A setup utility that lets you configure some features of the BIOS, using a clunky console-graphics GUI.

- A library of functions that control the core hardware devices such as floppy and hard disk, video adapter, keyboard, and serial port.

That last component meant that as well as controlling the booting up of your system, the BIOS was also supposed to keep running and do all the work that is today done by device drivers. The operating system would call BIOS routines in read-only memory to access the disk, make sounds through the speaker, drive the keyboard, and so on. Hence the "Basic I/O" name.

Around 1979 when this dual purpose was laid down, it seemed reasonable, but it was eventually found to be too inflexible and impractical. The runtime I/O responsibilities of BIOS were phased out around the days of the Intel 386. So nowadays it's more accurate to think of BIOS as representing "Boot It to OS".

The Order of the Boot

Use the BIOS setup utility to change the boot order so that the CD comes first. You access the BIOS setup by pressing one or two keys just after powering on. The precise key or keys depend on the version of the BIOS you have. The major BIOS suppliers today are Phoenix Technologies and American Megatrends Incorporated (AMI).

American Megatrends is standardizing on the DEL key. The Phoenix BIOS in my HP laptop PC uses the F10 function key. Others use keys or key combinations such as Esc, F1, F2, Ctrl-Esc, Alt-Esc, Ctrl-Alt-Esc, Ctrl-Alt-Enter, Ins, and others.

If you're stuck, go to the PC vendor's web site, click on **Support** and search for BIOS setup. If they don't have this information, or the manual for your model online, then at least you know to buy from a different vendor next time.

Figure B-1   Entering BIOS setup

Figure B-1 shows the screen, which gives you the chance to enter the BIOS setup utility on your PC. It flashes up for no more than a second early on in the boot process on my PC. You've got to be quick to catch it. I was never able to read the text until I took this photograph of the screen! The text at the bottom reads:

Press <ESC> to change boot order

Press <F10> to enter Setup, <F12> to boot from LAN

This BIOS offers you the chance to go directly to the Change Boot Order screen by pressing the ESC key, but most BIOS setups do not, so let's do it the longer, more common way. If you manage to press the F10 function key while this screen is showing, you will be taken to the main screen of the BIOS Setup Utility shown in Figure B-2. If you're too slow and miss it, let Windows complete booting then restart the system and try again.

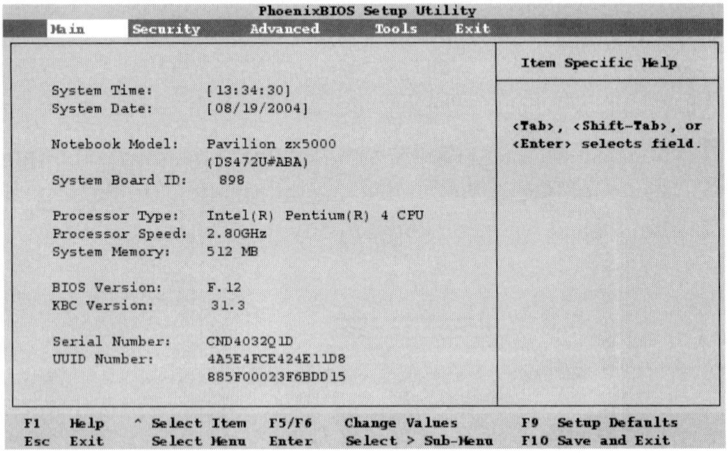

```
                        PhoenixBIOS Setup Utility
       Main    Security    Advanced    Tools    Exit

                                                  Item Specific Help
     System Time:      [13:34:30]
     System Date:      [08/19/2004]
                                               <Tab>, <Shift-Tab>, or
     Notebook Model:   Pavilion zx5000          <Enter> selects field.
                       (DS472U#ABA)
     System Board ID:   898

     Processor Type:   Intel(R) Pentium(R) 4 CPU
     Processor Speed:  2.80GHz
     System Memory:    512 MB

     BIOS Version:     F.12
     KBC Version:      31.3

     Serial Number:    CND4032Q1D
     UUID Number:      4A5E4FCE424E11D8
                       885F00023F6BDD15

     F1   Help    ^ Select Item   F5/F6  Change Values     F9  Setup Defaults
     Esc  Exit      Select Menu    Enter  Select > Sub-Menu F10 Save and Exit
```

Figure B-2   BIOS setup utility

The BIOS setup screen on your PC may look quite different from this one, which is the Phoenix BIOS, version F.12. But all the BIOS setup utilities offer similar functionality. This screen (and probably your BIOS setup utility too) provides a key along the bottom of the screen explaining how to interact with it. When you explore BIOS setup, be careful not to change any settings other than the one you intend. Some of the values can have a big effect on your PC.

There is no **Change boot order** shown on this initial screen, so look at the other menu items, laid out along the top of the screen. The instructions don't tell you that you move to other menu items by using the left and right cursor keys, but that's a fair guess.

Pressing the **Return** key while on the Advanced menu brings you to a screen where you can change the boot order. It's the second entry on that screen, shown in Figure B-3.

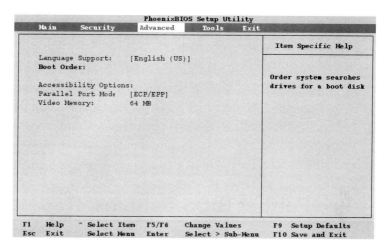

Figure B-3   Selecting boot order

Press **Return** to bring up the Boot Order screen shown in Figure B-4. Press the
keys indicated in the on-screen instructions to move the CD drive to the top of the
list. The word "ATAPI" listed with the CD drive is the name of the standard
interface by which the CD talks to the rest of the system. It's not a very helpful
piece of information to add by itself, and demonstrates why BIOS programmers
should not design GUIs.

```
                         PhoenixBIOS Setup Utility
                           Advanced

            Boot Order:                           Item Specific Help

        ATAPI CD-ROM Drive                    Keys used to view or
       +Hard Drive                            configure devices:
        Network Adaptor                       <Enter> expands or
        Floppy Diskette Drive                 collapses devices with
                                              a + or -.
                                              <Shift + 1> enables or
                                              disables a device
                                              <F6> and <F5> moves the
                                              device up or down.


    F1   Help    ^ Select Item  F5/F6   Change Values     F9  Setup Defaults
    Esc  Exit      Select Menu   Enter   Select > Sub-Menu  F10 Save and Exit
```

Figure B-4   Boot Order screen

While you're changing the CD boot order, you might as well move the floppy drive to the bottom of the list as well. Some systems don't have a floppy any more, and when they do you almost never boot from it, so why waste time trying to read it during a boot? If you ever need to boot from floppy, you can always change the configuration back.

After changing the boot order list to put the CD first, exit the screen, making sure to save the changes (not discard them). You will probably be asked to confirm them. When you exit the setup utility main screen (here with an F10 key), the system will continue booting.

Two Further BIOS Settings

You might also find it helpful to Linux to turn off Plug-N-Play in the BIOS if you have an option for that. Plug-N-Play is a feature that is only used in Windows, and it doesn't contribute anything to Linux.

If your BIOS supports several speed settings for your video card (typically 2x, 4x, and 8x for an Advanced Graphics Processor), select the slowest setting at first. You can always go back and speed it up later. You can check whether you have this setting by looking at the choices you are offered in the BIOS hardware configuration screens.

BIOS bugs

Over the last quarter century, the BIOS has been forced to adapt to many different roles as PC technology has evolved and changed. As a result, most BIOS programs have become disorganized, buggy, and hard to maintain. In several cases, the Linux kernel was changed to work around a BIOS bug.

For example, one task of the BIOS is to build a table of information about the motherboard and how its interrupt lines are connected to interrupt controller chips. Some of AMD's Geode line of motherboards had a BIOS bug that put faulty data into this table. The Linux community quickly developed a software fix for the AMD hardware bug. Linux version 2.4.19 and later recognizes incorrect motherboards, corrects the data, and works perfectly! Windows never had the interest nor the ability to do the same. It is just not that agile.

If You've Still Got Trouble

If you've followed all the previous steps, then it's over to the forums to search for the symptoms you are seeing. If you can't find the answer, then post a question.

Troubleshooting Balky Devices

You might find that your PC boots under the live CD, but you have a problem with one specific device. For example, you might find that sound doesn't play, or your wireless networking adapter doesn't connect, or the printer doesn't print. In the rest of this appendix, I'll describe how to deal with individual peripherals that don't work under Linux.

The basic process is as follows:

1 Identify in great detail the make and model of any peripheral that is not working when you boot up.

2 Check the peripheral make and model against the hardware that is supported by the distro.

3 If that hardware *is* supported by the distro, it's a software configuration problem. Use the Control Center application, described in Chapter 4, "Onto the Net," on page 93, to resolve it.

4 If that hardware *is not* supported by the distro, it's a missing device driver problem. The three choices for solving this are:

♦ Find a device driver on the net and install it (hard for novices)

♦ Make do without that device (unsatisfying)

♦ Get a replacement device that is supported (easy but costs money).

What Is a Device Driver?

Every computer peripheral needs a device driver to make it work correctly. The device driver is a piece of software that controls or "drives" its peripheral and manages the resulting flow of data between the peripheral and the operating system. It allows the operating system to be relatively independent of specific hardware. A device driver gives the OS a standard view of the peripheral it drives.

To the operating system, talking to the device driver is very similar to reading or writing a file. The operating system has the same interface to every device driver, so it doesn't need to know anything at all about a driver or its peripheral. It just has to be able to access and load the right device driver when someone tries to use the peripheral.

Most device drivers tell the peripheral what to do by writing to special hardware registers or addresses in the peripheral. The data that the driver writes, and the different registers that the driver uses, tell the peripheral what to do and allow it to report its status back to the driver. See Figure B-5.

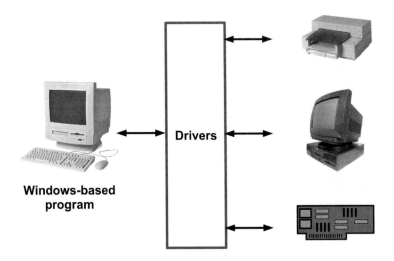

Windows-based program

Drivers

Figure B-5   How an application uses drivers to connect to peripherals

Each driver is specific to one operating system. You generally can't use Windows drivers on Linux, although you might be able to re-use the parameters contained in a Windows .inf configuration text file.

Each driver is specific to one piece of hardware. You can't use a keyboard driver to drive a video card, and you can't use one vendor's video driver to control a different vendor's video card. There's a huge variety of PC hardware, most of it low quality, built down to a price, and often with uneven compliance to industry standards. The specific hardware knowledge and workarounds that make a device work are pushed into the driver software.

Device drivers are regarded as part of the operating system, but they are typically supplied by the peripheral manufacturer, not the operating system manufacturer. You've probably seen this when you buy a new printer or DVD drive. It usually comes with a CD containing the Windows driver to run that device.

Peripheral manufacturers produce a driver for Windows, and then stop. Too often, they don't even release the hardware specification that would enable the Linux community to give them a Linux driver.

Linux Device Drivers Are Also Modules

Linux has the software concept of a module. A Linux module is a program or library that can be compiled separately from the kernel and loaded at runtime into the kernel address space while the kernel is running.

Loadable modules are very convenient for software like a device driver that has to run with kernel privileges, but that is created at a different time and by a different organization than the one that created your kernel. As you might guess, Linux modules are typically used to implement device drivers, so drivers follow both the device driver interface and the module interface conventions. Modules are just ordinary object files created by the compiler, and that follow a few rules about names.

Linux modules are kept in files with an extension of .o or .ko, in a folder under the folder /lib/modules. If you have to install a Linux driver, the last step is to put it somewhere under there. There's usually a script to put it in the right place. Figure B-6 shows the file manager looking at a directory of Linux device drivers.

These happen to be the device drivers that control various wireless network cards. The window displays the details of the file containing the driver for the Atheros wireless device. That driver uses a rate control algorithm developed by Atsushi Onoe, a programmer for Sony in Japan. The code was written by Sam Leffler. Getting the proper credit is how we keep the score in the world of open source developers, so Sam chose a file name ath_rate_onoe.ko to reflect that. The file is quite small, only 10K bytes, but absolutely vital to running a wireless card with the Atheros chipset on Linux.

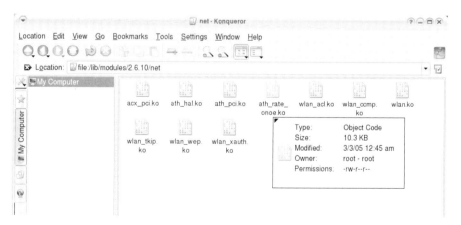

Figure B-6   Linux device driver files

The Right Device Drivers Are Essential

Device drivers are the biggest single factor determining the success of an operating system installation attempt. If your installation CD has the device drivers needed for all your peripherals, the installation will be successful.

If some necessary drivers are missing, the corresponding hardware won't work. This is as true for Windows as it is for Linux.

Checking Hardware for Linux Compatibility

One aspect of getting Linux set up, or of adding devices or hardware, is ensuring compatibility. Here's how to find out what you have and how to ensure that you can make it, or something else, perform its function on your Linux system.

Finding Out What Hardware Your PC Has

If you boot from the live CD, and notice that a specific peripheral (such as a wireless card) isn't working, it may be because its device driver is not present. If you know exactly what hardware makes up your PC, you can confirm whether your distro bundles a driver for it, and hence whether or not this is the problem.

You need to identify the manufacturer and model number of the hardware that isn't working. Then you can check the distro's hardware compatibility list for, e.g., a Yamaha OPL3-SA3 AC97 Audio Controller chip. That's the level of detail you will need.

You don't have to do this level of checking, but if you decide not to, don't let the reason be because no one told you how. Windows comes with a program called Device Manager that helps you find out exactly what hardware your PC has.

Under XP and 2000, it's quickest to start Device Manager from the command line. Click **Start** > **Run**. In the Run window, type the command name devmgmt.msc as shown in Figure B-7, and click **OK**.

Figure B-7   Running the Device Manager program

You can also start the Device Manager program by clicking through half a dozen panels, starting at the control panel.

Under Windows 9x and Me, the command to type is:

```
control sysdm.cpl ,1
```

Be careful to put a space before the comma and no space between the comma and the digit one. (That program was clearly written by someone at Microsoft who didn't have a lot of development experience.)

Many PC companies aren't PC companies

Many of the companies commonly thought of as PC manufacturers, like Dell, are really just warehousing and online ordering companies. Not many PC manufacturers design their own electronics these days, or indeed have any serious amount of technical expertise. There are a few real computer companies left, such as Apple and Sun Microsystems.

IBM is not on the list of "real PC companies" anymore, since their bold decision in February 2005 to exit the PC business altogether. It has just become too cut-throat and the margins are too slim. IBM finally got realistic about what business they are really in (high-margin mainframes and allied services) just the way Intel did in the mid-1980s when they had to cede the memory market to Asia. IBM will still sell PCs, maybe even under their own brand. They'll just be reselling PCs from a Chinese company.

Vendors like Dell mostly buy off-the-shelf components like motherboards, chips, memory, disk, and so on, from different vendors, and coordinate their assembly by others into a PC. Striving for the lowest possible cost drives everything.

This is why Linux customers are so poorly served in the computer industry. Drivers come from as many different places as there are device manufacturers, Each device vendor has its own policies, standards, schedules and priorities. But they know one thing—without a driver that works under Windows, they're dead.

The PC company usually doesn't have the technical expertise to produce Linux drivers for the products they integrate. By the time they've thought about it, they've changed suppliers to someone who bid a unit cost 10 cents lower and who needs a different driver. That's what you get from warehousing and online ordering companies.

Read the Output of Windows Device Manager

The Device Manager in Windows shows an expandable tree structure of all the hardware components that make up your PC. It shows individual devices, like printers, and also other low-level components like the real-time clock, the CPU and the buses that devices plug into.

Examining the Problem Devices

1   Go down the device manager list and double-click on any problematic device you have, such as the video adapter or the wireless network adapter.

2   Double-clicking opens up a little more detail on the device. Your device manager panel should now look somewhat like Figure B-8, but showing the devices that your PC has. If you don't see a display like Figure B-8, choose **Device Manager's View** > **Devices by type,** the default.

Reading this from the top down, Jupiter is the host name of my computer. The first device is Batteries, tipping you off that this particular system is a laptop.

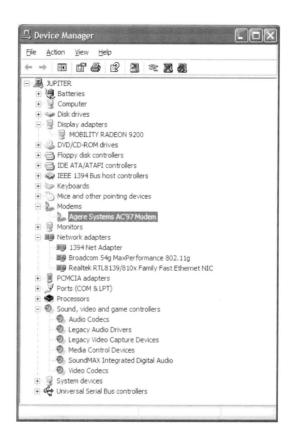

Figure B-8   Device Manager tree

3   Double-click on that **Mobility Radeon 9200** detail line in the Device Manager tree to bring up its Properties window. The Properties window lists the manufacturer. Figure B-9 shows what I get on my system.

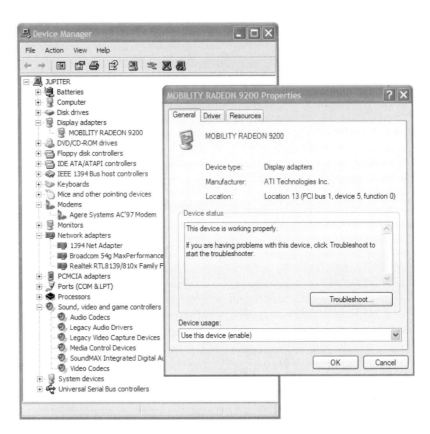

Figure B-9   Properties window for the selected device

Display Adapter Vendors

Nowadays there are just two big vendors of display adapters: ATI and nVidia. nVidia has very good Linux drivers; ATI recently got the message about Linux and has started releasing Linux drivers for its products.

You can find the manufacturer and model number for a problematic device in your computer this way. That allows you to phrase a support enquiry as "Does this distro support the ATI Mobility Radeon 9200 graphics card?" That has vastly more chance of attracting helpful suggestions than "Why does my screen go blank when I try to boot Linux?"

You could also print out the device manager display (it's under the Action menu item). I don't recommend you do that, as it gives you more than a dozen pages along with a huge amount of irrelevant detail.

You can see my system has three devices listed under network adapter. This means that my laptop has three different hardware devices that can be connected to a network. In the order of appearance in the Device Manager, these are 1394 networking, wireless networking, and Ethernet cable networking.

The name of the first network adapter, 1394 Network Adapter, is not a maker/ model number like the others. 1394 is the name of a high-speed bus, also known as FireWire. In this PC, the 1394 network adapter allows me to network two computers together using FireWire instead of Ethernet cable. top-tier

Nobody does that in practice. People only use 1394 for attaching disks and camcorders. Ignore a 1394 network adapter device if it shows up on your PC. You'll only be concerned with wireless networking and Ethernet cable networking from here on. Similarly if other unfamiliar devices show up in your device tree, you can either ignore them with the expectation that the device might not work with Linux, or add them to the list of devices to double-check and see if there's a Linux driver for them.

Sound Controller Vendors

If you look at sound controllers you'll probably also see several entries. You are not interested in capture devices, legacy devices, or codecs (coder-decoders). In the example, that leaves just the SoundMAX Integrated Digital Audio device, and the property panel shows it is made by ADI—Analog Devices Inc. All you're doing is getting a list of any non-working peripherals you have and who made them.

Matching Your Hardware Against the Distro Hardware Compatibility List

Now that you have the hardware inventory, check that there are Linux device drivers for all these devices. This is also easy to do. Every distro has a web site. You can easily find it and many other details on a distro by doing a search at google.com, or by visiting the web site http://www.distrowatch.com and searching for the distro by name. Go to the web site for the distro and find the hardware compatibility list.

Practically every distro maintains a hardware compatibility list specifying the devices that are known to work with that distribution. A distro that doesn't maintain a hardware compatibility list is not a distro you want to use. If a device is listed as compatible with the distro, a Linux device driver is bundled with it.

The Linspire hardware compatibility list is located at the following web site:

http://www.linspire.com/linspire_hardware_compatibility.php

Rather than a long text list, the Linspire list is a web form, in which you select manufacturer name and hardware type from drop-down lists.

You have to be prepared to dig down a little for the information. If the distro says compatible or tested or believed to work, etc., for a device, count it as works OK. Otherwise mark it as not supported.

Alas, with wireless networking in particular, you cannot use the compatibility lists to help you purchase a card with 100% reliability. Wireless card vendors all too frequently change their products to use a different chipset, without changing the product model number. Rather than rely on a list of cards, go online and purchase a cheap Netgear card from somewhere you can return it if it doesn't work. Netgear has a good track record of being Linux-friendly. There are other good network companies too.

Decide What to Do About Your Unsupported Hardware

Matching Your Hardware Against the Distro Hardware Compatibility List gave us very specific information about what devices are and are not supported in this distro of Linux. In this step you will decide how to adapt to that.

One option is to collect any needed drivers individually from the web. You'll have to compile and install them. They usually come with a readme file that explains how to do that. You'll need to download the compiler first, which is explained in Chapter 6, "Web Tools," on page 171. Compiling is not challenging, but it looks a whole lot like random magic if you're not a software professional. Adding a missing driver is an option best deferred until you have a good familiarity with Linux.

The only devices that absolutely have to work are the display and keyboard. You can usually take the keyboard for granted. All devices other than the display and keyboard are in the "nice to have" category while you practice with the Linux window system. You don't need printing at all until you are ready to deploy Linux as your main system. If the sound card doesn't work, you'll miss out on playing music.

Sample Output from Wifi Network Commands

This appendix contains a series of commands that can be used to find out more information about your network connections. The first step in troubleshooting a wireless network connection is to confirm that you have a device driver for your wifi hardware. If the wifi hardware appears in your drop-down list of interfaces, then you have the device driver, otherwise you do not.

Once you have the device driver for the wifi hardware, you can try the following commands and compare the sample output with your results. This will help you determine where the problem lies. Output will vary from system to system depending on what hardware you have. You're looking for gross differences, not minor changes.

Bring up a command line terminal by clicking **Launch > Run command** and typing **xterm** in the text field. Then you can type commands like these in the terminal window that will appear.

ifconfig

Prints details and configures a network interface.

```
eth0    Link encap:Ethernet  HWaddr 00:02:3F:6B:DD:15
        UP BROADCAST MULTICAST  MTU:1500  Metric:1
        RX packets:0 errors:0 dropped:0 overruns:0 frame:0
        TX packets:2376 errors:0 dropped:0 overruns:0 carrier:0
        collisions:0 txqueuelen:1000
        RX bytes:0 (0.0 b)  TX bytes:812592 (793.5 KiB)
        Interrupt:11 Base address:0x9800


eth1    Link encap:Ethernet  HWaddr 00:02:2D:08:B0:CB
        inet addr:192.168.1.4 Bcast:192.168.1.255 Mask:255.255.255.0
        UP BROADCAST RUNNING MULTICAST  MTU:1500  Metric:1
        RX packets:503 errors:0 dropped:0 overruns:0 frame:0
        TX packets:482 errors:0 dropped:0 overruns:0 carrier:0
        collisions:0 txqueuelen:1000
        RX bytes:39892 (38.9 KiB)  TX bytes:64758 (63.2 KiB)
        Interrupt:3 Base address:0x100
```

```
lo       Link encap:Local Loopback
         UP LOOPBACK RUNNING  MTU:16436  Metric:1
         RX packets:238 errors:0 dropped:0 overruns:0 frame:0
         TX packets:238 errors:0 dropped:0 overruns:0 carrier:0
         collisions:0 txqueuelen:0
         RX bytes:57436 (56.0 KiB)  TX bytes:57436 (56.0 KiB)
```

dmesg -c

Prints the buffer of system log messages, then clears the buffer.

```
usb.c: USB disconnect on device 02:07.0-2 address 3
hub.c: new USB device 02:07.0-2, assigned address 4
input: USB HID v1.10 Mouse [Logitech USB Receiver] on usb3:4.0
eth1: New link status: Disconnected (0002)
eth1: New link status: Connected (0001)
```

iwconfig

Prints details and configures a wireless interface.

```
eth0     no wireless extensions.
eth1     IEEE 802.11-DS  ESSID:"home22"  Nickname:"(none)"
         Mode:Managed  Frequency:2.462GHz  Access Point: 00:0F:B5:1D:37:8C
         Bit Rate:11Mb/s  Tx-Power=15 dBm  Sensitivity:1/3
         Retry limit:4  RTS thr:off  Fragment thr:off
         Encryption key:off
         Power Management:off
         Link Quality:59/92  Signal level:-34 dBm  Noise level:-93 dBm
         Rx invalid nwid:0  Rx invalid crypt:0  Rx invalid frag:142
         Tx excessive retries:0  Invalid misc:0  Missed beacon:0
```

iwlist eth1 key

iwlist wlan0 key

Prints more details of a wireless interface.

```
eth1    2 key sizes : 40, 104bits
        4 keys available :
            [1]: off
            [2]: off
            [3]: off
            [4]: off
        Current Transmit Key: [1]
```

route

Prints routing tables and interfaces in use.

```
Kernel IP routing table
Destination    Gateway      Genmask        Flags Metric Ref    Use Iface
192.168.1.0      *           255.255.255.0  U     0      0       0 eth0
default        192.168.1.1   0.0.0.0        UG    0      0       0 eth0
```

dhclient

Requests an IP address when using DHCP.

```
Internet Software Consortium DHCP Client V3.0.1rc11
Copyright 1995-2002 Internet Software Consortium.
All rights reserved.
For info, please visit http://www.isc.org/products/DHCP
Listening on LPF/eth0/00:02:3f:6b:dd:15
Sending on   LPF/eth0/00:02:3f:6b:dd:15
Listening on LPF/lo/
Sending on   LPF/lo/
Listening on LPF/eth1/00:02:2d:08:b0:cb
Sending on   LPF/eth1/00:02:2d:08:b0:cb
Sending on   Socket/fallback
DHCPDISCOVER on eth0 to 255.255.255.255 port 67 interval 7
DHCPDISCOVER on lo to 255.255.255.255 port 67 interval 7
```

DHCPREQUEST on eth1 to 255.255.255.255 port 67
ip length 314 disagrees with bytes received 534.
accepting packet with data after udp payload.
DHCPACK from 192.168.1.1
bound to 192.168.1.4 -- renewal in 27280 seconds.

ping -c 10 192.168.1.1

Sends test packets on your own network. Use the IP address in the line starting DHCPACK from the previous command. This is the address of your router; you want to find out if you have two-way communication with it.

PING 192.168.1.1 (192.168.1.1): 56 data bytes
64 bytes from 192.168.1.1: icmp_seq=0 ttl=64 time=4.3 ms
64 bytes from 192.168.1.1: icmp_seq=1 ttl=64 time=2.3 ms
64 bytes from 192.168.1.1: icmp_seq=2 ttl=64 time=2.3 ms
64 bytes from 192.168.1.1: icmp_seq=3 ttl=64 time=2.3 ms
64 bytes from 192.168.1.1: icmp_seq=4 ttl=64 time=2.3 ms
64 bytes from 192.168.1.1: icmp_seq=5 ttl=64 time=2.3 ms
64 bytes from 192.168.1.1: icmp_seq=6 ttl=64 time=2.3 ms
64 bytes from 192.168.1.1: icmp_seq=7 ttl=64 time=2.3 ms
64 bytes from 192.168.1.1: icmp_seq=8 ttl=64 time=2.3 ms
64 bytes from 192.168.1.1: icmp_seq=9 ttl=64 time=2.3 ms
--- 192.168.1.1 ping statistics ---
10 packets transmitted, 10 packets received, 0% packet loss
round-trip min/avg/max = 2.3/2.5/4.3 ms

cat /etc/resolv.conf

Checks that your PC knows which host will resolve domain names. Again, check that this is the IP address of your router.

nameserver 192.168.1.1

ping -c 5 google.com

Checks that you can send test packets across the Internet.

```
PING google.com (216.239.39.99): 56 data bytes
64 bytes from 216.239.39.99: icmp_seq=0 ttl=245 time=92.3 ms
64 bytes from 216.239.39.99: icmp_seq=1 ttl=245 time=92.4 ms
64 bytes from 216.239.39.99: icmp_seq=2 ttl=245 time=91.2 ms
64 bytes from 216.239.39.99: icmp_seq=3 ttl=245 time=91.7 ms
64 bytes from 216.239.39.99: icmp_seq=4 ttl=245 time=91.7 ms
--- google.com ping statistics ---
5 packets transmitted, 5 packets received, 0% packet loss
round-trip min/avg/max = 91.2/91.8/92.4 ms
```

APPENDIX D

Commands for the Command Line

Getting Started

You don't have to become a command line wizard to use Linux, but you shouldn't be afraid of it either. It's like learning how to drive a stick shift car as well as an automatic—you'll understand the vehicle better, and get more from it when you need it. Too many people think the command line interface is hard to learn; it can be, if commands are presented as a long dreary list of mysterious incantations. But even a GUI is impossibly hard if you don't know it exists or how to start it running.

I'll come at it from another direction: instead of focusing on the command, consider the object that you're trying to look at or adjust. Is it a file? A folder? A filesystem? A running program? If you keep in mind what you are trying to work with, the number of applicable commands is smaller and much more manageable. Knowing and using a few commands raises you from the level of passenger ("Where do you want to go today, pal?") to commander ("Here's where I'm leading us").

When you get right down to it, the job of an operating system is to maintain your data (today that is done using files), and to run programs to process that data. Everything else is there to help with those two tasks. There are only about twenty or so frequently used commands, and they are all very similar on Windows, MacOS X, and Linux. Know these commands, and you'll be more effective with your PC.

About Commands Generally

There's nothing special or magic about the commands in Linux. They are ordinary programs that do ordinary things. You run any program by typing the complete pathname to the executable file.

Executable files don't need a special file extension, like .com or .exe seen in Windows. As an example, the file /bin/date contains an executable program. It prints the current date and time.

Try it. You can run the program like this.

```
/bin/date
Wed Jan 19 15:50:37 PST 2005
```

It's not very convenient to have to remember and type an entire pathname for each program you have to run. It would be easier if you could just remember the file name date, rather than the entire pathname /bin/date. So that's the way the OS designers made it work. They did it in a general way that works for everybody. You can specify the places (list of folders) where you want the system to look when you type a file name. A default list of folders is given in a file you might not even be aware of.

The Path

The file is called /etc/profile and it has a list of all the folders that the command line interpreter should look in to find any command that you type. The list of folders is called the path and if you look in /etc/profile, you'll see a line like this that gives an initial value to the string variable called PATH:

```
PATH="/usr/local/sbin:/usr/local/bin:/usr/sbin:/usr/bin:/sbin:/bin:/usr/bin/X11"
```

That's a list of directories, separated by colons. When you check the file, you'll see there are actually two such lines; one sets the path for the root user, the other for other users. The root user has a few extra directories in the path. Those directories contain administrator utility programs.

That PATH= line is saying "Whenever I type the name of some executable file, the command line interpreter should look in these folders in this order: /usr/local/sbin, then /usr/local/bin, then /usr/sbin, then /usr/bin, then /sbin, then /bin, finally in /usr/bin/X11."

If the command line interpreter finds an executable file with that name as it looks in those folders in order, it runs it. If it looks in all of those folders, and doesn't find a file with the name you typed, it prints an error message to the effect of "Command not found".

The /etc/profile file applies to all users on the system who are using the command line interpreter called bash. Linux has several command line interpreters, and they use different initialization files and syntax, but they all have some way to set the path. You can add to or change that system-wide path list in the file ~/.profile, which is pre-installed for root in root's home directory. Other users can copy /root/.profile to their home directories.

Watch out for that leading . in the name of ~/.profile—it makes the file invisible to default directory listings (more on that coming up). Every bash user starts with the same settings from the one /etc/profile file used by all. Each user has her own copy of the second .profile file so that she can customize her settings. The folders in the path are separated by colons, so if you add another folder to the path in ~/.profile, be sure to add the colon separator, too.

You can still type the entire pathname if you want, as you saw previously. /bin/date produces the same result as date.

The Path Is Saved in an Environment Variable

The concept of having a path or list of folders in which to look when you type something that might be a command name is pretty useful. Windows uses exactly the same concept in its command line.

However, it's a bit inconvenient if a file is the only way to set the path. You'd really like something that can store the string representing the path, and have a way to change it or add to it from the command line (without having to edit a file).

That's the purpose of environment variables. These are strings that the command line interpreter (also known as the *shell*) keeps track of on your behalf. Different shells use different syntax to set shells, but most of them let you retrieve the value in an environment variable by giving its name preceded by a dollar sign. The path is stored in an environment variable called PATH. You can see its value by typing the command:

```
echo $PATH
/bin:/usr/bin:/sbin:/usr/sbin:/usr/X11R6/bin
```

The bash shell syntax for changing the PATH environment variable is:

```
PATH=/bin:/usr/bin:/sbin:/usr/sbin:/usr/X11R6/bin
```

You'll see people apply a shortcut, using the old value to set the new value, like this:

```
PATH=$PATH:/new/folder/here
```

That just means "Take the existing value of PATH and cram :/new/folder/here on the end."

When you change the PATH (or any) environment variable, the change is immediately effective.

Typing the Full Pathname

Now, clearly, if you want to run a file that isn't in one of the folders on your path, you have to type the full pathname to the file. This often confuses new users. They install a program, and the installer puts it in a folder that isn't on the path. Then they try and run the program by typing the name, such as transmogrify. The command line interpreter gives the mysterious error message "sh: transmogrify: command not found", and the user gets mad and says "But it's right there—I just installed it!" (Other command line interpreters issue the message "No such file or directory.")

The error message would be a lot clearer if it just mentioned the path: "shell error: file called transmogrify not found in any of the folders in the path, /usr/local/sbin, /usr/sbin, etc". The current directory "." can be put into the path with a command like:

PATH=$PATH:.

Then a command of transmogrify would run a program of that name in the current working directory. Experienced users don't usually put "." in their path, because it can be a security risk. You might mistakenly execute something in a random directory that had the same name as a system command, like ls.

The Shell

I've mentioned the *command line interpreter* a couple of times. This is just another program, like all the rest. It is the program that takes input from the command line and carries out the commands, either directly or indirectly by running another program.

Linux has several command line interpreters, and the one you use by default is called bash. The name is a multi-level pun and joke that you can look up on the web if you're so disposed.

The bash command line interpreter is the executable file /bin/bash. A command line interpreter is called a shell in Unix. It's like a thin hard covering for all the real programs below it. A shell has the job of getting lines typed by the user, looking along the path to find the corresponding file, and then running that file. If the name isn't a file name, perhaps it is one of the built-in commands to the shell itself (like the command to set an environment variable, or to change directory). If so, the shell will carry out that command.

Another Use for Environment Variables

The shell also does other important tasks not covered yet: it expands wildcards in file names and supports pipelines of commands. Those will be covered. The shell also keeps track of a dozen or so settings for each process (running program) using environment variables. The PATH is one of these. The Present Working Directory is another.

Present working directory is the notion of where in the filesystem a running program is. In other words the directory it will use if it writes a file. This starts out as your home directory by default, but a program can change the present working directory (or *pwd*). Type

```
printenv
```

to see all your environment variables.

After the built-in command or executable program has completed, the shell will return to get the next line of input from the user, and repeat this over and over again.

Let's take a look at commands for doing things with files.

Working with Files

Whatever data a file contains—a word-processing document, a web page, an image—there are some common things you might want to do:

*   Copy a file
*   Move a file somewhere else
*   Give a file a different name
*   Delete a file
*   Find out what data is in the file
*   List the meta-data (ownership, permissions, etc) of a file
*   Type out the contents of a text file
*   Search through a text file for a particular string

Here's how to do these things. In each case I show the general form of the command, with the part you have to supply in italics. Then I show a typical example of running the command, complete with output (if any).

Copy a file

command: cp, meaning copy

general form: cp *existingfile copy-of-existingfile*

example: cp ~/.profile ~/.profile.bak

Move a file somewhere else

command: mv, meaning move

general form: mv *file-or-directory new-filename-or-directory*

example: mv ~/dogs.jpg ~/Desktop

Give a file a different name

Renaming a file is the same as moving it to a new name. See *Move a file somewhere else.*

example: mv resume.draft.doc resume.final.doc

Delete a file

command: rm, meaning remove

general form: rm *file*

example: rm /tmp/*

This is an example of wildcard use. Instead of typing the exact full name of a file, you can provide a partial name by using the asterisk character as a wild card. Before the program ever sees that argument, the shell expands the wildcard into a list of all the file names that match it. Most commands accept a list of files as well as just one file.

The shell does a text match of all the file names in the directory against the wildcard. The * matches any number of characters, and hence by itself matches all files in the directory. A ? matches any one character. So a wildcard of *.??? matches all files with an exactly three-character extension.

Here, the argument /tmp/* is expanded into a list of all files in the /tmp directory. This is a text list of the names (and not, say, a logical expression that magically stands for the same information). The list is then passed to the command as a command line argument.

A name of br* matches all file names that start with br such as brazil.txt, bright, and br. A name of br*.txt matches all files that start with br and end with .txt, such as brazil.txt.

Find out what kind of file it is

command: file, meaning tell me about this file

general form: file *somefile*

example: file ~/dogs.jpg

output: /root/dogs.jpg: JPEG image data, JFIF standard 1.01

Try running file /bin/date—what output do you expect to see?

List the metadata of a file

command: ls -l, meaning list, and the -l option says "in long form"

general form: ls -l *file-or-directory*

example: ls -l ~/dogs.jpg

output: -rw-r--r-- 1 root friends 993019 Jan 19 19:29 dogs.jpg

Explanation of output: -rw-r--r--

The line of output for each file has this information, from left to right:

-rw-r--r--

This field is called the mode of the file. It represents the file permissions and other metadata in a very compact form. The first character of the file mode will be d if this file is a directory. Since the first character here is not d, this is a file not a directory. There are other possible first characters; l (the lowercase letter L) means this is a link.

The rest of the file mode is three groups of three characters, which here have the values rw-, r--, and r--.

- The first group shows the permission that the owner has. The letter r represents permission to read the file. The letter w represents permission to write the file. The letter x means permission to execute the file. Although you can set it for any file, execute permission only makes sense for binary programs and shell scripts. This file is an image file, and so there is a dash, - meaning no permission where the x might otherwise appear.

- The second sequence of three letters, in this example, r-- shows the permission accorded to people who belong to the same group as this file. Here, that is read-only permission for users in group friends. There is no w and x, so there is no write permission and no execute permission for group users.

- The third sequence of three letters, in this example r-- is the permission that anyone, who is not the owner and not a user in the same group as the file, has. Here, that is read-only permission.

Explanation of output: 1 root friends 993019 Jan 19 19:29 dogs.jpg

1 The number of hard links to the file. A hard link is another directory entry for this file's contents. You use a hard link to get to the same file under a different (perhaps shorter) name, or to provide a different set of permissions.

root The owner name. Every file in the system has an owner. This file is owned by the system administrator, who has the login name root.

friends The group name. Users can belong to one or more groups. Every file belongs to exactly one group. The purpose of groups is to provide more flexible access to files than just owner and everyone else. This file is readable by the friends group. You can see what groups you belong to by typing the command groups.

If I have a payroll program that I want only Sally and George to be able to run, then I can create a group called payrollers and make Sally and George the only two users in that group. Make the payroll program owned by user payrollers and have execute permission only for the group. This means the mode will be as follows:

----r-x---

Now the program can only be executed by users who are in the group payrollers.

993019 The file size in bytes. This file is just under 1 MB in size.

Jan 19 19:29   The date and time when the file was last written.

dogs.jpg   The file name.

Try running ls -l /bin/date

What output do you expect to see?

Type out text file contents

command:	cat, meaning concatenate (this name has always been ill-fitting; it would have been named type except it is also used for joining several files together).
general form:	cat *somefile*
example:	cat ~/.profile
output:	the contents of the ~/.profile file, namely:

# ~/.profile: executed by Bourne-compatible shells.
if [-f ~/.bashrc]; then
. ~/.bashrc
fi
mesg n

Search through a text file for a particular string

command:	grep, meaning "globally search for regular expression and print"
general form:	grep *"some-string"* *somefile*
example:	grep ";" ~/.profile
output:	the lines in the file that contain the search string, namely:

if [-f ~/.bashrc]; then

The power of grep is its ability to search many files, not just one. If you remember that the string "dads birthday" appears somewhere in a file in your home directory, grep allows you to look at them all and identify which file. Here's an example.

grep "dads birthday" *
family-info.txt:dads birthday is Dec 22

To learn more about commands, download the man pages and man-db packages from CNR.

After installing the man pages and man-db (manual database), you can look at the man page description of any command by typing this:

man *command*

For example, man date produces a couple of pages of output, starting like this.

```
NAME
     date - display or set date and time
SYNOPSIS
     date [-nu] [-r seconds] [+format]
     [[[[[cc]yy]mm]dd]hh]mm[.ss]
DESCRIPTION
     date displays the current date and time when invoked without arguments.

     Providing arguments will format the date and time in a user-defined way or set the date.
     Only the superuser may set the date.

     The options are as follows:

     -r    Print out the date and time that is seconds from the Epoch.

     -u    Display or set the date in UTC (universal) time.
```

Whether or not you install the man pages, most commands will give you a brief summary of the options they expect. If you give them a single --help option, like this:

date --help

you'll get about a page of output, starting like this:

```
Usage: date [OPTION]... [+FORMAT]
  or:  date [-u|--utc|--universal] [MMDDhhmm[[CC]YY][.ss]]
Display the current time in the given FORMAT, or set the system date.
  -d, --date=STRING        display time described by STRING, not 'now'
  -f, --file=DATEFILE      like --date once for each line of DATEFILE
  -ITIMESPEC, --iso-8601[=TIMESPEC]  output date/time in ISO 8601 format.
                   TIMESPEC= 'date' for date only, 'hours', 'minutes', or 'seconds' for date
                   and time to the indicated precision.
                   --iso-8601 without TIMESPEC defaults to 'date'.
  -r, --reference=FILE     display the last modification time of FILE
```

```
-R, --rfc-2822        output RFC-2822 compliant date string
-s, --set=STRING      set time described by STRING
-u, --utc, --universal   print or set Coordinated Universal Time
   --help    display this help and exit
   --version  output version information and exit
```

Y r cmd nms so mystrsly shrt?

The architects of Unix, Ken Thompson and Dennis Ritchie of Bell Labs, obviously like very short names. Linux adopted the same conventions wholesale, so Linux commands are really not intuitive.

There's no getting away from it; command line Unix was designed to allow specialists to work with the minimum of typing. Ken Thompson was once asked if, in hindsight, there was anything he would change about Unix.

In a tongue-in-cheek acknowledgment that brevity can be taken too far, Thompson replied that next time around, he would spell the creat *system call with an* e *at the end.*

Only computer programmers ever see creat *and we can't spell anyway, so personally I'd be happier putting the* n *back into* umount.

Working with Folders

I mentioned the *present working directory*. This is the default directory used when a program reads or writes a file without giving a full pathname.

You might see someone type ./date when she wants to run the executable file called date that is in the current directory.

- The pathname . is an abbreviation for the current directory.

- The pathname .. is an abbreviation for the parent directory.

- The pathname ~ is an abbreviation for her home directory.

Here are some common commands used with folders.

Print working directory

command:	pwd, meaning print working directory
example:	pwd
output:	the directory in the filesystem that is your present working directory, e.g., :

`/root/Desktop`

pwd lets you see where you are in the filesystem.

Move into another directory

command:	cd, meaning change directory
general form:	cat *some-directory*
example:	cd ~/My\ Documents

This example illustrates the perils of spaces in file names. Most commands can accept one file name, or a list of file names separated by spaces. So the shell needs a way to distinguish between two files called my and data and one file called my data.

Here's how: spaces in one pathname must be escaped with a \ before each space. The \ tells the shell "the next character after the \ is still part of this file name." Or you can put the entire pathname in double quotes. It's better to avoid spaces in pathnames. Use a - to separate words, as in my-data.

List files in directory

Listing a directory is the same command as listing a file. Just give a directory name instead of a file name. No name means list the current directory. Wildcards are fine.

command:	ls *optional-file-or-folder-pattern*, meaning list
example:	ls /home/pvdl/Desktop

Files whose names start with . in a directory, such as .profile, are deliberately not listed. This lets you prevent small, rarely changed, configuration files from crowding out data files in which you are mostly interested. Just give them a name that starts with a period. To see all the files in a directory, including the dot-files, use ls -a. The -a means all files.

Create a directory

command: `mkdir`, meaning make directory

general form: `mkdir  some-directory`

example: `mkdir  My\ Documents/todays-work`

Delete directory

command: `rmdir`, meaning remove directory

general form: `rmdir  some-directory`

example: `rmdir  Draft-docs`

alternative: `rm -rf  Draft-docs`

The directory must be empty of all files and subdirectories to use the `rmdir` command. If you are certain that you want to delete a directory and all contents, you can use the `rm -rf` command to delete any directory, full or empty. It is wise to carefully check directory contents before using `rm -rf`. Unix treats you as an adult, and assumes that you mean what you say.

Move or rename a directory

Renaming a directory is the same as renaming or moving a file. See `mv` command.

Copy a directory

Copying a directory uses the same command as copying a file, with the addition that you must use the -R option. That option says copy recursively. The second directory gets a copy of the first directory and everything in it, including subdirectories, and everything in those, and so on.

command: `cp`, meaning copy

general form: `cp -R  existing-directory  copy-of-existing-directory`

example: `cp -R  ~  /homedir-backup`

If you forget to use the -R option when copying a directory, the command will assume that you want to copy a directory as a file and further assume that is a mistake, and not do it. You'll get a cryptic message saying `cp: omitting directory`.

Doing a `cp -R` is potentially a large amount of work. It may take some minutes to duplicate a directory with gigabytes of files.

Working with Samba

In an effort to simplify file sharing for users, the Linspire folks never refer to Samba and never show the Samba command line. They describe everything in terms of the Network Share Manager (which is just another incarnation of the Konqueror file manager, tweaked slightly to make it convenient for opening network shared folders). However, for those who want to go one step beyond, I'll present some command line-oriented Samba details in this section.

Showing the Available Shares and Printers

You can reveal the shares and printers available from other computers in your workgroup with this command:

smbtree

You will be prompted to provide a password, and the output will have this general appearance:

```
HOME
        \\LUNA   mist (LindowsOS)
                        \\LUNA\PSC_2200_Seri          PSC 2200 Series
                        \\LUNA\local-hp               HP PSC 2210
                        \\LUNA\Bluetooth-Mod          Bluetooth-Modem
                        \\LUNA\Internal_Mode          Internal Modem
                        \\LUNA\ADMIN$                 IPC Service (luna (LindowsOS))
                        \\LUNA\IPC$                   IPC Service (luna (LindowsOS))
                        \\LUNA\fromLinux
                        \\LUNA\print$                 Printer Drivers
        \\LINDEN                                      Mac OS X
                        \\LINDEN\ADMIN$               IPC Service (Mac OS X)
                        \\LINDEN\IPC$                 IPC Service (Mac OS X)
```

luna and linden are the names of two sharing hosts in my workgroup. Luna is running Lindows, and Linden is running MacOS X. Underneath the URL for each host is a list of the services they are exporting.

Stopping and Starting Samba Manually

You might want to stop and start the Samba software manually to give some configuration changes a chance to take effect. You can do it with these commands:

```
/etc/init.d/samba   start
/etc/init.d/samba   stop
```

Mounting a Shared Folder Manually

You can mount a shared folder manually with the following command line.

```
mount -t smbfs -o username=name,password=pass //192.168.1.5/sharename  /mnt/winshare
```

Substitute:

- The actual user name for name
- The actual password for pass
- The actual IP address for 192.168.1.5
- The actual folder name for sharename
- Any empty directory for /mnt/winshare is where the shared folder contents will appear.

By default, files shared from another PC show up in your Linux filesystem in folder /root/Network/hostname-or-ip-address/sharedfoldername.

Filtering Service by IP Address

You can restrict printer and file sharing to specified IP addresses by adding a line to Samba's configuration file.

1 As with any system configuration file, make a backup copy before changing it. Make sure you are the root user, and then enter:

   ```
   cp /etc/samba/smb.conf /etc/samba/smb.bak
   ```

2 Use your favorite editor to edit the file smb.conf. If you don't known any Linux editors, use the Kate GUI editor reached by clicking **Launch** > **Programs** > **Software Development** > **Advanced Text Editor**.

   Open the file /etc/samba/smb.conf and adjust the window width so you can see the full length of each line.

3 The file is only a couple of hundred lines long. Locate the section that starts with this comment header:

```
#======================= Global Settings =====================
```

```
[global]
```

4 After that comment header, add a couple of lines giving a comment and a list of the IP addresses you want to allow. For example, if you are allowing clients at 192.168.1.2 and 192.168.1.3, but not 192.168.1.5, add these lines:

```
## Filter IP addresses of clients
allow hosts = 192.168.1.2 192.168.1.3
```

5 Stop and start Samba manually (explained previously) to put the change into effect.

Sharing Folders That Aren't Under /root

This is something of an advanced technique, but it is worth its weight in gold for people who need it. There is a restriction on Linspire file sharing: you can only share folders that are somewhere underneath the /root folder. You can work around this restriction using the command line.

Usually, you don't need to share folders outside the /root tree. But you might have a dual boot installation that allows you to choose to boot either Linspire or Windows. Your Windows disk partition shows up as a read-only folder, usually /mnt/hda1 in Linspire, which is not under /root.

It would be handy if you could share these Windows folders to other Windows PCs on your local network even while you're running in Linux. You cannot do this directly, because of the /root restriction mentioned previously. You can, however, unmount the partition, and mount it again underneath /root. Then you can share it as usual. Here are the commands to achieve that.

First, determine the physical name of the partition you want to remount. Type the command mount. For each mounted partition, Linux will print a line saying what the physical pathname of the disk is, and where it has mounted it in Linux.

For example, my system shows this output for my Windows partition:

/dev/ide/host0/bus0/target0/lun0/part1 on /mnt/hda1 type ntfs (rw,noatime)

Write down the physical partition name (in larger type in the example) from your system. Where I refer to this name as *partition* later, you will use the actual string.

Similarly, make a note of the *mount point*, which is /mnt/hda1 here. The mount point is the directory in your filesystem where this partition is grafted in (mounted). I will refer to that as oldmountpoint; you will use the actual pathname.

Type these commands:

mkdir /root/winxp

umount *oldmountpoint*

mount -t ntfs *partition* /root/winxp

Type the following:

ls /root/winxp

You should get a directory listing for your Windows partition. Then share the folder /root/winxp.

Note – This will enable you to share the folders, but possibly with read-only permission. It depends on how the Windows partition was formatted when it was originally installed (either by you, or at the factory). There are two filesystems in common use on Microsoft products: NTFS and the older FAT32.

If your Windows partition was formatted as NTFS (as Microsoft recommends) instead of the more compatible FAT32, then you will not have the ability to write to it or delete files in it. Microsoft has not released the specifications needed for other operating systems to write to NTFS. There are some experimental implementations of a Linux file adapter for NTFS. One of these is captive-ntfs authored by Jan Kratochvil, but there is nothing ready for production use as of 2005.

Filesystem Utilities

Continuing the progression of file, and folder, there are half a dozen common commands that deal with a filesystem as a whole. They include commands like mount and umount (to make a filesystem active or inactive). There's a gotcha with umount—the command won't succeed if any file in the filesystem is in use. So you have to use cd to get out of all directories in the filesystem you are trying to umount, and stop all processes that are reading or writing to files in the filesystem.

You can run the filesystem checking utility reiserfsck on an unmounted reiser filesystem to confirm or restore its consistency. You might run reiserfs after an unscheduled power off. You can run it to check your main disk by booting under a live CD (you cannot check a hard disk that is in use, and the live CD leaves your disk unused). Then issue the command:

```
reiserfsck --fix-fixable /dev/hda1
```

You should use the device name for your actual hard disk partition, which might or might not be /dev/hda1 as in the example.

I've also omitted mentioning utilities that let you look at processes, change their priority, stop them, find out what files they have open, and so on. The command pstree is a particularly effective one for finding out which processes started other processes.

The Most Powerful Part of Linux (Not Included)

It's possible to write for a decade and halfway into the next about the power and flexibility Linux gives you. This would of course result in a book larger than most people. So, regretfully, I will not be able to include a few of my favorite features. But I do want to at least tell you what I'm not covering. Before ending this book I need to mention—just mention—a few powerful tools.

PC Hardware Commands

I'd love to go into detail about the commands that describe your PC hardware, like the ones in the following list:

- dmesg – Displays the system message buffer. If you ever get a kernel panic, this is the first command you should run on reboot to see if there is any information about the cause.

- /sbin/lsmod – Shows information about all loaded modules (device drivers).

- /sbin/modinfo *somemodule* – Shows more about *somemodule.*

- lspci – Shows information about all devices on the PCI bus.

- lsusb – Shows information about all devices on the USB (-v option is available but gives far too much information).

- cardctl info – Shows information about PCMCIA ports.

- netstat - List IP connections – Checks what's coming through your firewall.

- free - Shows the amount of physical and virtual memory.

A Linux module is a program or library (usually a low-level one) that can be compiled separately from the kernel, and is loaded at runtime into the kernel address space while the kernel is running. Modules are typically used to implement device drivers, so drivers follow both the device driver interface and the module interface.

Legends and lore of Unix—How powerful are Unix commands?

```
rev  lewis.txt  |  sort  |  rev  >  lewis-rhymes.txt
```

How powerful are standard Unix commands? Let me show you something that was shown to me 20 years ago when I joined a fast-growing start-up company called Sun Microsystems.

If you have a list of English words, how easy is it to create a rhyming dictionary from them? A rhyming dictionary is used by poets. It lists words in order of what they sound like, not how they are spelled. In a regular dictionary, the word "ride" is near the words "rice" and "rife". In a rhyming dictionary "ride" is near "glide", "hide", and "slide".

Perhaps your first thought, like mine, was that it cannot be done at all. Judging whether or not something rhymes takes human intelligence. Well, it turns out you can get a pretty good approximation by noting that words that are spelled similarly at the end probably rhyme (like "shoot" and "loot").

So if you run a Unix command on your world list to reverse the order of every word, then sort it so that words with the same letters at the end come next to each other, then reverse the letter order of each word again (without changing which word is adjacent to which other word)—well, then you've got yourself a pretty good rhyming dictionary.

The Linux command line to do exactly that is the subheading on this sidebar. The word list can be downloaded from http://afu.com/linux/lewis.txt. *This word list is a compilation of all the words that appear in Lewis Carroll's* Alice in Wonderland *popular books (a cheap and quick way to whisk up a manageable wordlist). Download the wordlist and try it yourself. The result is in file* lewis-rhymes.txt.

An extract from the rhyming list is:

- *hiding*
- *gliding*
- *sliding*
- *riding*
- *scolding*
- *folding*
- *holding*
- *handing*
- *landing*
- *standing*
- *ending*
- *bending*
- *defending*
- *sending*
- *pretending*

How long would it take you to create a rhyming dictionary in a Windows GUI?

Overview of I/O Redirection, Filtering, and Pipelines

The biggest piece that I omit in this book is the piece that gives the Unix command line its greatest power. I am referring here to the shell constructs known as I/O redirection, filtering, and pipelines.

Old hands don't simply prefer the Unix command line because they are stubborn die-hards. Well, maybe that's true for some of them. But most of them use the command line because almost all the commands give simple text output, and there are exceptionally good tools for taking the text output from one program and feeding it into another program, and the results of that into another program, and so on.

The Unix philosophy is that commands should be small, and do just one thing well. Complex results are obtained by stringing a series of commands together with pipes. The sidebar *Legends and lore of Unix—How powerful are Unix commands?* shows an example of a command pipeline.

```
rev lewis.txt | sort | rev > lewis-rhymes.txt
```

That command runs the rev command on file lewis.txt. Feed the output directly into the sort command. And feed the output from the sort into the rev program again, putting the output from that into the file lewis-rhymes.txt. The vertical bar or pipe symbol | connects the output of one program into the input of the next.

By learning 20 or 30 basic commands and the ways to glue them together, you can build up very powerful composite tools that tell you what a system is doing, keep it running, analyze your data, and so on.

If you want to learn more about these fascinating topics, Linspire has a thorough and lengthy guide at http://info.linspire.com/lindowsoscommands.html. You can also do a web search for "Unix command line guide".

Beyond even that, there is shell programming. In shell programming you write scripts of commands that can be invoked by typing the name of the script file. The installation of the operating system (any Unix operating system) is accomplished by running elaborate and extensive shell scripts that invoke the regular Unix commands.

APPENDIX E

Disk Basics and Partitioning

Partition Overview

The goal of this appendix is to explain more about partitions, and show you how to partition a disk.

The storage on a hard disk is divided into one or more regions called partitions. A partition is like a fenced-in field. There is a definite size and some boundaries to it. There may be parts of the disk that have not yet been turned into a partition; these are called "unallocated space".

Each partition acts like an independent disk. Each partition can be unformatted (not useful) or formatted with a filesystem. There are different kinds of filesystem with different properties. Microsoft's NTFS (NT File System) is not writable with current Linux tools, though people are working on this and there is experimental quality code. Linspire uses the reliable and high-performance Reiser filesystem.

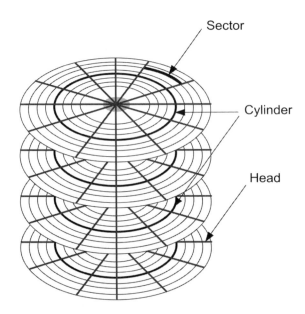

Figure E-1   A schematic disk drive

Figure E-1 shows, schematically, the components of a disk drive. There will be one read/write head for each surface used (the outer surfaces, top and bottom, are sometimes not used). Your disk may have as few as one platter, but modern disk drives usually stack up multiple platters. It's a simple cheap way to increase capacity without increasing disk diameter (and hence disk head movement times).

A *sector* is the smallest addressable unit of data on the disk, typically 512 bytes. A track is a complete ring of sectors—everything that will pass under one stationary head during one one disk rotation. A *cylinder* is the tube formed by considering the same specific track on each platter. The disk heads are linked together so that they all move in or out to a particular track at the same time.

Disks are read and written in blocks of a sector at a time. A complete disk address specifies the head (the platter), the cylinder (how far in or out the head should be positioned) and the sector number (where on each track in that cylinder the desired sector lies).

This is an idealized disk. The disk controller inside the disk drive actually decides what gets written to disk, where, and in what size blocks. The number of heads parameter no longer corresponds to physical disk heads. I have a disk drive that claims to have 255 heads. In reality, the manufacturer is just using the head part of the address to maximum effect, and the controller will figure out what physical heads to use.

Right at the start of your hard disk (head 0, cylinder 0, sector 1) is a master boot record, a disk sector containing some boot code, and a table with room to store position and size information for up to four partitions. That limited-size MBR table is the reason that you can have only four primary partitions on a PC disk. The MBR cannot be a regular file or part of the operating system, because it has to be accessed before the operating system has booted up.

The MBR and Partition Table

The first 446 bytes of the Master Boot Record are a little boot loader program, GRUB in the case of Linspire. The partition table starts at byte 447 of the MBR. It has four entries of 16 bytes. Each entry describes one primary partition, and has this structure; see Table E-1 on page 556.

Table E-1   A partition descriptor of the master boot record

Offset	Length	Content
00h	1 byte	Windows Active Marker: 08h if this is the active partition, 0 otherwise. Windows will boot the active partition by default.
01h	3 bytes	Head, cylinder, and sector of the partition start
04h	1 byte	The type of the filesystem in the partition: 00=empty, 05=contains logical partitions, 0C=FAT32, 07=NTFS, 82=linux swap, 83=any of the Linux filesystems. There are dozens of other types, too.
05h	3 bytes	Head, cylinder, and sector of the partition end.
08h	4 bytes	Offset, in sectors, to jump over the sector partition record and reach the partition filesystem.
0Ch	4 bytes	Total sectors in the partition.

If you want more than four partitions, the additional ones have to be set up as "logical" or "extended" partitions that are contained within the fourth primary partition. Each partition that contains an operating system will start with a "partition sector" or "volume boot record" that has more of the boot program.

The extended partition type, type 05, differentiates it from a basic partition. The partition that this entry describes is treated like a completely separate hard disk. The extended partition starts with another MBR. This MBR usually contains no code, only a partition table.

The advantage of an extended partition is that it can be used to divide a hard disk into an arbitrary number of logical drives. Extended partitions weren't originally intended to be bootable, and Windows still can't boot from them. But Linux and other modern operating systems can be booted even when they are installed on an extended partition.

Looking at an MBR

Once you have Linux running, it's easy to look at the MBR with this command:

```
dd if=/dev/hda count=1 bs=512 | od -x -A x
```

Windows is somewhat badly behaved. If you install Windows after Linux, Windows will overwrite your master boot record with its own version that doesn't offer the choice of booting into other operating systems. You can save a copy of the GRUB MBR from Linux, with this command:

```
dd if=/dev/hda of=/boot/boot.MBR bs=512 count=1
```

The MBR can be restored with:

```
dd if=/mnt/hda3/boot/boot.MBR of=/dev/hda bs=512 count=1
```

You'll need to do the restore while booted from the live CD, so that the MBR is not in use and protected from overwriting. The input file pathname will be something like /mnt/hda3/boot/boot.MBR depending what partition it is and where the live CD mounts it.

You can also use a Microsoft utility to look at the master boot record on your hard disk. Download the Windows "sector inspector" text utility from:

```
http://www.microsoft.com/downloads/details.aspx?FamilyID=dd3ef22a-a586-4079-9489-
c3ea14573fc4
```

You can also go to http://microsoft.com and search for "sector inspector".

Now that you know all about the MBR, you're ready to proceed with partitioning.

Reducing the Size of the Windows Partition

Follow these steps for repartitioning your Windows hard drive.

1   Delete all unwanted files, such as browser caches.

2   Defragment the disks.

3   Run the Windows chkdsk utility.

4   Then follow the steps in this section for repartitioning.

Deleting Unnecessary Files

Start by deleting any unnecessary files on your Windows partition. Boot up in Windows, then uninstall unwanted programs, archive old data, delete outdated files, and flush browser caches.

Then run Disk Cleanup by clicking **Start** > **All Programs** > **Accessories** > **System Tools** > **Disk Cleanup**.

Defragmenting Disks

Defragmentation is intended to allow your hard disk to work more quickly and efficiently, by moving the parts of files together. Chkdsk checks and repairs Windows filesystem metadata.

In truth, the original reasons for defragmenting disks no longer apply to today's larger, more sophisticated drives. However, some partition editing tools still expect to find defragmented disks, and may refuse to repartition disks unless you defragment them first. You might want to start the defragment process at night, since the process can easily take several hours.

Run the Windows defragmenter by clicking **Start** > **All Programs** > **Accessories**, **System Tools** > **Disk Defragmenter**. That brings up the window shown in Figure E-2. Click **Defragment**. After it completes, repeat until there are no red lines (representing what Windows thinks are fragmented files) in the window.

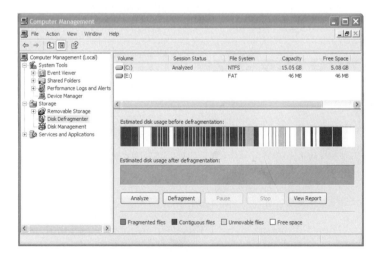

Figure E-2   The illusory Windows defragmenter

Disk defragmentation is largely an Illusion

Disk defragmenting is largely an illusion with modern multi-hundred GB disks. The premise of defragmenting is that access is more efficient when the data and metadata of individual files is compacted into a smaller space, not spread out over the partition. It minimizes the amount of time-consuming disk head movement when reading an entire file.

There are three logical flaws, two big and one small, that prevent this premise from being true. The little flaw is the assumption that you only have one disk access going on at a time, and so you can rely on the disk head staying put if you don't move it. On all but the most lightly loaded PC, there are many other disk accesses going on all the time, from the virtual memory pager, from delayed cache flushes, from other files your programs are writing, and from system processes.

The first big logical misconception with fragmentation stems from the fact that the operating system doesn't really know where sectors are on disk. It thinks it does, but it doesn't. The operating system tells the disk controller "write this block to address abc". The disk controller can and does put blocks anywhere it likes, as long as it remembers where the operating system thinks they are. Disk manufacturers have elaborate and secret algorithms for laying out data and re-ordering disk requests to improve performance. The disk also automatically detects and remaps bad sectors using a sector substitution table kept inside the drive.

None of the information about where data actually goes on disk ever leaves the disk controller. So although the OS believes the blocks of a file are coalesced, they may actually be spread out across the physical disk.

Finally, since the disk controller misreports the number of disk heads, the operating system does not have an accurate idea of the disk geometry, and hence does not have an accurate idea of block adjacency. The misreporting is done to take maximum advantage of every field in addressing sectors. If the controller tells the OS it has eight disk heads, it can use the numbers 0 to 7 in addressing the disk. Disk addressing is done with fixed size fields of head, track, and sector. If the controller truthfully reports it only has one head, disk addressability is reduced to one eighth of its potential. But old habits die hard, and people will be selling Windows disk defragmenters, and memory doublers, and snake oil, for years to come.

Run the Windows chkdsk Utility

Run the chkdsk command in Windows to check the integrity of the partition, and repair any errors found. In a Windows command terminal, type:

```
chkdsk /R
```

Windows will reply with a message saying that the volume (partition) is in use. It will ask if you want the volume to be checked on your next reboot. Reply **Yes**, then restart the system.

Unix and Linux manage disk space more efficiently. They have never had nor needed defragmentation utilities.

Repartition the Hard Drive

Once you've mollified the gods of Windows metadata with a bogus defragmentation, you can go on to take some space away from Windows and give it to Linux.

Use QtParted to Shrink a Windows Partition

Linspire has long included a couple of utilities that will create or delete partitions: fdisk, and a console graphics version, cfdisk. These programs are simple and good, but they don't support an essential feature: a way to resize a Windows partition.

That's why Linspire now includes an advanced partitioning tool on the live CD, starting with Linspire 5. (If you're using a pre-5.0 release of Linspire, you'll need to download the system rescue disk ISO image from http://www.sysresccd.org. Confirm its MD5 checksum, burn that ISO image onto a CD, boot from the CD, and run QtParted that way.)

If you're using Linspire 5.0 or later, you will boot from the live CD, and use QtParted to change your partitions. The following section, *Changing Your Partitions Using QTParted*, walks through that process.

Changing Your Partitions Using QTParted

QtParted is a clone of the commercial Partition Magic product. The name of the product is an object lesson in why marketing managers should name products instead of software developers. QtParted is based on an earlier command line tool called Parted, meaning partition editor. Parted was updated with a GUI that uses the Qt application framework, and so became QtParted.

Start QtParted running by following these steps:

1   Boot from the Linspire live CD. Click through the license agreement, timezone setting, and so on, until you arrive at the desktop.

2   When the Flash tutorial starts, click on **Exit Tutorial** in the top right corner of the window. Exit any other programs that start automatically.

3   QtParted won't work on disk partitions that are mounted, as that means the partitions may be in use and it is not safe to change the partitioning. Unmount all hard drive partitions that the live CD may have mounted for you. You can see the mounted partitions by typing:

```
mount | grep mnt
```

That might give some output showing the mounted partitions like this:

```
/dev/ide/host0/bus0/target0/lun0/part1 on /mnt/hda1 type ntfs
/dev/ide/host0/bus0/target0/lun0/part2 on /mnt/hda2 type vfat
/dev/ide/host0/bus0/target0/lun0/part5 on /mnt/hda5 type vfat
```

In this case you would unmount the partitions with these commands:

```
swapoff -a
umount /mnt/hda1
umount /mnt/hda2
umount /mnt/hda5
```

A filesystem won't unmount if a process is using some file in it (e.g., if it is the current working directory of a shell). You can tell which processes are using a filesystem with the command:

```
fuser -m /mount/point
```

4   Start the QtParted partition editor by clicking **Launch > Run programs > Utilities > QTParted**. Note that you are running directly from CD, which is significantly slower than disk. You might need to wait for a couple of seconds for menus to appear after you click on them.

5   The QtParted main window will appear. Maximize the window by dragging the lower right corner on your screen.

At the top left of the main window, QtParted will show a list of all the hard disks it has detected. If your PC only has one disk, there will only be one entry in the list, probably reading /dev/ide/host0/bus0/target0/lun0/disc.

6   Click on the disk you want to partition. The program will take a moment or two to analyze that disk, then it will display all its partitions, as shown in Figure E-3.

There is a bar graph of partitions on the top right, and underneath it a list of partitions. This disk has one Windows NTFS partition covering the whole disk. This is typical of the way many PCs come from the factory. You might also see a second, Windows recovery partition. Be careful not to wipe that out inadvertently (assuming you are going to keep this PC even though it has inadequate recovery support).

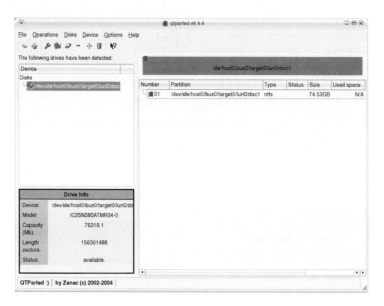

Figure E-3   Clicking on the disk to reveal its partitions

7   Highlight the NTFS partition. In Figure E-3 it is labeled as number 01.

8   Choose **Operations** > **Resize** (see Figure E-4).

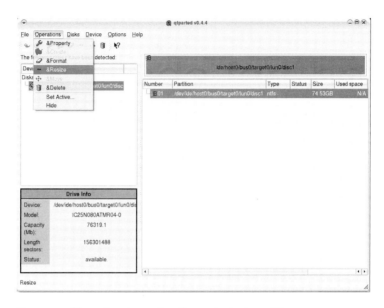

Figure E-4   Choosing to resize the selected partition

9 The Resize partition window will appear. Type the new size for the partition in the **New Size** field; as shown in Figure E-5, shrink it to 14 GB. Click **OK**.

Figure E-5   Specifying the new, smaller size for the NTFS partition

10 Get QTParted to put the change into effect by choosing **File** > **Commit** (see Figure E-6). (QTParted makes you use a two-step process of first describing all the changes you want to make, and then telling it to actually do them.)

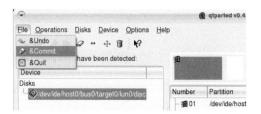

Figure E-6   Committing the size change

11 You will see a warning dialog about the possibility of losing data. Click **Yes** to confirm you want to go ahead.

12 Another dialog will state "Operations completed successfully". Click **OK** to dismiss that dialog. A series of progress dialogs will appear, showing the steps in completing the partitioning change.

Creating a Linux Partition

Any of the applications—QtParted, cfdisk, or fdisk—can create a Linux partition from the empty space you just made by shrinking the Windows partition. Cfdisk is much simpler than QtParted, but can only create and delete partitions, not shrink them.

Using QtParted

You might as well use QtParted since you are already in the program.

1   At this point your screen should look like Figure E-3 on page 562.

2   You'll create a partition for Linux out of the space you freed. Click on the list entry for the free space, and choose **Operations** > **Create**.

3   A Create Partition dialog will appear, showing the steps in completing the partitioning change. See Figure E-7.

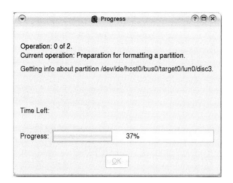

Figure E-7   Operations completed successfully

4   Choose **File** > **Quit** to leave the QtParted program.

That puts you back at the live CD desktop.

5   Click **Launch** > **Logout/Turn Off** > **Restart Computer**, and eject the CD by pressing the button on the front of the drive. (You might have to wait until your system is rebooting.)

Alternative to QtParted: Using cfdisk to Partition

If you instead want to use cfdisk to create a partition, follow these steps.

1   Boot from the live CD and type cfdisk in a command window. Cfdisk has a main window similar to that shown in Figure E-8.

2   The **up and down cursor keys** let you highlight and select the partition of interest. The left and right cursor keys let you highlight some of the operations you can do on that partition, such as toggle the bootable flag, delete the partition, etc.

Your first action should be to move the cursor over to the **Help** tag at the bottom of the screen. (Ignore the menu item **Help**, which only provides help on the command tool.)

3   Press **Enter** to see a couple of screens of commands. You typically type **N** to create a new partition, then type **T** to lay out a filesystem on it.

4   Finish by pressing **W** to write the partition table to disk. The cfdisk program is quite basic, and has no bells and whistles.

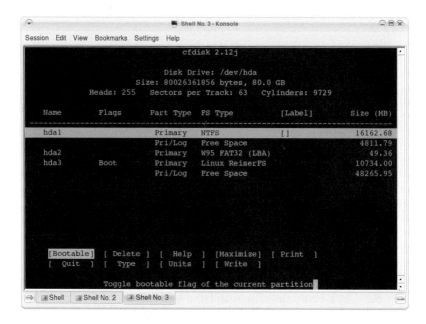

Figure E-8   cfdisk is an easy tool to create and delete partitions

If you restrict yourself to four or fewer partitions, then they can all be primary partitions. This is the limitation imposed by the fixed size partition table in the MBR.

If you need more than four partitions (you can go up to at least 26, though no one does in practice). You can read about some of the other archaic rules for partitions at http://www.pcguide.com/ref/hdd/file/structPartitions-c.html.

Partitioning just creates entries in the partition table. To use a partition, you will need to format it with a filesystem. The installation process will do this. If you want to use a partition without an OS installed in it, look up "mkfs" in the man pages for details.

Restoring the Windows MBR

This sequence of actions will restore your original Windows MBR.

1 Insert your WinXP install CD, reboot and let it load.

2 Select the **Recovery Console** option.

3 Select the Windows installation that you want to repair (normally 1). You might be prompted for an administrator password at this point.

4 A text console will appear on screen. Type `fixmbr` and `fixboot`. (As you probably guessed, you are using the XP install CD as a live CD while you fix up the hard drive that contains Windows.)

5 Then restart, removing the CD before it boots again, The `fixmbr` command will put the Windows MBR back on the disk, and the `fixboot` command will rewrite the volume partition code.

This procedure doesn't remove any Linux partitions you have on disk, but because the Windows MBR doesn't recognize non-Windows partition, it will prevent you from booting into Linux.

GRUB Procedures

GRUB is the grand unified boot loader responsible for managing the transfer of control between the BIOS and an operating system. Unlike LILO, the other common Linux loader, GRUB has the ability to navigate filesystems, not just disk block addresses. Thus GRUB can find files by name, making it easier to use.

Restoring GRUB

If you reinstall Windows after Linux, you will find that Windows has overwritten the MBR, thus preventing you from booting into Linux. You can restore operating system choice by writing the GRUB code back into the MBR.

Boot from the live CD and use these commands

```
grub
find /boot/grub/stage1
```

The output from the second command will be the disk and Linux partition where the GRUB files were found, something like:

(hd0,2)

GRUB uses a different disk and partition naming scheme to that of Linux. GRUB identifies hard disks by hd and floppy disks as fd followed by a number starting from 0. In commands, the disk references are always enclosed in parentheses, thus the first hard disk is referenced as (hd0). Disk partitions are separated from the hard disk by a comma and identified as 0–3 for the primary partitions and 4 and up for partitions inside an extended partition.

Disk names in Linux and GRUB

I asked Erich Boleyn, the developer of GRUB, why he didn't use the standard Linux form for disk-and-partition names. Erich patiently explained that he gets that question a lot.

GRUB can only see the disks through the inadequate and outdated BIOS interface. BIOS does not provide information about what kind of disks they are.

If you have, for example, an IDE and a SCSI disk on the machine, what do you name them? The BIOS, and therefore GRUB, only knows that it has disks 0 and 1. So rather than be wrong and confusing in the general case, Erich used a naming scheme that expresses only the information GRUB has: disk and partition. GRUB doesn't try to guess or invent disk-type information that it doesn't have.

Table E-2 shows the details.

Table E-2   Partition names

Physical partition	Linux name	BIOS name	GRUB name
IDE disk 1, partition 1	/dev/hda1	disk0, p0	(hd0,0)
IDE disk 1, partition 2	/dev/hda2	disk0, p1	(hd0,1)
USB disk 1, partition 1	/dev/sda1	disk1, p0	(hd1,0)

To restore a good copy of GRUB into the MBR, use the disk and partition name in these commands.

First, determine what disk and partition contains your Linux installation, from where you will get a good copy of the boot loader. If it is the third partition on the first disk, that is referred to as (hd0,2). While still booted off the live CD, and in the GRUB program you started earlier, confirm that by typing:

root (hd0,2)

You might see output like the following:

Filesystem type is reiserfs, partition type 0x83

Then state that you want GRUB installed into the MBR of this drive, by typing:

setup (hd0)
    Several lines of output
    including "succeeded"
quit

If your BIOS has antivirus features designed to stop modifications to the hard drive boot blocks, you must disable it before making any changes to your boot blocks.

Changing GRUB Defaults

The main menu of GRUB is shown in Figure E-9.

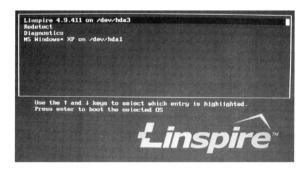

Figure E-9   The GRUB menu lets you determine what or how to boot

The menu is generated from lines in file /boot/grub/menu.lst. GRUB reads the file and displays the menu of operating system choices it finds there. After you have installed Linspire, you can edit that file to change the choices offered, or the order in which the operating system choices appear, or other defaults like the "timeout before proceeding with the default boot".

You can change the delay and the default OS to boot by editing the lines

default=*ordinal-position-in-list*

or

timeout=*number-of-seconds*

As you might see from Figure E-9, the boot screen labels any version of Windows as Windows XP. If you are using Windows 2000, you can correct the entry on the boot screen by editing the /boot/grub/menu.lst file.

It used to be the case that if you changed anything in the menu.lst file, you had to prevent a program called jiffyboot from running, because it would reset menu.lst to its original contents.

The jiffyboot program is a Linspire invention. It tries to anticipate when your boot possibilities have changed, and then updates menu.lst accordingly. You could stop jiffyboot running by renaming it

mv   /sbin/jiffyboot   /sbin/NOjiffyboot

Jiffyboot has a companion program called jiffymount that updates the configuration file /etc/fstab specifying which partitions should be mounted on boot. Again, you can prevent jiffymount from overwriting your changes by renaming it.

Recent versions of Linspire 5 detect when the user has manually changed one of the configuration files, and they are no longer overwritten. As long as this remains the default behavior, it will not be necessary to rename jiffyboot or jiffymount.

The GRUB Command Shell

Enter the GRUB command mode by pressing **c** when the GRUB menu is displayed on your screen. This will bring up the screen shown in Figure E-10.

```
[ Minimal BASH-like line editing is supported.  For the first word, TAB
     lists possible command completions.  Anywhere else TAB lists the possible
     completions of a device/filename.  ESC at any time exits. ]

grub> help
background RRGGBB                         blocklist FILE
boot                                     cat FILE
chainloader [--force] FILE               clear
color NORMAL [HIGHLIGHT]                 configfile FILE
displayapm                               displaymem
find FILENAME                            foreground RRGGBB
geometry DRIVE [CYLINDER HEAD SECTOR [   halt [--no-apm]
help [--all] [PATTERN ...]               hide PARTITION
initrd FILE [ARG ...]                    kernel [--no-mem-option] [--type=TYPE]
makeactive                               map TO_DRIVE FROM_DRIVE
md5crypt                                 module FILE [ARG ...]
modulenounzip FILE [ARG ...]             pager [FLAG]
partnew PART TYPE START LEN              parttype PART TYPE
reboot                                   root [DEVICE [HDBIAS]]
rootnoverify [DEVICE [HDBIAS]]           serial [--unit=UNIT] [--port=PORT] [--
setkey [TO_KEY FROM_KEY]                 setup [--prefix=DIR] [--stage2=STAGE2
splashimage FILE                         terminal [--dumb] [--no-echo] [--no-ed
terminfo [--name=NAME --cursor-address   testvbe MODE
unhide PARTITION                         uppermem KBYTES
vbeprobe [MODE]

grub> █
```

Figure E-10   Entering the GRUB command shell

The GRUB command shell lets you pass arguments to the kernel you are about to boot. This is only necessary in special circumstances. The GRUB command for specifying a kernel image is:

kernel path-to-kernel-on-a-partition boot-params-to-pass-to-kernel

You might do this to specify the screen resolution or a graphics driver to use. The Linux kernel accepts certain command line options, or boot-time parameters, at the moment it is started. In general this is used to supply the kernel with information about hardware parameters that the kernel would not be able to determine on its own, or to override the values that the kernel would otherwise assign. For example the parameter

xdriver=vesa

tells X Window to assume the basic dumb graphics hardware (this avoids problems with fancy cards that have bugs in the driver).

It's possible that you'll see an error from GRUB either now or in the future. GRUB is better than the older LILO (LInux LOader) software. LILO effectively issued "error letters" (individual letters). GRUB uses error numbers and a list of numbers. You can find out what they mean using the following document:

http://www.fifi.org/doc/grub-doc/html/grub_14.html

The GRUB manual is located here:

http://www.gnu.org/software/grub/manual/grub.html

APPENDIX F

Troubleshooting with Strace

Using Strace (For Experts Only)

Strace is a very powerful, little-known debugging command line utility that has no equivalent in Windows, which you can use to prefix any command. It has the effect of printing all the system calls that the command makes (with the arguments and return values). It lets you see what a program is trying to do as it does it.

The Desktop folder is the GUI desktop and that's that!

It would be cool if you could select the folder that is displayed as the GUI desktop, and maybe change it on the fly, instead of being tied to the specific folder called ~/Desktop. But this would probably generate way too many calls to support lines asking "Hey, where did my files go?"

Strace isn't for everyone. Its output is only meaningful to people who know (or are willing to learn) the Linux system call library and the C programming language. But it is so quick and easy to use, you might want to try it regardless.

Strace is another in a long line of great ideas and code that Sun Microsystems has freely given to the computer industry, along with NFS, Java, OpenOffice.org, grid computing, and so on. Paul Kranenburg, inspired by the trace facility of SunOS, reimplemented it in open source as strace. Branko Lankester then ported that version to Linux and enhanced it.

When a program needs some service from the kernel, like opening a file or writing a block of data, it makes the request in the form of a system call. If you understand software you can follow the progress of a program, particularly an open source program, by looking at the sequence of system calls and their arguments. You can sometimes resolve simple issues like file access or permissions problems from looking at strace output. Most system calls return 0 if everything went smoothly, and non-zero in the event of an error. Just looking for non-zero values returned by system calls can take you quite a long way.

It can be useful to capture the output from strace in a file. Type the command:

```
script filename.txt
```

to record all subsequent typing in that terminal window in the file filename.txt. Type Control-d to exit the script recording.

As an example, to see what's going on inside a very simple command. An example is the command touch -a foo to update the access time of file foo.

```
strace touch -a foo
```

The last few lines of the strace output will look like this:

```
time([1105226803])                = 1105226803
open("foo", O_WRONLY|O_NONBLOCK|O_CREAT|O_NOCTTY|O_LARGEFILE, 0666) = 3
fstat64(3, {st_mode=S_IFREG|0644, st_size=0, ...}) = 0
close(3)                          = 0
utime("foo", [2005/01/08-15:26:43, 2005/01/08-15:19:10]) = 0
_exit(0)                          = ?
```

Each line represents a system call that the program made.

There are always many setup system calls at the start of the strace output, things like opening dynamic libraries, mapping memory, stack handling, signal set up, break adjustment, and so on. All that is omitted here for clarity. Once you get past that and into the code of the program, things are easier to follow.

In the previous example, the code calls time() and gets a value of 1105226803 returned. The time() system call returns the number of seconds since the start of the day Jan 1, 1970. There are about 31557600 seconds in a year, and working out 1105226803/31557600 gives us 35.02252, which puts us 35 years on from 1970, which is 2005. So that seems right.

The code then opens the file foo and uses fstats to get the file metadata. This is so that it can put back unchanged the two other time of last... fields when it updates the time of last access field. The code then closes the file and issue the utime() system call to update the file metadata of times. Notice that strace has translated the time_t values into meaningful date/time strings.

The Corresponding Source Code of "touch.c"

To complete the example, here is part of the source of touch.c. This code is the static, compile-time program; some of the lines are executed at runtime. The first system call, the time(), is in another part of the code, not shown here. The next three system calls in the sample output are executed in order as the flow of control goes through the touch() function.

```
static int
touch (const char *file)
{
  int status;
  struct stat sbuf;
  int fd = -1;
  int open_errno = 0;

  if (! no_create)
    {
      /* Try to open FILE, creating it if necessary.  */
      fd = open (file, O_WRONLY | O_CREAT | O_NONBLOCK | O_NOCTTY,
              S_IRUSR | S_IWUSR | S_IRGRP | S_IWGRP | S_IROTH | S_IWOTH);
      if (fd == -1)
        open_errno = errno;
    }

  if (! amtime_now)
    {
      /* We're setting only one of the time values.  stat the target to get
         the other one.  If we have the file descriptor already, use fstat.
         Otherwise, either we're in no-create mode (and hence didn't call open)
         or FILE is inaccessible or a directory, so we have to use stat.  */
      if (fd != -1 ? fstat (fd, &sbuf)  : stat (file, &sbuf))
        {
          if (open_errno)
            error (0, open_errno, _("creating %s"), quote (file));
          else
            error (0, errno, _("getting attributes of %s"), quote (file));
          close (fd);
          return 1;
        }
    }
}
```

Where to Find Linux Source Code

You can find the source code for the Free Software Foundation commands that are bundled with Linux at http://directory.fsf.org. The source for touch.c is in the fileutils package at http://ftp.gnu.org/gnu/fileutils/fileutils-4.1.tar.gz.

You can find the Linux kernel source code at http://www.kernel.org/. To compile device drivers, you don't need the kernel source, but you do need the header files. These can be downloaded from CNR, or installed with Debian packages. The Linspire kernel source is also in CNR.

See which version of the kernel you have by typing the command:

uname -r

The result will be a string like "2.6.9" so you need to install the headers or kernel source that matches, e.g., Linux kernel version 2.6.9 (use the version that matches what you have on your own system). There are also different versions of the header files for different architectures, and this command tell you what is available:

```
apt-cache search kernel-headers-2.6.9
kernel-headers-2.6.9-1 - Header files related to Linux kernel version 2.6.9
kernel-headers-2.6.9-1-386 - Linux kernel headers 2.6.9 on 386
kernel-headers-2.6.9-1-686 - Linux kernel headers 2.6.9 on PPro/Celeron/PII/PIII/PIV
kernel-headers-2.6.9-1-686-smp - Linux kernel headers 2.6.9 on PPro/Celeron/PII/PIII/PIV SMP
kernel-headers-2.6.9-1-k7 - Linux kernel headers 2.6.9 on AMD K7
kernel-headers-2.6.9-1-k7-smp - Linux kernel headers 2.6.9 on AMD K7 SMP
kernel-headers-2.6.9-2 - Header files related to Linux kernel version 2.6.9
kernel-headers-2.6.9-2-386 - Linux kernel headers 2.6.9 on 386
kernel-headers-2.6.9-2-686 - Linux kernel headers 2.6.9 on PPro/Celeron/PII/PIII/P4
kernel-headers-2.6.9-2-686-smp - Linux kernel headers 2.6.9 on PPro/Celeron/PII/PIII/P4 SMP
kernel-headers-2.6.9-2-k7 - Linux kernel headers 2.6.9 on AMD K7
kernel-headers-2.6.9-2-k7-smp - Linux kernel headers 2.6.9 on AMD K7 SMP
kernel-headers-2.6.9-9 - Header files related to Linux kernel version 2.6.9
kernel-headers-2.6.9-9-amd64-generic - Linux kernel headers 2.6.9 for generic x86_64 systems
kernel-headers-2.6.9-9-amd64-k8 - Linux kernel headers for version 2.6.9 on AMD64 systems
kernel-headers-2.6.9-9-amd64-k8-smp - Linux kernel headers for version 2.6.9 onAMD64 SMP
systems
kernel-headers-2.6.9-9-em64t-p4 - Linux kernel headers for version 2.6.9 on Intel EM64T systems
kernel-headers-2.6.9-9-em64t-p4-smp - Linux kernel headers for version 2.6.9 onIntel EM64T SMP
systems
los-kernel-headers-2.6.9 - Lindows kernel header package
```

The correct one for Lindows 5 early access is los-kernel-headers-2.6.9, which you install in the usual way by typing:

apt-get install los-kernel-headers-2.6.9

You can also get much version information about the kernel and X Window by typing:

X -version

When you click **Launch** > **Settings** > **Control Panel**, you'll see the user, host name, and Linspire version name in the right hand panel.

You can find the Linux man pages, describing all system calls and commands at http://www.rt.com/man. You can also install the man pages from CNR. If you CNR the aisle "pvdl", you'll find the man pages and tools to compile drivers and applications.

Finding the Pathname for a GUI Application

You have to be able to start a program from the command line to use strace. Luckily, all GUI applications can be started from the command line—if you know the pathname to their executable.

1   The easiest way to find the pathname for a GUI is to look for it in the menu editor. Right-click on the **Launch** button and select **Menu Editor**. That brings up the Menu Editor window.

2   Double-click **Programs** (left side of Menu Editor) and keep going until you come to the application you want.

3   Highlight the application, and read off the command line to start it from the field marked **Command** on the right side of the Menu Editor.

4   Click in the **Command** field and scroll left/right to get the full name. You can also click on the open folder icon to the right of the **Command** textfield.

5   That will open a KDE Menu Editor 2 window in Figure F-1, which you can drag wider to show the folder and file name of the application.

Figure F-1 shows an example of this. Putting together the folder name (item 3) and the file name (item 4), the command line to start Lsongs is:

`/usr/lib/python2.3/site-packages/Lsongs/lsongs`

The command to start it under strace is:

`strace /usr/lib/python2.3/site-packages/Lsongs/lsongs`

Another approach is to use the top command to get the process ID of a process of interest, and attach strace to it while it is running, with:

`strace -p process-id`

Figure F-1   Using KDE Menu Editor to get the pathname for a GUI application

I don't want to give you a false impression of the power of strace—it can produce an overwhelming amount of output, particularly for a windowing program. On the other hand, if you can easily locate the point at which something fails (say, because the program hangs there) you can quickly see what it was doing right before that.

Strace is so quick and easy, there's no reason not to use it to troubleshoot. In the worst case, you might not get any new information, but you'll be no worse off than before. You can go a step further by recompiling the source code for debugging, and using gdb to run the code in debugging mode. But that's a subject best left for another book.

Index

inform**IT**

www.informit.com

YOUR GUIDE TO IT REFERENCE

Articles

Keep your edge with thousands of free articles, in-depth features, interviews, and IT reference recommendations – all written by experts you know and trust.

Online Books

Answers in an instant from **InformIT Online Book's** 600+ fully searchable on line books. For a limited time, you can get your first 14 days **free**.

POWERED BY
Safari
TECH BOOKS ONLINE®

Catalog

Review online sample chapters, author biographies and customer rankings and choose exactly the right book from a selection of over 5,000 titles.

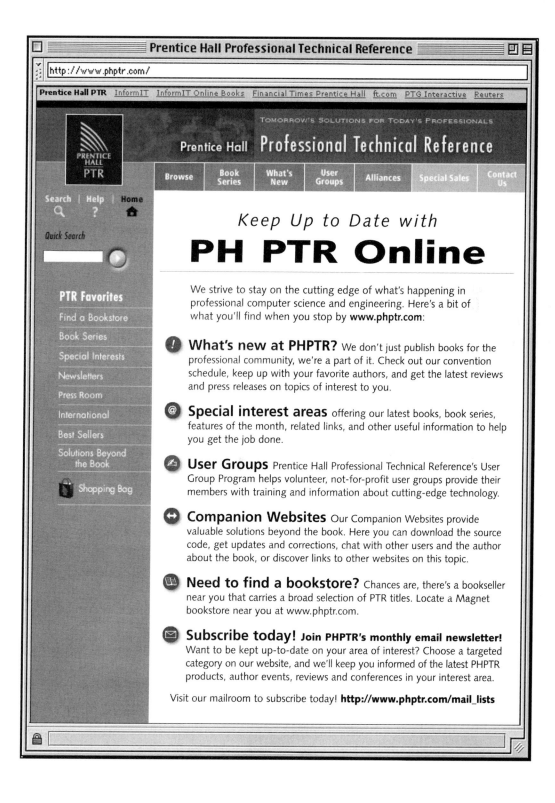

About the CD

This book includes a Linux CD for PCs that run Windows. It doesn't require any installation, and it doesn't run under Windows or affect it in any way.

Using the CD

When you're ready to try Linux, put the CD in your CD drive and reboot your PC (choose **Start** > **Turn off computer** > **Restart**).

For complete instructions, please refer to Chapter 2, "Running the Linux Live CD," on page 25.

CD-ROM Warranty

Prentice Hall PTR warrants the enclosed CD-ROM to be free of defects in materials and faulty workmanship under normal use for a period of ninety days after purchase (when purchased new). If a defect is discovered in the CD-ROM during this warranty period, a replacement CD-ROM can be obtained at no charge by sending the defective CD-ROM, postage prepaid, with proof of purchase to:

> Disc Exchange
> Prentice Hall PTR
> Pearson Technology Group
> 75 Arlington Street, Suite 300
> Boston, MA 02116
> Email: AWPro@aw.com

Prentice Hall PTR makes no warranty or representation, either expressed or implied, with respect to this software, its quality, performance, merchantability, or fitness for a particular purpose. In no event will Prentice Hall PTR, its distributors, or dealers be liable for direct, indirect, special, incidental, or consequential damages arising out of the use or inability to use the software. The exclusion of implied warranties is not permitted in some states. Therefore, the above exclusion may not apply to you. This warranty provides you with specific legal rights. There may be other rights that you may have that vary from state to state. The contents of this CD-ROM are intended for personal use only.

More information and updates are available at:

http://www.phptr.com/